CITIZENSHIP AND ACCOUNTABILITY OF GOVERNMENT:

AN ISLAMIC PERSPECTIVE

Mohammad Hashim Kamali

CITIZENSHIP AND ACCOUNTABILITY OF GOVERNMENT: AN ISLAMIC PERSPECTIVE

THE ISLAMIC TEXTS SOCIETY

First published 2011 by
THE ISLAMIC TEXTS SOCIETY
MILLER'S HOUSE
KINGS MILL LANE
GREAT SHELFORD
CAMBRIDGE CB22 5EN, U.K.

Reprint 2013

British Library Cataloguing-in-Publication Data.
A catalogue record for this book is
available from the British Library.

ISBN 978 1903682 60 9 cloth
ISBN 978 1903682 61 6 paper

Note on the "Fundamental Rights and Liberties in Islam" Series

The present volume is the last in a seven volume series on 'Fundamental Rights and Liberties in Islam: Principles and Applications' by Mohammad Hashim Kamali. The entire series of seven volumes is made up of the following:

Volume 1: *The Dignity of Man: An Islamic Perspective* (2002);
Volume 2: *Freedom, Equality and Justice in Islam* (2002);
Volume 3: *Equity and Fairness in Islam* (2005); and
Volume 4: *Freedom of Expression in Islam* (1997).
Volume 5: *Right to Life, Security, Privacy and Ownership in Islam* (2008);
Volume 6: *Right to Education, Work and Welfare in Islam* (2009); and
Volume 7: *Citizenship and Accountability of Government:*
         An Islamic Perspective (2010).

The revised order in which the seven titles are now arranged reflects their division under the two categories of 'Principles and Applications'. The first three volumes, namely *The Dignity of Man: an Islamic Perspective*, *Freedom, Equality and Justice in Islam*, and *Equity and Fairness in Islam* contain the general discussions of the Principles, while the remaining four titles address the special Applications of fundamental rights and liberties.

The reader may be interested to know that *Freedom of Expression in Islam* contains separate chapters on freedom of religion, freedom of association, and a chapter also on blasphemy and apostasy.

ABOUT THE AUTHOR

Mohammad Hashim Kamali is the Founding Chairman and CEO of the International Institute of Advanced Islamic Studies (IAIS) Malaysia. He studied in the UK from 1969 to 1976 and obtained an LLM and a PhD in Law from the University of London. He was Professor of Islamic Law and Jurisprudence at the International Islamic University Malaysia (1985–2004), and also Dean of the International Institute of Islamic Thought and Civilisation (ISTAC) from 2004 to 2006. Dr Kamali was previously Assistant Professor at the Institute of Islamic Studies, McGill University in Canada; he was a Visiting Professor at the Capital University, Ohio, and also at the Institute for Advanced Study (Wissenschaftskolleg) of Berlin. He was a member of the Constitution Review Commission of Afghanistan (2003) and also served as a UN expert on constitutional reform in the Maldives (2004). He advised on the new constitution of Iraq (2004–2005) and is currently on the UN Alliance of Civilisations Global Experts panel. He now serves on the boards of 13 local and international academic journals. Kamali has addressed over 130 national and international conferences, and he has published 17 books and over 140 academic articles. His books *Principles of Islamic Jurisprudence*; *A Textbook of Hadith Studies*; *Freedom of Expression in Islam*; and *Shariʿah Law: An Introduction* have been adopted as textbooks at leading English-speaking universities worldwide.

Contents

Acknowledgements   ix

CHAPTER ONE: Freedom of Movement: an Islamic Perspective   9

   I. Introductory Remarks   9

  II. Affirmative Evidence   13

Hijrah: Juristic and Historical Analysis, 16 · Whether *Hijrah* is a Continuing Requirement, 20 · *Hijrah* in Recent Times, 28 · Concluding Remarks on *Hijrah*, 32 · What of *Dār al-ḥarb*?, 33 · Migration and Asylum, 35 · Travel: Obligatory and optional, 37 · Travel in Search of *Ḥadīth*, 43 · The Quest for Knowledge, 48 · Right of Passage, 51 · Social Visits, 53 · Concessions for Travellers, 55

 III. Restrictions on Freedom of Movement   59

Considerations of Privacy and Health, 59 · Prohibition of Espionage, 61 · Considerations of *Maṣlaḥah*, 64

  IV. Conclusion   74

CHAPTER TWO: Citizenship   82

   I. Summary and Literature Review   82

  II. Concept and Terminology   88

 III. Islamic Conception of Citizenship   96

 IV. Citizenship Laws: Past and Present   101

  V. *Dhimmī* and *Musta'min*   109

 VI. Second Class Citizens Among Arabs—the *Mawāli*   117

VII. *Dār al-Islām* and *Dār al-Ḥarb* Revisited   120

VIII. *Ummah*, Nation–State and Citizenship: Modern Opinions   127

IX. Unity and Equality: Re-Examination of *Fiqh* Rules   134

X. *Dār al-Ḥarb*: An Unwarranted Designation!   141

XI. What of *Dār al-ʿAhd* (Abode of Treaty)?   145

XII. Rights of Citizens   147
The Franchise, 151 · Right to Nomination, 153 · Right to Consultation, 157 · Right to Criticise, 158 · The Right to Disobey the Deviant Ruler, 160 · Right to Basic Necessities, 163

XIII. Duties of Citizens   166

XIV. Women and Citizenship   170

XV. Conclusion And Reform Proposals   175

CHAPTER THREE: Accountability of Government   193

I. Introductory Remarks   193

II. Basic Postulates of Accountability   195
Ummah as Locus of Authority, 196 · Accountability: The Early Precedent, 198 · Accountability and Consultation, 203 · *Ḥisbah* and *Naṣīḥah*, 207 · Government As A Trust (*Amānat al-Ḥukm*), 210 · Selection of Officials, 216 · Criteria of Accountability: Personal and Corporate, 222 · The Limits of Obedience, 227 · Right of Complaint (*Ḥaqq al-Shakwah*), 233 · Holding Oneself to Account (*Muḥāsabat al-Nafs*), 237 · Corruption and Bribery (*Fasād wa-Rashwah*), 241 · Disobedience and Defiance, 250

III. Deviation and Departure from Precedent   253
Despotism and Dynastic Misrule, 253 · Misuse of Public Funds, 258

IV. Institutional Developments   262
Overriding Role of the Judiciary, 263 · *Dīwān al-Maẓālim* (Court of Grievances), 267 · Accountability and the *Muḥtasib*, 274 · Impeachment, 280 · Other Institutions of Accountability, 284 · Ottoman Constitutional Reforms, 286

Glossary   297

Bibliography   301

Index   315

Acknowledgements

Some parts of the research on this volume were carried out during my one-year fellowship at the Institute for Advanced Study in Berlin, better known as Wissenschaftskolleg zu Berlin (2000-2001). I went to Berlin with unfinished work on a larger project: *Fundamental rights and liberties in Islam; principles and applications*, which I had started much earlier. I needed full time concentration to press ahead with the research and my stay in Berlin provided me with that opportunity. Although ten months was too short a period to complete the needed research on my larger project, I did manage to make significant inroads in its various themes. The financial support I received from Wissenschaftskollegg facilitated this progress in research and, at present, I would very much like to acknowledge that support. I would also like to acknowledge the co-operation and support of the then Rector of the Kolleg, Professor Dr. Wolf Lepenies, and his efficient Deputy, Herr Joachim Nettleback, the Head Librarian, Ms Gesine Bottomly, and Head of the computer unit, Herr Hans G. Lindenberg.

My research on the larger project had actually begun in 1983 when I won a strategic research award from the Social Sciences and Humanities Research Council of Canada. The award allowed me to concentrate on completing my book proposal, *Freedom of Expression in Islam*, which now constitutes volume four of my larger series on fundamental rights and liberties in Islam. It was initially published in Kuala Lumpur (1995) and later by the Islamic Texts Society (ITS) of Cambridge, UK in 1997. I would like to take this opportunity to acknowledge the financial assistance of Canada Council that covered one year of my reseach on the early portions of this project in 1983-84 and the first few months of 1985. The research I conducted for this project during my stay in Montreal following my employment as an Assistant Professor at McGill University, Institute of Islamic

Studies, continued to be useful in the various themes and stages of this extended project.

The remaining portions of the work on the larger series, and on the present volume, were carried out largely at the International Islamic University Malaysia where I have been employed ever since 1985. My long-term association with this University offered me the much-needed continuity in which to focus on writing side by side with teaching and administrative work. During the last two years (July 2004–June 2006) I assumed increased administrative responsibilites as Dean of the International Institute of Islamic Thought and Civilisation (ISTAC) where I also had the good fortune of having the assistance of a highly accomplished P.A., Mrs. Salmah Ahmad, and also of my Research Assistant, Mr. Nirwan Syafrin, who is currently engaged in completing his Ph.D studies at ISTAC. I take this opportunity to thank them both for their valuable assistance and support. I would also like to mention the help I received with the computer work from Sister Diwi Abbas who is currently completing her M.A studies at ISTAC and would like to thank her most warmly for her assistance.

Lastly, I would like to acknowledge the generous cooperation and support of Fatima Azzam, the ITS Director, in this and in virtually all the other compendium volumes of this seven volume work. Her helpful suggestions and initiative in the detailed preparation of these titles and the sourcing of funds for their publication has been heartwarming and I take this opportunity to thank her most warmly for all her support. The fine quality of ITS publications, their careful attention to editing and design provided me with incentives to continue my fruitful engagement with Fatima and her colleagues which goes back to almost two decades. I am happy and fortunate to have enjoyed very good relations with them throughout these years.

International Institute of Islamic Thought and Civilisation
April 2011

Introduction

Though the present volume mainly focuses on citizenship and accountability of government in Islam, I have chosen to precede these discussions with that of freedom of movement in Islam which completes the individual freedoms that previous volumes in this series have covered. The reason for its inclusion here is because, like citizenship and accountability, this freedom was never discussed as a separate topic in the *fiqh* manuals and therefore fits in with the two other subjects of this volume. The freedom of movement from an Islamic perspective is here analysed in two sections and numerous subheadings. The two main contours of the discussion consist of a presentation of affirmative evidence in the *Sharīʿah* in support of the freedom of movement, which is then followed by a review of the restrictions that the law supposes on the exercise of this freedom. The subheadings that appear under each of these two themes tend to reflect the thematic engagement of the readers and jurists of *Sharīʿah* on the valid exercise of this freedom for a variety of purposes that are for the most part indicated in the Qur'ān and *Sunnah*.

Our discussion of the affirmative evidence is thus presented in twelve sub-sections. It begins with a review of the basic guidelines in the Qur'ān and *ḥadīth* that validate the freedom of movement. The review will briefly address the general and specific conditions under which freedom of movement is validated. The specific conditions include migration (*hijrah*), travel in pursuit of work and education, travel (in earlier times) in the search of *ḥadīth* (*riḥlah fī ṭalab al-Ḥadīth*), travel for purposes of visiting one's parents and relatives, and travel to a safer place to escape from imminent danger to one's life and safety, seeking asylum in another country, or becoming a refugee in stressful situations. Freedom of movement and travel from place to place in most of these situations is geared toward fulfilment of a religious duty, which may either be obligatory (*wājib*) or recommended (*mandūb*). In certain cases it may simply consist of a permissible activity, which is what freedom is really all about. It is by open and unhindered movement of the individual for pleasure or self-fulfilment that he can exercise the true freedom of movement.

Restrictions on the freedom of movement under Islamic law are usually meant to achieve certain specific objectives. These objectives may consist of, for example, securing the rights of others, upholding the public interest, and ensuring one's own safety in hazardous situations. There is also no validity to freedom of movement if it means indulgence in espionage or violation of the right of ownership of another individual. Public interest may also impose restrictions in the event, for example, of an outbreak of contagious disease that may necessitate restrictions on people's movement.

A question also arises with regard to the requirement of veiling for women and limitations on their mobility outside the home. There is also a similar debate over the freedom of non-Muslims, namely, whether they can freely enter the Muslim places of worship. In fact, a special case has been made in this connection regarding the precincts of the Ka'bah and the holy mosque in Mecca. So we will consider this topic in detail.

Because freedom of movement has not been treated as a designated topic in the *fiqh* manuals, my presentation here depends on scattered and unconsolidated evidence, which was sometimes excavated from unexpected places. All along, my purpose has been to provide a full coverage of the relevant themes and, hopefully, a concise yet self-contained read on the subject.

Chapter two of this volume advances an Islamic perspective on citizenship by putting together a picture that is composed of a number of related themes of concern to the contemporary understanding of this concept. Whereas the majority of commentators, both Orientalist and Muslim, subscribe to the view that citizenship is not recognised in the *Sharī'ah*, a few have taken the opposite view. They say that if citizenship consists of personal identity for the individual and a sense of belonging on his part to a larger community while enjoying a set of recognised rights, then this notion existed in Islamic thought and praxis to the same extent as it existed in the Greek polis or Roman civitas. The Islamic equivalent of citizenship can even be dated back to the renowned Constitution of Medina (623 CE). Being the earliest of its kind, this document laid the foundation of a new community (*ummah*) and the city state of Medina whereby the native individuals and tribes of Medina and the newly arrived migrants (i.e., the *muhājirūn*) were granted certain protections as well as a set of rights and duties toward one another and the emerging state of Medina. The advocates of this view of Islamic citizenship also tend to look at the potential for greater unity among Muslims and are suspicious of the divisive consequences of the European model of nation state, which, in their view, represents a departure from the Islamic concepts of *ummah* and *khilāfah*.

I have, however, not taken this view because of the historical changes including, for example, the disintegration of *ummah* as a political unity that was precipitated by the downfall of the Ottoman caliphate in 1924. It seems unrealistic, even unfeasible, to base an understanding of the prevailing concept of citizenship on a framework that no longer exists. The nation state has become an inescapable reality and what we have today is a multiplicity of some fifty-seven Muslim majority nation states that are neither politically united nor maintain the level of cooperation that is strong enough to sustain the notion of a common citizenship for all of their inhabitants. Yet in my concluding section, I return to the theme of unity and propose a plan as to how the Muslim countries and governments can cooperate and address issues of concern to unity and cooperation within the *ummah* and work for the realisation of the basic rights and welfare of their citizens. My reform proposals for greater unity are, in turn, based on ʿAbd al-Razzāq al-Sanhūrī's ideas which he formulated in the 1920s, following the downfall of the caliphate, for the establishment of an Organization of Oriental Society which he elaborated in his Sorbonne doctoral dissertation, *Le Califat*, later published in Arabic with the title *Fiqh al-Khilāfah*. I have taken up the basic outline of al-Sanhūrī's proposal for theme-specific and piecemeal approaches to cooperation among Muslim countries that include matters of relevance to citizenship. Yet I have also taken his proposal a step forward and updated it since the basic framework of his proposals was formulated in a different historical setting that preceded, for example, the formation of the United Nations and also perhaps that of the Organisation of Islamic Conference. But al-Sanhūrī's proposal and my addition to it are predicated on prospects of cooperation among nation states to the extent that one has witnessed in the formation of, for example, the European Union.

Citizenship as a theme of concern to the modern student of constitutional law does not feature in the writings of Muslim jurists of earlier times. The *fiqh* literature in the areas of *al-aḥkām al-sulṭāniyyah* (sultanic ordinances) and that which appear under the general heading of *al-siyāsah al-sharʿiyyah* (Sharīʿah-oriented polity) do not address the subject. Only during the early decades of the 20th century, Arab writers and jurists who wrote on the Islamic system of government (*niẓām al-ḥukm fi'l-Islām*), and the human rights-related literature under the general heading of *ḥuqūq al-insān fi'l-Islām* began to address the subject of citizenship. Yet even in these writings, it is not often that one can find an in-depth or exclusive treatment of the subject. Many Arab writers who have addressed the subject are inclined to fall back on earlier writings on *khilāfah* (caliphate), *dār al-Islām* (abode of Islam) and *dār al-ḥarb* (abode of war) and often subsume citizenship under one or the other of these concepts. There is a brief section, for example, on citizenship in Mawdūdī's *Islamic Law and Constitution* which advances an understanding of citizenship according to the Qur'ānic passages on migration (*hijrah*) and other passages which make conversion to the faith as a precondition for grant of protection under an Islamic polity. The conclusion is thus drawn that anyone who embraces the faith and takes domicile in *dār al-Islām* (read also Islamic state for *dār al-Islām* as Mawdūdī tends to draw a parallel between them) is a citizen of the Islamic state.

I have also discussed in some detail the problems that tend to arise from this binary division of the world into the abode of Islam and abode of war and reached the conclusion that they cannot accommodate citizenship as is understood through our reading, for example, of the applied constitutions of the present-day Muslim countries. I have attempted in the meantime to extricate citizenship from the religion-dominated themes and address it as a civilian concept and a part of the basic rights of all citizens, Muslims and non-Muslims alike.

Citizenship is also not a monolithic concept in that it tends to subsume a number of rights and obligations. In my attempt to distinguish the religious from the civilian aspects of citizenship, I have drawn attention to certain ambiguities in the existing writings of Muslim scholars on the subject. Of the two well-known 20th century figures who wrote on citizenship, namely Muhammad Hamidullah and Abū'l-Aʿlā Mawdūdī, only the latter made brief observations as to certain rights and obligations, which, in his view, are borne only by the Muslim citizens, but not by their non-Muslim compatriots. This is a theme that I have taken up in the latter part of my presentation. My attempt in this part has been to identify a set of rights and obligations for citizens in the light of evidence that I draw from the Qur'ān and *Sunnah*.

Chapter three of this volume develops an Islamic perspective on accountability of government, a theme which somewhat like citizenship, does not receive an exclusive treatment in the existing *fiqh* literature under the general headings either of *al-aḥkām al-sulṭāniyyah* or *al-siyāsah al-sharʿiyyah*. Arabic treatises in these areas as well as the more recent works on principles of government in Islam (*niẓām al-ḥukm fi'l-Islām*) do not include accountability in their familiar range of topics. Certain aspects of the subject have been addressed in a piecemeal and unconsolidated fashion in these works but the evidence needed to be put together, consolidated and developed, which is what I have attempted. Once again, like citizenship, accountability of government is basically a civilian concept and needs to be treated in this light, yet this subject has shown a similar tendency to be enmeshed in religion-dominated themes that required a great deal of sifting through in order to give it a substantive grounding in positive law. I have made an attempt to do this but there is scope for further research to address in greater depth some of the themes of this exceedingly wide-ranging subject.

The present attempt to develop an Islamic perspective on accountability is also thematic in that it develops the subject by identifying a number of principles and themes of concern to accountability and then addresses them each in some detail. The discussion thus begins with the basic postulates of accountability and continues to develop the theme by presenting a combination of both juristic and historical data on the subject. The latter portion of the discussion explores institutional developments such as the *maẓālim* jurisdiction under the Abbasids that made accountability a visible aspect of governance.

Many of the basic postulates and indicators of this model of accountability of government can be found in the Qur'ān as well as the early precedent of the pious caliphs. The system of rule that the Qur'ān has envisaged is founded in a number of principles, including trust (*amānah*), justice (*ʿadl*), consultation (*shūrā*), the rule of law, namely the *Sharīʿah*, as well as the principle of vicegerency (*khilāfah*), bidding good and forbidding evil (*amr bi'l-maʿrūf wa-nahy ʿan al-munkar*), *bayʿah* (pledge of allegiance), representation (*wakālah*) and so forth. The principal audience of these and similar other teachings is also the Muslim community (*ummah*), which is the locus of political authority and the basic constituent of government. I have attempted to advance a certain understanding of these principles and how they can be utilised for the purpose of providing a blueprint for a government's accountability.

Regarding this subject, I proceed on the assumption that theoretical guidelines on accountability envisage a civilian government that is elected by the people and can be deposed by the popular vote if it fails to fulfil its mandate of establishing justice and good governance, or if it deviates and falls short of the *Sharīʿah* or its constitution. This is an aspect of my presentation that is often ignored under the plethora of unverified generalisations in many juristic works. Commentators often tend to take for granted that an Islamic government is a theocracy, or a government of the theologians and jurists by definition. I try to address these mostly inaccurate assertions and then expound the framework and principles that I can find in the source evidence of the Qurʾān and *ḥadīth*.

There is no requirement in Islamic law for statesmen to be designated from the ranks of religious leaders and ʿulamāʾ. The typical textbook expression used for those who qualify for leadership is the *ahl al-ḥall wa'l-ʿaqd* (those who loosen and bind, those who make binding decisions). These are people of influence who enjoy public confidence in their decision-making abilities. People, in other words, who give counsel in community affairs and are themselves capable of leadership, which is why they are also known as the *ahl al-shūrā* (those who are competent to give counsel). They are basically civilians who may or may not be ʿulamāʾ and religious leaders. It is not a requirement to include the latter, though.

The head of the state is elected by the people through consultation and pledge of allegiance (*bayʿah*), which translates into an elective procedure. The head of state acts as a representative (*wakīl*) of the people and his success and failure in office is also judged by reference to people's welfare, or *maṣlaḥah*. The head of state is admittedly the patron and protector of religion, but he is also a civilian officer who is required to conduct the community affairs in consultation with the people.

Justice is one of the cardinal duties of government and its application must be guided by the spirit of impartiality and fairness and without the consideration of race, language, social status or religion. The court of *Sharīʿah* is bound to treat the litigants before it with total impartiality and may not favour one party over the other on grounds of piety, knowledge, and religion. A pious litigant or a learned one stands in exactly the same position before the court as one with questionable piety or one who may be totally illiterate. In administering justice and in matters of trial and evidence the court of *Sharīʿah* may similarly not discriminate between Muslims and non–Muslims, and must treat everyone equally before it. Trial and evidence procedures before the courts of *Sharīʿah* are also positivist in character and are guided by considerations of objectivity and fairness and do not pay attention to knowledge and piety. One may add on a more general note that in the sphere of civil transactions (i.e. *muʿāmalāt*), which constitute almost the entire bulk of the court business, the proceedings of *Sharīʿah* courts are dominantly civilian and not theocratic. Matters of religious rituals and *ʿibādāt* are basically not justifiable before the *Sharīʿah* courts as they are of concern mainly to the relationship of man with his Creator and as such fall outside the jurisdiction of courts and governments. The government does have administrative powers in respect of the *ʿibādāt* which relate mainly to the affairs of the mosques and public observances of events such as Friday prayers and rules of abstention in public places, the proper performance of the fasting month of Ramadan, etc. Thus it remains to be said, as declared succinctly in a legal maxim of *fiqh* that 'the affairs of the head of state are judged by reference to people's welfare—*amr al-imām manūṭ bi'l-maṣlaḥah*.' It is a mere extension of the same logic to say that *maṣlaḥah* and people's welfare constitute the basic framework of accountability in an Islamic government.

Maṣlaḥah is a broad concept, just as it is utilitarian in substance, it is also one of the major themes of Islamic jurisprudence. *Maṣlaḥah* is classified into several types, one of which is the class of *maṣlaḥah* known as essential benefits (*ḍarūriyyāt*). Muslim jurists have identified the *ḍarūriyyāt* under the five headings of religion, life, property, intellect, and family. To promote, protect and advance these values constitute a principal assignment of government in Islam, and by the same token constitute the basic criteria of accountability in government. It will be noted further that except for the first of these, the other four headings in this classification of benefits relate primarily to the people's welfare in the positivist sense of the word. There is, in sum, a civilian and positivist aspect to the *Sharīʿah* which is often overlooked by many a commentator who is inclined to see the *Sharīʿah* as religious law in toto that recognises no lines of distinction between law and religion.

Accountability of government is based on a set of principles that are neither theological nor dogmatic, but which can be ascertained and implemented on positivist grounds. I must nevertheless add that my purpose in making these preliminary remarks is to draw attention to an often neglected aspect of the *Sharīʿah* without wishing, however, to underestimate the strong links between law, morality and religion in *Sharīʿah*. Here, there are no black and white categories that one can speak of. Moral values, religious norms and juristic doctrines often tend to overlap and influence one another within the rubric of the *Sharīʿah* and they can often be an extension of one another. This is generally acknowledged and there is no need for the elaboration of this basic feature of Islamic law and government, yet it would be equally incorrect to say that no lines of distinction between the religious, the moral and the legal subject matter exist in the *Sharīʿah*. Accountability in government can similarly not be isolated from the combination of these influences. Yet I still maintain that the civilian side of the *Sharīʿah* tends to be a dominant influence, in certain areas at least, of public law and that includes the subject of our immediate concern here. Accountability of the bearers of public office is a part of the *muʿāmalāt* aspect of the *Sharīʿah* and it is as such open to a myriad of influences, including the textual guidelines of the Qurʾān and *Sunnah*, consideration of public interest or *maṣlaḥah*, rationality (*ʿaql*) and independent reasoning (*ijtihād*). Accountability of government also takes into consideration the reservoir of discretionary powers that the government is vested in under the Islamic law doctrines of *siyāsah sharʿiyyah*, and I shall have occasion to elaborate on it in the following pages.

CHAPTER ONE

Freedom of Movement: an Islamic Perspective

I. Introductory Remarks

Freedom of movement refers to the right of the individual to move and travel within his home country, to leave it for another place, or return to it without any restrictions except for consideration of public interest.[1] Public interest in this case may include safeguarding other people's rights such as their right to privacy, right of ownership, unhindered access to public facilities, and considerations of public health.

Freedom of movement may be seen as the first and most fundamental of all personal liberties. To be free to move is an expression of the natural desire of every human being; it is the opposite of imprisonment; and it is instrumental in enabling a person to work and earn a living. One can hardly give a complete list of the objectives that may be pursued by the exercise of this freedom. Some of the most significant of these objectives that have been highlighted in the Islamic juristic literature are escape from tyranny and oppression, pursuit of knowledge, the quest for a better life—or one which is in harmony with one's conscience, and fulfilment of religious duties. These are among the salient uses of the freedom of movement; they are not mutually exclusive, just as they are also in many ways related to personal dignity and a person's ability to lead an honourable life.

The evidence in the Qur'ān and *Sunnah*, which is reviewed in the following pages, shows that Islam's perspective on freedom of movement underlines the crucial role that this freedom plays in pursuit of a host of other values that can hardly be realised without the person's freedom to move and travel from place to place. Islamic law also envisages certain situations where leaving a particular place and migrating to another becomes a duty if it proves to be the only way to safeguard the integrity of one's faith, escape tyranny and degradation.

If freedom of movement were to mean simply the freedom to 'come and go,' as it does in the Arabic phrase *al-ghuduww wa'l-rawāḥ*, one could say that some limitation may be justified on 'coming in' especially for settlement and residence in a particular place or country. There is, however, no corresponding justification to be found for laws that forbid people to 'go out' of a place or country, yet it is exactly such laws that have caused suffering to countless numbers of people in many parts of the world. In earlier times, it was the particular fate of slaves to be forbidden to leave their place of domicile. Although slavery has disappeared, when a government ordains that its people may not leave their country without some special exit visa given as an act of grace, that government is in effect restricting the freedom of the entire people within the boundaries of its territory.[2]

Legal history has followed rather a negative course on freedom of movement, which may be said to be a function largely of the increasingly assertive stance that nation states have taken on sovereignty and nationalism. Prior to 1914, freedom of movement was wider and far less encumbered by so many restrictions as it is today. It is ironic that as long as the means of travel were restricted, travel itself was free. When the means of transportation improved and travel became faster, man's freedom to avail himself of these facilities was subjected to 'arbitrary and vexatious restrictions. In this respect, there has been a visible retrogression.'[3]

The recognition in the Universal Declaration of Human Rights (UDHR) of the freedom of movement and asylum as rights of every individual undoubtedly represented an achievement of civilisational proportions. Yet it will be noted that the UDHR measures have also not escaped the strictures of nationality and nation state. This is clear in the text of Article (13) which provides:

(1) Everyone has the right to freedom of movement and residence within the borders of each state.

(2) Everyone has the right to leave any country, including his own, and to return to his country.

The right to asylum is recognised for everyone in the most abstract of terms in Article (14) which stops short of imposing an obligation of any kind on the sovereign state, even in stressful humanitarian situations. Article (14) thus declares:

> Everyone has the right to seek and to enjoy in other countries, asylum.

Prior to the advent of the nation state, 'Muslims used to move about and travel within the boundaries of *Dār al-Islām* without restrictions . . . It was not unusual for a person to be born in one city, grow up in another, and reside in yet another place.'[4] Imām al-Shāfiʿī's name comes to mind here as he is known to have travelled widely in the Hijaz and Iraq. He is the founder of two schools, the Old School he founded in Iraq and the New School he founded when he settled in Egypt. Even during the early stages of the modern nation state, there were fewer restrictions on travel among Muslim countries, but then the situation began to change. While people are now experiencing more and more restrictions on travel being imposed by both Muslim and non-Muslim countries. The world of post 9/11 has seen unprecedented compromises on the free movement of people and the unceasing restrictions as to what a person can or cannot carry on a flight, especially to the United States and European destinations.

It is not difficult for a developing, or an industrialised country for that matter, to advance a plausible argument that it needs the skills of its managerial and professional classes, and if they were allowed to emigrate in substantial numbers, the country's economy will suffer. Utilitarian considerations of this sort may well be seen as valid grounds of public policy and interest, but only on an ad hoc or transitory basis. Considerations of this kind would, however, fall short of justifying denial in principle of freedom of movement to an entire population. For this is likely to amount to unwarranted imposition on the people's freedom, and tolerating oppression, in the hope of producing benefit for some future generation.[5]

Freedom of movement is admittedly not an absolute value that can be vindicated at all cost. Some sacrifice of public interest and a certain degree of compromise of individual rights is just as warranted in regard to this freedom as it is with respect to most other recognised liberties. One may not perhaps be ready to allow an exodus of skilled labour force to another country, yet it may still be inadvisable to impose a total ban on all qualified individuals to travel in pursuit of better opportunities. Within reasonable bounds, one may still be able to ascertain a basic order of priority between a present reality and a future hope. In the event of a direct clash between the individual freedom of movement and utilitarian prospects of the society's future, one ought to give priority to the first. A review of the source evidence of *Sharīʿah* and historical practice indicates that this order has occasionally been reversed, in individual cases at least. The Head of State is authorised to exercise a certain amount of discretion, within the general framework of a *Sharīʿah* oriented policy (*siyāsah sharʿiyyah*) in such matters. Yet it appears that instances of vindicating the public interest at the expense of the individual right to freedom of movement in the early history of Islam, especially during the period of the Khulafāʾ Rashidūn, represent exceptional departures from the basic norm and do not, therefore, alter the normative sanctity of the individual's right to freedom of movement.

Even though everyone has the right to move, few people would have the natural desire to be always on the move. They have a natural desire also for a base or a homeland. The natural right of movement is thus connected with the right to nationality and domicile. The prevailing realities of the national state at the dawn of the twenty-first century are such that an individual can no longer find a home in a place beyond territorial boundaries where no state claims jurisdiction. Under the present conditions the right to a domicile entails the right to a formal nationality. It is due mainly to this linkage that some writers view the freedom of movement as an integral part of the right of domicile. This can clearly be seen in the alternative Arabic phrase for this freedom, that is, *ḥurriyyat al-maʾwā* (lit. freedom to reside). Many Arab writers have preferred to use this term over *ḥurriyyat al-tanaqqul* (freedom of movement). Freedom of movement thus signifies the freedom of the individual to reside where he wishes. Both expressions may however be seen as the two facets of the same liberty as they are to all intents and purposes inseparable extensions of one another.

Our discussion in the following pages characterises the basic evidence and outlook of the Qurʾān and *Sunnah* on freedom of movement, which is then followed by a review of the more specific evidence on migration (*hijrah*), the Hajj pilgrimage, and the minor Hajj of ʿumrah, travelling in pursuit of knowledge, travel to visit family and friends, and the right of passage. The discussion ends with an exposition of restrictions that the *Sharīʿah* has envisaged on the freedom of movement. The main restrictions we review are concerned with the privacy of the private home where strangers have no freedom to enter. The *Sharīʿah* also forbids espionage which means that freedom of movement does not exist when it is exercised for the purpose of spying on others. Considerations of public interest (*maṣlaḥah*) may also require limitation on freedom of movement. This also raises the question as to the validity of banishment and incarceration as instruments of *maṣlaḥah* as they are the two most obvious instances of official restrictions on freedom of movement. The question as to whether Muslims have the freedom to travel into *dār al-ḥarb* (abode of war) also calls for new consideration and review. Other instances of restrictions on freedom of movement that call for discussion concern women and non-Muslims. Whether veiling is accepted as a *Sharīʿah* requirement and whether it represents a lawful restriction on freedom of movement are among the issues we address. The question that concerns the non-Muslims in this connection is focused on a basically single Qurʾānic verse, which disallows 'the associators' to stay in the vicinity of the sacred mosque of Kaʿbah.

II. Affirmative Evidence

The affirmative evidence I have examined below is related to a variety of special themes, although some of it is also of a general nature. In fact, it will be helpful to begin with a brief review of general evidence in the Qurʾān and *Sunnah* on freedom of movement, whereas evidence on special themes, such as *hijrah* (migration), obligatory and optional travel, and the quest for knowledge etc., will be discussed each in their relevant places.

It will be noted at the outset that basic evidence in the Qurʾān and *Sunnah* on movement and travel is not premised on the nation state as a basic framework nor does it convey any awareness of official permissions and visa formalities. The *Sharīʿah* outlook may as such be said to be free of some of the strictures that are associated with the nation state and the exclusive authority it might exercise over a geographical unit. The outlook under review is not even predicated on *ummah*, for *ummah* is not envisaged as a territorial unit but as a unity in faith. The world is thus seen as a monolithic entity that is subservient to God's entrusted vicegerency in man, whose basic task is to establish justice, build the earth, promote good and prevent evil. Within that framework, human beings are granted unrestricted freedom to traverse the earth and utilise its resources for beneficial purposes. The legal principles of the Qurʾān and its directives on personal liberties, including the freedom of movement, also seek to promote the fundamental values of human dignity, the liberality of individual conscience and moral virtue on a universal plane. This is an outlook that bears little affinity with sectarian or nationalist identities. Although divisions do exist and they are recognised, yet they do not command normative validity and cannot therefore compromise the wider horizons of these teachings.

Many Muslim scholars recognise the fact that biases of a nation-state and its restrictions on freedom of movement are just as much a reality of contemporary Muslim life as they are of the world beyond. However, they also believe that the Qur'ānic outlook holds a strong appeal and may well be translated into a reality that, in turn, may help to restore the freedom of travel. Of course, they also view the twentieth century's exchange of freedom of travel in favour of sovereignty and nationalism as regressive. The Qur'ānic discourse tends to focus on the individual character that is envisaged as the basic source of motivation for virtuous conduct and beneficial exchange. The text is also clear in its affirmation of the fraternity of humans and their common predicament as bearers of responsibility to God and to their fellow humans. To quote the holy Book:

يآيها الناس اتقوا ربكم الذى خلقكم من نفس واحدة وخلق منها زوجها وبث منهما رجالا كثيرا ونساء واتقوا الله الذى تسألون به والأرحام

O mankind! Be mindful of your Lord who created you from a single soul, and created from it its spouse, and from them men and women in large numbers that were scattered (all over the earth). Be mindful of your Lord by whom you claim your rights from one another, and observe the ties of kinship. (4:1)

God thus created men and women from a single soul and scattered them on the planet earth, that is, in all places and everywhere, without any notion of barriers and divisions as to their places of residence, and regardless of imposing any restrictions on their freedom to travel and explore various parts of earth. This is the outlook characteristically of openness that nurtures the spirit of unity and cooperation among human beings. Faithful men and women are also united in their belief in one God, which is yet another level of unity that binds them to one another.

There is recognition in the Qur'ān, nevertheless, of the division of mankind into groups, tribes and nations. It is, however, conveyed in a spirit of unity and cooperation rather than of divisiveness and separation, as in the text below:

يأيها الناس إنا خلقناكم من ذكر وأنثى و جعلناكم شعوبا وقبائل لتعارفوا إن أكرمكم عند الله أتقاكم

O mankind! We created you from (a single pair of) a male and a female and made you into nations and tribes that you may know each other (not that you may despise each other). Truly the most honoured of you in the sight of God is the most righteous of you. (49:13)

If divisions into groups, tribes and nations are for the purpose of mutual recognition and knowledge of one another, then freedom of movement and mutual contact among people become the implied requirement of this declaration. This is known, in the language of jurisprudence, as the requirement of the text (*iqtiḍā' al-naṣṣ*), because denial of the freedom of movement would frustrate familiarity and recognition, which is the explicit purpose of that text. The text before us begins with a note on unity and then speaks of mutual recognition, which should be for positive purposes that promote unity and cooperation. For recognition and exchange can easily follow a negative course and instead of serving the noble objectives of humanity can also generate hostility and rancour. The verse under review thus envisages mutual recognition among people as a means of promoting positive values among them.

Further endorsement of this open outlook on movement and travel is found in other Qur'ānic verses, such as: 'The earth belongs to God and He gives it as heritage to such of His servants as He pleases, and the end is (best) for the righteous' (7:128; see also 21:105 to the similar effect). It is then declared in another passage: 'O My servants who believe! My earth is truly spacious, therefore serve Me (wherever you may be).' The text thus encourages unrestricted movement of people to travel and reside wherever they please and lead a virtuous life of devotion to positive values. For service to God in the Qur'ānic idiom is best manifested in advancing the causes of God and his messages. And finally, the artificiality of any divisive efforts that seek to restrict the individual's freedom of movement and migration is underscored in another passage as follows: 'Say! To God belongs the East and the West. He alone guides to the right path those whom He pleases' (2:142).

قل لله المشرق والمغرب يهدى من يشاء إلى صراط مستقيم

This is in line with the open outlook Islam maintains that no one except God the Most High can claim ownership of the earth and that in His illustrious eyes the east and the west and all in between is open for all human beings to move about and explore. The latter portion of the text seems to suggest that despite these reminders, there will still be men who will not follow the right path nor will they recognise the limits established by God. The Qur'ān also contains more specific invitations, as will presently be reviewed, addressing the people to travel as they please, and in some cases, it becomes an obligation for them to do so. Travel that is undertaken for a good cause, such as earning a lawful living, or in the way of God, such as propagation of beneficial knowledge, is also an act of merit that invokes God's pleasure. There is a promise of reward for such activities, as in the following *ḥadīth*:

من أغبرت قدماه فى سبيل الله حرمه الله على النار

Anyone whose feet are covered with dust for the cause of God Most High (*fī sabīl Allāh*), God shall forbid him to the fire of Hell.[6]

ḤIJRAH (MIGRATION): A JURISTIC AND HISTORICAL ANALYSIS

Being the verbal noun of *hajara*, *hijrah* literally means 'to abandon', 'to boycott and break ties with someone,' such as breaking a bond of kinship or other personal association. *Hijrah*, in the sense of 'migration' refers primarily to the Prophet's migration from Mecca to Medina in 622 AD. *Hijrah* in the early history of Islam is also discussed in conjunction with the migration of a group of Muslims from Mecca to Abyssinia in 615 AD. Although the *hijrah* to Abyssinia was voluntary and somewhat limited in scope, the *hijrah* to Medina was obligatory and involved almost the entire Muslim community at the time. No Muslim was supposed to stay behind in Mecca, except for the very weak among them, women, children and the sick who could not afford to travel the 270 km distance to Medina. A question that arises in this connection is whether *hijrah* is a religious requirement of a permanent nature that demands compliance even from the present-day Muslim individuals and communities. Another question to be discussed in the following pages is over the binary division of the world into *dār al-Islām* and *dār al-ḥarb* and its implications on freedom of movement and *hijrah* respectively.

To migrate from one's homeland to another country where one finds protection and livelihood is the more common application of *hijrah* in our times. The word *hijrah* in the Qur'ān is used in the sense of departure, abandonment or boycott, usually implying the idea of abandonment physically or mentally, from an existing undesirable state for something better.[7] *Hijrah* differs from its allied but more general concept of *safar* (travel, journey) in that *safar* signifies travel with the intention of coming back within a short period, the minimum for which, according to some jurists is three days. A journey of this kind may be for any purpose and usually falls under the general category of *mubāḥ* (permissible) but can partake in an obligation when it is undertaken for due performance of a duty such as travelling to the *ḥajj*.

Hijrah or migration normally consists of travel which is not attended by an intention to return to one's place or country and one's permanent home. *Hijrah* has an Islamic connotation and one who undertakes it is a *muhājir* or a Muslim migrant. The parallel term to *muhājir* is *musta'min* for a non-Muslim migrant who seeks refuge in an Islamic country.[8]

The historical *hijrah* was a manifestation of the open outlook of the Qur'ān on the individual's freedom of movement and how it could be utilized to bring about change in the sense of turning a new page in the life of a community. Freedom of movement was on that occasion utilised for such a purpose. The event of the *hijrah* also generated a momentum that played a vital role in consolidating the unity of the nascent community of Muslims in their new habitat. The Prophet's migration to Medina helped to unite the community not only in their faith in Islam but also in the physical sense of exodus of the whole of the Muslim community to a new destination and environment. The *hijrah* moved the centre stage of events in the early history of Islam from Mecca to Medina and marked a turning point in the eventual success of the Prophet's campaign, which is why it features so prominently in the history of Islam.

In the early years of the advent of Islam, Muslims were subjected to persecution by the pagans of Mecca. So much so that the Prophet advised some of his followers to seek asylum in Ethiopia where they could live in peace under the Christian emperor Negus. A number of them thus immigrated to Abyssinia/Ethiopia and resided there until several years later when the time was right for them to join the Prophet in Medina. As the persecution of Muslims continued to mount in Mecca the Prophet feared for the physical safety of his followers and decided therefore on a general exodus to Medina. The Prophet consequently instructed that everyone capable of undertaking the journey to Medina should emigrate. This was after some thirteen years of campaign in Mecca, which the Prophet left for Medina under conditions of imminent threat to his life. Whereas the migration to Ethiopia was optional, migration to Medina was a requirement, mainly because of the hostility and persecution that made it impossible for the Muslims to uphold and propagate their beliefs. Migration to Medina was consequently made obligatory for all of them except for those who were unable to undertake the journey. The Qur'ān and *Sunnah* consequently treated the *hijrah* both as a physical journey and a principle that had bearings on faith and loyalty of the believers. The principle that it signified was one of sacrifice for a cause, and willingness to turn a new page even if it meant abandoning one's home, family and friends. To take a challenge of that kind was an act of faith and it demanded the strength of conviction. It is in this light that the *hijrah* was seen as an obligation and no longer a mere expression of individual freedom.

The obligatory *hijrah* was arguably a time-bound phenomenon which came to an end after the conquest of Mecca some eight years later, but the principle it advocated gave *hijrah* a variety of meanings in the Qur'ān and *ḥadīth*. Many have concluded that the basic freedom of movement may become value-specific at times and elevated to the degree of something recommendable (*mandūb*), even obligatory (*wājib*), if it could be used as a means of securing the freedom of conscience or one by which to escape from persecution and injustice. To quote a Qur'ānic passage:

إن الذين توفهم الملائكة ظالمى أنفسهم قالوا فيم كنتم قالوا كنا مستضعفين فى الأرض قالوا ألم تكن أرض الله واسعة فتهاجروا فيها

And when the angels take the soul of those who die while unjust to themselves and then they are asked in what (plight) were you? They will say: we were weak (and helpless) in the earth. Then they (the angels) say: was not God's earth spacious so that you could have migrated therein? (4:97)

The text continues to predict a painful predicament for those who were able to emigrate but chose not to. 'As for such, their habitation will be Hell, an evil journey's end.' An exception has been made, however, for 'the weak among the men, women and children who did not have the means nor could they find a way (to escape)' (4:98).

$$\text{إلا المستضعفين من الرجال والنساء والولدان لايستطيعون حيلة}$$

The text then continues to praise those who migrate in the way of God (*fī sabīl Allāh*) and assures them of the abundant space and plentiful resources of the earth while granting them, in the meantime, a concession to shorten the obligatory prayer during the journey (4:100–101).

Further on the subject of *hijrah*, the Qur'ān praised those who migrated with the Prophet to Medina and became the rightful founders of the new community. It is thus provided in an address to the Prophet that 'those who embraced the faith and migrated and struggled hard in God's way with their lives and properties, they are friends and supporters of one another. And those who believed but did not migrate, you are not responsible for their protection until they migrate' (8:72).

$$\text{ان الذين آمنوا وهاجروا وجاهدوا بأموالهم وأنفسهم فى سبيل الله والذين ءاووا ونصروا أولئك بعضهم أولياء بعض والذين آمنوا ولم يهاجروا ما لكم من ولايتهم من شيئ حتى يهاجروا}$$

The Qur'ān thus made it clear that migration was of key significance in determining individual loyalty and membership of the new community in Medina.

These passages were revealed at a time when the pagans of Mecca had stepped up their persecution of the early Muslims and the Prophet had reached the conclusion that continued residence in Mecca threatened their physical safety. Pagans of Quraysh had hatched a plot to kill the Prophet himself. The passage under review addressed that specific situation. A careful reading of the text also indicates that it basically visualised three groups of Muslims at the time of its revelation.

The first of these three groups were the early Companions of the Prophet who embraced Islam at an early stage, and remained steadfast in their faith, and supported the Prophet in his plan to migrate to Medina. They were also fit to undertake the journey with or without their families and were also willing to leave their property and livelihood behind for the sake of their religion. These were the people whom the Qur'ān praised for their sacrifice and promised them great rewards (cf. 9:100).

The second group was the so-called *mustaḍ'afūn,* or the weak among Muslims who were eager for Islam, and like the first group, were willing to emigrate and strengthen the cause of the *hijrah,* yet were unable to do so due to old age, failing health and poverty. They stayed behind in Mecca but remained faithful and eager to secure their freedom from oppression. It was to them that the latter portion of the verse was addressed—those who did not have the means nor could they find a way to escape.

There was yet a third group of people who were fit and capable to undertake the *hijrah,* but were influenced by their family and clan, and also attachment to their property persuaded them to reside in Mecca and put up with their predicament. It was basically to this group that the first portion of the verse was addressed in such terms that they were unjust to themselves and their plight was self-imposed despite the excuse they gave that they were weak and helpless. Their unhappy predicament was vividly described in the verse in that they subjected themselves to oppression and spiritual torture in both their earthly lives and the hereafter.[9]

It is quite obvious that the Qur'ānic references to *hijrah* were basically circumstantial as they addressed a time-bound reality that changed course within almost the same generation. Yet since the text does not clearly declare this, the question has arisen whether the *hijrah* remains essentially a permanent feature of the Qur'ānic dispensations on the subject. We turn to this next.

WHETHER *HIJRAH* IS A CONTINUING REQUIREMENT?

Maḥmūd Shaltūt has drawn the conclusion from the text under review that *hijrah* is neither a circumstantial nor a time-bound phenomenon. Instead, it is a principle of permanent validity that is of relevance to the lives even of Muslims in the twenty-first century. He then specifies the various applications of *hijrah* under three categories.

Firstly, *hijrah* is obligatory on individual Muslims who live in non-Muslim countries that oppress them and deny them the freedom to practice their religion. If they are able to migrate and go to a place where they can avail themselves of that freedom they are under obligation to do so, failing which they would have qualified themselves for the warning that the text has conveyed: 'They would be unjust to their own souls.'[10]

Secondly, on those individuals who live in Muslim countries that are occupied or colonised by the enemy forces that rob the people of their right to self-rule and impose their own culture and values on those under their rule. The occupiers are oppressive as they deny Muslims the liberty to uphold their faith and the right to own their properties. It is the duty of these Muslims to resist these oppressors and refuse to endorse their rule and 'emigrate in their hearts and minds to join their brethren in the faith' so that they become a unified force to expel the coloniser. If they refuse to do this when they are able to do so, they also call upon themselves the sorry predicament that the verse under review has warned. Here we have a reference to a mental/psychological migration in the sense that true Muslims must refuse to associate themselves with the oppressors and denounce them in their thoughts if they are unable to repel them otherwise.

Thirdly, on Muslims who live in various Muslim towns and cities that are ruled by the enemy forces and who are unable to emigrate or form a united force to expel and resist the oppressor. They should nevertheless disassociate themselves in their hearts and minds from oppression and refuse to endorse it. If they can unite and be effective to repel oppression, they should do so to regain their integrity and freedom.

The basic message in all of this, Shaltūt adds, is that Muslims should not accept oppression that compromises their liberty and their faith and spare no effort to repel it. Shaltūt then adds that many scholars of earlier times, including, for example, al-Zamakhsharī (the author of *Tafsīr al-Zamakhsharī*, d. 538/1180) have reached the conclusion that *hijrah* is advisable, even from Islamic lands, if it means escape from a climate where heresy and evil proliferate. This is, in fact, one of the many conclusions derived from the texts we have just reviewed.[11]

Having discussed the verses in some detail, Shaltūt raises the question: 'Where are we today and what is happening to our community and people?' Some of us are helping the colonisers, and our religion is being subjected to the caprice of the oppressors. Shaltūt ends this series of questions with a supplication for Divine mercy and guidance to save the Muslims and the oppressed from the oppressors.[12] It would appear from the tone of this ending that Shaltūt himself was not convinced whether the conclusions he drew and advocated in his discussion were feasible and realistic! He was most probably aware of the difficulties of successfully resisting a powerful but unsympathetic government through the use of *hijrah*. How can one resort to *hijrah*, one may ask, against one's own despotic leaders?

In his article 'The Obligation to Migrate,' Muhammad Khalid Masud discusses the same Qur'ānic passage (i.e. 4:97) from which he draws the following conclusions: 1) the historical *hijrah* was an obligation that required physical movement of Muslims to join the nascent Muslim community in Medina. It was a movement also toward a new self-definition in a newly emerging context. Refusal to migrate also meant exclusion from membership of the nascent community; 2) *hijrah* was closely associated with *jihād* as those who migrated 'in the way of God' were assured of God's pleasure and reward; 3) *hijrah* established a bond of relationship among Muslims, especially between the newcomers to Medina (i.e. the *Muhājirūn*) and the residents of Medina, the *Anṣār*.[13]

Among the several *hadīth*s on the subject of *hijrah*, at least one treats *hijrah* as a principle of permanent validity that applies to all Muslims at all times:

لاتنقطع الهجرة حتى تنقطع التوبة ولاتنقطع التوبة حتى
تطلع الشمس من مغربها

Migration (*hijrah*) will not end until repentance ends and repentance will not end until the sun rises in the West.[14]

The parallel between repentance and migration in this *hadīth* seems to visualise the mental/psychological dimension of *hijrah* in the sense that both signify a mental renunciation and departure from a certain state of mind toward self-renewal and reform. In several *hadīth*s, *hijrah* has also been identified as a continuing obligation, except for one *hadīth* which provides that it ceased to be an obligation after the conquest of Mecca, which took place in the year 8 Hijrah. The *hadīth* simply declares that: 'There is no *hijrah* after the Conquest—*lā hijrah baʿd al-fatḥ*.'[15] One can imagine that even this *hadīth* can be given a metaphorical meaning as it has indeed been given in the sense that conquest puts an end to *hijrah*: say, if the Muslims conquer the enemy then obviously *hijrah* would become redundant—in its physical sense at least. Muslim jurists and *ḥadīth* scholars are still divided on the purport of this *ḥadīth*, but historical developments tend to confirm that *hijrah* came to end after the conquest of Mecca. Some have held the view that the obligatory *hijrah* may have even been terminated with the pact of Hudaybiyyah in 628 AD, some three years before the conquest of Mecca, since Hudaybiyyah allowed the Muslims to stay behind in Mecca.

The Shāfiʿī jurist, Ibn Daqīq al-ʿĪd (d. 625/1228) commented that in the *ḥadīth* under review the Prophet only nullified the obligation of *hijrah* from Mecca to Medina. The reasoning behind this nullification was that Mecca became *dār al-Islām* after it was conquered. But this *ḥadīth* only put an end to the obligatory *hijrah* from Mecca to Medina. As for the *hijrah* to leave *dār al-kufr* and for Muslims to migrate to *dār al-Islām*, that is a continuing obligation and remains intact. This was also the view of the Ḥanafī jurist, Abū Bakr al-Jaṣṣāṣ (d. 370/980) who regarded it an obligation to migrate from *dār al-kufr*. The Mālikī jurist Ibn Rushd (d. 595/1199) was of view that the obligatory *hijrah* had ended, but only in the narrow sense of leaving Mecca for Medina. The wider concept of *hijrah*, which requires Muslims to leave *dār al-kufr*, remains to be of permanent validity. The Ḥanbalī jurist, Ibn Qudāmah (d. 620/1223) asserts that 'the jurists have unanimously agreed' to the effect that migration from *dār al-kufr* to *dār al-Islām* is a firm obligation of Muslims.[16] The contemporary Walid Sharaiyra who has quoted a cross-section of scholastic opinion on the subject has, however, reached the opposite conclusion that: 'there is not the slightest indication in the often-quoted *ḥadīth* of 'no migration after the conquest' to support the view that *hijrah* from *dār al-kufr* to *dār al-Islām* is an eternal obligation.'[17]

Abū Sulaymān Ḥāmid al-Bustī (d. 996 AD), a scholar of *ḥadīth*, reconciled this difference of opinion and argued that *hijrah* was actually meant to support and strengthen the abode of Islam (*dār al-Islām*) in its early days. After the conquest of Mecca in 630 AD the Muslims became strong and victorious and migration was no longer required. Yet the *hijrah* may become obligatory again whenever change of conditions make it necessary for it to be reinstated.[18]

Ibn Khaldūn (d. 1406 AD) explained the texts under review to say that *hijrah* was a requirement for Muslims to join the Prophet Muhammad in Medina. Even if *hijrah* is said to have continued after the conquest of Mecca, it was definitely not a requirement after the Prophet passed away.[19]

Ibn Ḥajar al-ʿAsqalānī (d. 1449 AD), a renowned *ḥadīth* scholar, scrutinised this debate and concluded that a number of prominent Companions, including Ibn ʿAbbās, Tāʾus, ʿAṭāʾ, Ibn Jurayj, and ʿĀʾishah perceived *hijrah* as a migration from Mecca to Medina. After Mecca was conquered, no *hijrah* was required any longer.[20]

Thus there was a change in the perception of *hijrah* even within the first generation of the advent of Islam. *Hijrah* was obligatory at first, then it became optional, but it was not discouraged as its continued practice meant weakening Mecca and strengthening Medina. But even that situation changed after the conquest of Mecca. Then people began to discuss the wider *hijrah*. The question was then asked whether *hijrah* should be understood such that migration from outside to *dār al-Islām* was an obligation. No simple answer can be given, as the precedent on this tends to be divergent. The *hijrah* to Abyssinia, for instance, was not to *dār al-Islām*; the Hudaybiyyah pact allowed Muslims to stay in Mecca, which was also not *dār al-Islām*, and the Prophet did not require the Bedouins around Mecca and outside Medina to migrate to Medina. Instead of pledging themselves to migrate, the Bedouins pledged to join the *jihād* against the unbelievers. This seems to imply as if *hijrah* was a *jihād*-related requirement.[21]

Imām al-Shāfiʿī held the view that *hijrah* was not obligatory for all because the Prophet permitted the Bedouins not to migrate if they did not wish to. Shāfiʿī argued that *hijrah* became an obligation only after the declaration of *jihād*, and then only on those who had the ability to do so. A Muslim was allowed, therefore, to stay in *dār al-kufr* as long as he was free to practice his religion.[22]

Early responses to the question of migration are complex. The issue of movement to the Islamic territory by Muslims who resided in *dār al-kufr* invoked responses from various groups that reflected their particular views and circumstances, as well as the outbreak of civil war and violence even during the period of the Pious Caliphs (632–661 AD). Both the rebels and pro-community groups justified their positions within the Islamic framework.

The Kharijites who rebelled against the caliph ʿAlī and subsequently also opposed the Umayyads (661–750 AD) maintained that a territory became *dār al-kufr* if its rulers denied the sovereignty of God or committed major sins, in which case, they became unbelievers, or *kāfir*. In these circumstances, *hijrah* from such a territory and *jihād* against it became obligatory. There were some differences of opinion among the sub-groups of the Kharijites, such as the Ibādiyyah who were more moderate and did not term all the territories outside their own camp as *dār al-kufr*. According to the Ibādiyyah, inability to migrate was not an excuse but a condition that one should strive to remove.[23]

The Muʿtazilah leader al-Jubbāʾī (d. 916 AD) held the view that as long as it was possible to stay in a territory without being forced to commit acts of disbelief, the territory was *dār al-īmān* (abode of faith), but added that this condition did not prevail in Baghdad at the time. The Shīʿites who opposed the Umayyads and the Abbasids (750–1250 AD) did not take the extreme position of the Kharijites and regarded the territories under these dynastic regimes as *dār al-hudnah* (abode of truce) from which *hijrah* was not obligatory.[24]

The majority of Muslims favoured the *status quo* and disagreed with the extremist views on *kufr* and *hijrah*. They took a moderate view and considered different options within the concept of *hijrah*. In doing so, they referred to the renowned *ḥadīth* which recommended that one should combat evil by one's hand, or by one's tongue, depending on the nature of the evil and one's ability to combat it. If one was unable to do either, one should denounce it in one's heart and distance himself from it. But that would be the weakest level of faith.[25] The majority thus took the view that *hijrah* was *jihād*-related, and *jihād* was a collective duty (*farḍ kifāyah*), not a personal obligation of every Muslim, which may or may not be undertaken individually. The only *hijrah* that could be individually performed was withdrawal in the heart. The Sufis also embraced this esoteric and interiorised understanding of *hijrah*.[26]

The Sufi commentators of the Qurʾān maintained that the obligation of physical *hijrah* was repealed, and only the spiritual *hijrah* remained. There were accordingly three types of *hijrah*: 1) that of the *ahl al-dunyā*, migration of the 'people of the world' for the purpose of trade; 2) that of the ascetics (*zāhidūn*) toward the hereafter through piety and spiritual refinement; and 3) that of the mystics (*ʿārifīn*) from the evil of the self to the heart, then to the soul, and ultimately to the Beloved. The first of these is the outwardly *hijrah* (*hijrah ẓāhirah*), and the latter two consist of inwardly migration (*hijrah bāṭinah*).[27] Many commentators have held that *hijrah* means abandonment of sin, which may be in a physical sense or otherwise. Some have added to this that *hijrah* also means abandoning the habitual sinners after advice and reminders fail to make any impact on them. In his Qurʾān commentary, Sayyid Quṭb (d. 1966) urged his readers to dissociate themselves from corrupt society. *Hijrah* to him was thus primarily a spiritual concept involving mental dissociation (*ʿuzlah shuʿuriyyah*), but he asked his readers in the meantime to work hard to eliminate corruption from society.[28]

Earlier, the renowned al-Ghazālī, who is known for his mystical orientations, read a similar meaning in a Qur'ānic passage which praises the faithful for their humility and *iʿrāḍ*, that is, turning away from the ignorant (*al-Furqān*, 25:63). When a Muslim realises that it is useless to persuade the ignorant, he should abandon them by refusing to greet them or associate with them. A different course of action is indicated here which is that the faithful is not required to migrate and abandon his homeland for another country.[29]

The jurists were also caught in a web of ambiguities and defined *dār al-ḥarb* as a vague and amorphous category, which need not be elaborated here, as I shall briefly return to it in the following pages. I shall nevertheless specify some of their basic positions on *hijrah*.

The majority of the Mālikī jurists agreed with the Shāfiʿīs that *hijrah* was not an obligation after the conquest of Mecca. Some even held that *hijrah* was not required after Hudaybiyyah. A Muslim was thus allowed, to remain in *dār al-kufr* with a legitimate excuse, or for the propagation of Islam. The Mālikī jurist Ibn al-ʿArabī (d. 1148 AD) provided a detailed analysis of *hijrah* and specified the circumstances in which the *hijrah* continued to be a requirement. He presented six scenarios and argued that migration was obligatory in the first three and basically permissible in the rest—as explained below:

(1) Migration from *dār al-ḥarb/dār al-kufr* (abode of war) to *dār al-Islām* (abode of Islam). It is said that the principle of *hijrah* remains valid notwithstanding the *ḥadīth* which proclaimed 'there is no *hijrah* after the conquest.' Ibn al-ʿArabī added: since a clear distinction between the two abodes may now be difficult to sustain, the early juristic position on them should be reviewed. One way to resolve this hurdle may be to take *dār al-ḥarb* literally and say that when war breaks out between two countries, it would be necessary from a rational viewpoint, and obligatory from the *Sharīʿah* perspective, for a Muslim to travel away from the enemy territory to a safer place.

(2) Abandoning the land of heresy and *bidʿah*. Ibn al-Qāsim, a disciple of Imam Mālik reported that he heard the Imam saying that it was not permissible for a Muslim to live in a place where the leaders of the faith (*al-salaf*) are being constantly reviled, insulted and abused.

(3) Migration from a place wherein *ḥarām* prevailed such that earning a lawful living becomes impossible and indulgence into *ḥarām* unavoidable for a Muslim.

(4) When migration means escape from fear and persecution to a safe place where a Muslim can live in peace and avoid being the victim of injustice. This is because protecting oneself against oppression and persecution is a *Sharīʿah* requirement. An example of this in the Qurʾān may be when the Prophet Abraham feared persecution from idolaters, he declared his intention and told them: 'I am a migrant—*muhājir*—unto my Lord' (29: 26). A similar response to fear and persecution was given by Prophet Moses who 'escaped from them (the oppressors), fearing violence and said: My Lord! Deliver me from the wrongdoing folk' (28:21). Both these examples tend to validate *hijrah* in the sense of escape from oppression and injustice.

(5) Leaving a place which is infested with illness and disease for a place that is safe and clear of disease. An exception to this is made in a *ḥadīth* with regard to a plague that has already been contracted, in which case one should not leave the locality where the plague broke out.

(6) When one's property is no longer safe in a particular locality or place. This is because the *Sharīʿah* equates the sanctity of the property of a Muslim to that of his life and honour, all of which call for protection in the face of destruction and violence.[30]
None of the first three scenarios in which Ibn al-ʿArabī has considered *hijrah* to be obligatory are self-evident, which means that they cannot provide the basis of an obligation. From a juristic viewpoint, there must be no ambiguity on what constitutes an obligation and what does not, so that the duty bearer knows precisely when he is required to comply. We can accept the rational suggestion that *dār al-ḥarb* should be literally understood. But that alone cannot establish a religious obligation. There is also a difference between a 'collective obligation (*farḍ kifāʾī*) and a personal obligation (*farḍ ʿaynī*). We know that *jihād* is a collective obligation, but the juristic debate on *hijrah* seems to be premised on *hijrah* being a personal obligation. It may be that one way out of this debate is to extend the concept of collective obligation to *hijrah* and say that it is also a collective obligation. The other two scenarios in al-ʿArabī's discussion can also be only understood in a general sense, but they cannot lend themselves to clear definitions. It is difficult enough to give precise definitions to *kufr*, apostasy and blasphemy, let alone insult to the leaders of the faith, or the upright predecessors (*al-salaf*).[31] What exactly amounts to reviling or an insult? And who are precisely the faith leaders and *al-salaf*? These are some of the inevitable questions

one has to answer when one imagines the second and the third scenarios presented by Ibn ʿArabī. Since that level of precision is not available in the doctrine of *hijrah*, all one can say is that moving away from such and such a place is recommended, or that it is a collective obligation, and this would leave an element of flexibility as well as scope for the personal judgment of the individual concerned.

Moreover, all the schools of law have recognised the role of necessity where compliance to the laws of *Sharīʿah* can become unfeasible due to stressful situations. Thus according to a *fatwā* by Imam Mālik, in the event where all the means of earning a lawful living are made inaccessible to a Muslim, and he is also unable to escape to another place and the only way for him to earn a living is to engage in an unlawful occupation, he may do so to the extent necessary for his survival but no more.[32]

HIJRAH IN RECENT TIMES

Subsequent developments in the Mālikī school oscillated between the two positions of considering *hijrah* as a continuing obligation, or a mere permission. Of relevance here are developments in Nigeria, especially in the work of Shehu ʿUthman Dan Fodio (1754–1817 AD) who restated the Mālikī doctrine of *hijrah* in the context of historical circumstances in which he was compelled to fight syncretism and injustice of the Hebe Muslim rulers. Dan Fodio argued for *jihād* and migration and went against the tide of the *ʿulamā'* opinion that was supportive of the Muslim rulers in power. Dan Fodio relied mainly on the Kharijite precedent and went so far as to apply the concept of *dār al-kufr* to a Muslim country wherein the rulers were corrupt and observed pagan practices. Dan Fodio's views 'had a far-reaching impact on the *jihadist* movements in West Africa and it continued to influence the Nigerian response to British hegemony.'[33]

The question of *dār al-Islām* and *hijrah* acquired fresh significance in the wake of the British occupation of India and Nigeria. Attahiru, the last Sultan of the Sokoto Caliphate resorted to Dan Fodio's formulation of *hijrah* when faced with the British invasion from 1900 onwards when Kano was also taken. Attahiru rallied his forces against the British, resorted to *hijrah* and asked his followers to follow him to Mecca. He fought the British at the battle of Burmi where he was killed and the British occupied Nigeria. After Attahiru's death, Mālikī scholars returned to the position that *hijrah* was not a requirement.

Whereas the majority view of *dār al-Islām* and *dār al-kufr* contemplates the personal affinity of the individual, the Ḥanafīs consider ter–

ritorial affinity as a determining factor in this distinction. *Dār al-Islām* to the Ḥanafīs changes into *dār al-ḥarb* under the following circumstances: (a) when the laws of disbelievers replaces the *Sharīʿah*; (b) when the occupation forces cease to observe their treaties with the Muslim; and (c) when the land in question is adjacent to *dār al-ḥarb* with no territory in between.[34]

The Ḥanafī majority view has been that if the Friday and religious holidays can be observed in a place, it is *dār al-Islām*. The non–Muslim rulers can also appoint Muslim governors and judges to enforce the Islamic law. It was on this basis that many Muslim scholars in India considered British India as *dār al-Islām*. But there were others, such as Shah ʿAbd al-Azīz (d. 1824) and Mawlana ʿAbd al-Bari Farangi Mahli (d. 1828) who considered India as *dār al-ḥarb*, but did not call for *hijrah*. Sayyid Ahmad Barelwi and Abū'l-Kalam Azad considered *hijrah* and *jihād* necessary, on the other hand, to restore India's status of *dār al-Islām*. Many scholars from the Deoband and Barelwi schools advocated a refrain from *hijrah*. Yet the upsurge in the Khilāfat movement and views of Kalam Azad and Shawkat ʿAlī persuaded thousands of Indian Muslims to emigrate from India to Afghanistan in the 1920s. Yet it was clear that the traditional *ʿulamā'* opinion was against *hijrah* and the experience of *hijrah* to Afghanistan was not all that successful. Most of the immigrants went unprepared, 'hundreds died on the way . . . others returned to India destitute and frustrated.'[35]

Migration of Muslims into the Ottoman lands is mainly concerned with the movement of Muslims from Russia and the Balkans due to hostile policies, colonisation and war. Migration into the Ottoman state began at the time of Russia's annexation of Crimea in 1783. Muslims began to leave their ancestral homes largely because they desired to live under the authority of a Muslim ruler rather than the Russian Orthodox Czar. Migration intensified after the wars of 1806–19 and 1829, especially after the Crimean War of 1853–56 in which Muslims had supported the Ottomans in the hope of regaining their old autonomy and independence. The Turko-Russian War of 1877 and the Balkan war of 1912 brought waves of migrants from the Balkans. The total number of emigrants into the Ottoman Empire between 1860 and 1914 is estimated between five to seven millions.[36]

In addition to political and historical causes, the 'concept of *hijrah* has exercised a profound influence on Muslim thought and practice over the centuries.' *Hijrah* became an intrinsic part of the Ottoman intellectual heritage, and it was given a new meaning in the late 1880s when the Sultan was persuaded to declare the empire open to all Muslims who wanted to migrate and settle there.[37] However notwithstanding the interest the Muslims of Russia and the Balkans showed in migrating to Ottoman lands for historical, political and religious reasons, for many the empire was always the final destination. The religious elites from Central Asia, Afghanistan and the Caucasus migrated and settled in Mecca and Medina where many of their descendants, although 'Arabised' survive as distinct groups until today. It is also important to note that for 'the Muslims of Central Asia the *ḥajj* was considered somewhat incomplete without a stop, sometimes for years, in Istanbul;' it was almost like a 'second-tier *ḥajj*.'[38]

The initial Ottoman immigration policy was devoid of religious significance. The early Muslim migrants, mostly ethnic Turks from the Balkans but also Slavic-speaking Bosnians, Herzegovinians, Montenegrins etc., were accepted as part of the traditional Ottoman practice of granting asylum to anyone, Muslim or non-Muslim. By 1880, however, the government's immigration policy had changed in favour of Muslims. The old policy was officially changed in 1887 after the Shaykhul Islam wrote to the Caliph Sultan Abdulhamid II that the lives of Muslims under foreign rule had become intolerable and that 'every Muslim wishing to live in an Islamic country should be allowed to immigrate.' The change of policy that followed was reflected in the naming of the office charged with immigration matters, which was renamed as of that date, as Muhacirin-i Islamiyah Komisyonu Alisi (High Islamic Immigration Commission) and was placed directly under the Sultan.[39]

In many areas the local Muslims helped to build homes for the newcomers. Although there were unpleasant clashes, caused by negative perceptions and attitudes, they were the exceptions. The manner in which the native population welcomed them further solidified the migrants' Muslim consciousness and eventually facilitated their integration into the new society.[40]

A new dimension of *hijrah* that emerged in the nineteenth century is *hijrah* to non-Muslim countries. For reasons of higher education, training, employment and escape from oppression in their own countries Muslims have travelled and migrated to non-Muslim countries and their numbers have increased over the years. This was by and large a new type of *hijrah* with different motives and objectives.

As noted earlier, *hijrah* is permitted from a land of persecution, disease, and financial insecurity. There were also those who permitted *hijrah* to non-Muslim lands for the propagation of Islam. Oppression and tyranny, insecurity of life and property also became more and more stressful in the case of refugees. This was the story in recent decades also of the dislocated Afghans, for example, who migrated to foreign lands including Europe and America. Some of the refugees were associated with a previous regime and fell out of favour with a change of government and saw no other alternative but to leave the country for fear of persecution and even death in obscure circumstances. Although genuine cases of this kind are likely to be covered by the principle of necessity (*darūrah*), one also sees, in the case of Afghanistan, that economic necessity due to continued fighting for over twenty years compelled many to flee the country in search of a livelihood.

Most of them went to the neighbouring countries, but some also emigrated to Australia, Europe and America. Most of the Afghan refugees would seem to qualify one or the other of the valid grounds of *hijrah*. Then there remains the case of economic migrants and those who have settled in non-Muslim lands for employment, education either of themselves or their children and family.

Khalid Masud has quoted ʿAbd al-Azīz al-Ṣiddīq[41] to the effect that remaining in Europe and America for purposes of education and employment was not only allowed but was often obligatory. The main argument being that education and training in modern science and technology are obligatory for the progress of Muslim societies, as they would otherwise remain dependent on developed countries.

The effective cause and reason of migration away from *dār al-ḥarb* in Islamic law is the apprehension that the faith, life and property of Muslims would not be safe there. But then one might say that there is no such fear now. It has even been noted that, 'the prospects of propagation of one's religion are better in Europe and America than they are in most Muslim countries.'[42] Added to this is also the point that Western countries cease to be *dār al-ḥarb* since they have entered treaties with Muslim countries and a peaceful pattern of relations now prevails between them. This was the conclusion ʿAbduh had reached earlier when he declared that Muslims were allowed to reside in Britain so long as they had the freedom to practice their religious duties.[43] Many distinguished scholars of Islamic law in the Middle East such as Abū Zahrah (d. 1974), ʿAbd al Qādir ʿAwdah (d. 1954) and the living author Wahbah al-Zuḥaylī have offered similar interpretations of the doctrine of *hijrah*.[44]

CONCLUDING REMARKS ON *HIJRAH*

Having lived for many years in the West, I can confirm that the lives and properties of Muslims are not under threat there. I also conclude from it that the *dār al-ḥarb* of medieval times is no longer sustained by the pattern of relations that currently prevails between the Muslim countries and their Western counterparts. Broadly speaking, the laws of *Sharīʿah* in the sphere of human relations and *muʿāmalāt* apply when their effective causes are present and they cease to apply when they become absent as applying them then would be an exercise in futility. *Hijrah* is a doctrine that combines both religious and humanitarian grounds. The humanitarian dimension of *hijrah* is no less important than its religious bearings. If *hijrah* can bring the humanity together on compassionate grounds of some giving shelter to others and accepting them in their lands at times of distress without religious oppression, then *hijrah* itself has undergone a change or we have seen it operating in a new direction. Thus it would be reasonable to say that we retain the original doctrine and hold it applicable if and when the situation and predicament of Muslim and non–Muslim relations change again. But *hijrah* should otherwise not be seen as an obstacle in the way of expanding the compassionate dimensions of human relations.

The emergence of the nation state also presented the *ummah* with a new reality. After independence from colonial rule, Muslims have emerged divided into a number of nation states. The Muslim world of earlier times now consists of nation states looking after their own national interests. Unlike the situation that prevailed in medieval *dār al-Islām*, a Muslim cannot now freely travel, migrate, or settle in any Muslim country of his choosing. Some of these countries are secular and many others have reformed their religious and personal laws, which might add to the element of doubt as to whether they can now be seen as *dār al-Islām* in the sense this concept was understood. *Dār al-Islām* can, in any case, retain its meaning when there is a *dār al-ḥarb*. Under the present conditions where *dār al-Islām* has been replaced by the plurality of nation–states, the idea of *hijrah* in terms of movement from *dār al-ḥarb* to *dār al-Islām* becomes basically meaningless if all of them apply a system of visa or entry by permission to their territories. The question that now arises is not only from where one must migrate but also to where? Another relevant question that has been asked is: from where does one not need to migrate? If the place where a Muslim resides is not only physically safe but also presents no hindrance to the practice of his faith, then the answer could well be that, from such a place, a Muslim does not have to migrate. This logic would also apply even more so if the non-Muslim country in question has entered a covenant or treaty with its Muslim counterpart that offers protection to the Muslims and recognise their freedom of religion and other rights.

There are obviously many new and unresolved questions, most of which seem to hinge upon a clearer understanding of the early doctrine and its application to the present times. This is what is addressed next.

WHAT OF *DĀR AL-ḤARB*?

Muslim jurists have tended to apply *dār al-ḥarb* to every non–Islamic country or territorial domain. Our inquiry into this shows that *dār al-ḥarb* should only refer to a hostile country which may or may not involve a non-Muslim power. A certain amount of diversity in juristic opinion over the substance of this binary division had obviously existed among the schools of law.

In addition to the typical division of the world into *dār al-Islām* and *dār al-ḥarb*, the Shāfiʿī and the Zaydī jurists introduced the two intermediate terms of *dār al-ʿahd* (abode of treaty, or abode of truce) and *dār al-fisq* (country of transgression and disobedience) respectively. The Ḥanafīs perceived *dār al-ḥarb* as every state that was not governed by the *Sharīʿah* and held that they should be invaded and subdued by Muslims. Others have held that *dār al-ḥarb* is a place where neither the *Sharīʿah* applies nor does it offer security for Muslims who might reside therein.[45] Some contemporary scholars have on the other hand employed the term *dār al-daʿwah* as an equivalent to *dār al-ʿahd* signifying a place where Muslims are allowed to preach and propagate Islam.

Although the word *ḥarb* and its derivatives are mentioned in six different places in the Qur'ān, none of them seem to correspond with the notion of placing all non-Muslim countries under the monolithic category of *dār al-ḥarb*. A country may be designated as *dār al-ḥarb* only when it is hostile and dangerous for Muslims to reside in, otherwise these terms should be replaced by what Fakhr al-Rāzī has suggested as *dār al-daʿwah*, and *dār al-ijābah* (the land of propagation, and land of receptivity or response).[46] This labelling is drawn from the Qur'ānic guidelines on *daʿwah*, or invitation to the faith, which should be peaceful, and courteous:

ادع إلى سبيل ربك بالحكمة والموعظة الحسنة وجادلهم
بالتى هى أحسن

Invite to the way of thy Lord with wisdom and good exhortation, and argue with them in ways that are best and most gracious. (16:125)

This is a normative guideline for *daʿwah*, and it is clearly one of courtesy and friendship. As for determining whether a place can be designated as *dār al-ḥarb*, the Qur'ān provides only some guidelines, one of which is persecution and injustice that deny Muslims the freedom to practice their faith.

Historical records indicate that the basic concept of *dār al-ḥarb* relates to the threat that the Quraysh of Mecca presented to the nascent Islam, for they were the guardians of the Kaʿbah at the time and dominated the socio-economic life of Mecca. The spread of Islam was a direct challenge to their privileges, which they were determined to protect through recourse to violence, including persecution of the new converts to Islam who were eventually compelled to abandon their homeland in Mecca. It was in this context that the following Qur'ānic verse was revealed:

أذن للذين يقاتلون بأنهم ظلموا وأن الله على نصرهم
لقدير الذين أخرجوا من ديارهم بغير حق

To those against whom war is waged, permission is granted for them (to fight back) because they were wronged. They were expelled from their home in defiance of their right. (22:39-40)

Ibn ʿAbbās stated in conjunction with this verse that Mecca was as a result considered hostile territory (*dār kufr, dār ḥarb*), and it was then that this verse was revealed. Aggression and injustice were thus the main feature and hallmark of *dār al-ḥarb*. Another characteristic that is shown in the Qur'ānic record of events may be noted in the following verse:

ربنا أخرجنا من هذه القرية الظالم أهلها

Our Lord! Rescue us from this town, whose people are oppressors. (4:75)

The phrase 'this town whose people are oppressors' was a reference, according to Fakhr al-Rāzī, to Mecca as the original *dār al-ḥarb*. Fighting the Meccans was permitted in order to repel oppression and restore justice.[47] This is, however, a status that can be changed by means of agreement and treaty, just as the Prophet did by signing the renowned peace treaty of Hudaybiyyah with the Meccans. Mecca was, as a result, turned into *dār al-ʿahd* (abode of treaty) as Muslims were eventually able to conduct *daʿwah* and practice their religion in Mecca. This is the prevailing contemporary opinion of many leading scholars. Abū Zahrah, ʿAbd al-Salām Madkūr, Wahbah al-Zuḥaylī, Ṭaha Jābir al-ʿAlwānī and others maintain that the previous *dār al-ḥarb* has now all become the abode of treaty and *dār al-ʿahd*. No country that is now a member of the United Nations can consequently be considered as *dār al-ḥarb*.[48]

Our review of the basic evidence thus points to the conclusion that every non-Muslim state that does not apply the *Sharīʿah* is not automatically *dār al-ḥarb*. Since there is no *dār al-ḥarb* now as it used to be in medieval times, the term should consequently be reserved only for a state or country that is engaged in actual hostility and war against Muslims. And then again, the term can only be applied when Muslims are persecuted in the territory in question and are denied the freedom to practice their religion.

MIGRATION AND ASYLUM

The nearest Arabic expression for asylum is *istiʾmān* (also *istiʾjār*) which literally means asking for safe conduct. The starting point of *hijrah* and *istiʾmān* are almost identical in that the migrant and the person who seeks asylum both leave their place of residence with the intention of finding a new home and a safe place in a foreign territory. Both migration and asylum also tended to occur due to problematic and compelling circumstances. However, the jurists have reserved *hijrah* and *muhājir* for Muslim migrants whereas *istiʾmān* and *mustaʾmin* refer to non-Muslims who seek shelter and protection in Muslim lands under similar circumstances.

For Western jurists 'asylum' implies refuge and protection for persons who have left their own countries for fear of being persecuted.[49] 'Refugee' on the other hand refers to a person who has been displaced from his or her home and community for reasons that are not under his or her control.[50]

The historical origins of *hijrah* and asylum in Islam date back to the lifetime of the Prophet and his companions, when they migrated from Mecca to Medina. The Qur'ān and *Sunnah* took an affirmative stance on the right of protection and refuge for both Muslims and non-Muslims. To quote the text:

وإن أحد من المشركين استجارك فأجره حتى يسمع كلام الله ثم أبلغه مأمنه

> If one amongst the pagans ask you for asylum (*istajārak*) grant it to him (*fa-ajirhu*) so that he may hear the word of God, and then escort him to where he can be secure. (9:6)

Non-Muslims have thus been granted the right of asylum and security in Muslim lands, and this includes, according to commentators, grant of asylum even to a person who might have been hostile to the Muslims. For asylum is usually sought under contentious circumstances often involving hostility and persecution.[51] The verse above effectively directed the Islamic government to grant a request for asylum when it is solicited by a non-Muslim. It varies in this respect from the language of the UDHR (Art. 14) which recognises the right of the individual to request asylum, but granting it is subject entirely to the sovereign authority of the State.[52] The Islamic government is also entitled, like other sovereign states, to identify the grounds of asylum so as to ensure that it is grated on genuine grounds, but when these have been ascertained, then the request from asylum seekers must be granted. According to al-Zamakhsharī, it is binding on the Muslim state to respond to a request for asylum from non-Muslims just as it must provide them with education in the principles of Islam. If the person embraces Islam, he or she will have the right to full citizenship, but if he does not embrace Islam, he will require double protection: first from the Muslim forces that might be engaged in hostility against their people; and second, from their own folk as the asylum seeker would have detached himself from his kith and kin. Both levels of protection should be extended to him and should consequently be escorted to a safe place.[53]

Muslim jurists have divided the contract of granting safe conduct (*amān*) into two types: temporary, which is referred to as *isti'mān*, and the person bearing it is known as *musta'min*. The second type of *amān* is known as *'aqd al-dhimmah*, which is concluded between a non-Muslim and the Islamic government on a permanent basis, and the person bearing it is consequently called *dhimmī*. The temporary contract of *amān* is also divided into two types. It may be concluded between a non-Muslim individual and the Islamic government, which is what is known as *isti'mān,* or it may be between a Muslim government and a non-Muslim government. This latter is known as *muwāda'ah* or truce, being a peace treaty for a limited period between its signatories. It is usually resorted to in order to put an end to war. If a *musta'min* wishes to reside permanently in the Muslim country, he becomes a *dhimmī.*[54]

To grant asylum to a non-Muslim is also not confined only to the 'hearing of the word of God,' for this is not stipulated as a condition but is seen as a likely consequence. The purpose is to enable the non-Muslim to live in the Muslim community, travel around, learn about Islam and experience the Muslim way of life. The notion of asylum is thus broad enough to encompass all legitimate purposes for a long and peaceful period of time, still enjoying the freedom to leave and return to his country of origin whether or not he chooses to become a Muslim.[55] This conclusion is in line with a conversation that is reported to have taken place between the renowned Companion 'Alī b. Abū Ṭālib and a non-Muslim who asked him 'if one of the non-believers came to do something else other than listening to the word of God, would his life be secure?' 'Alī responded that the life of such a visitor would be safe because God Most High said 'if one amongst the pagans asks you . . .' without, that is, specifying the purpose or ground of asking for asylum.[56]

TRAVEL: OBLIGATORY AND OPTIONAL (THE *ḤAJJ* AND *'UMRAH*)

The *hajj* pilgrimage to Mecca is a religious obligation that is ranked as one of the five pillars of the faith. This is to be performed by every Muslim who is physically and financially capable of doing so. It is a once-in-a-lifetime obligation, but additional visits, although optional, are recommended. As a religious duty, the *hajj* evidently takes for granted the freedom of the pilgrim to travel to Mecca regardless of the distance or the pilgrim's country of origin. This duty, in turn, entitles every Muslim to a corresponding right, which the ruling authorities at both ends may neither deny nor obstruct. The origins of the *hajj* date back to Prophet Abraham, who laid the foundations of the Ka'bah, as the Qur'an declared:

$$\text{وإذ بوّأنا لإبراهيم مكان البيت . . . يأتوك رجالا وعلى}$$

$$\text{كل ضامر يأتين من كل فـج عميق}$$

And when We pointed to Abraham the site of the House . . . (and asked him) to proclaim to people the pilgrimage (and said): they will come to thee on foot and on every lean camel coming from every remote path—so as to partake in its benefits and mention the name of God on appointed days. (22:26–27)

This verse contained the prophecy, when it was revealed, that Mecca will become the centre to which men will come from all directions. The verse was revealed at a time when the Prophet was being forced by the pagan Arabs to leave Mecca. The reference to 'lean camel' indicated the great distances that the pilgrims would undertake to travel and 'from every remote path' evidently showed that people would come to Mecca from the remotest parts of the earth.[57] The great Islamic tradition that was so instituted has been maintained by Muslims of the world to this day, and has remained uninterrupted over the many centuries since its inception.

Another religious purpose that involves travelling to Mecca is the supererogatory *'umrah*, which is a minor *ḥajj*. Some jurists have held that *'umrah* is also a duty (*wājib*) to be performed once in a lifetime by Muslims who are capable of performing it. Two prominent Companions, 'Abd Allāh b. 'Umar, and 'Abd Allāh b. 'Abbās have held that *'umrah* is an obligation. The latter is quoted to have said that 'the *'umrah* is mentioned side by side with the *ḥajj* in the Book of God.' (Cf. 2:196).[58]

Unlike the *ḥajj*, which is time-bound, *'umrah* may be performed at any time of the year. The *ḥajj* is evidently an obligation whereas *'umrah* is optional and every Muslim is in principle free to visit Mecca for performance of *'umrah* and no one may be said to have the authority to prevent him or her. The first *ḥajj* is an obligation but Muslims are also entitled to repeat it and perform it a second time or even more. According to a *ḥadīth*, a person asked the Prophet if *ḥajj* was to be performed annually or only once. The answer was 'only once, and if anyone performs it more often, he perform a supererogatory act.'[59]

يأيها الناس قد فرض الله عليكم الحج فحجوا، فقال رجل

أكلّ عام يارسول الله! فسكت، حتى قالها ثلاثا، فقال

رسول الله (صلعم) لو قلت نعم لوجبت ولما استطعتم

Another aspect of travelling for religious purposes is travelling to the mosque for congregational prayers, which is highly recommended on a regular basis, and it is a requirement in the case of the Friday prayer (*ṣalāt al-jumʿah*). There is much encouragement in the *ḥadīth* that one should try also to perform the early morning and late evening prayers (i.e. *fajr*, and *ʿishāʾ*) in congregation, and those who persistently neglect to attend the mosque for prayers call upon themselves a moral blame. Friday congregational prayer is the subject of a Qurʾānic directive addressed to all believers who must close business and diligently perform the noon prayer in congregation (cf. 62:10). Villages and localities that are too scarcely populated for congregation prayer to be convened, their people are advised to travel to the nearby village or town where Friday prayers are held.

During his journeys from Mecca to Medina, and vice-versa, the Prophet used to stop and pray in certain places, including the mosque of Qubah outside Medina. The Prophet's Companions also followed this practice and prayed in the same places. Concerning Qubah the Prophet reportedly said that 'performing a single prayer at the mosque of Qubah equals (in reward) the performance of a *ʿumrah*.'[60] The Prophet built the mosque of Qubah when he migrated to Medina and named it as Masjid al-Taqwā (mosque of piety). He used to visit it frequently and Muslims have also kept that practice alive to this day. In another *ḥadīth*, the Prophet spoke in praise of the Masjid al-Aqṣā in Jerusalem and said that a single prayer performed at that mosque earns reward one thousand times that of prayer in other mosques.[61]

Pious Muslims have throughout the ages vied for the opportunity to breathe their last in the vicinity of the two holy mosques in Mecca and Medina. Many have sought to take permanent residence and the idea of finding a place of rest in the holy land has had a special appeal to Muslims. There is encouragement for this in the *ḥadīth* such as 'there will be migration after migration, and the best of people are those who cling closely to the places of migration of Abraham.'[62] The faithful are thus encouraged not only in the context of *hijrah*, but in a variety of other contexts, to undertake a certain amount of travel as a part of his or her religious duties and gain spiritual merit by it. In a recent case, the Federal Shariat Court of Pakistan quoted several passages from the Qurʾān and unconditionally declared the following:

> The right of free movement from one place to another of all human beings has been fully recognised in Islam. This right has not only been recognised by the Holy Qurʾān, but in several *āyāt*

a clear incentive has been given to undertake the journey and to travel on the earth.[63]

The Qur'ān also refers to another facet of Arabian life, the fact that they were a trading nation and used to travel to distant places such as Sham (Syria) and the Yemen with their trade caravans that regularly crossed through alien territories. Mecca was a major business centre and the caravans that travelled between Mecca and other destinations were organised on a seasonal basis. Business was often combined with worship which is why the caravan journeys coincided with the *ḥajj* season. The Qur'ān spoke approvingly of the existing pattern of seasonal journeys and the treaty arrangements which facilitated them:

لإيلاف قريش إيلافهم رحلة الشتاء والصيف فليعبدوا رب

هذا البيت الذى أطعمهم من جوع وآمنهم من خوف

For the covenant (of security and safe conduct) enjoyed by the Quraysh, and covenants that facilitated their travelling (*riḥlah*) in winter and summer—let them be and let them worship the Lord of this House, who provides them with food against hunger and with security against fear. (106:1–4)

The free movement of trading caravans and the then existing levels of cooperation between the Quraysh and other distant tribes were thus to continue unhindered and continue to bring benefit to all concerned. The word *riḥlah*, which in the familiar Arabic usage, is associated with travel in search of knowledge is here used in the Qur'ān in connection with the special accomplishment of the tribe of Quraysh and how much they owed their success to God's providence. The text thus conveys the message that the Quraysh, above all, with their talent for journeys south and north (to Yemen and Syria) should accept God's commands to worship Him. That trading should not be their sole preoccupation and that they should express their allegiance to the Lord of the Ka'bah.[64]

Travel in its broadest sense ensured the bonds of unity in the Muslim community. The *ḥajj* pilgrimage manifested this, especially in pre-modern Muslim societies. The pilgrimage in itself was a complex phenomenon that enabled its participants to share most of their everyday life with their co-religionists during travel. The journey to Mecca was not only a religious enterprise. Because of its length over a period of several months the pilgrims also observed and experienced common local practices. For instance, in most of the important parts of the journey, Moroccan pilgrims converted their merchandise into cash, and purchased the different commodities that they needed for the journey. For this reason many *rihlah* texts are in the form of market guides, advising future pilgrims about the best way to carry on advantageous trade on the way to the *Hijāz*. These guides show how business and pilgrimage were intimately connected.

At the main stages of the journey from Africa-Tripoli, Cairo, Mecca, and Medina the pilgrims stopped for longer periods than they did at other places. They were able to go to libraries, buy books, attend classes at al-Azhar in Cairo, or give lectures at the Prophet's mosque and shrine in Medina. They could also participate in the topical religious debates of the time.[65]

Some Moroccan pilgrims preferred to settle permanently in Mecca or in Cairo. One Moroccan scholar, Abū Salim ʿAbd Allāh al-ʿAyyash (d. 1090/1659) travelled three times to the Hijaz in 1639, 1653 and 1661 and stayed for long periods in Mecca and Medina, as well as Jerusalem and Cairo. Everywhere he participated actively in theological debates, both learning and teaching, which led him to write his two-volume *rihlah* text on the subject.[66]

Recent decades have seen the numbers of *hajj* pilgrims swell up from almost all Muslim countries. Modern means of transportation have facilitated the *hajj* and the total number of pilgrims has increased to up to two million a year. This has also brought changes in the practical experiences of pilgrims. Until the early 1930's the *hajj* was a physically unsafe, insecure journey of long duration in cramped and crowded conditions. Country by country survey might reveal differences in the experience of pilgrims, but on the whole, the vast improvement in transportation, medical and welfare facilities has reduced the death and destitution figures.

In the case of pilgrims from Malaysia, the destitution rate for the pilgrims was about 0.85 per cent in the 1880s. Since the Second World War, destitution is claimed to have been completely eradicated through severe government measures to restrict pilgrimage to those who are financially able to make the journey without jeopardising their own, or their family's, financial security. Death rates have also declined dramatically since statistics became available in the 1920's. At that time, rates fluctuated widely, peaking to roughly 13 per cent. By the 1950s, this figure stood at 8.8 per cent. In the 1970s and 80s, the highest rate has been 3.7 per cent, and rates more often range between 1.5 per cent and two per cent.[67]

Improvement in *hajj* preparation facilities in Malaysia were stepped up with the setting up in 1969 of the Hajj Management and Savings Corporation, known as Tabung Haji, which helps the pilgrims save and prepare effectively for the event. It organises such practical matters as registration, visas, passports, transportation and medical care, as well as saving plans for would be pilgrims.

By the 1920s the average stay of the Malaysian pilgrims was about six months, and it was becoming more common for pilgrims to reside in Mecca permanently after retirement. Since the end of WWII, the length of the *hajj* journey has shortened, and it is now reduced to a well-controlled, four-week event.[68] Whereas previously the pilgrims came mainly from the middle aged and elderly groups, today the *hajj* participants include younger age groups, and also an increased number of women.

Pilgrims discuss 'an intense feeling of belonging to a community of Muslims. The communal bond developed during the journey is still strong,' although it is perhaps now perceived in relation to the Malay community. Because the *hajj* is performed within an almost wholly Malay context, shepherded and buffered by Malay officials, it is seen as a shared national experience as well as a religious one.[69]

Broadly speaking, travelling can be divided into the three varieties of praiseworthy (*maḥmūd*), reprehensible (*madhmūm*) and neutral (*mubāḥ*) depending on the purpose of travel and the intention (*niyyah*) of the traveller. The praiseworthy travel can be in the nurture of an obligation (i.e. *wājib*) such as *hajj* , which is obligatory on those who can afford it. Al-Ghazālī has also included travelling for acquisition of knowledge under the category of *wājib* based on the *hadīth* that 'pursuit of knowledge is an obligation of every Muslim.' Travelling may be recommendable (*mandūb*), such as visiting the learned and benefiting by their company, and also visiting the graves of prophets and saints. Most other travelling falls under the category of *mubāḥ* with the proviso that *mubāḥ* can become praiseworthy and *mandūb* if the intention is to gain the pleasure of God. Thus when a person travels in order to earn a living and help his family and dependants in need, it would earn him a spiritual reward. Travelling can become reprehensible, even if it is for the *hajj* , if it is motivated by ostentation and hypocrisy. Travelling away from a place where plague breaks out is also reprehensible for an afflicted person if it means spreading the disease. But if vaccination or protective medication is available and it is duly taken, than there should be no objection to travel. Intention and change of conditions thus play an important role in raising the *mubāḥ* to *mandūb* or reducing the *makrūh* to *mubāḥ* in travelling.[70]

Travel in order to visit the living is preferable than visiting the dead because greater benefit can be gained from the company of the living, whether it is in respect of knowledge or other beneficial purposes, or simply as a way to show fraternity and affection for someone. As for visiting places, a territory or land, and whether pilgrimage to a place or a building may bring a spiritual reward, al-Ghazālī's response to this is that it does not. Exceptions are the three holy mosques, namely the holy mosque of Kaʿbah in Mecca, the mosque of the Prophet in Medina, and the Masjid al-Aqṣā in Jerusalem. No other building or site has such merit or spiritual ranking. Visiting these places is obviously meaningful if one actually prays in them.[71]

TRAVEL IN SEARCH OF *ḤADĪTH*

Riḥlah fī ṭalab al-ḥadīth (travel in search of *ḥadīth*) became a standard phrase and a genre of the *ḥadīth* literature that became the theme and focus of writers on *ḥadīth*. One of the well-known works of *ḥadīth* by al-Khaṭīb al-Baghdādī (d.429/1039) bears this very title. Al-Baghdādī wrote that travel in search of *ḥadīth* was prompted by the fact that the Companions travelled away from Medina and took residence in various outlying regions. They were the carriers of *ḥadīth* and people began to travel to meet with them to verify *ḥadīth* they had received from the Prophet. During the time of the Pious Caliphs, many of the leading Companions were sent as teachers and judges to other places. ʿAbd Allāh b. Masʿūd was thus sent to Iraq and Abū Dardā' was sent to Syria. Their disciples among the successors intensified the search and interest in the subject grew further which is why al-Baghdādī, like many others, devoted works to this subject.

As is well known, doubts about the authenticity of *ḥadīth*s were expressed from the very early times. ʿUmar b. al-Khaṭṭāb and ʿAlī b. Abū Ṭālib went on record to warn the people against indiscriminate reporting of *ḥadīth*. The more frequent the instances of doubt became concerning the veracity of *ḥadīth*, the greater became the need to verify its authenticity. Travelling in search of *ḥadīth* gained momentum until it became a feature of Islamic scholarship in this area.[72]

Another factor that stimulated travel in search of *ḥadīth* was due to the distinction drawn between the connected (*muttaṣil*) and disconnected (*mursal*) *ḥadīth*s. Had they both been treated on an equal footing, the writers of *ḥadīth* would not have had the incentive to undertake the hardship of extended journeys, to establish that a certain *ḥadīth* is connected to a certain chain of narration (*isnād*) and therefore reliable.[73]

Islamic scholarship in the area of *ḥadīth* is thus a product largely of intensive travelling by *ḥadīth* scholars. Ever since the time of the Companions, travelling in search of *ḥadīth*, and then travelling by seekers of knowledge to distant centres of learning set in place an attitude whereby travelling was associated with knowledge. To give an example, one of the Companions, Jābir b. ʿAbd Allāh, is reported to have travelled for a whole month, on camel back, from Medina to Egypt, together with ten of his fellow Companions in order to verify just one *ḥadīth* they had received from ʿAbd Allāh b. ʿUnays al-Anṣārī who had received it directly from the Prophet.[74] There are other examples. The renowned follower Saʿīd b. al-Musayyib travelled frequently in search for a single *ḥadīth*. Al-Baghdādī has quoted Ibn al-Musayyib as saying: 'I used to travel for several days at a time in search of a single *ḥadīth*.' Imam Mālik has also confirmed this report.[75] The Companion al-Shaʿbī was quoted to have said that travelling in search of even a word that shows the way to enlightenment or clarifies confusion is never wasted.[76]

Travelling in search of *ḥadīth* became a salient feature of the works of the third/ninth century compilers of *ḥadīth* such as al-Bukhārī and Muslim who spent many long years (in the case of al-Bukhārī over ten years) to collect and authenticate the *ḥadīth* with narrators who had narrated a *ḥadīth* for the first time or who could confirm and verify the authenticity of an existing *ḥadīth*.[77] Travelling in search of knowledge became 'a normative feature of medieval Muslim education, at least until the sixth AD/twelfth AD century.'[78] The incidental benefit of travel is the exposure one gains to the world and the cultures and traditions of people, something that gives insight and stimulates reflection in general. Viewing and hearing, as Ghazālī comments, can be external or internal. Perhaps with mystical undertones, al-Ghazālī says that people of wisdom have often advised others to 'open your eyes so that you can see' but 'I say to them to close your eyes so that you can see.' Both of these statements convey a meaning, and both tend to stress the reflective side of man. Hearing and sight are both enriched by travel, which has a spiritual meaning in the sense of transcendental movement or journey to the higher echelons of spiritual and intellectual attainment.[79]

Another benefit of travel is that it develops the quality of patience and resilience in the face of difficulties that travellers tend to en-counter. Al-Baghdādī thus commented that a traveller in search of knowledge goes away from his home and leaves his loved ones behind. Then he is also likely to meet with different people and feel the need to communicate and get on well with people of different cultural orientations. He needs to be courteous and know the place and standing of people; if he succeeds and becomes close to people of knowledge and experience, his travel would have become a source of benefit for him. Travelling is also a useful means of making new friends who then become one's mediators to a new culture of the town and city in which the traveller resides.[80]

Among the etiquettes of *rihlah* (*ādāb al-rihlah*) one that al-Baghdādī has noted is that the search for knowledge must surely begin with one's own town and areas nearby before one undertakes a journey further out. For it is less arduous and good for the locality if one values the teachers and the learned of one's own town. When this is done and the benefit from local sources of learning is obtained, one may then branch out to other places.

One of the leading successors, 'Ikrimah, while quoting Ibn 'Abbās, is reported to have said that the word '*al-sā'ihūn*' (travellers) in the Qur'ān refers to travellers who went in search of the *hadīth*. '*Al-sā'ihūn*' occurs in the Qur'ān where the text declares that 'triumphant are those who turn repentant to God, those who worship Him, those who praise Him and the *sā'ihūn*.' (9:112)

Qaradāwī has also quoted this episode and commented that 'Ikrimah's interpretation can be read also in the *hadīth* of the Prophet: 'One who sets out in pursuit of knowledge, he is engaged in the cause of God (*fī sabīl Allāh*) until he returns.'[81] But since the text does not specify the meaning 'Ikrimah has given to *sā'ihūn*, it may be said that travelling in pursuit of religious knowledge, indeed all knowledge that is pursued with good intention, is included within the meaning of *al-sā'ihūn*.

History has not known of a nation that has engaged so extensively in travel at such an early stage in the search of knowledge as the Muslim *Ummah*. Medieval Muslims really knew no boundaries in their desire to master the subjects of their learning, which comprised among others, the Qur'ān, *hadīth*, *tafsīr* (commentary on the Qur'ān) and *qira'ah* (correct recitation of the Qur'ān). Scholarly peregrinations were frequent and often long, in terms of both time and distance. A man could study in twenty different cities with as many different teachers in each and return home yearning for yet another trip. A representative example of this was a Cordovan shaykh who went to the east in 330AH/941AD at the age of fourteen. During his

trip, he followed an extensive itinerary that included Mecca, Medina, Jeddah, Yemen (San'a, Zabid, Adan), Fustat, Jerusalem, Gaza,
Ashkelon, Tiberias, Damascus, Tripoli, Beirut, Caesaria, Ramla,
Farama, Alexandria and Qulzan. This tidal flow of scholars and
scholarship across the Islamic lands eventually established the primacy
of certain cities and regions as learning centres.[82]

A shifting hierarchy of learning centres emerged and, depending on
political and economic conditions, different cities in different periods
could vie for pre-eminence. Whereas Baghdad set the standard in
the third-early fourth AH/ninth-early tenth AD centuries, it was Cairo
under the Fatimids and Nishāpur in the succeeding two centuries
which attracted Muslim scholars. This hierarchy also depended to
a lesser degree on circumstances, such as distance to one's place of
origin, personal knowledge of places and teachers. But it is evident
that travelling scholars were well informed. They knew where the
leading scholars lived, how to contact local 'ulamā' and where they
would be most rewarded.

The special virtues (faḍā'il) assigned to Mecca and Medina in the
Qur'ān and ḥadīth established a precedent and a paradigm for newly
established Muslim communities. Mecca, of course, possessed both a
privileged pre-Islamic status and a central place in Muslim tradition.
This was in many ways emulated by other Muslim societies and
stimulated, in turn, a level of cultural competition among them.

The tradition of riḥlah was also influenced by the outlook and
origin of the traveller himself. For example, a scholar who left
Cordoba or Seville to perform the ḥajj and study with the learned
men of North Africa and Egypt was usually a man of 'solid middle
class background and some local intellectual of renown'.[83] He was
imbued with the value of his native land. Although he marvelled
at the sights he saw in Mecca, and classes he attended in Fez or
Damascus, he returned home still convinced that no other land
surpassed the merits of al-Andalus.

Spain, Egypt and Khurasan were three examples of intellectual
centres with strong local identities. Each contributed to the riḥlah
tradition. A Muslim in search of knowledge could find a warm
reception in each region and it would cement his ties to the wider
Muslim community of which he was a member.[84]

Muslim rulers were also drawn into the competition spawned
by the riḥlah. The fourth/tenth century was the height of Spanish
Umayyad power and visits by Spanish Mālikī scholars to Egypt. Reports indicate that the Caliph 'Abd al-Raḥmān III al-Nāṣir regularly

sent 10,000 dinars for the maintenance of Mālikī *fuqahā* in Fustat (now Cairo). Not to be outdone, the Egyptian ruler Abū al-Mask Kafūr ordered that 20,000 dinars be distributed among the Shāfiʿīs.[85]

The pharaonic view of Egypt as the centre of the universe became part of its cultural heritage. As a centre of Islamic studies, however, Egypt initially did not match the rate of development that Iraq enjoyed, but by the fourth/tenth century it was a much-respected centre of Islamic learning. Fustat was a magnet for Muslims from all over the Mediterranean, and Egyptians themselves saw little reason to seek knowledge elsewhere. The scarcity of Egyptians in the lists of *ghurabā'* (foreign scholars) in Spanish, Iraqi and Persian bibliographical works underlines this attitude. Fustat was a teeming, sophisticated reception centre and destination for *riḥlah*, but the *riḥlah* as a self-defining concept in Egyptian Muslim life seems to have played a minor role.

Spain was the exact opposite of Egypt. The *riḥlah* was the central feature of Spanish Muslim intellectual life. This was due partly to Spain's geographical location at the Western reaches of the Medieval Islamic World, and partly also to its proximity and contact with the Christian World. With the possible exception of its coreligionists in Sicily, Spanish Muslims had more contact with Christians than any other region of the Muslim World.

Although Muslims were the dominant group, Spain had a large population and maintained economic ties with the Christian west. Spanish Muslims had every reason to seek spiritual refreshment in areas where Islam was the majority culture. Egyptians could afford, so to speak, to remain home, whereas for Spaniards, *riḥlah ṭalab al-ʿilm* truly meant the survival of Islam as a coherent, *Sharīʿah*-based way of life. What began as a refreshment that conferred social benefit in the third/ninth century gradually became an unavoidable necessity by the sixth/twelfth century, given the changing political and military conditions and the increasing emigration of the corps of Mālikī *ʿulamā'* to North Africa and Egypt.

The Muslims of Spain, Tunisia and Egypt also turned to some extent to centres of learning in Iraq. Whereas the study of *fiqh* developed locally in Spain from an early date, *ḥadīth* did not. Hence a substantial number of Muslims went east to immerse themselves in that field. If a sense of intellectual periphery (Spain) and of centre (Iraq and increasingly Egypt and Tunisia) did exist, it was not highlighted in the biographies, yet these same biographies tend to indicate this. *Ṭalab al-ʿilm* was in the Andalusian context a way of expressing how their peripheral Islamic society related to the more central heartland of the *ummah* especially after the fall of Toledo (478/1058) and steady progress of the Reconquista. *Riḥlah fī ṭalab al-ʿilm* thus became 'the most important aspect of Spanish learning and the concept permeated the language of the Spanish biographical dictionaries.[86]

Nishapur was home to an influential network of *ʿulamāʾ* who controlled much of the political activity of Nishapur. People from Nishapur travelled in pursuit of knowledge, particularly in the realm of *hadīth*, but the nature of their travel differed from both their Spanish and Egyptian counterparts. They travelled but not with an urgent sense of 'mission' which characterised the Spanish preoccupation with *riḥlah*. Travel for the sake of knowledge was more of a routine for the scholars of Nishapur. It was taken for granted in a way that was not the case in Spain. In Spain it was a primary aspect of one's identity as an *ʿālim* and reflected the country's peculiar status at the periphery of the Islamic World. The Egyptians also respected *riḥlah* but felt little obliged to pursue it. Nishapur, and its environs were never even remotely threatened by the likes of a Christian Reconquista and had enjoyed a self-assured and prosperous past, despite the Mongol ravages in Khurasan. Nishapur and the Iranian/Central Asian culture zone generally looked more towards India and China rather than the Mediterranean, although they also travelled within Khurasan, Iraq and Central Asia.[87]

THE QUEST FOR KNOWLEDGE: AN OVERVIEW OF THE
QURʾĀN AND *HADĪTH*

The Qurʾān recommends travel as a means of self-development, discovery, and education. Valuable lessons could be drawn from the contemplations of history and experiences of bygone nations, as stated in the following text:

قد خلت من قبلكم سنن فسيروا فى الأرض فانظروا كيف
كان عاقبة المكذبين

> Surely there have been examples before you, so travel in the earth and see what was the end of the rejecters (who accused God's messengers as liars). (3:137)

Elsewhere, the people are encouraged to 'Travel in the earth and observe how He (God) originated the creation' (29:20).

قل سيروا فى الأرض فانظروا كيف بدأ الخلق

And then again attention is drawn to the rise and fall of nations as the text put it:

أفلم يسيروا فى الأرض فينظروا كيف كان عاقبة الذين من قبلهم

'Have they not travelled in the land that they might observe the end of those who were before them?' (40:82). Al-Baghdādī has quoted Aḥmad b. Ḥanbal to have said that ascertaining and establishing a higher *isnād* (*ʿuluww al-isnād*), that is, a higher chain of narrators for *ḥadīth*, partakes in religion and merits therefore as an act of piety.[88]

As can be seen from these passages, travelling is not only permitted but strongly recommended for the advancement of knowledge. 'What God has permitted,' ʿAbd al-Karīm Zaydān pointed out 'the Islamic state must also permit.' Abū Zahrah has also made a similar remark that since Islam has encouraged travelling, Muslims must uphold that spirit and impose no restrictions on it unless public interest dictates otherwise.[89] This relationship between travel, knowledge, and education is highlighted in a *ḥadīth* in which the Prophet instructed the faithful to 'seek knowledge even if it takes you to China'.

اطلب العلم ولو كان بالصين

In another *ḥadīth*, the Prophet is reported to have said:

ما من رجل يسلك طريقا يطلب به علما الا سهل الله له طريق الجنة

'Not a single man travels in pursuit of knowledge that God does not guide his path to Paradise'.[90] China was obviously not a place of religious knowledge, nor had there been any prospect of its receptiveness to Islam. The Prophet, in other words, encouraged travel to a non-Muslim territory to impress upon his followers that religion must not come in the way of acquiring beneficial knowledge.

Qaraḍāwī has claimed the *ḥadīth* (on travel to China) to be a statement of one of the Companions, yet I noted a detailed discussion of it in al-Baghdādī who traces its *isnād* to the Companion Anas b. Mālik through three different channels all reaching Anas b. Mālik. Al-Baghdādī's modern commentator, Nūr al-Dīn ʿAtr also added that the same *ḥadīth* has been recorded by Ibn ʿAbd al-Barr in his *Jāmiʿ Bayān al-ʿIlm*, and also in *al-Kāmil* by Ibn ʿAdi. Anas b. Mālik's version of the *ḥadīth* reads: 'Seek knowledge even if it be in China, for the search of knowledge is an obligation of every Muslim.'[91]

Another aspect of the freedom of movement which the Qurʾān has singled out is prospects of earning a lawful income. Here again the believers are strongly encouraged to utilise the resources of the earth in order to improve their share of its bounties: 'God has made the earth subservient to you. So go about in its tracts and eat of its sustenance' (67:15).

هو الذى جعل لكم الارض ذلولا فامشوا فى مناكبها وكلوا
من رزقه

On the relationship of worship and work, it is provided in another verse with reference particularly to congregational prayers: 'When the call is made for Friday prayer, then rush to the remembrance of God and abandon trade. But when the prayer is over, then scatter in the land and seek of the bounty of God' (62:9–10).

إذا نودى للصلوة من يوم الجمعة فاسعوا الى ذكر الله
وذروا البيع . . . فإذا قضيت الصلوة فانتشروا فى الارض
وابتغوا من فضل الله

It is thus indicated that after performing the obligatory prayer, people may go after their business and work. They are not, in other words, required to spend any more time in the mosque than what is required for the prayer.

This practical attitude to work and worship is also reflected in another Qurʾānic verse that permits the people to do their business even during the days of the *ḥajj* pilgrimage: 'There is no blame if you seek the bounty of God (during the pilgrimage). Then when you descend from the Mount of Arafat, celebrate the praises of God at the sacred monument' (2:198). Worship, remembrance of God, and journey to the *ḥajj* may, in other words, be combined with lawful trade and the daily activities of life. The message conveyed here is that there is no harm in conducting trade in Mecca during the pilgrimage season. The story behind this verse is that prior to the advent of Islam trade fairs were held during the *hajj* season. Some of the most well-known of these fairs, namely ʿUkaz, Madinah and Dhuʾl-Majāz, attracted many visitors from the outlying areas. After the advent of Islam, there were some among the early Muslims who thought that doing business for worldly gain was inconsistent with the spirit of worship during the pilgrimage. This verse was then revealed to inform them that it was not so and that trading activities, meetings and conferences may be combined with acts of worship during the same period.[92] The *Sunnah* of the Prophet has also emphasised the virtue of work and self-application in pursuit of earning a living so much so that work is often equated with devotion and ʿibādah. Freedom of movement and freedom to earn a living thus go hand in hand and the evidence in the Qurʾān and *Sunnah* is generally affirmative on both.

RIGHT OF PASSAGE

Another theme of the *Sharīʿah* evidence concerning the freedom of movement relates to the upkeep of public thoroughfare for the convenience of passengers. Keeping the streets clear and safe is a requirement and the purpose is naturally to ensure that travellers and the general public are not hindered in the conduct of their daily activities. It is reported that on one occasion the Prophet noted some of his Companions sitting so that they were crowding the street; they were told: 'You must avoid sitting on public thoroughfare.' To this they replied: 'O Messenger of God! These are our venues and we cannot avoid them.' Then the Prophet said: 'If so, then give the street its right.' 'And what is its right?' they asked. To which the Prophet replied: 'To turn your gaze away, to avoid harming others, to return the greeting (*salām*) of those who pass by and to bid good and forbid evil.'[93]

إياكم والجلوس فى الطرقات، فقالوا يارسول الله مالنا مجالسنا بل نتحدث فيها، فقال اعطوا الطريق حقه، قالوا وماحق الطريق يارسول الله، قال غض البصر، وكف الأذى، ورد السلام، والأمر بالمعروف والنهى عن المنكر

The message of this *hadīth* is that people should avoid obstruction and congestion of public passages as far as possible and should allow the passengers to enjoy free and unhindered passage. But if traders and others have to use them, they may be allowed to do so provided they refrain from annoying others or limit their freedom of movement and also treat the users with courtesy.[94] The caliph ʿUmar b. al-Khaṭṭāb evidently considered the message of this *ḥadīth* to be more than a persuasive advice when he punished with flogging one Iyās b. Salāmah for obstructing the public thoroughfare. The Umayyad Caliph, ʿUmar b. ʿAbd Al-ʿAzīz, is also reported to have instructed his officials to 'open the doors of migration to the Muslims. Let the people carry their goods by land and sea and obstruct not God's servants from earning their living.'[95]

Muslim jurists have drawn the conclusion that anyone who encroaches on the public path, erects or builds something on it, the authorities may demolish it in order to clear the path. It is also the duty of the *muḥtasib* (market inspector) to ensure that in summer and in winter and at all other times, the property owners and residents take good care of the safety and cleanliness of public paths in their areas.[96] Shopkeepers, traders and property owners are not allowed to bring their goods out in the street such that they restrict public passages. Nor are property owners entitled to build premises adjoining the street such that they violate the 'right of the street' (*ḥaqq al-ṭarīq*) or cause inconvenience to the public. It is the duty of the *muḥtasib* to prevent these and similar other conduct that may cause inconvenience to the street users.

Since public paths and streets are for the use of the general public, everyone is entitled to use them to the extent they need to but no one may use them in such a way that inconveniences others. Thus if someone ties animals in the middle of the street, or throws rubbish or refuse water that causes obstruction and inconvenience the *muḥtasib* may stop him. The *muḥtasib* may also impose limits on the use of streets by porters and carriers of bulky items, such as straw and stacks of hay etc., that obstruct the street or soil and tear people's clothes. All of these partake of *munkar*, which the *muḥtasib* is required to regulate and prevent. The *muḥtasib* is also within his rights to regulate the activities of property developers so that public passages are not exposed to excessive smoke and smell and that toilets and bathrooms are not constructed such that they violate the safety and cleanliness of the streets.[97]

Highway robbery (*qaṭʿ al-ṭarīq*, also known as *ḥirābah*) is a capital offence for which the Qurʾān prescribes a three-fold punishment depending on whether it involves murder and robbery, or terrorising the passengers without loss of life and property. A detailed account of these will not be attempted here. Suffice it to point out that the Qur'ān penalises with banishment anyone who obstructs public passages and terrorises the people, even if the perpetrator does not commit any violence. There is a general agreement among jurists to the effect that the prescribed punishment of *ḥirābah* applies to terrorists who threaten people with arms and obstruct their free access to public passages both within and outside residential areas and towns. The Qur'ān provides a three-fold punishment that culminates in death penalty and mutilation of limbs of the terrorist if his act of terror actually destroys innocent life. Banishment, which amounts to a denial of the freedom of movement is, in other words, a punishment, itself a testimony to the inviolability of the freedom of movement.[98] Moreover, in Islamic law, banishment for one year is a supplementary punishment for fornication, which is added to the principal punishment of one hundred lashes. This is the position of the majority; Imam Abū Ḥanīfah has, however, taken an exception and held that it is for the head of state to decide whether or not to banish the convict. This is because of the questionable effects of banishment as a deterrent, a subject which will later be discussed in further detail.[99]

SOCIAL VISITS

Muslims are encouraged to maintain close relations with their family and friends and one of the ways in which this is achieved is to exchange visits and undertake the travel they might entail. Maintaining the ties of kinship (*ṣilat al-raḥim*) with one's close relatives is more than recommended in Islam, indeed it is an obligation. Close relatives in this sense are broadly defined as persons who are prohibited from marrying one another. It is due to this emphasis that the subject has received in the Qur'ān and *ḥadīth* that Muslim jurists were prompted to hold that observing the ties of kinship is a *wājib* and severing them is *ḥarām*.[100] The Qur'ān thus enjoins the believers:

$$\text{واتقوا الله الذى تسألون به والأرحام}$$

Be mindful of your duty to your Lord in whom you claim (your right) against one another, and observe the ties of kinship. (4:1)

Al-Bukhārī has recorded several *ḥadīth*s on the subject. In one *ḥadīth* on the authority of Abū Ayyūb al-Anṣārī, it is provided that,

'A man asked the Prophet, if he could tell him of a deed (so virtuous) that will earn him entry to Paradise. In answer the Prophet mentioned three things: worship of God through prayer, charity (*zakāh*) to the poor and "keeping good relations with your kith and kin".'[101]

فقال النبي صلى الله عليه وسلم تعبد الله ولاتشرك به شيئا وتقيم الصلاة وتؤتى الزكاة وتصل الرحم

The subsequent portion of the same *ḥadīth* simply declared that 'one who severs the bond of kinship will not enter Paradise.'

Al-Bukhārī has also recorded a *ḥadīth* narrated by Abū Hurayrah wherein the Prophet is reported to have said:

عن النبى صلى الله عليه وسلم قال الرحم شجنة من الرحمن. فقال الله من وصلك وصلته ومن قطعك قطعته

Al-raḥim (lit. the womb) is a derivative of (God's illustrious name), al-Raḥmān. God addressed *al-raḥim* and said 'I will keep good relations with the one who keeps good relations with you and I will sever relations with him who severs ties with you'.[102]

The Prophet visited his family and relatives and encouraged others to do the same. New converts to Islam were also encouraged to maintain good family ties with their non-Muslim relatives by visiting them and giving them financial support when they were in need. Ties of kinship that are mentioned in the *ḥadīth* also included foster relations. Thus it is reported that the Prophet used to visit Umm Ayman who nursed him during his early childhood years.

Visiting friends and keeping good relations with them stand next in order of priority to one's family and relatives. Honouring the friends of one's parents has also been recommended in a *ḥadīth* in which the Prophet is quoted to have said that one way of honouring one's parents is 'to be reverent to one's father's close friends.'[103]

عن عبد الله ابن عمر . . . انى سمعت رسول الله صلى الله عليه وسلم يقول إن من أبر البرّ صلة الرجل أهله ودّ أبيه بعد أن يولى

To show affection to one's friends should not be for the sake of personal gain and material benefit; it should be for the sake of God. This is the message of a *ḥadīth* Muslim has recorded from Abū Hurayrah wherein the Prophet recounted an anecdote that 'a man went to visit his brother' in a nearby village. God Most High sent an angel on his route who asked the man where he was going and the answer was 'I am going to visit my brother (the word brother seems to be a euphemism referring to a friend) in the next village.' He was then asked whether this was for some gain or material benefit, to which the man replied 'No. Only because I love him in God's pleasure.' The angel then said 'I am God's Messenger to you to say that God loves you in the same way as you loved your brother through Him.'[104]

اريد أخا لى فى هذه القرية، قال هل لك عليه من نعمة ترد بها؟ قال لا، غير أنى أحببته فى الله عز وجل، قال فاني رسول الله اليك بأن الله قد أحبك كما أحببته فيه

Muslims are also recommended to visit men of knowledge and piety to gain from their company and advice. The Prophet's Companion Abū Bakr has thus been noted to have reminded 'Umar b. al-Khaṭṭāb to visit persons that the Prophet used to visit when he was alive. It thus becomes a part of Islamic ethos to enhance ties of friendship by means of social visits on every suitable opportunity. To do so is a commendable way of exercising one's freedom of movement and travel. Hence no Islamic government would be within its rights to take a negative stand on them.

CONCESSIONS FOR TRAVELLERS

Travelling qualifies the traveller to certain concessions in respect of the religious duties such as prayer and fasting. These are meant to help the traveller sustain the possible hardship he might experience in the performance of such duties.

Travelling (*safar*) for the purposes of utilising these concessions is defined as a movement away from one's usual domicile for a lawful purpose that is premeditated and intended. In this way travelling for no purpose and wandering without a definite destination and some idea of the time that may be taken by it is not taken into account in the juridical meaning of *safar*. Travel that invokes juridical concessions is also one that absorbs a minimum of three days of travelling by camel back or any equivalent means, covering a distance that was estimated at about 100 kilometres. It is also noted that *safar* should take the traveller outside the city and residential quarters to areas where normal amenities are not available, and also the proviso that the traveller plans to stay for three or more days at destination, be it a town, residential area, or wilderness.

There is also a maximum limit of fifteen, according to one *ḥadīth*, and of eighteen days, according to another, beyond which the concessions terminate, and do not apply if one knows the length of one's stay in advance. Thus when a traveller intends to stay at destination for fifteen days or longer, he is considered a resident (*mustawṭin*), as opposed to a traveller (*musāfir*).[105] To qualify for any concession, travelling must also be permissible (*mubāḥ*) and this would exclude, for example, a criminal who flees due to fear of arrest, or a young person who runs away from home without the permission of his parents, or worse still, when it is contrary to their wishes. Included in this is also an indebted person escaping from his creditors at a time when he is in no hardship and is able to repay. A terrorist who is on the move terrorising people and spreading corruption in the land also does not qualify for any of these concessions. This is the preferred view of the majority, which is upheld by the Shāfiʿī school. The Ḥanafī's, on the other hand, have entitled the traveller to concessions regardless of the purpose or type of journey. They ground their argument in their reading of the Qurʾānic verse on the subject, which declares 'and any of you who is ill or travelling may count the days and observe them later' (2:184).

فمن كان منكم مريضا أو على سفر فعدة من أيام أخر

This verse is said to have been conveyed in absolute and unqualified (*muṭlaq*) terms, which applies equally to all cases. The effective cause (*ʿillah*) of concession that is granted therein for the traveller and the sick in respect of fasting is without any further qualification. Hence the conclusion that it includes all cases where the effective cause or *ʿillah* of the concessions obtains.[106]

The general position as earlier stated is that concessions are all optional that may or may not be utilised and this includes the one concerning the fasting of Ramadan, which the traveller may observe at a later date. But some jurists have held a different opinion, according to which, breaking the fast is obligatory for the traveller.

This opinion is based on a somewhat literal reading of the Qur'ānic verse (2:184), already cited, which can be read so as to mean that the concession is made into an obligation. This is further re-enforced by a certain *ḥadīth*, quoted by al-Kāsānī, to the effect that 'one who fasts while travelling, disobeys the Prophet—*man ṣāma fi'l-safari fa-qad ʿasa Aba'l-Qāsim*.' Al-Kāsānī then follows with a comment: 'all that we know is that the Prophet, peace be on him, has travelled while fasting just as he also broke the fast during travel. This pattern is also endorsed by the practice of his Companions.' Since the purpose of the concession is to lighten the burden of the people, they should have a choice in the matter, and making *iftār* (breaking fast) obligatory would go against the spirit of flexibility and concession.[107] The only proviso that al-Kāsānī has added is: 'according to us—ʿ*indanā*—it is preferable to observe fasting if the journey is light and does not involve hardship.' The issue then runs into some technicality due to the fact that the Ḥanafīs consider fasting during travel as the normal law (ʿ*azīmah*), and *iftār* as a concession (*rukhṣah*). The Shāfiʿīs have held the reverse of this and consider *iftār* as normal law, which merits preference.

The *Sharīʿah* also grants a concession with regard to shortening the quadruple prayer (*al-qaṣr*) from four units (*rakʿat*) to two. This would apply to three of the five daily prayers only as the other two consist of two and three units of obligatory prayer each. Being a concession, *qaṣr* is also optional, and not, as it were, obligatory. One who does not observe it therefore is not blameworthy. Another concession that applies to obligatory prayers is combining of two prayers at one and the same time (i.e., *al-jamʿ*), which, like *al-qaṣr*, is meant to relieve the traveller of hardship. The two afternoon prayers of *ẓuhr* and ʿ*aṣr* (i.e., those of early and late afternoon) may thus be combined and performed either at *ẓuhr* time or ʿ*aṣr* time, but preferably at the latter. This may also be done with regard to the early and late evening prayers (i.e. *maghrib* and ʿ*ishā*), which can both be performed at either of these two time segments. The majority of the leading schools have upheld the concession of *al-jamʿ*, except for the Ḥanafīs, who do not apply it due to their differential understanding of timing in prayer. *Qaṣr* and *jamʿ* can also be combined and both taken advantage of together.

Another point of concession relating to prayers for travellers is abandonment of the Friday congregational prayer in favour of the usual *ẓuhr* prayer. And lastly in the event of fear of attack from predatory animals or enemy forces and the like, prayers may be performed while on the move or riding, in a combination of gestures and bodily movements that are expounded in the *fiqh* manuals. This last concession is also available in situations of necessity even when one is not travelling.

Two other concessions are also granted concerning the ablution (*wuḍū'*) in preparation for obligatory prayers, one of which replaces the normal ablution with dry ablution (*tayammum*) that consists of wiping ones hands and face with clean dust or sand. The *tayammum* so performed is a total substitute to *wuḍū'* and acts in the same capacity as *wuḍū'*. *Tayammum* is permitted in the absence of water or when reaching water involves risk to one's personal safety. The other concession concerning the *wuḍū'* is that a traveller may wipe his feet instead of washing. Ablution may thus be performed by wiping over the boots that cover the ankles instead of washing the feet, provided that the foot and boot are clean at the time of wiping. Wiping (*mash*) is valid for a maximum of three days after which the feet must be washed once at least for another three days of concession to be resumed. Socks which are fortified with leather are also counted as boots for purposes of this concession. The concession pertaining to *mash* terminates as soon as the journey comes to an end and washing by normal method is resumed even if it is prior to the expiry of three days.

Further on the fasting of Ramadan, it will be noted that if the journey is planned as of the previous night, there is no requirement of fasting on the following day of Ramadan. When the journey actually begins, but is unplanned and the day has been started with fasting as usual, the fast that has already begun must be completed and the concession concerning it starts as of the following day.

Some disagreement has arisen on the position of persons who travel during the month of Ramadan and on the possibility that some may take advantage of the concession and plan their travels so as to circumvent the fasting. The general response here is that the *Sharī'ah* has granted a concession that applies whenever its effective cause (*'illah*) is present, regardless as to the motive behind the travel. This is once again the position the Ḥanafīs have taken and Kāsānī has said it to be in conformity with the practice of the Companions. A variant view on this has been recorded from two Companions, namely 'Alī b. Abū Ṭālib, and 'Abd Allāh b. 'Abbās who hold that when a person starts the fasting month during normal residence and travels afterwards, he is not allowed to take advantage of the concession. This is to prevent undue advantage being taken of the *Sharī'ah* concessions. The position here is said to be analogous to one who starts the day fasting and then starts travelling on the same day—he has to complete the fast on that particular day. Having recorded this view, Kāsānī has once again referred the matter to the fact that the Qur'ānic verse, cited above, on this is couched in absolute (*muṭlaq*) terms, which stipulates no conditions and the minority view on this is therefore not supported.[108]

Most of the foregoing concessions are also available for the sick and the invalid, as well as in situations of necessity, not only during travel but also in normal times. Some of the limitations that apply to the traveller do not, in fact, apply in the same way to the sick. For concessions granted in the case of illness continue for the duration of that illness. In the case of fasting, an elderly person who is ill may, for instance, be unable to fast even after recovery from illness, in which case a charity may be given as compensation. But the details of this fall beyond our immediate purpose here.

And lastly, the concession regarding the combination of prayers (*jamʿ*) is also extended to rainfall when *jamʿ* may prove to be particularly convenient. This is a standard Mālikī view, which the Shāfiʿīs have also adopted, whereas others have recorded certain reservations on this.[109] Basic authority for this is found in a *ḥadīth* wherein it is reported that the Prophet combined the *ẓuhr* and *ʿaṣr* prayers together, and the *maghrib* and *ʿishā* prayers together, and this was said to be on a day when it was raining.[110]

III. Restrictions on Freedom of Movement

The main restrictions on freedom of movement to be noted here relate to the right of privacy, the sanctity of private property, protection of public interest such as prevention and containment of disease, espionage and banishment. Then there are issues over the status of women, such as segregation and veiling, which have bearings on their freedom of movement. And lastly an attempt is made to verify the scope of the limitations that the Qur'ān and *Sunnah* have imposed on the residence of non-Muslims in the two holy places, namely Mecca and Medina.

CONSIDERATIONS OF PRIVACY AND HEALTH

The Qur'ān is unequivocal on the sanctity of the private dwelling and respect for the privacy of the home. There is, in principle, no freedom under the *Sharīʿah* to trespass, pry upon, or violate the private homes and properties of others. Entering the property of others or visiting their homes must be with the permission of its owners and occupiers (cf. *al-Nūr*, 24:27). The right of privacy is the subject of a separate volume of the present series and need not therefore be elaborated here.[111] I shall merely attempt, however, to recapitulate, in the following paragraphs, the main Qur'ānic evidence on the privacy of the home. The text thus provides:

يأيها الذين آمنوا لاتدخلوا بيوتا غير بيوتكم حتى تستأنسوا وتسلموا على أهلها . . . فإن لم تجدوا فيها أحدا فلا تدخلوها حتى يؤذن لكم وان قيل لكم ارجعوا فارجعوا

O believers! Enter not houses other than your own unless you familiarise yourselves and greet the inhabitants. Should you find no one therein, you should (still) not enter until a permission is granted to you. And if you are told to turn back then turn back. (24:27–28)

This verse clearly stipulates that entry into a private dwelling must always be with the permission of its occupant which should be obtained in a courteous manner. Only the occupants have the prerogative to grant permission and it matters little whether they are owners, tenants, temporary or long-term residents, and whether the house is large or small. All are equally protected. In the event where one hears no reply from within, one still needs to obtain a permission either from the owner, or from a government authority to enter a private home. There may be people inside who are not in a presentable state and do not welcome visitors. One should therefore wait, and the fact of not receiving a reply does not entitle one to enter without permission. If one is actually asked by the inmates to withdraw, one should accede and withdraw. The rule here does not apply to shops, offices and public places, a point which is indicated in the succeeding verse immediately following the one quoted above. An exception to this general rule is, however, granted in emergency situations, such as fire and flood, in which case entry with the purpose of providing help may be without obtaining a prior permission of either the inhabitants or government authorities. Under normal circumstances, however, it is a part of the required courtesy of visiting private homes that the visitors should not take the inmates by surprise. Instead, they should familiarise themselves by saluting the occupants.

Another aspect of the courtesy of visiting a private home that the Qur'ān has specified is that it should be in the normal way, which is to use the front door or the main entrance that is assigned for that purpose:

$$ليس البر بأن تأتوا البيوت من ظهورها ولكن البر من اتقى وأتوا البيوت من أبوابها$$

It is no virtue to enter the houses from the rear. Virtuous is one who fears God and enters the houses through the proper doors. (2:189)

This is because entry by the back door arouses suspicion as it is also indicative of secrecy and surprise, contrary to the courteous and upright behaviour that is generally recommended. The occurrence of two words in this verse namely of 'decency and fear of God' (*birr* and *taqwā*) suggest that respecting the privacy of the home is integral to Islamic ethos and a duty that all Muslims must observe.

The requirement of obtaining permission also applies to family and relatives, and also to children that have attained a certain age, especially among people who live in the same household or who live in close proximity to one another. This is confirmed in the Qur'ān (*al-Nūr*, 24:27–28) where the text identifies night time, that is, the time between the late evening ('*ishā*') and early morning (*fajr*) prayers as time of rest in which freedom of movement is naturally restricted and entry even by relatives and children must be with the permission of the inmates. The same applies to times when one is likely to be changing or putting on clothes. This is also confirmed in a *ḥadīth* in which a Companion by the name 'Atā' bin Yasar reported that a man asked the Prophet whether he needed permission from his mother to enter her apartment, to which the Prophet replied that he did. The man then said that he lived in the same house with his mother and often had occasion to serve her. To this the Prophet posed the question 'Do you wish to see her naked?' And the man answered 'of course not.' 'You must obtain permission then,' said the Prophet.[112]

PROHIBITION OF ESPIONAGE

Espionage is forbidden by the explicit injunctions of the Qur'ān and *Sunnah*, hence there is no freedom of movement at the expense of prying on the privacy of others and collecting information that seeks to expose their weaknesses. Spying is forbidden regardless of the objective that might be pursued by it. Even a lawful objective, such as discovery of truth and evidence with which to administer justice, does not validate espionage. The main guideline of *Sharīʿah* here is to ascertain the legality of both the means and the ends of evidence that is used against another person. Lawful ends should be realised and pursued only through lawful means and not otherwise.[113] The Qurʾānic denunciation of espionage is conveyed in a particularly striking language as follows:

ولا تجسسوا ولا يغتب بعضكم بعضا أيحب أحدكم أن ياكل لحم أخيه ميتا فكرهتموه

Spy not and defame not one another behind your backs. Does anyone of you like to eat the flesh of his dead brother? Surely you would abhor it. (49:12)

Whereas this verse juxtaposes espionage and backbiting (*ghībah*) and prohibits them both, in the *hadīth* that follows there is a juxtaposition of three inter-related activities: suspicion, espionage and exposing the weaknesses of others:

إياكم والظن فإن الظن أكذب الحديث، ولا تحسسوا ولا تجسسوا

Beware of suspicion, for suspicion may amount to the worst form of lying, and spy not on one another, nor try to bare each other's hidden failings.[114]

It thus appears that the three evils mentioned in this *hadīth* often occur together in that espionage begins in suspicion and it involves exposing the weaknesses of others without either the knowledge or ability of their victims to protect themselves. The *hadīth* thus prohibited espionage together with its preliminaries and end results.

According to another *hadīth*, a Bedouin Arab came to the Prophet's house and started peeping through the crack of the front door and it caught the Prophet's attention, at which point, he picked up a rod and startled the Bedouin through the aperture. The Prophet attempted to poke the peeping eye but missed it and the man fled. The Prophet then said: 'If I had succeeded, I would have gouged your eye.'[115]

لو ثبت لفقعت عينك

On yet another occasion the Prophet is reported to have said 'If someone pries over another person's home without the latter's permission and he gouges the spying eye, there is no *diyyah* in compensation (of the injury inflicted).'[116]

من اطلع فى بيت قوم بغير اذنهم ففقعوا عينه فلا دية له

The *'ulamā'* have, however, disagreed on the import of this *ḥadīth*. Some are of the view that this *ḥadīth* has been abrogated by the Qur'ānic verse which demanded that 'if you decide to punish, then punish the like of the pain that has been inflicted on you' (*al-Naḥl*, 16:126).

وإن عاقبتم فعاقبوا بمثل ما عوقبتم به

There is also the view that the manifest meaning of the *ḥadīth* quoted above is not intended and that it is typical of the Arabs to use metaphorical language for purposes of emphasis—like the expression *iqtaʿ lisānahu* (cut his tongue), which has occurred in the *ḥadīth* as a metaphorical expression. Thus it is said that 'gouging the eye'—*faqʿ al-ʿayn*—in the above *ḥadīth* means a deterrent punishment that would prevent repetition.[117] It is provided in another *ḥadīth* that 'permission must be obtained prior to viewing.'[118] Hence anyone who looks into the privacy of one's neighbour's house, even without entering it, is in violation of his neighbour's right of privacy.

There is also a report that, on one of his night patrols of Medina, the caliph ʿUmar b. al-Khaṭṭāb heard noises coming out of a house. The caliph peeped over the wall and saw that a man who was engrossed in wine drinking was making the noise. When the caliph tried to admonish the culprit, he was met with this response: 'O commander of the faithful! I may have committed one sin but you have committed three: you spied, you peeped over the wall instead of coming through the front door, and then you did not familiarise yourself. God has ordained that you greet the inmates, and you failed to do that'. Upon hearing all this, the caliph apologised and simply left.[119] An offence was committed but since the means of detecting it (through spying) was contrary to the rules of *Sharīʿah*, the caliph evidently decided not to pursue it.

CONSIDERATIONS OF *MAṢLAḤAH*

A. Contagious Disease

Considerations of public interest (*maṣlaḥah ʿāmmah*), public policy and morality may also require imposing restrictions on the freedom of movement. One of the clear instances of this, which is the subject of a *ḥadīth*, is concerned with the prevention and containment of contagious disease. The *ḥadīth* thus provides 'when a plague breaks out in a locality while you are in it, do not leave, but when you hear of it while you are outside, do not enter it.'[120]

اذا ظهر الطاعون فى بلد وأنتم فيه فلا تخرجوا منه ، واذا سمعتم به وأنتم خارجه فلا تدخلوه

ʿUmar Ibn al-Khaṭṭāb followed the instruction of this *ḥadīth* when he was on a journey to Sham (Syria) and received the news that plague had broken out in Sham. He consulted the leading Companions in his entourage. After some discussion in which different opinions were expressed, he decided that they should all return to Medina.[121] The Mālikī jurists have held that this *ḥadīth* conveys the value of *makruh* (reprehensible) which is a degree below prohibition. To travel or migrate from a place where plague is broken out is thus held to be reprehensible, but not forbidden.[122]

B. Banishment

Banishment has been stipulated as a supplementary punishment for the crimes of highway robbery (*ḥirābah*) and adultery (*zinā*). The former is prescribed in the Qurʾān (*al-Māʾidah*, 5:33) where the text provides a four-fold punishment for armed robbers, the last of which is 'banishment from the land'. Banishment is a supplementary punishment for *zinā* when committed by an unmarried person. It is stipulated in a *ḥadīth* that such a person should be subject to 100 lashes of the whip and exile of one year.

Muslim jurists are however, in disagreement over both of these provisions. With regard to the Qurʾānic text on highway robbery, the wording of the text is open to interpretation of the part that stipulates 'to remove (the offender) from the earth (*yunfaw min al-arḍ*)'. The Ḥanafīs have equated removing the robber from the (face of) the earth with imprisonment and argued that banishment to another place without imprisonment will expose the new locality to a menace.

Hence the intention of the text must be to imprison the culprit. The majority of jurists have understood the reference to banishment here in its usual sense, which would mean that the criminal should be transferred to another place away from his homeland by a distance of at least a whole day of travel by foot. A minority opinion has it that the highway robber should be banished to a non-Muslim country, that is, the *dār al-kufr* as was conventionally understood at the time.[123]

Muslim jurists have also questioned the authenticity of the *ḥadīth* that stipulates banishment as an additional punishment for adultery. It is the only *ḥadīth* on the subject and it is also considered, by the Ḥanafīs at least, to be somewhat obscure. The majority have followed the ruling of the *ḥadīth* but have differed on whether banishment for *zinā* becomes a part of the prescribed (*ḥadd*) punishment, or whether it is provided in the manner of discretionary (*taʿzīr*), something which is subject to discretion and *maṣlaḥah* and has to be determined by the ruler. Others have suggested that one year of banishment in question should be converted to imprisonment. There is also disagreement over the procedure of banishment, the distance and place to which a person is sent.[124] Since banishment in this case is a supplementary punishment to the standard 100 lashes that is stipulated in both the Qur'ān and *Sunnah*, and the two sources vary only on the supplementary provision of an unconfirmed *ḥadīth*, the best one can say is to consider it as an additional and discretionary provision that may be enforced by the express decision of the court. General precedent in the Muslim countries, to the best of my knowledge, has not enforced the banishment provision for *zinā*.

Two other instances of *maṣlaḥah*-based restrictions on freedom of movement that occur on the precedent of the Caliph ʿUmar were as follow: The caliph made a decision that the leading *ʿulamā'* and Companions should remain in Medina so as to be available for consultation. In another decision, he exiled a man named Naṣr b. al-Ḥajjāj from Medina to Iraq. The latter decision was a preventive measure to protect public morality and was obviously intended to put an end to temptations that Ḥajjāj's exceptionally good looks had created for the women of Medina. Ḥajjāj had evidently not committed an offence and reports indicate that he himself said this to the caliph and the caliph's reply was that he wanted 'to protect the abode of *hijrah* against corruption.'[125]

As already indicated, banishment is a rather controversial issue and many leading *ʿulamā'*, especially of the Ḥanafī school, have expressed reservations about its basic validity and effectiveness. The evidence is nevertheless clear to the effect that the Pious Caliphs have invoked it as an instrument of public policy and *maslahah* notwithstanding its restrictive effect on the freedom of movement. Reports also indicate that one of the leading Companions, Abū Dharr al-Ghaffārī was banished, on the order of the third caliph ʿUthmān, from Sham to Medina, for an apparently political reason, which was to isolate him and his controversial teachings that could have incited civil strife and *fitnah*. Textual authority on the enormity of *fitnah* is found in the Qurʾānic proclamation that '*fitnah* is worse than killing' (*al-Baqarah*, 2:217). Abū Dharr held the view that the enormous wealth of governors and leading officials should be confiscated and divided among the poor. Then the governor of Sham, Muʿāwiyah, requested the caliph to banish Abū Dharr and the caliph complied. Abū Dharr consequently spent the rest of his life in exile in the vicinity of Medina.¹²⁶ This was an example of imposing restrictions on freedom of movement in order to prevent a mischief (*mafsadah*), and prevention of *mafsadah* also partakes in *maslahah*.

A report also has it that the caliph ʿUmar b. al-Khaṭṭāb sentenced to banishment from Medina one Rabīʿah b. Ummahyah, because of his indulgence in wine-drinking. He was exiled to Khaybar, but then it was reported that he fled from there, renounced Islam, and embraced Christianity. When the caliph learned of this, he said, 'I shall never sentence a Muslim to exile again.' It is accordingly suggested that imprisonment is preferable to banishment, for banishment to another place leaves open the possibility of recurrence of the feared conduct. It is also stated that the banished individual is no longer exposed to the same social pressure, as he might be when he continues to live in his own community. This may explain why the Hanafī jurist Ibn ʿĀbidīn observed that 'banishment tends to open the door to corruption.'¹²⁷

C. Imprisonment

Imprisonment is not a typically Islamic concept. Yet references to imprisonment and detention are found in the Qurʾān and one of the words used for it is *sijn* which occurs in the story of Joseph in the 12th *Sūrah*, and again in reference to Pharaoh who threatened Moses with imprisonment (26:29). The other expression used in the Qurʾān is from the root word *habasa* (to detain) although not specifically in reference to imprisonment (cf. 5:106). Then it is noted, in reference to the use of the word *asīr* in some *hadīths*, that the Prophet does not refer to a real prison but merely to detention. This may have justified the use of the word *asīr* (one bound in fetters) for a detained person and prisoner.

Although prisons were historically known and were in existence in pre-Islamic times almost everywhere, imprisonment was seen as a dubious and impractical measure in the Bedouin environment of Arabia: a device that could be more burdensome to those who applied it than to those to whom it applied. The Prophet is only said to have detained someone on suspicion for a day or less and it seems in any case to be an isolated incident. The Prophet did not have a prison, and it was in Caliph ʿUmar's time when due to the increased population of Medina, a house was converted into a prison.

Juristic opinion has reflected this Arabian heritage and considered imprisonment basically as a supplementary punishment to *ḥudūd* and *qiṣāṣ* penalties. The tenth century Mālikī jurist, Ibn Abī Zayd al-Qayrawānī, advised in his famous *Risālah* that in the case of murder, without intention of robbery, and after forgiveness has been granted by the next of kin of the victim, the murderer should be lashed 100 times and sentenced to one year in prison. In the case of highway robbery, punishment may generally be left to the discretion of the head of state but the culprit may be kept in prison until he repents. A third and subsequent repetition of theft was also punishable by flogging and imprisonment. In the early juristic literature, imprisonment is also stipulated in conjunction with apostasy. It is noted in this connection that the second caliph ʿUmar recommended three days' stay in prison for the apostate, during which attempts were to be made to persuade him to recant.[128]

The most widely discussed application of imprisonment in the works of *fiqh* occurs in reference to imprisonment of a defaulting debtor. Affluent debtors who refused to clear their debts were frequently sued by their creditors and the courts sent the debtors to prison if they were not bankrupt. But if the debtor established his inability to pay he would be declared bankrupt by the judge and could be set free—in accordance with a Qurʾānic directive on the subject (2:280). An early precedent, recorded from the Companion Abū Hurayrah, on this issue suggested a totally different course of action. Abū Hurayrah preferred not to imprison the debtor, solvent or otherwise, but to permit him to go free so as to be able to earn money and repay his debt—and also to support himself and his family.[129] This opinion is supported, at least partially, by the Ḥanafīs and it manifests the basic anomaly that is involved in sending debtors to prison. Yet all the various schools of Islamic law have validated imprisonment of a solvent defaulter on the authority of a renowned *ḥadīth* which simply declared 'procrastination by an affluent debtor is an act of injustice' (*maṭl al-ghaniy ẓulm*).

The twelfth century Ḥanafī jurist Qāḍī Khān validated imprisonment for a defaulting debtor who is able to pay with one or two exceptions in favour of close relatives: parents, male and female direct ancestors of the creditor may not be imprisoned for unpaid debts.[130]

Muslim jurists have viewed imprisonment basically as a *maṣlaḥah*-based restriction on the freedom of movement that consists of a deterrent device or *taʿzīr*. Thus it is held that the ruler and judge may determine appropriate sanctions, including imprisonment, for crimes and violations that are not covered by the *Sharīʿah*. Notwithstanding the circumspect and hesitant view that Muslim jurists have taken of imprisonment, it is noted that political authorities and dynastic rulers of the subsequent periods have not hesitated to send their political opponents to prison. As already noted, among the range and types of punishment that Islamic Law recognises, imprisonment does not occupy a prominent place and is hardly recognized as a punishment in its own right. The Qurʾān has recognised banishment as a punishment for highway robbery that does not entail injury and loss of life but merely intimidate the people. Due to lack of any direct reference to it as a punishment variety in the Qurʾān, the jurists have validated imprisonment as a mode of punishment by analogy to banishment, both of which they have classified under the broad category of *taʿzīr*. Many jurists have also regarded banishment as a *ḥadd* punishment simply because the Qurʾān has made a reference to it.

The Qurʾān does contain references to imprisonment as already noted. Yet among the prescribed, or *ḥadd* penalties that occur mainly in the Qurʾān, imprisonment is not mentioned. The reference in the Qurʾān (4:15) about the detention of women convicted of fornication is reportedly abrogated and replaced by flogging (24:2). Such detention was to be at the home of the woman concerned and it was also referred to by a derivative of *masaka* (to detain), which is not the typical Arabic expression for imprisonment. It is only in the works of the Muslim jurists of later periods, such as Ibn Ḥazm, al-Qayrawānī and Ibn ʿĀbidīn that imprisonment is discussed as a punishment variety in some detail. Two types of imprisonment have been recognised: short term, and indefinite.

Early practice basically favoured short-term imprisonment, which tends to find support in the *Sunnah* of the Prophet who is reported to have detained odd individuals for a day. The Caliph ʿUmar also authorised short-term imprisonment that was basically for preventive detention purposes. Many jurists have suggested a limit of one day for short-term imprisonment as a *ta'zīr* punishment to be meted out to first time offenders. There is disagreement as to the maximum length of a long-term imprisonment. The Shāfi'īs have suggested one year as maximum by analogy to banishment (in the case of *zinā*), whereas other schools do not agree with that analogy in the first place and hold that imprisonment should not exceed six months. A third opinion on this leaves the maximum up to the discretion of the judge.[131]

The second type of imprisonment is for an indefinite period which is meted out to dangerous criminals. Such criminals may be imprisoned until they repent and show signs of remorse and the resolve to reform themselves. Hardened criminals who do not show signs of remorse may be held in prison indefinitely.[132]

Ibn Ḥazm al-Ẓāhirī (d. 456/1064) and his commentator, the judge Abū'l-Wasīm b. Riḍwān advised that the authorities should separate dangerous criminals from those who are merely held for failure to pay their debts or serve a light corrective sentence. Hardened criminals should be placed in maximum security prisons, whereas others should be held under more relaxed conditions. The authorities should also maintain a separate prison for women, and even in this category, it is recommended that a special prison should be maintained for respectable women as opposed to those who are held on charges of infamous crimes.[133]

D. Ḥijāb (Veiling)

The question to be addressed here is whether women enjoy equal freedom of movement to that of men, or whether their freedom is limited on account of veiling and family obligations. Muslim jurists have given two different responses, one of which maintains that women must reside in their homes. Since their husbands, in the case of married women, are under obligation to support them, they must therefore devote themselves to their husbands and families.[134]

The rules of *fiqh* entitle the husband to prevent his wife from leaving the home for purposes of travel or employment, if such activities interfere with the rights of the husband and the interests of the family. The wife, on the other hand, is entitled to visit her parents and close relatives without the permission of her husband. She may also travel to perform the *hajj* pilgrimage with a close relative, and consult a learned person in order to seek guidance over any problem she might have. And lastly the wife may leave the marital home without any permission in emergencies and situations that endanger her personal safety. But outside these circumstances women do not enjoy unrestricted freedom of movement.[135]

The proponents of the foregoing view have mainly relied on the two Qur'ānic passages, which provide, in an address to the wives of the Prophet, that they should stay at home and avoid inappropriate encounter with strangers of the opposite sex. What is required of the wives of the Prophet, the advocates of this view maintain, is also required of all Muslim women. Their place, in other words, is at home and they have no liberty to leave it at will. The two Qur'ānic verses which the advocates of this view quote in support are as follows:

> (1) O wives of the Prophet! You are not like any other women. If you keep your duty, do not be soft in speech, lest one in whose heart is a disease yearn, but speak a good word, stay in your houses, and display not your beauty like displaying of the ignorance of yore. (al-Aḥzāb, 33:32)

يانساء النبي لستن كأحد من النساء ان اتقيتن فلا تخضعن بالقول فيطمع الذى فى قلبه مرض وقلن قولا معروفا وقرن فى بيوتكن ولاتبرجن تبرج الجاهلية الاولى

> (2) O Prophet! Tell your wives and daughters and the believing women that they should cast their outer garment over themselves when they leave home. That is most appropriate... (al-Aḥzāb, 33:59).

يأيها النبى قل لأزواجك وبناتك ونساء المؤمنين يدنين عليهن من جلابيبهن ذلك أدنى أن يعرفن

The first verse is evidently a specific address to the wives of the Prophet and the text itself is exclusive of other women, whereas the second verse is couched in a persuasive language that provides an appropriate course of action rather than a definitive command. In another Qur'ānic passage, the believers are asked to 'lower their gaze and guard their modesty, for this is in the interest of greater purity for them' (al-Nūr, 24:30). This last Qur'ānic directive to the believers 'to lower their gaze' actually takes for granted women's presence and participation in public life. For if they were to be physically confined to their homes, there would be no real occasion for asking anyone to lower their gaze. But the advocates of the view under discussion have ignored the specific import of the text and have instead chosen to extend it by analogy to all women. The conclusion drawn from this manner of text reading is that women do not enjoy full freedom of movement beyond the limited range of activities that the *fiqh* books have attempted to specify.

The second view that is supported by the advocates of equality maintains firstly that the Qur'ānic verse (the first of the two verses quoted above) is specifically addressed to the household of the Prophet and should therefore not be generalised. This verse was meant to protect the sanctity of the Prophet's home and the etiquette of visiting him, and it was not meant to apply to the rest of the Muslim community. Secondly, it is stated that the *Sharīʿah* has entitled women to manage their own financial affairs, conclude contracts and transactions and testify as witnesses in the court without the need to obtain permission from anyone. Women are also not under any obligation that they should manage their affairs through their relatives or representatives.[136] If the *Sharīʿah* entitles women, as it indeed does, to manage their own property and business affairs, then this right would be frustrated if they were at the same time required to remain at home.

Thirdly, it is noted that the first of the two Qur'ānic verses under review was revealed in the fifth year of the Hijrah whereas the Prophet permitted women to participate in the battle of Ḥunayn in the ninth year of the Hijrah. This would show that the directive in this verse was not an absolute requirement and the Prophet had not treated it as such.

And lastly, it is suggested that segregation and veiling is neither a genuine Islamic nor an Arab tradition. It was an ancient Persian practice that was subsequently adopted by some Muslim communities but then it was taken to such excess that it became a mark of dignity and class and acquired different attributes. It is therefore less than justified to bring all this under the umbrella of *Sharīʿah* and attribute normative validity to veiling in isolation from, or at the expense of, some of the other equally valid rules of *Sharīʿah*.[137]

The facts of history also reveal that during the Prophet's time women were not confined to their homes and they generally understood the Qur'ānic verse that addressed the Prophet's wives not to be of general application to all women. There are numerous reports recorded in the *ḥadīth* collections of al-Bukhārī and Muslim which confirm women's participation in the various walks of life in the presence of men during the Prophet's time.

There is little doubt that the *Sharīʿah* requires covering of the private parts (*ʿawrah*) of both men and women. In the case of women, it is also clear that the face and the hands are not included in *ʿawrah*. This is the general understanding of the Qurʾānic text with reference to women that 'they do not expose their beauty except for the part that is apparent' (*al-Nūr*, 24:31). The last phrase in this verse is understood to be a reference to hands and face. This understanding is conclusive as it is supported by the *Sunnah* of the Prophet and general practice during his time.[138] The reference to exposure of beauty by women in this verse is to provocative exposure which is prohibited, but not to that which is customary and moderate.[139]

The ruling of some jurists that advocate total veiling including, that is, the covering of face and hands is based on their *ijtihād* and their attempt at blocking the means (*sadd al-dharīʿah*) to temptation and *fitnah*.[140] It should be noted in this connection, however, that the Qurʾān identifies three main sources of *fitnah*, namely property, offspring, and women,[141] all of which are indispensable to human life, and the *Sharīʿah* makes detailed provisions concerning them. Property and wealth are a source of great temptation and yet they are also a pillar and foundation of life and recognised as one of the five essential interests (*al-maṣāliḥ al-ḍarūriyyah*). The Lawgiver has also warned the faithful against the *fitnah* of women, which is also regulated by the rules pertaining to deviant behaviour and *zinā*. But the dignified presence and participation of women in public life without covering their faces is lawful and it would be excessive to say otherwise. The Lawgiver has not forbidden it and it is not for the jurists to change this to its opposite. The Qurʾānic directive to the believers to lower their gazes at times of encounter with members of the opposite sex (*al-Nūr*, 24:30, quoted above) shows that the fear of *fitnah* over women was present during the time of the Prophet, just as it has remained so ever since, yet the Qurʾānic order is confined to lowering the gaze, and it is here where the position remains.

E. Non–Muslims in the Hijaz

There is basically no difference in the position of Muslim and non-Muslim citizens in regard to their freedom of movement. This is also confirmed by historical evidence which is generally supportive of equality in this respect.[142] The only exception that might be mentioned here relates to travel and stay in the Arabian peninsula that is known as the Hijaz (Mecca and Medina), although some jurists have actually reduced this virtually to the four walls of the Ka'bah. The following Qur'anic verse was revealed on the occasion of the Prophet's return from the battle of Tabūk which was preceded by a concentration of the enemy forces around the Arabian Peninsula. This was seen as a threat not only to the security of Muslims but to Islam itself. The verse states:

يأيها الذين آمنوا انما المشركون نجس فلا يقربوا المسجد
الحرام بعد عامهم هذا

> O believers, the associators are impure so let them not come near
> the sacred mosque after this year (*al-Tawbah*, 9:28).

The jurists have disagreed over the precise import of this verse as well as the actual definition of sacred mosque (*masjid al-ḥarām*). Did it refer to the building of the Ka'bah only or did it also include its surrounding areas, which might mean the entire city of Mecca? Questions have also arisen about who exactly were the associators (*mushrikūn*) and whether this term only referred to the pagans of Mecca or it also included the People of the Book. The precise understanding of this text had been made more difficult by some references to the subject in the *hadīth*. For al-Shāfi'ī the sacred mosque only meant the mosque of Ka'bah, the area that the Prophet called sacred land and that included the area where the *hajj* pilgrims performed their rituals of worship. Two renowned Qur'an commentators, al-Ṭabarī and al-Qurṭubī, have held that *mushrikūn* included the pagans as well as Jews and Christians. Imām Abū Ḥanīfah and his disciples have held, and I believe rightly so, that *mushrikūn* only applies to idol worshippers and does not include Jews and Christians who may enter any mosque, including the mosque of Ka'bah. Moreover, the term impure in the verse in question refers to those who do not possess a Divine scripture, which the Jews and Christians do.

Another aspect of this debate is related to security.[143] The Prophet has accordingly stated in a *hadīth* that 'I shall evict the Jews and Christians from the Arabian Peninsula until I leave no one but only the Muslims.'[144] 'The purpose of the proposed eviction', wrote al-'Ilī 'was to protect the Muslim army against . . . their conspiracies.'[145] The caliphs Abū Bakr and 'Umar pursued the policy of evacuation of the *dhimmī*s from Mecca and Medina to Kufa and Sham. The policy that was actually followed, according to al-Shawkānī, was to evacuate the whole of the Arabian Peninsula from its non-Muslim inhabitants, whereas al-ʿAsqalānī has stated that the evacuation policy was confined only to Mecca and Medina.[146] Others have recorded the view that the purpose was to prevent the pagans and associators settling as groups and communities in these areas, but their presence as individuals was not prohibited. The Ḥanafīs have held that slim residence of non-Muslims in the Hijaz is permissible except for the sanctuary of the holy mosque. Imam Mālik has also held that their entry to Mecca and Medina for visitation and trade is permissible. Imam Shāfiʿī has held that they may only enter with the permission of the head of state on grounds of *maṣlaḥah* for Muslims. Reports also suggest that the Caliph ʿUmar permitted Christian traders to stay in Medina for three days. According to the Ḥanbalī school, this period may be extended until they can sell their goods and the time period for their stay can be determined on grounds of *maṣlaḥah* and *ijtihād* by the authorities. The practice today in Saudi Arabia is, of course, dependent on obtaining a visa, not just for non-Muslims, but for non-Saudi Muslims as well. Temporary visit and travel is generally permitted but long-term residence for non-Muslims in Mecca and Medina is discouraged.[147]

It thus appears that the initial ruling of the Qur'ān was predicated on considerations of *maṣlaḥah*, defence and security of the nascent community at the time. The juristic view which began on a slightly different note eventually recognised this and referred the matter to the discretion of the ruling authorities and *ijtihād*. The more specific terms of the Qur'ān and *Sunnah* have thus been regarded as *tashrīʿ zamanī*, or time-bound legislation, which envisaged the prevailing *maṣlaḥah* at the time, and *maṣlaḥah* remains the principal criterion that juristic opinion has taken into account in the travel and visitation of non-Muslims to the holy places.

IV. Conclusion

It may be said that the *Sharīʿah* recognises freedom of movement as an integral part of human dignity and self-expression, as well as a means toward the attainment of valid objectives. The normative validity of this freedom is evidenced by the fact that its denial is equated with punishment and torture. The *Sharīʿah* also imposes minimal restrictions on the free movement and travel of people, be it for pleasure, pursuit of earning a living or other lawful objectives.

Freedom of movement is, in other words, recognised as a value in itself as well as a means that may be necessary for the attainment of other goals. The evidence we have reviewed in the Qur'ān and *Sunnah* is predominantly affirmative on the normative validity of this freedom, and there is much encouragement for the individual to utilise freedom of movement as a means of self-development and growth, acquisition of knowledge, enquiry and observation, fulfilment of religious duties, as well as a means of escape from oppression. The *Sharī'ah* limits on the exercise of this freedom are mainly concerned with respect for the rights of others, preservation of public interest, and prevention of contagious disease. There is little recognition, on the other hand, of the strictures that are associated with territorial sovereignty and nationalism of the kind that have characterised the nation–state phenomenon that has led to ever widening range of restrictions on freedom of movement.

The *Sharī'ah* would not seem to support restrictions on the free travel of Muslims in the territorial domains of Islam and one can find but little support for visa regulations that are applied as an expression merely of the national sovereignty of Muslim states. But if these are deemed necessary in order to prevent criminality and disease, they may be validated on the grounds of *siyāsah shar'iyyah*, that is, public policy which bears harmony with the *Sharī'ah*, or on the basis of public interest. The general trend of the *Sharī'ah* evidence remains to favour open borders among Muslim countries and probably also for the whole world. A valid application of *siyāsah shar'iyyah* might favour the principle of reciprocal treatment among the nations of the world generally. The basic evidence and guidelines of *Sharī'ah* is inclined toward encouraging openness and discouraging unwarranted restrictions on freedom of movement, both for Muslims and non-Muslims, especially when openness is considered to be for the benefit of all and in harmony with considerations of public policy and *maṣlaḥah*.

NOTES

1. Cf. 'Abd al Mun'im Aḥmad, *Uṣūl Niẓām al-Ḥukm fi'l-Islām*, 261.
2. Cf. Cranston, *What Are Human Rights*, 34.
3. Zafrulla Khan, *Human Rights*, 85.
4. Fatḥī 'Uthmān, *Ḥuqūq al-Insān*, 83.
5. Cranston, *Human Rights*, 36.
6. Bukhārī, *Ṣaḥīḥ* (Khan's tr.), vol. II, *ḥadīth* 30.

7. *Al-Muʿjam al-Wasīṭ*, bāb laja'.

8. Cf. Hasan, *Principles*, I, 356.

9. Cf. Maḥmūd Shaltūt, *al-Fatāwā*, 431–32.

10. Id., 433.

11. Id., 434.

12. Id.

13. Cf. Khalid Masud, 'The Obligation to Migrate,' in Eickelman, edr. *Muslim Travellers*, 32.

14. Al-Ḥāfiẓ al-Mundhirī, *Mukhtaṣar Sunan Abū Dāwūd*, ed. Aḥmad Muḥammad Shakir and Ḥamid Muḥammad al-Faqī (Beirut: Dār al-Maʿrifah), *ḥadīth* 3369.

15. Bukhārī, *Ṣaḥīḥ al-Bukhārī* (Khan's tr.) V, 155, *ḥadīth* 239.

16. Ibn Qudāmah, *al-Mughnī*, X, 513. See also Sharaiyra, *Right*, 172–73.

17. Sharaiyra, *Right and Freedom of Movement in Islam* (Originally a Ph.D dissertation, International Islamic University Malaysia, 1998), 179.

18. Quoted in ʿAsqalānī, *Fatḥ al-Bārī*, VI, 378; see also Masud, 'The Obligation to Migrate,' 33.

19. Ibn Khaldūn, *Muqaddimah*, I, 256 (Routledge, London, 1958).

20. ʿAsqalānī, *Fatḥ al-Bārī*, VI, 378.

21. Cf. Masud, 'The Obligation to Migrate,' 36.

22. Shāfiʿī, *al-Umm*, IV, 84.

23. Ashʿarī, *Maqālat*, II, 137; Shahristānī, *al-Milal*, I, 170; Masud, 'The Obligation to Migrate,' 35.

24. Ashʿarī, *Maqālāt*, II, 137.

25. Muslim, *Mukhtaṣar Ṣaḥīḥ Muslim*, p.16, *ḥadīth* 34.

26. Cf. Masud, 'The Obligation to Migrate,' 35.

27. Cf. Ahmad Ghazi, *The Hijrah, Its Philosophy and Message*, 71; Bābillī, *al-Hijrah fi'l-Islām*, 92.

28. Quṭb, *Fī Ẓilāl al-Qur'ān*, IV, 69f.

29. Al-Ghazālī, *Iḥyā'*, II, 149.

30. Ibn al-ʿArabī, *Aḥkām al-Qur'ān*, I, 486; see also al-Ghazālī, *Iḥyā'*, II, 248; Masud, 'The Obligation to Migrate,' 37. Fu'ād Aḥmad, *Uṣūl*, p. 262, Shīshānī, *Ḥuqūq al-Insān*, 381.

31. Cf. Kamali, *Freedom of Expression in Islam*, chapter on Blasphemy, 212–50, especially 212–25.

32. Shāṭibī, *al-Iʿtiṣām*, II, 300; see also Kamali, *Principles of Islamic Jurisprudence*, 280.

33. Masud, 'The Obligation to Migrate', 38.

34. Cf. Zuḥaylī, *Athār al-Ḥarb*, 175.

35. Masud, 'The Obligation to Migrate,' 43.

36. Karpat, 'The Hijra from Russia and the Balkans,' in Eickelman ed, *Muslim Travellers*, 133.

37. Id.

38. Id., 133–34.

39. Id., 138.

40. Id., 139.

41. The treatise bears the title *Ḥukm al-Iqāmah bi-bilād al-kufr wa-bayān wujūbihā fī baʿḍ al-aḥwāl* (Legal view of staying in the land of Unbelief and the explanation why it is obligatory in certain cases) quoted in Masud 'The Obligation to Migrate', 42.

42. Cf. Masud, 'The Obligation,' 43, quoting al-Ṣiddīq's treaty (the previous note, 30).

43. Riḍā, *Tafsīr al-Manār*, v, 361.

44. Masud, 'The Obligation,' in Eickelman, *Muslim Travellers*, 43.

45. Cf. Ghunaymī, *Qanūn al-Salām*, 110; Sharaiyra, *Right and Freedom*, 96.

46. Al-Rāzī, *Tafsīr*, I, 187.

47. Al-Rāzī, *Tafsīr*, x, 188.

48. Abū Zahrah, *al-ʿIlāqāt al-Dawliyyah*, 56; Zuḥaylī, *Athār al-Ḥarb*, 175; Madkūr, *Maʿālim*, 115.

49. Levin, *Human Rights*, 62.

50. Nanda, *Refugee Law*, 3.

51. Cf. Shāfiʿī, *Aḥkām*, II, 64.

52. Cf. Levin, *Human Rights*, 62.

53. Zamakhsharī, *al-Khashshāf*, II, 164; also discussed in Sharaiyra, *Right and Freedom*, 136.

54. Kāsānī, *Badāʾiʿ*, vII, 106; ʿAwdah, *Al-Tashrīʿ al-Jināʾī*, I, 530–31.

55. Cf. Ghanoushī, *Ḥuqūq al-Muwāṭanah*, 60.

56. Id., 60–61; Sharaiyra, *Right and Freedom*, 135.

57. Yusuf Ali, *The Holy Qur'an*, fn. 2799.

58. Bukhārī, *Ṣaḥīḥ al-Bukhārī* (Muhsin Khan's tr.).

59. Abū Dāwūd, *Sunan Abū Dāwūd*, ed. Al-Ḥāfiẓ al-Mundhirī, vol. II, *ḥadīth* 1647.

60. Ibn Mājah, *Sunan*, *ḥadīth* 1411.

61. Ibn Mājah, *Sunan*, *ḥadīth* 1406.

62. Abū Dāwūd, *Sunan*, *ḥadīth* 2476.

63. In the Passport Act 1974 {1989} FSC 41. The following *āyāt* were cited: 3:137; 22:46; 29:20; 4:97 and 100.

64. Cf. Gellens, 'The Search for Knowledge,' in Eickelman, ed., *Muslim Travellers*, 53.

65. El-Moudden, 'The Ambivalence of *Rihlah*,' in Eickelman, ed., *Muslim Travellers*, 75.

66. Id., 77.

67. McDonnell. 'Patterns of Muslim Pilgrimage from Malaysia', in Eickelman, ed., *Muslim Travellers*, 114.

68. Id., 117.

69. Id., 121–22.

70. al-Ghazālī, *Iḥyā'*, II, 248.

71. The *ḥadīth* in question is as follows: 'Pack not your bags except for three mosques, my mosque, the *Masjid al-Ḥarām* and *Masjid al-Aqṣā*.' Al-Ghazālī, *Iḥyā'*, II, 246.

72. Al-Khaṭīb al-Baghdādī, *al-Riḥlah fī Ṭalab al-Ḥadīth*, 18.

73. Id., 23.

74. Ghazālī, *Iḥyā'*, II, 245. This is also a *ḥadīth* al-Bukhārī has recorded. Neither the names of the ten companions, nor the subject of *ḥadīth* have been given in any of the reports. Al-Bukhārī simply wrote that Jābir b. ʿAbd Allāh travelled for one month to get a single *ḥadīth* from ʿAbd Allāh b. Unays. (*Ṣaḥīḥ al-Bukhārī* (Muhsin Khan's tr.), I, 65, *ḥadīth* 76). Al-Khaṭīb al-Baghdādī (*al-Riḥlah fī Ṭalab al-Ḥadīth*, pp. 110–115) has quoted this *ḥadīth* in detail through several *isnād*s and says that it was on the subject of just retaliation (*qiṣāṣ*) on the Day of Resurrection, which is as follows: 'God Most High resurrects the people on the Day of Resurrection naked, uncircumcised, and in bare essence, and then He calls from His Throne with a voice that is equally audible by the near and the far and says "I am the Lord this Day and I shun injustice (*ẓulm*), and I make sure that every one who has committed acts of injustice, even a slap or a strike by the hand inflicted on another will be retaliated."' To a question the Companions asked the Prophet on how *qiṣāṣ* was possible in that state when everyone is in bare essence, naked—the Prophet replied it would mean addition of the good deeds of the oppressor to those of the oppressed, and deduction of the sins of the oppressed that are then added to the account of the oppressors.

75. Al-Khaṭīb al-Baghdādī, *al-Riḥlah fī Ṭalab al-Ḥadīth*, 128.

76. Id.

77. For details, see Kamali, *A Text Book of Hadith Studies*, esp. the chapter On Collection and Documentation of Hadith.

78. Gellens 'The Search for knowledge,' in Eickelman, ed., *Muslim Travellers*, 55.

79. Id., II, 245–246.

80. Al-Baghdādī, *al-Riḥlah fī Ṭalab al-Ḥadīth*, 27–28.

81. Qaraḍāwī, *Al-ʿAql wa'l-ʿIlm*, p. 222. The *ḥadīth* is reported in al-Tirmidhī, *Sunan al-Tirmidhī*, Kitāb al-ʿIlm, *ḥadīth* 26–49.

82. Gellens, 'The Search for Knowledge,' in Eickelman, ed., *Muslim Travellers*, 55.

83. Id., 56.

84. Id., 56.

85. Id., 58.

86. Id., 61.

87. Id., 63.

88. Al-Khaṭīb al-Baghdādī, *al-Riḥlāh fī Ṭalab al-Ḥadīth*, 87–89.

89. ʿAbd Al-Karīm Zaydān, *Majmūʿat Buḥūth Fiqhiyyah*, Baghdad: Maktabah al-Quds, 1976, 121; Muḥammad Abū Zahrah, *Tanẓīm al-Islām li'l-Mujtamaʿ*, Cairo: Maṭbaʿah Mukhaymar, n.d., 196.

90. Abū Dāwūd, *Mukhtaṣar Sunan Abī Dāwūd*, K. al-ʿIlm, b. al-ḥathth ʿalā ṭalab al-ʿilm, *ḥadīth* 3643.

91. Al-Khaṭīb al-Baghdādī, *al-Riḥlāh fī Ṭalab al-Ḥadīth*, 71–76; al-Qaraḍāwī, *Al-ʿAql wa'l-ʿIlm*, 224.

92. Yusuf Ali, *The Holy Qur'an*, fn. 219.

93. al-Bukhārī, *Ṣaḥīḥ al-Bukhārī*, K. al-Isti'dhān, bāb 2 (narrated by Abī Saʿīd al-Khuḍrī).

94. Cf. Shīshānī, *Ḥuqūq al-Insān*, 385–86.

95. al-ʿĪlī, *Al-Ḥurriyyat al-ʿĀmmah*, 324; Shīshānī, *Ḥuqūq al-Insān*, 381.

96. Ibid., 376; Ismāʿīl al-Badawī, *Daʿā'im al-Ḥukm*, 85.

97. Ibn al-Ukhuwwah al-Qurshī, *Maʿālim al-Qurbah fī Aḥkām al-Ḥisbah*, 78–79; Shīshānī, *Ḥuqūq al-Insān*, 387.

98. Cf. Ghazāwī, *Al-Ḥurriyyah al-ʿĀmmah fi'l-Islām*, 32.

99. Ibn Kathīr, *Tafsīr Ibn Kathīr*, commentary on *Sūrah al-Nūr* (24:2).

100. Qurṭubī, *Tafsīr al-Qurṭubī*, vol. v, 7.

101. Bukhārī, *Ṣaḥīḥ al-Bukhārī* (Khan's tr.), vol. vIII, *ḥadīth* 10.

102. Bukhārī, *Ṣaḥīḥ al-Bukhārī* (Khan's tr.), vol. vIII, *ḥadīth* 13, *ḥadīth* 17. A slightly different version of this *ḥadīth* has also been reported by ʿĀ'ishah (Id., *ḥadīth* 18).

103. Muslim, *Mukhtaṣar Ṣaḥīḥ Muslim*, 470, *ḥadīth* 1759.

104. Muslim, *Mukhtaṣar Ṣaḥīḥ Muslim*, 472, *ḥadīth* 1769.

105. Abū Dāwūd, *Sunan Abū Dāwūd*, K. Ṣalāt al-Safar, b. matā yutimm al-musāfir, *ḥadīth*s 1229–1232.

106. Kāsānī, *Badā'iʿ*, II, 1018.

107. Kāsānī, *Badā'iʿ*, II, 1019; Ibn Rushd, *Bidāyah*, I, 160; Shīshānī, *Ḥuqūq*, 386.

108. Kāsānī, *Badā'iʿ*, II, 1018.

109. Cf. Al-Mazarī, *al-Muʿlim*, I, 280.

110. Abū Dāwūd, *Sunan*, K. Ṣalāt al-Safar, b. al-jamʿ bayn al-ṣalatayn, *ḥadīth* 1211.

111. Cf. Kamali, *Right to Life, Security, Privacy and Ownership in Islam*.

112. Imām Mālik b. Anas, *Muwaṭṭā*, 32.

113. Ibn Qāyyim al-Jawziyyah, *Iʿlām al-Muwaqqiʿīn*, III, 147.

114. *Ṣaḥīḥ Muslim*, K. al-Birr wa'l-Ṣillah, b. al-nahy ʿan al-tajassus.

115. Al-Bukhārī, *Ṣaḥīḥ al-Bukhārī*, n. 7, K. al-diyyah, vol. IX, 13.

116. Al-Bukhārī, *Ṣaḥīḥ al-Bukhārī*, n. 7, K. al-diyyah, vol. IX, 13.

117. Cf. Al-Ghannūshī, *Ḥuqūq al-Muwāṭanah*, 96.

118. Al-Bukhārī, *Ṣaḥīḥ al-Bukhārī*, n. 7, K. al-diyyah, vol. IX, 13.

119. Sulaymān al-Ṭamāwī, *ʿUmar al-Khaṭṭāb wa-Uṣūl al-Siyāsah wa'l-Idārah al-Ḥadīthah*. Cairo: Dār al-Fikr al-ʿArabī, 1969, 126; Al-ʿĪlī, *Al-Ḥurriyyah*, n. 8, 374; Ghazāwī, *Al-Ḥurriyyah*, 48.

120. Mālik, *Muwaṭṭā*, ch. 45, ḥadīth 7, 23; al-ʿĪlī, *Ḥurriyyat*, 378.

121. Muslim has recorded this as a *ḥadīth* as it includes reference to *ḥadīth*: Muslim, *Mukhtaṣar Ṣaḥīḥ Muslim*, ed. al-Albānī, 385, *ḥadīth* no. 1463.

122. Ibn al-ʿArabī, *Aḥkām*, vol. 485.

123. ʿAwdah, *al-Tashrīʿal-Jināʾī*, I, 543; Badrān, *Uṣūl*, 66; see for a discussion also Kamali, *Principles*, 22f.

124. ʿAwdah, *al-Tashrīʿ*, I, 639.

125. Ibn ʿĀbidīn, *Ḥāshiyah*, IV, 15; Al-Sarakhsī, *Al-Mabsūṭ*, VI, 3; Shīshānī, *Ḥuqūq al-Insān*, p. 384. Reports indicate that on one of his night tours of Medina, the Caliph heard a woman singing in such terms: 'O if I would have wine to drink, and would I find a way to be with Naṣr b. al-Ḥajjāj.' The Caliph summoned Naṣr the following day only to find how good looking he was, especially his hair that caught the caliph's attention. The caliph initially asked Naṣr to shave his hair, which he did but instead of detracting from his looks, this added to his beauty, hence even a greater source of temptation for women. The caliph then decided to banish Naṣr to Iraq. This is, however, taken as a personal *ijtihād* of the caliph without giving rise to any such assumption that personal beauty or good looks constitutes a valid ground of banishment.

126. Muḥammad Abū Zahrah, *Al-Jarīmah*; al-ʿĪlī, *Al-Ḥurriyyah*, 379.

127. Ibn ʿĀbidīn, *Ḥāshiyah*, IV, 65.

128. Cf. L. Bercher's edn. and trans. of the *Risālah*, 3rd edn. Algiers, 1949, 242; See also Kamali, *Freedom of Expression in Islam*, 234.

129. Cf. Rosenthal, *The Muslim Concept of Freedom*, 49.

130. Cf. Sarakhsī, *al-Mabsūṭ*, XX, 88.

131. Ibn Farḥūn, *Tabṣīrah*, II, 284; Ibn Qudāmah, *Mughnī*, X, 348.

132. Ibn ʿĀbidīn, *Ḥāshiyah*, III, 260; Ibn Farḥūn, *Tabṣīrah*, II, 264; ʿAwdah, *al-Tashrīʿal-Jināʾī*, I, 697.

133. Abū'l-Wasīm b. Riḍwān, *al-Shuhub al-Lamiʿah fi'l-Siyāsah al-Nāfiʿah* as quoted in Rosenthal, *The Muslim Concept of Freedom*, 59.

134. Al-Sarakhsī, *Al-Mabsūṭ*, n. 18, V, 181.

135. Zayn al-Dīn Ibn Nujaym, *Al-Baḥr al-Rāʾiq Sharḥ Kanz al-Daqāʾiq*, IV, 194; Ghazāwī, *Al-Ḥurriyyah*, 38.

136. Cf. Zaydān, *Al-Mufaṣṣal fī Aḥkām al-Marʾah*, III, 427.

137. Mutawallī, *Mabādi' Niẓām al-Ḥukm fi'l-Islām*, 31ff; Ghazāwī, *Al-Ḥurriyyah*, 40ff.

138. Muḥammad al-Ghazālī has referred to at least ten *ḥadīths* to the effect that the Prophet met with women without any cover on their faces and did not disapprove of it: *Sirr Ta'akhkhur al-ʿArab wa'l-Muslim*, p. 19; see also Zaydān, *Al-Mufaṣṣal fi Aḥkām al-Mar'ah*, III, 167.

139. Cf. Abū Shaqqah, *Taḥrīr al-Mar'ah,* IV, 263; Zaydān, *Al-Mufaṣṣal fī Aḥkām al-Mar'ah*, III, 96.

140. Abū Shaqqah, *Taḥrīr,* IV, 302 and 327.

141. Cf. *Sūrah al-Taghābun*, 64:15; *Āl-ʿImrān*, 3:14.

142. Osmān, *Ḥuqūq al-Insān*, 83; Ghannūshī, *Ḥuqūq al-Muwāṭanah*, 93.

143. Al-Jassās, *Aḥkām al-Qur'ān*, III, 88. See for a discussion also Sharaiyra, *Right and Freedom*, 113–115.

144. Muslim, *Mukhtaṣar Ṣaḥīḥ Muslim*, 308, *ḥadīth* no. 1153.

145. Al-ʿĪlī, *Ḥurriyyah*, 329.

146. Cf. Al-Shawkānī, *Nayl al-Awṭār*, VII, 73–74.

147. Cf. Al-ʿĪlī, *Ḥurriyyah*, 324; al-Ghannūshī, *Ḥuqūq al-Muwaṭanah*, 94–95.

CHAPTER TWO

Citizenship

I. Summary and Literature Review

I start the discussion here with a brief note on the meaning and scope of citizenship, a literature review and a note on terminology for 'citizenship' in the English and Arabic languages. The discussion continues to explore aspects of *fiqh* literature that relate to the concept of citizenship. Early juristic writings in *fiqh* do not articulate this subject and often tend to subsume citizenship under the twin concepts of *dār al-Islām* and *dār al-ḥarb*, Abode of Islam and Abode of War. This has only complicated matters as the division of the world into *dār al-Islām* and *dār al-ḥarb* is itself open to questions and cannot in any case provide a sound basis for citizenship. Added to this picture is the fact that the contemporary concept of citizenship is in many ways an epiphenomenon of the nation-state and cannot be meaningfully understood under the controversial dichotomy of *dār al-Islām* and *dār al-ḥarb*. The basic notion of citizenship is not repugnant to Islam, yet some of the ultra-nationalistic features of citizenship may be said to be less than compatible with the basic tenets of Islam on equality and justice. The whole topic of citizenship has remained so underdeveloped in the juristic writings of *fiqh* that one can hardly speak of a clearly defined concept of citizenship in Islamic law. Due to the absence of subject-specific literature on citizenship in the *fiqh* sources, writers have tended to subsume citizenship under *dār al-Islām* and thereby make citizenship an extension of religious identity of the person. My own treatment of the subject does not follow this line of discourse, and I also part ways with the conventional *fiqhī* coverage of the subject in the latter part of this presentation. Sections four and five of this chapter expound the *fiqh* literature on the status, in an Islamic polity, of Muslim and non–Muslim citizens respectively. Under the *fiqh* rules, Muslim residents of *dār al-Islām* are granted automatic citizenship whereas the status of non–Muslims is, on the whole, discussed within the rubric of *dhimmī* and *musta'min*. A discussion of these topics is followed, in section six, by an analysis of *ummah* and nation-state and how the latter has inevitably become the principal frame of reference on citizenship.

The historical unity of the Muslim community within the rubric of *ummah* now stands in contrast with its division into a multiplicity of nation states that take their origin not in Islam or in *ummah* but in European thought of the 18th and 19th centuries, especially following the French revolution of 1789. Muslim writers have generally considered nationalism and nation-state to be inimical to Muslim unity and disagreeable with Islam. Yet there are also views that see no inherent conflict between Islam and nationalism. A summary of these views appears in section seven, which is then followed by a discussion of unity and equality in the Qur'ān and *Sunnah* as the cardinal principles and goals of Islam, and the understanding, therefore, that all citizens are entitled to be accorded equal treatment under the law. A direct recourse to the sources of Islam on citizenship is necessary to propose a reform of the *fiqh* rules in the direction of equality and justice. This would also necessitate a fresh analysis of *dār al-Islām* and *dār al-ḥarb*, which is attempted in sections eight and nine. I then raise the basic question, in section ten, as to why are we talking of *dār al-ḥarb* if we find that peace rather than war commands normative validity in the Qur'ān, especially with reference to the status of citizens who are not engaged in hostility and war with the outside world nor with the state of their domicile. A question is also posed about whether the intermediate concept of *dār al-ʿahd* (abode of treaty) can actually provide us with relevant answers. I then draw attention to certain historical aberrations from the norms of equality in the poor treatment of non-Arab Muslims, the *mawāli*, under the Umayyad state. What is said here tends to confirm that in the matter of citizenship the record of government policy has been one of disequilibrium and was at best a poor representation of the normative guidance of Islam. Our reading of history also needs to be adjusted due to many changes. I note in this connection that the historical division of the world into the House of Islam and the House of War and the somewhat less than egalitarian treatment that was visited on the *dhimmīs* reflected the political and military superiority of Muslim powers. The rules of *fiqh* have not totally escaped this and a review of some of its provisions in the light of the guidelines of the sources has therefore been attempted.

The rights and duties of citizens are addressed in the succeeding sections, twelve and thirteen, respectively. Here too I have proposed a slightly different scheme of citizens' rights to that which I have found in the relevant literature. Six basic rights have been discussed in this connection including the right to candidacy and nomination to government positions, right to election, right to be consulted in community affairs, right to criticise political leaders, right to disobey a deviant command, and right to welfare and education. This is followed by a discussion of the basic duties of citizens. A separate section is devoted to a discussion of the disabilities women have experienced under the prevailing statutes and how they are in contrast to the normative rules of equality and justice in Islam. Why should only the father, but not the mother, of a child be entitled to pass on his identity, including his nationality, to their offspring is a question that I have raised and discussed. The conclusion that follows rounds up the discussion and puts forward reform proposals that were once suggested by the renowned Egyptian scholar, ʿAbd al-Razzāq al-Sanhūrī (d. 1971) who looked into the prospects of unity within the rubric of the *ummah*. I have only adjusted certain aspects of his basic proposal in the light of changes that the world has witnessed since then.

It is perhaps due to the controversial nature of the subject and the wide gap that has developed between the rules of *fiqh* and contemporary realities that even modern writers on Islamic constitutional law hardly include citizenship in their treatment of the subject. There is no discussion of citizenship, for example, in Mutawallī's *Mabādi' Niẓām al-Ḥukm fi'l Islām*, or ʿAbd al-Majīd al-Khālidī's, *Qawāʿid Niẓām al-Ḥukm fi'l-Islām*. This is also the case with regard to Muḥammad Fārūq al-Nabhān's *Uṣūl Niẓām al-Ḥukm fi'l-Islām*. Taqī al-Dīn al-Nabhānī's *Muqaddimāt al-Dustūr* has a brief discussion which subsumes citizenship under the twin division of *dār al-Islām* and *dār al-ḥarb*. Anyone who resides in *dār al-Islām* is a citizen and anyone who resides in *dār al-ḥarb* is an alien, unless he migrates to *dār al-Islām* and resides in its territory.[1] But since Muslim jurists are not in agreement on the definition of *dār al-Islām*, the parallel that is drawn between *dār al-Islām* and citizenship status of Muslims is consequently not devoid of ambiguity and can also be misleading.

Muhammad Hamidullah's treatment of the issue of citizenship is once again subsumed under the conventional juristic categories of *dhimmī, musta'min* and *ḥarbī* (permanent resident, temporary resident under permit, and alien at war) respectively. This manner of treatment is also entrenched in the same dichotomy that has become one of the main hurdles in reaching an appropriate understanding of citizenship within the nation-state framework of today. Unlike the earlier writers who either ignored the subject totally, or continued the conventional format, Hamidullah has mentioned that citizenship in some countries like Saudi Arabia is governed by different rules and that Saudi Arabia is no longer the same *dār al-Islām* in the way jurists of the past have considered it, as the original home and abode of the Muslims. Hamidullah acknowledges that this is dictated by necessity and the realities of international relations in the twentieth century. But having raised the main issue over citizenship, Hamidullah too leaves it where it is and proceeds with the discussion of *dhimmī* and *musta'min, dār al-Islām* and *dār al-ḥarb*. Hamidullah's main preoccupation is admittedly to expose the Islamic law of nations (*al-siyar*), the international law of Islam. However, it sidesteps the issue of citizenship in its new framework, that is, the nation-state that prevails throughout the Muslim world today.[2]

A more recent work which seems to feature in many juristic writings on the Islamic principles of government is that of Mawdūdī's *Islamic Law and Constitution*, which has a brief section on citizenship. Mawdūdī's treatment also follows the conventional format of *fiqh* but maintains the somewhat unprecedented view that Islamic law prescribes two types of citizenship, one being reserved for the Muslims and the other for *dhimmīs*.[3] The only difference that is noted here is that Mawdūdī no longer speaks of *dār al-Islām* and *dār al-ḥarb*, but simply replaces '*dār al-Islām*' with 'Islamic State,' and then expounds the rights and duties of citizens within that framework.

Mawdūdī's treatment of citizenship is also controversial in that it tends to create a 'second class' citizenship category, as it were, for non-Muslims, and tries to reinforce this by such additions, as he does, in reference to employment to government positions. For example, he says that the non-Muslim citizens of an Islamic state are not entrusted to appointment in 'key posts'. Mawdūdī's treatment of this subject may be said to be at odds with the Qur'ānic ideals of justice and fair treatment for non-Muslims.

Haitham Manna's book, bearing the title *Citizenship in Arab Islamic History* published by the Cairo Institute for Human Rights Studies (1996) underscores the size and scope of the challenge to address citizenship from the Islamic perspective. She explained that her attempt to write a book on the subject was faced with many challenges: there is a 'huge gap in this topic,' there is not a single definition of citizenship; there is no single model in legislation within states today that we can consider our frame of reference, and many orientalists have settled the issue by announcing the absence of this concept in Arab Islamic history.[4] As indicated in its title, Manna's work is basically historical and it is in the author's own phrase 'a mere contribution to the debate around the topic,'[5] and does not, as such, address juristic issues on citizenship beyond occasional references to them and highlighting the absence of research on them.

Having highlighted the problems in the existing works, my own presentation provides an exposition of the citizens' rights and obligations against the background of the basic Qur'ānic ideals of equality and justice. This approach marks a departure from Mawdūdī's two citizenships idea as this proposal is less than harmonious with Islam's commitment to equality. Equality is thus taken as a basic postulate of citizenship. The national state, which is the principal unit of political organisation in the Muslim world, is also taken as a basic framework of analysis. This is not intended, however, to mean an unquestioned acceptance of the nationalistic and sometimes divisive propensities of the nation-state phenomenon. It is proposed instead to visualise nation states and national identities as divisions that would hopefully promote recognition, familiarity, and friendship in the wider *ummah*. It may be justified perhaps to see the nation state as a manifestation of the Qur'ānic declaration 'O mankind! We have made you into tribes and nations so that you may know one another. The most honoured of you in the eyes of God is the most righteous of you' (49:13).

يأيها الناس إنا خلقناكم من ذكر وأنثى وجعلناكم شعوبا وقبائل لتعارفوا إن أكرمكم عند الله أتقاكم

The extent to which the rights of citizens are adequately protected in Islamic law is a matter of some controversy, especially with reference to the non-Muslim citizens. Islam clearly recognises Christianity and Judaism as true religions, yet embracing the faith of Islam has been treated by writers such as Mawdūdī as an overriding factor in determining the legal framework of citizenship. This is an erroneous assumption simply because the Qur'ān recognises the validity of other great religions and advocates freedom of religion as a basic right of their followers. There remains no basis then for the assumption that a non-Muslim cannot be a full citizen. To embrace Islam may still qualify a person for citizenship, but not in the exclusive sense, perhaps, of disqualifying a non-Muslim of the same. The latter may also qualify on other grounds such as naturalisation and domicile. The *Sharī'ah* entitles every human being to justice and the protection of a number of basic rights and liberties without any discrimination. Notwithstanding this basic unitarian outlook of *Sharī'ah* on fundamental rights there is much diversity over details among the various legal schools and jurists of Islam. Since the rules of *fiqh* were developed mainly by the leading *'ulamā'* of the scholastic period, these works were influenced by the prevailing conditions of their time. Some of the rules that were formulated tended to be discriminatory in regard to the rights of the *dhimmīs*. But the realities of contemporary life in the Muslim world have followed a different course. States and governments in the Muslim societies of today are no longer fashioned, as they used to be, on the basis only of religion. The era of democracy and constitutionalism has placed a fresh emphasis on the basic rights and liberties of the citizens. These changes have in turn been reflected in the works of Muslims jurists of the twentieth century, many of whom have advocated parallel changes in the rights and duties of citizens, both Muslim and non-Muslim, which are indicative of a commitment to the higher objectives of equality and justice as are upheld in the Qur'ān and *Sunnah*.

In political history, citizenship represents a transition from the obedient subject, the subservient individual and taxpayer to one who participates in the making of socio-political life in all its manifestations. Citizenship as such represented a rupture with the medieval world and marked a transition from 'divine' rights to citizen's rights, from a political system based on the survival of the strongest to a sharing of interests and common belonging to a civil society. Having said this, one also wonders whether citizenship offered a response to the need for equality between members of a religious, national and geographical community, or whether it tacitly expressed the desire for exclusivism and protection against the others. The historical experience of citizenship shows that this term has not served the purpose to provide all with common and equal rights. The nation state phenomenon which laid emphasis on the exclusivist content of citizenship may be said to have been a backward step for equality and the egalitarian call of international human rights law that rejects considering the citizen a special case and an exception, as it were, to human rights laws.[6]

Whether citizenship is based on the right of blood (*jus sanguinis*) or territorial right (*jus soli*), it is treated as a purely national issue that comes wholly under the general framework of national sovereignty. The only non-national text on nationality, the Hague Convention of 12 April 1930, stresses this point:

(1) Every state is entitled to define, according to its own legislations, its nationals.

(2) It is only these legislations that determine whether an individual is a national or not.

A perusal of the nationality and immigration laws of contemporary states also shows the various ways in which different states deal with the issue: *de facto* nationality and *de jure* nationality (as in the case of Poland), naturalization, nationality obtained through marriage, kinship or adoption, nationality based on family reunification, and honorary citizenship.[7]

The word 'citizen' did not formally appear until the French Revolution of 1789. Before that time, people were grouped in terms of religion, language, ethnic or tribal backgrounds. People did not affiliate themselves with the earth on which they lived. This kind of attachment has only subsequently featured as the central theme of nationalism and its associated concept of the nation state.[8] What I am saying is that the basic postulates of citizenship laws that now obtain in the national states, both Muslim and non-Muslim, call for a review in the light of a more egalitarian approach of international human rights laws and the fundamental principles of equality and justice.

II. Concept and Terminology

The term 'citizen' comes from the Latin word *civitas*, meaning city. The ancient Greeks were the first to explore the idea and practice of citizenship. Their society was based on *polis*, or city state. Aristotle believed that man was a political being and could not, therefore, reach his full potential without participating in the *polis*. However, the opportunity to take part in the *polis* did not extend to everyone. Women, children, resident foreigners, some labourers and slaves were not regarded as citizens and were excluded from the privileges of rule.

For Aristotle the main basis of distinction between a citizen and a non-citizen was his participation in giving judgment and in holding office. He further added that as soon as a man became entitled to participate in the affairs of *polis* or state and hold an office, he is deemed to be a citizen of that state. In Rome, citizenship was the basic criterion which served to distinguish between the civil and political rights of the Roman citizens (*cives*) and those of the populations of the conquered territories to whom citizenship was only partially and gradually extended.[9]

The link between education, welfare support, and citizenship has been frequently highlighted in recent years, in addition to participation in government which has traditionally been the focus of citizenship rights.

Citizenship is admittedly a complex idea and connotes a wide range of meanings. So much so that it does not lend itself either to a simple or a comprehensive definition.[10] As a concept, citizenship is also dynamic and evolutionary in that it tends to vary from community to community and remains open to the circumstantial changes of place and time. The rights that are acquired by citizenship are primarily of a political nature which contemplate participation in the political life of the community. At the present time, they may be said to include, above all, the right to participate in rule-making institutions and the right not to be arbitrarily or unfairly treated by those in positions of authority.[11] Citizenship is thus described as a means of identifying some of the most critical aspects of the relationship between the individual and the state.[12] Citizenship under contemporary law is established on the basis of blood tie or place of birth, or both. The reference to blood tie means that a child acquires the nationality of his father, whereas reference to the place of birth would entitle a child to the citizenship of the country of his or her birth even if the parents are not citizens of that country. Naturalisation is also recognised as a basis on which citizenship is acquired.

The modern meaning of citizenship, with a special reference to the English experience, underlines three components of citizenship and suggests that they were institutionalised in the following sequence: first, the civil rights, which mainly referred to individual liberties and the rule of law; next, the political rights, which were associated with democratic franchise and participation; and last, the social rights which referred mainly to welfare and education. With reference to the role of social factors in the development of citizenship, four successive waves, namely property, sex, kinship ties, age, and currently environmental issues are noted to have played a role in the definition of citizenship.

The very idea of citizenship, throughout its evolution has been premised on the existence of a state, the recognition of a status for the individual, and the relationship between them based on membership. This membership entitled the individuals to certain rights and required them to discharge certain duties.

Modern citizenship has aimed at eliminating all forms of hereditary or group privilege and requires that all citizens should be equal before the law. Yet in its core values, citizenship is not opposed to social and economic inequalities as such, but only to illegitimate inequality, to inequality which cannot be justified on a basis of equal citizenship rights.[13]

In the United States while the expressions 'citizenship' and 'nationality' are often used interchangeably, the term 'citizen' is, as a rule, employed to designate persons endowed with full political and personal rights. The expression 'nationals' is used in reference to persons who owe allegiance to the United States, but do not possess full rights of citizenship in the United States. A difference is also noted in the usage of words 'subjects' and 'citizens' in the United Kingdom, when one hears, for example, of British 'subjects' and Commonwealth 'citizens'. The word 'subject' in this usage implies entitlement to full political and personal rights in the United Kingdom. In some Latin American countries the expression 'citizenship' denotes the sum-total of political rights of which a person may be deprived, by way of punishment or otherwise, and thus lose citizenship without being divested of nationality as understood in international law.[14] Oppenheim apparently used the terms 'national', 'subject' and 'citizen' interchangeably when he defined nationality and wrote that 'the nationality of an individual is his quality of being a subject of a certain state, and therefore its citizen.'[15]

Notwithstanding the generally acknowledged merits of democracy and constitution, one should not overestimate the state of progress on citizenship issues in Western countries. The biases of history and culture still persist, so much so that many commentators have expressed dissatisfaction over the treatment of minorities, citizens or otherwise, in countries like Germany, Britain and France. Germany has accordingly been described as 'very much an ethnic state with citizenship conceived of in relation to an ethnic consciousness of kind.' A powerful idea of shared ethnic identity is therefore reflected in Germany's citizenship policy.[16]

The dividing lines between native and other citizens are so apparent that commentators have drawn a distinction between two types of citizenship, namely 'formal citizenship' which simply signifies 'membership in a nation-state' and 'substantive citizenship' which entails an array of rights, including participation in the business of government.[17]

The formal framework of French citizenship policy is not influenced so much by ethnicity and religion as by history and culture, including the revolutionary iconography of the tricolour Marianne, Liberty, Equality and Fraternity.[18] The Law of 22 December 1789 in France associated political rights with taxes paid by citizens. While in the United States, African-Americans did not get the right to vote until the 1960's. Fascist Italy prohibited marriage between 'Italian' citizens and the 'colonial subjects' in order to preserve the purity of their race. During the war with Iran, the Iraqi authorities requested Iraqi women to file for divorce from their Iranian husbands to 'put an end to inter-marriage between Arabs and Persians,' and most surprisingly, a founder of the Committee for the Defence of the Legitimate Rights in Saudi Arabia declared the Shiite Twelvers as apostates.[19] Citizenship may thus be said to be the last 'civilised' expression of depriving particular individuals in society of the rights given to the native people. In this sense, citizenship is a formula for marginalisation and exclusion, irrespective of the nature of the rights granted or withheld.[20]

Neither the conservative monarchy of England, nor revolutionary France, nor the American democracy provided equal rights to all those who lived in their territorial boundaries. Britain's self-image of monarchical continuity and parliamentary democracy entailed a certain absence of a rigid policy since Commonwealth nationals had a common allegiance to the Monarch. But the 1981 Nationality Act and subsequent legislation have sought to exclude non-white immigrants and progressively moved from 'an open democratic concept of citizenship towards one based on an ethnic-state concept.'[21] Exclusivism and alienation are noted as common predicaments of minority life in all the three countries. Thus in Germany, very substantial numbers of German born Muslim residents of Turkish background are excluded from formal citizenship, while in France, working class North African Muslims, who are French citizens, are made to feel culturally alien. And in Britain, following the 'Rushdie Affair', the Gulf War, and the currently ongoing anti-terrorism euphoria of post 9/11, British Muslim citizens have been challenged to demonstrate their 'Britishness.'[22]

While discussing the relevant Arabic terminology for citizenship, ʿAbd Allāh Basyūnī draws a distinction between *al-sukkān*, *al-shaʿab*, *al-riʿāyāh* and *al-muwāṭinūn*, that is, inhabitants, populace, citizens and compatriots respectively. Whereas the inhabitants (*al-sukkān*) of a state include both citizens, aliens and all who reside in its territory, the term 'populace' or 'population' (*al-shaʿab*) refers only to those who enjoy a recognised status as citizens. But since the word 'people' or 'populace' (*al-shaʿab*) is inherently generic, it may be qualified in Arabic as *al-shaʿab al-siyāsī* (people with a political status), in contradistinction with *al-shaʿab al-ijtimāʿī* that envisages the populace as a social group only. Then there is the distinction to be noted in passing between *al-shaʿab* (populace) and *al-ummah* (nation, in one of its usages) in that *ummah* literally signifies a natural relationship between a multitude of people which does not necessarily give rise to legal consequences; for it may be based on a common language, religion, history, culture or geography. This is however different to *al-shaʿab* which signifies a politico-legal relationship that entitles the individuals to protection by the state of their lives, properties and other rights as well as placing them under duty to obey its laws.[23]

The Arabic equivalent of 'nationality' is 'al-jinsiyya' but 'muwāṭanah' is the preferred term by modern Arab writers for citizenship, and *muwāṭin* for 'citizen.' The root word here is *waṭan* (home where one lives). It is the individual's place of residence, *riʿāyā* (sing. *raʿiyyah*) or subjects signifies a protected status that is accorded by the ruler to the ruled. According to Ibn Manẓūr in *Lisān al-ʿArab*, to reside in a territory means to consider it one's home, one's nation and hence be its native. Another derivative of *waṭan* is *istiṭān* (settlement) as well as *waṭaniyyah* (nationalism) although this last literally means patriotism. Nationality is basically a term of exclusion that demarcates the boundaries of participation whereby participation in certain rights and social interactions is denied to outsiders. The grounds of exclusion tend to vary. Religion and culture as well as ethnicity and language are some such factors, but more than one is often combined as a basis of exclusion. The Saudi Kingdom founded by King Abdul Aziz used to appoint Arab Ministers from outside the peninsula. The Kingdom of Abdul Aziz's successors 'enriched by oil wealth, is a perfect model of seclusion.'[24] Israel rules out both the blood and the territorial rights of a great number of Palestinians who are the real owners of the land. At the same time, Israel sanctions the principle of the Jews return to the Promised Land, as religion becomes the fundamental, albeit not the sole, frame of reference for the concept of nationality.

The problem here may be said to be not so much over the use of terms as it is over the role and meaning of citizenship in the transition between two eras, the first of which is the pre-World War I period and the decline and eventual demise of the Ottoman Caliphate. The second starts with the end of WWI, the emergence of independent Arab states, and the UN Universal Declaration of Human Rights. The interval between the two dates represents a crossroads between the two eras.

In Ottoman Turkey the proclamation of the Imperial Edict, the *Hatt-I Serif* of Gulhane of 3 November 1839 was a landmark development for citizenship rights in recent Islamic history. The Edict declared the need for new reforms, known as the *Tanẕīmāt* reforms along the following lines:

(1) The guarantee ensuring to our subjects perfect security for life, honour and fortune.

(2) A regular system of assessing and levying taxes.

(3) An equally regular system for the levying of troops and the duration of their service.

The Edict clearly stated that 'these imperial concessions shall extend to all our subjects, of whatever religion or sex they may be; they shall enjoy them without exception.'

These were promises which, though not entirely fulfilled, strengthened the voice of Ottoman reformists which led to the proclamation of another edict, the *Hatt-i Humayun* on 18 February 1856. It reaffirmed the principles laid in the 1839 edict and included more specific guarantees regarding the equal treatment of all Ottoman subjects in matters of taxation, military service, education, and admission to public employment. The prohibition of discrimination was also to cover 'every distinction or designation tending to make any class whatever of the subjects of my Empire inferior to another class, on account of their religion, language or race.'[25]

Whereas these edicts still spoke of the subjects of the Empire and the millet system that went in some ways against the notion of equality and integration, the 1876 constitution that followed affirmed the idea of Ottoman nationality for all alike. According to Article (7) of this constitution 'All subjects of the Empire are called Ottomans, without distinction, and whatever faith they profess, the status of an Ottoman is acquired and lost, according to conditions specified by law.'[26]

The Ottoman Caliphate had been under pressure from Europe over many long years to renounce its religious legacy that linked citizenship to religious identity. The abolition in Turkey of the Caliphate in 1924 disrupted the historical model and what followed in the next wave was the second era of the emergence of states, such as Saudi Arabia and the Islamic Republics of Pakistan and Iran. Despite their evidently religious character, they still lack the fundamental constitutional conditions that would guarantee natural growth into a society that protects the individual against fanaticism of various groups (tribe, clan, sect) and shields him against the excesses of coercive power. In short, the Ottoman concept of citizenship, as explained above, was buried without acceptance of a substitute that would fill the gap with either the western concept, or with a newly formulated one by the emergent states.[27] Due to historical and constitutional uncertainties, Haitham Manna observed that 'there is not a single definition of citizenship; there is no single model in legislation within states today that we can consider our frame of reference.' This observation is evidently not confined to the Islamic context but includes western legal traditions. Manna went on to highlight the wider aspect of the issue by saying that 'The human race has not yet settled the question of abolishing the borderline between the human and citizen rights. Not every human being is a citizen, and there is no nominal equality of rights between humans.'[28]

None of the Arabic terms reviewed above occur in the Qur'ān. But the notion of belonging to a place in the Qur'ān is conveyed in words such as *diyār* and *balad*. References to *ummah* and *qawm* also occur in the Qur'ān as groups to which an individual may have a sense of belonging and attachment. In a passage where the text allowed the early Muslim community of Medina to wage war in the cause of God and against oppression, a reference is also made to homeland and family:

ومالنا ألا نقاتل فى سبيل الله وقد أخرجنا من ديارنا وأبنائنا

How could we refuse to fight in the cause of God, seeing that we were turned out of our homeland (*diyārinā*) and our families (2:246).

Elsewhere the text refers again to these factors and on this occasion enjoins justice and fair treatment for those who 'never fought you over religion nor evicted you from your homes (*diyārikum*)' (60:8).

لا ينهاكم الله عن الذين لم يقاتلوكم فى الدين ولم يخرجوكم من دياركم أن تبروهم وتقسطوا إليهم

The Qur'ān also addressed the Prophet Muhammad in the following terms: 'Remember (when) Ibrahim said: O my Lord: make this city (*balad*) one of peace with security.' (14:35)

The idea of belonging to a place highlighted by a sense of affinity with its landscape, fruits, and safety is also depicted in the following verse: 'By the fig, and the olive, and the mount of Sinai, and this city of security (*al-balad al-amīn*)' (*al-Tīn*, 95:1–3).

والتين والزيتون وطور سينين وهذا البلد الأمين

The sense of attachment to one's *balad* is further accentuated when this becomes the object of a divine oath-taking in a verse addressed to the Prophet Muhammad, in a *sūrah* which also bears the name '*al-Balad*.'

لا أقسم بهذا البلد وأنت حلّ بهذا البلد ووالد وما ولد

I do call to witness this city, and you are a freeman of this city, and the ties of parent and child . . . (90:1–3)

The parent and child bond is clearly read into the notion of *balad*, the homeland, and the freedom that is enjoyed as a result of belonging to it. By virtue of this reference, this *sūrah* is also known to be a Meccan *sūrah*, as this was the place where the Prophet and his parents resided. The Prophet himself went on record to express his love for his birthplace Mecca when he was compelled to leave it. Ibn ʿAbbās reported in this connection that grief had overcome the Prophet when on his way to Medina, he paused for a moment at Ḥazwarah near the marketplace of Mecca and said:

والله إنك لخير أرض الله وأحب أرض الله إليّ، لولا أني أخرجت منك ما خرجت

> By God! You are the best of all places in the eyes of God and most beloved on the face of God's earth to me. Had it not been for the fact that your inhabitants evicted me, I would not have left you.[29]

Commentators have drawn the conclusion that the forced eviction of Muslims from their homeland was the basic cause of the Qur'ānic validation of armed struggle and *jihād*. This was not allowed during the first twelve years of the Prophet's campaign in Mecca where he propagated Islam through peaceful means. Only when the Muslims were subjected to persecution and thrown out of their homeland were they allowed to resort to *jihād*.

III. Islamic Conception of Citizenship

One of the general attributes of Islam that needs to be taken into account is its claim to universality and the assertion that its standards of equality transcend the particularities of tribe and nation and for that matter of the nation state. This is because of Islam's rejection of all racial, ethnic, and hereditary criteria of distinction that constitute the foundations of nationalism. The only valid ground on which an individual may be deemed superior to another in Islam is God-consciousness and piety (*taqwā*).

One may or may not agree with Enayat that what Islam gives with one hand, it takes away with another by imposing civic deprivations on the non-Muslims living in an Islamic state. Yet Enayat has himself noted that virtually no egalitarian school of political thought provides for absolute equality. With reference to modern democracies, for example, Enayat stated that all of them impose certain implicit or explicit discriminations in favour of those who pay allegiance to a set of ideals, whether it be the 'American way of life' or 'scientific socialism' or liberal monarchical democracy. With reference to Islam, Enayat observed that there are also limitations to equality, but unlike the limitations based on race, colour, and caste 'the limitations placed by the *Sharī'ah* on the rights of non-Muslims are not permanent and irremovable, because non-Muslims always have the option to convert to Islam and thereby overcome their political incapacity.'[30]

Enayat may have a point, which is, however, rather a weak one, and it goes, in the final analysis against the Qur'ānic mandate that 'there shall be no compulsion in religion.' For what Enayat has said is prejudicial to non-Muslims who may feel under perpetual pressure to embrace Islam if they wish to become full citizens.

Despite the awareness the Qur'ān has conveyed of the reality of people's attachment to their place of birth and residence, it makes no direct reference to citizenship. This may be indicative of a certain openness of outlook above the restrictive framework of citizenship in modern times. 'The Qur'ān recognises man (*insān*),' as Enayat explains, 'irrespective of his beliefs and political standing, but has no word for citizen'.[31] This also explains the fact that Muslim writers have had to invent new terms for the concept: '*muwāṭin*' in Arabic, '*shahr-vand*' in Persian, and '*vatandas*' in Turkish, all of which are neologisms. The Qur'ān may have left the subject of citizenship undefined, but the position of man himself, in his pre-social state, is ennobled in the Qur'ān as God's 'vicegerent on the earth' (2:30). Conversely for the Romans, the Latin word '*homo*' the equivalent of man, 'suggested originally somebody who was nothing but a man, a rightless person, therefore, and a slave.'[32]

The following Qur'ānic verse is often quoted in evidence to the effect that religion and domicile are the basic requirements of citizenship:

إن الذين آمنوا وهاجروا وجاهدوا بأموالهم وأنفسهم فى سبيل الله والذين ءاووا ونصروا أولئك بعضهم أولياء بعض والذين آمنوا ولم يهاجروا ما لكم من ولايتهم من شيئ حتى يهاجروا

Surely those who believed and fled (their homes) and struggled hard in God's way with their wealth and their lives, and those who gave shelter and helped—these are friends of one another. And those who believed but did not migrate, you are not responsible for their protection (*wilāyah*) until they migrate. (8:72)

The reference to protection in this verse has been a matter of some discussion among the commentators. The basic meaning of the text seems to be clear, and the reference is, of course, to the Migrants and Helpers, *Muhājirūn* and *Anṣār*. The migrants were the early believers who were persecuted, fled their homes and then formed a community in Medina alongside those who gave them shelter and helped them (i.e., the *Anṣār*). But there were some who chose to remain in their homes and did not migrate to Medina. The nascent community in Medina could not undertake to protect the interests of such persons, and this is what is meant by 'you are not responsible for their protection.'

Mawdūdī has quoted this verse and drawn the conclusion that 'the basic qualifications for citizenship as prescribed in this text are two, namely faith in Islam and original or acquired domicile in an Islamic state. 'If a person, even though he may be from amongst the faithful, does not renounce his allegiance to a non-Islamic state and does not migrate to Islamic state, he is not and cannot be its citizen.'[33]

There may be some weakness in this analysis in that it draws a direct analogy between two somewhat different situations, namely of migrating under the threat of persecution, as in the early days of Islam, and migrating in peacetime that may well be a matter of choice. The text also makes no direct reference to citizenship, but if one were to equate the meaning of protection and support (*wilāyah*), which is the principal theme of this verse, with citizenship, then the verse may provide textual authority on the subject. The two main points of the text before us are embracing Islam and migration to Medina under circumstances that were evidently hostile, which is perhaps why migration played a crucial role in determining the faith and loyalty of individuals to Islam. A direct analogy of the kind that Mawdūdī has drawn would be relevant and justified perhaps in the case, for example, of India and Pakistan, as the course of events in the late 1940's in the Indian sub-continent showed a striking resemblance to those of the early history of Islam. But generally speaking, migration may or may not be under hostile conditions. Naturalisation due to birth or long-term residence, for instance, does not involve migration. It is submitted instead to take domicile as one of the basic requirements of citizenship. Although the text under review requires migration, the main purpose of that migration may be said to be domicile. The early Muslims were thus enjoined to migrate to Medina and make it their home. Domicile thus became the basic requirement of citizenship. The element of persecution and hostility that actually prompted the flight of the migrants to Medina may also be relevant in a negative sense, which is that the Islamic state may refuse to confer citizenship on persons who might be hostile to the Muslim community, naturally including those who might have persecuted the Muslims.

One may add to this analysis the information from the *Sunnah*, especially the *ḥadīth* which simply declared that 'there is no *hijrah* (migration) after the conquest (of Mecca).'[34]

لا هجرة بعد الفتح

Migration of the kind that the Qur'ān has referred to has therefore come to an end as of the conquest of Mecca, which took place in the year 8 after Hijrah. Mawdūdī's analysis of migration does not seem to have taken the purport of this *ḥadīth* into consideration and tends to attach to migration the meaning that it could only carry during the first two decades or so of the advent of Islam. To equate domicile with migration and take the latter rather than the former to be the basic requirement, as Mawdūdī has done, may be somewhat restrictive. It is thus proposed to take domicile instead of migration as a basic requirement. Due to the circumstantial nature of the text under discussion, it may be said to be a manifest text, or *ẓāhir*, which is in the nature of probability, rather than a decisive injunction on the subject. It is a source of guidance generally in so far as it can be relied upon to determine general policy on citizenship, but it is not a clear text, or *naṣṣ*, on the subject. It seems thus reasonable to conclude that residence and domicile for a period of time constitutes a basic requirement of citizenship, regardless as to whether it has come about as a result of migration in the sense of escape from enemy persecution, or migration caused by other factors.

The second requirement of the text under discussion, namely embracing Islam, may also be seen as a general policy guideline and it is most likely to be given a favourable consideration by an Islamic polity. Yet its application strictly as a prerequisite is hardly sustainable. This is partly due to the fact that religion is no longer the sole ideology or doctrinal foundation of the nation state in the Muslim world today, and this is obvious from a perusal of any of their numerous constitutions. Embracing Islam should not be a requirement in any case. For such a requirement is likely to clash with the Qur'ānic principle that 'there shall be no compulsion in religion' (2:256).

لا إكراه فى الدين

Besides, the Prophet-cum-head of state himself did not insist on embracing Islam as a precondition of citizenship. The Constitution of Medina acknowledged and declared the Jews of Medina as part of the *ummah* which the Prophet organised immediately after his migration to Medina. Moreover, there is nowhere a requirement in the sources of *Sharī'ah* to say that a non-Muslim resident, the so-called *dhimmī*, must become a Muslim first before he or she can become a citizen of an Islamic state.

Citizenship is entrenched in the recognition of a status for the individual and a certain degree of independence he or she must enjoy from the group to which he or she belongs. A positive valuation of one's personal life and family ties and a degree of moral autonomy are deemed necessary as basic foundations of citizenship. It will be noted that Islam takes an affirmative stand on these and provides much support for the individuality of the believer. Franz Rosenthal thus wrote that 'Islam in principle stresses the unique worth of the individual' yet it places equal emphasis on the maintenance of the social structure of which he is a part.[35] There is a profound awareness in the sources of Islam and in Arabic literature of the personality and personal attributes of the individual. 'The profuse richness of the Arabic language in words for character and character traits proves that the ancient Arabs had a keen eye for the personality of an individual with whom they had dealings.'[36] The same awareness obtains in the Qur'ān which makes frequent references to the upright character of the individual, his unique status as the prize of God's creation, and the affirmation that God favoured him 'far above most of Our creation.' Man is above all dignified with God's affirmation of having breathed into him of His spirit (32:9) and honoured him as his vicegerent (*khalīfah*) in the earth. Man in the Qur'ān is also made aware of his responsibility for his deeds, and his accountability 'for an atom's weight of good, and . . . an atom's weight of evil.' (99:7–8).

فمن يعمل مثقال ذرة خيرا يره ومن يعمل مثقال ذرة شرا

يره

It is further provided that 'no bearer of burden shall be made to bear another's burden' (53:38).

ألا تزر وازرة وزر أخرى

Moreover, since there is no church or priesthood in Islam, the believer's relationship with God should remain unmediated, thereby confirming the former's individuality in his aloneness before the Creator.[37] It is of interest also to note Schacht's characterisation of Islamic law in such terms that 'the solutions provided by Islamic law go decisively and consistently in favour of the rights of the individual, of the sanctity of contracts and of private property and

the political and religious community were concurrent, borne out by the fact that the word 'Muslim' was the nearest equivalent of 'citizen.' To say that the two were concurrent is not the same as to say that a political community, or citizenship for that matter, did not exist. Attention is drawn in this connection to a *hadīth*, recorded in both Bukhārī and Muslim, which declared that 'the lives of Muslims are equal (in respect of retaliation and *diyyah*) and they are a unity against their opponents. When the least among them offers safe conduct to someone, it becomes a commitment on all of them.'[44]

المسلمون تتكافؤا دماؤهم وهم على يد من سواهم

ويسعى بذمتهم أدناهم

'The least among them,' according to commentators, include women and children, although most have excluded the latter. Some of the confusion seems to have been caused by the notion of a 'political community' (*al-mujtama' al-siyāsī*) and how it is understood by critics and commentators. Modern critics seem to associate citizenship with a political community, a requirement which is not met by a religious community and the conclusion therefore that citizenship is alien to Islam.

The realities of unity within the ranks of the *ummah* have drastically changed over time and the freedom of travel and residence that they once enjoyed in all parts and territories under Muslim rule does not exist any more. Much of this, one might say, is a consequence of economic and political changes that were witnessed as a result of the prevalence of the nation state. Economic differentials among Muslim countries have given a new dimension to the exclusivities of nationalism. Yet the basic sentiment of *ummah*'s unity that is grounded in religion may still be said to be a reality, and a hope, according to Ḥassan al-Saffār, 'in the hearts of Muslims that can be utilized for greater cooperation and closeness within the framework of the currently prevailing conditions.'[45] This unitarian sentiment is upheld by Hamidullah who was, however, equally aware of the gap that had developed between the rules of *fiqh* of medieval origin and the prevailing state of international relations. Hamidullah thus observed that 'geographic nationalities are making certain discriminations. Even the orthodox Saudia Arabia has promulgated laws as to how a foreign Muslim may acquire citizenship in her dominion.' The author then simply wrote that 'prevalent international conditions have necessitated that.'[46] Hamidullah has nevertheless considered these rules to be anomalous and unworthy of serious attention: 'There are provisions on how to treat foreigners, and they apply to Muslims as well. We need not take notice of them as they are not rules of Muslim law.'[47] One may or may not agree with Professor Muhammad Hamidullah's light dismissal of the 'provisions' he has referred to; it is quite obvious now, as it was in 1953 when Hamidullah wrote it, that the gap between the rules of *fiqh* and the applied laws of Muslim countries on nationality and citizenship had grown so wide that they had become incompatible.

The lines of division between countries and nations, including Muslim countries, have become more obvious since and have struck root during the second half of the twentieth century. This is due to a variety of factors. Chief among them may be said to be the economic factor and the unwillingness of the richer countries to share their wealth with the poorer nations. Among the Muslim countries, Saudi Arabia and the Gulf countries are perhaps well known for their stringent policies on nationality and immigration. With the exception of some limited concessions that are granted to citizens of the Gulf states in the area of commerce,[48] it is generally quite difficult for Muslim foreigners to settle in Saudi Arabia and obtain citizenship.[49] Saudi Arabia is here cited as an example in order to pursue the discussion over Hamidullah's conclusions, but Saudi Arabia is by no means an exception. The citizenship laws of almost all Muslim countries have departed from the open door attitude and receptiveness of the kind that is associated with the Qur'ānic concept of *ummah*, by introducing restrictions that have altered the whole picture of openness to one of its opposite.

There is little doubt that the necessity which Hamidullah referred to as an explanation for the drastic changes of citizenship policies of Muslim governments has now become the general rule. Nationality and citizenship laws that are currently in force in the Muslim countries have marked a near-total departure from the rules of *fiqh* that were formulated in earlier times, that is, prior to the advent of the nation–state. The *fiqh* provisions were generally premised on the idea of unity within the boundaries of *dār al-Islām*, the abode of Islam, and by implication, the Muslim homeland. Yet the juristic rules of *fiqh* may also be said to have been premised on an equally questionable basis of dividing the world into the binary division of *dār al-Islām* and *dār al-ḥarb* (abode of war, also referred to as *dār al-kufr*). Apart from the fact that no clear authority for this classification could be found in the Qur'ān or the *Sunnah*, the classification seems to proceed on the acceptance, in principle, of belligerency and war as the normal pattern of relations between Muslim and non–Muslim powers. A fuller discussion of this issue will presently be attempted, but to continue with the debate over Hamidullah's point on the subject of necessity, we may refer to a legal maxim of *fiqh* which clearly specifies that 'necessity must be measured in accordance with its true proportions' (*al-ḍarūrah tuqaddaru bi-qadrihā*). What this means is that the situation of necessity should be carefully measured and brought to an end at an early opportunity when there is a change toward normality. The rules of necessity, and the emergency situation that invokes those rules, must in other words not be allowed to continue under normal conditions. It is perhaps instructive to draw attention to this and raise the question whether one can see any signs of change in the realities of the era of nationalism and nation state, which came hot on the heels of the colonialist distortions of relations among Muslim nations. The rising tide of nationalism, national sovereignty, and independence may be said to have been somewhat of an exaggerated exercise in exclusivity and self–assertiveness. Although nationalism has by no means given way to a more open regime of immigration laws, and there is little reason for optimism over the prospects of open immigration and citizenship policies among Muslim countries, yet there are signs to suggest that further changes are needed in order to rectify and moderate the exclusivities of the era of nationalism.

Under the 30-articled Royal decree of 22nd February 1974, Saudi Arabian nationality may be conferred on an alien who is adult and sane and has, at the time of application, acquired a permanent resident status in Saudi Arabia. The applicant should have resided in the country for a minimum of five years, and must possess a clean personal record and should be financially able to support himself (Art. 9).

The Egyptian law of 1975 empowers the Minister of Internal Affairs to confer Egyptian citizenship on an alien who is in possession of his normal faculties and has lived a minimum of ten consecutive years in Egypt. The applicant must be able to communicate in Arabic and also possess a good character and financial ability to support himself (Art. 4). It is further provided that marriage with an Egyptian man or woman does not qualify the alien spouse to Egyptian citizenship, but the Minister may grant an application after two years of marriage by such a person (Art. 6). But even when an alien does acquire Egyptian citizenship under these provisions, he or she is still not entitled to election to a representative assembly or political office for another five years (Art. 9).

There is no reference in either the Saudi or the Egyptian laws to the religion of the applicant for citizenship which would naturally mean that rules of nationality and citizenship under these laws apply to Muslims and non-Muslims alike.

The Tunisian law of 28 February, 1963 requires five years residence prior to application for citizenship by aliens, which may, however, be waived in the case of an applicant who is married to a Tunisian citizen, or when the person concerned has rendered valuable service for the country (Art. 20, 21).

The Bahrain law of September, 1963 requires no less than twenty five consecutive years of residence for an alien, or ten years for an Arab, to qualify for acquisition of Bahraini citizenship. One other somewhat unusual qualification required under this law is ownership of land in Bahrain (Art. 6). The applicant must also qualify a number of other conditions relating to a clean personal record and 'sufficient knowledge of Arabic.'

The United Arab Emirates law of 1972 requires thirty years of residence in the country for a non-Arab alien to qualify for citizenship, which is, however, reduced to seven years for an Arab, and to only three years for citizens of Oman, Qatar and Bahrain. Other qualifications pertaining to personal integrity and financial ability must also be met (Art. 5, and 6). The Head of State is entitled nevertheless to confer UAE citizenship to anyone on the basis of excellent service even without fulfilment of residential requirements (Art. 9).

The Syrian Cabinet Ordinance (no. 276) of November 1969 regulated nationality-related issues in 35 sections and permit acquisition of Syrian nationality to an alien who has completed a residency requirement of five years prior to application. The applicant must be clear of contagious disease and criminal record, be able to read and write Arabic and possess a skill to enable him to earn a lawful living (S. 4). The residency requirement of five years is then reduced, in the case of persons of Arab origin to 'ordinary residence (*al-iqāmah al-ʿādiyah*)' at the time of application and authorizes the Minister of Home Affairs to make a decision whether or not to entertain the application (S. 16).

The Iraqi law of July, 1963 stipulates a long list of conditions including fifteen years of residence in Iraq for a non-Arab and ten years for a person of Arab origin (Art. 1 and 4). Among the conditions that are listed for this purpose, there is one which provides that 'Iraqi citizenship may not be conferred on Palestinians until the liberation of Palestine and return of the refugees (to their homeland)' (Art. 8). In granting citizenship, the Minister considers the public interest and meritorious service that the applicant might have rendered for Iraq (Art. 2). The exclusion of Palestinians as a single category under this law was probably due to the large number of Palestinian refugees in Iraq at the time.[50]

The Federal Constitution of Malaysia 1957 stipulates four ways by which citizenship may be acquired: These are 1) by operation of law; 2) by registration; 3) naturalization; and 4) incorporation of territory. Acquisition of citizenship by operation of law takes place automatically in respect of persons who were born in Malaysia on or before Malaysia Day (i.e. September 16, 1963) and those born after and who fulfill certain requirements (Art.14). Citizenship by registration applies mainly to foreign wives of Malaysian citizens and their offspring. Citizenship through naturalization envisages persons who apply for citizenship after residence of 'not less than ten years in the twelve years immediately preceding the date of the application' (Art.19). Malaysia does not permit dual citizenship and the constitution provides for a number of grounds, including crime and fraud, whereby citizenship granted by registration and naturalization may be withdrawn by executive order (Art. 24–28 Federal Constitution).

It is evident that migration and citizenship laws of the present day Muslim countries are generally premised on nation state as a basic framework and the national interests of the country concerned. Religion does not appear to play a prominent role. It may be noted in passing, however, that residency and citizenship decisions are strongly influenced by policy considerations which may or may not be consistent with what the legal text might stipulate.

Greater openness in immigration laws is to some extent dictated by the need for greater cooperation in such areas as protection of the environment, more cooperative production and marketing strategies, and a move away from protectionist trade policies, labor relations and so forth. Regionalism and formation of economic and trading blocs such as the EEC (now EU, which is also a political union), ASEAN etc., have marked a departure from the ultra-nationalist strategies of the earlier decades not only in the areas of trade and agriculture but also nationality and citizenship laws among the EEC (and now the European Union) member countries. Muslim countries have too become aware of the importance of similar cooperation and of nurturing more open policies within the framework of organisations such as the OIC, NAM, D-15, and prospects for greater South-South cooperation. These and similar other factors may be seen as harbingers of further changes and adoption of more open immigration policies among Muslim countries.

Despite a basically open door policy that Muslim powers of earlier times practiced within Muslim lands, the *dār al-Islām*, there were ambiguities, and the rules of *fiqh* concerning certain issues were neither comprehensive nor well defined. There were instances when the rulers sent special missions to purchase goods, manuscripts, educational materials and the like, but as Hamidullah noted, 'they do not seem to have given rise to any legal arrangements for their treatment...'[51]

Following a relatively brief period in its early history, the Muslim world has ever since the latter Abbasid period been practically divided into a plurality of political and geographical entities. The Arab segment of the Muslim world, the Maghreb, the Andalus, Africa, and Transoceania operated as autonomous entities with their separate political and military establishments. Pluralism on operative levels did not, however, create barriers on the free movement and residence of Muslims, whether in the quest for knowledge, trade or employment.[52]

The Universal Islamic Declaration of Human Rights, 1981, does not contain a separate clause on citizenship. There are now fifty-seven independent Muslim states and although they maintain levels of cooperation in various organizations, and there is awareness and recognition of unity in faith among them, they are totally separate otherwise. There were initial hopes that the advent of globalisation would encourage openness and the prospects of better relations among nations to enable their people to enjoy better access, freedom of movement and residence. But those hopes have not been realized, and the world of post-9/11 is considerably less receptive to the idea of harmony and bringing nations and peoples closer to one another.

Islamic law recognises the existence of independent non-Muslim states and the prospects of them having peaceful relations with the Muslim states. A Muslim state has no right to interfere in the affairs of a non-Muslim state that may or may not have a Muslim minority population. Their relations would normally be in accordance with the terms of passport if they wish to enter each other's territory for temporary purposes.[53] A non-Muslim state which enters treaty relations with the Muslim state becomes a *dār al-ʿahd*, the abode of treaty, and its subjects need no extra permission from the Muslim state to enter the latter's territory for a sojourn. Foreign visitors, both Muslim and non-Muslim, are under the jurisdiction of Muslim courts during their stay, and Islamic law was generally applied to them.[54]

V. *Dhimmī* and *Musta'min*: A Juristic and Historical Perspective

Non-Muslim residents of a Muslim majority state are divided into two categories, namely those who have taken permanent residence and the Muslim state is committed to their protection (i.e. the *dhimmīs*), and the *musta'min*s, those who come to the Islamic lands for temporary residence. I shall have more to say on whether the word *dhimmī* should be abandoned in favour of *muwāṭin* (compatriot), but I present the gist of the conventional discourse over the status of 'dhimmīs' first.

Dhimmī is a derivative of *dhimmah*, which means commitment, and it applies to those who enter a contract, known as *ʿaqd al-dhimmah*, which entails mutual commitment on their part and on the part of the Islamic state. This is why the *dhimmīs* are also known as *al-muʿāhidūn*, or parties to a covenant. They commit themselves to loyalty and the state is in return committed to their protection and support. The contract of *dhimmah* basically entitles non-Muslim citizens to equal rights and obligations to those of their Muslim compatriots. It is a permanent contract which can only be concluded by the head of state or his delegates, and once concluded, it cannot be revoked, but the law provides for certain eventualities whereby the contract may be terminated.

Dhimmah is binding and permanent as far as the Muslims are concerned, but it is revocable as far as the non-Muslim party is concerned. The Ḥanafī's have, however, confined the grounds of revocation to three, namely when the *dhimmī* embraces Islam, when he joins the enemies, or when they act in consort and jointly declare war on the Muslims. Outside these three situations the contract of *dhimmah* is not revocable even when the *dhimmī* commits blasphemy, refuses to pay the poll-tax (*jizyah*) or commits murder, adultery and theft. This is the Ḥanafī view, but the majority of Sunni and Shīʿi jurists have held refusal to pay the *jizyah* as a ground for revocation of the contract of *dhimmah*.

All non-Muslim residents, whether temporary or permanent, are required to submit to the authority of the Islamic government and observance of its laws, except for personal and customary matters such as marriage, divorce, and inheritance where the *Sharī'ah* allows them to practice their own customs and traditions.[55] The *dhimmīs* are entitled to retain and practice their own religion without any hindrance and should they choose, at any point of time, to embrace Islam, their status of *dhimmah* is automatically terminated and they become full-fledged citizens as of that time. Notwithstanding some juristic rulings to the contrary, the position has prevailed that the status of *dhimmah* may be conferred not only on Christians and Jews, known as the *ahl al-kitāb*, but on all non-Muslims, indeed anyone who applies for it regardless of religious following.[56]

The basic requirement of acquiring the *dhimmī* status is taking domicile in the Muslim territory and payment of a poll-tax. A fuller treatment of *jizyah*-related issues in the context especially of contemporary conditions will later be attempted. Suffice it to note here that the lawful government and the *ūlū al-amr* may specify the requirements of conferring citizenship on non-Muslim applicants in the light of prevailing conditions, considerations of fairness and *maslahah*, all within the framework of a *Sharī'ah*-oriented policy (*siyāsah shar'iyyah*).[57] The Muslim state is authorised to enact appropriate rules and procedures that apply to the various modes of conferment of citizenship. It can be conferred through birth, naturalisation, marriage, domicile, grant on application, re-integration, subjugation, acquisition of territory and so forth.[58]

The *musta'minūn* are aliens who seek safe conduct to facilitate their entry and temporary stay in Muslim territories. They are admitted by permission and passport on the basis of contract, known as *'aqd al-amān*, or contract of safe conduct. The *musta'min* (lit. one who has been granted safety) thus enjoys the same rights that are recognised for the *dhimmī*, except that he or she is not required to pay the *jizyah* if the period of stay is less than one year. The contract of *amān* guarantees safe conduct to the person and property of the *musta'min* and to his family. The *musta'min* enjoys total freedom of movement within Muslim territories and that includes, according to the Hanafīs, but not the Shāfi'ī and Hanbalīs, freedom to visit and enter the mosques, and also residence in the vicinity of Ka'bah in Mecca for three days without any prior permission. The *musta'mins* are under similar obligations, as are the *dhimmīs*, to observe the laws of the land. Unlike the contract of *dhimmah*, which is permanent, *amān* is temporary and revocable by the authorities. Again, unlike *dhimmah*, which is only offered by the state authorities, *amān* can be offered and concluded both by the state authorities and any Muslim citizen, men and women alike.[59] The procedure of giving *amān* is very simple and there is no disagreement among the Muslim jurists on it. Once the intention of the person requesting *amān* is known, regardless of the language spoken, any word or sign of approval is enough to confer the status of *amān*. [60]

With the exception of the Ḥanafīs who recognise the right of giving safe conduct to aliens that may be granted by both the Muslim and non-Muslim citizens (the latter with permission of the authorities) the majority have confined this right to the Muslim citizens only.[61] This is yet another instance perhaps where the more egalitarian position of the Ḥanafī School is preferable and could be adopted by a simple permission that the head of state might extend to the non-Muslim citizens.

Basic authority for *amān* is found in the Qur'ānic verse which provides in an address to the believers: 'if one of the idolaters seeks your protection, protect him so that he hears the word of God, then convey him to his place of safety.' (9:6)

وإن أحد من المشركين استجارك فأجره حتى يسمع كلام الله ثم أبلغه مأمنه

The general (*ʿāmm*) declaration of this text is then confirmed in the above-quoted *ḥadīth* which provides:

المسلمون تتكافؤا دماؤهم وهم على يد من سواهم ويسعى بذمتهم أدناهم

The lives of Muslims are equal (in respect of retaliation and *diyyah*) and they are a unity against their opponents. When the least among them offers safe conduct to someone, it is a commitment on all of them.[62]

Muslim women are equally entitled to grant *amān*. This is confirmed in a clear *ḥadīth* where the Prophet endorsed the *aman* that was granted by Umm Hānī, the daughter of Abū Ṭālib, to one of the pagan Arabs on the day of the conquest of Mecca. Umm Hānī's brother had wanted to kill this man, at which time she went to the Prophet and informed him about it, and the Prophet addressed her

by saying 'we protect the one to whom you have offered protection
O Umm Hānī.'[63]

قد أجرنا من أجرت يا أم هانئ

The status of *amān* might be repudiated by the Imam at any time if
it is discovered that the *musta'min* has used it for harmful purposes or
when termination is deemed to be in the interest of the community.
The *amān* normally terminates when its period is expired or when the
musta'min leaves the *dār al-Islām*. If he or she wanted to return to *dār
al-Islām*, he or she would need to obtain another *amān*.[64] The *dhimmī*s
and *musta'min*s lose all claim to protection and their status is revoked
in the following two situations: 1) when they leave the Muslim state
and go over to the enemies, and 2) when they openly revolt against
the Muslim government and try to sabotage it.[65]

The majority of Muslim jurists have held that it is not permissible
to compel a *dhimmī* or a *musta'min* to profess Islam. As for the belligerent (*ḥarbī*), although the majority have held forced conversion permissible in their case, the preferred view is that of a minority group of
jurists who considered it impermissible to compel anyone into Islam.
Zuḥaylī and Khallāf who quoted both these views also considered the
latter preferable, for there is clearly a difference between the permissibility of fighting the *ḥarbī*s to repel their aggression and mischief, and
compelling or subjugating any of them to embrace Islam. This would
be unreasonable as it cannot lead to a valid outcome.[66]

The wife, under the *fiqh* rules, automatically acquires the citizenship of the country of her husband. Thus if a non–Muslim alien
woman marries a Muslim or even a non–Muslim citizen of the Muslim state, she becomes the citizen of that state. The husband on the
other hand does not acquire the status of his wife. This would mean
that when a non–Muslim alien marries a woman who is the subject
of a Muslim state, he does not automatically become the subject of
that state. But the husband may apply for naturalisation which the authorities may grant. Muslim jurists have not suggested a probationary
period but it is a discretionary matter for the government to determine whether the applicant should reside for a certain period and
have a clean record of upright conduct during that time.[67] Having
discussed the *fiqhī* position on *dhimmī*s I now propose to discuss the
impact of historical developments and the extent to which they affect
the legal status of the *dhimmī*s.

As already noted, *dhimmī* is a derivative of *dhimmah*, a contract that is concluded between two parties. It is not an enactment or *ḥukm* of *Sharīʿah* of permanent standing and has no independent existence unless it is created by the contracting parties. *Dhimmah* comes into existence when the parties to it are in existence. In historical terms the *dhimmah* came to an end, as el-Awa has rightly observed, with the onset of colonial rule in the Muslim lands because the parties to it did not exist, hence neither the *dhimmah* nor its bearer, the *dhimmī*, existed any longer. This was because the western colonial state did not apply the regime of *dhimmah* and no *dhimmīs* could therefore be said to exist as of that time. The whole concept of *dhimmah* has therefore been replaced and substituted by *muwāṭanah* (citizenship).[68] Although Muslim jurists have identified *dhimmah* as a permanent contract, yet it cannot exist unless it is concluded in the first place, and it comes to an end or dissolved under certain conditions which the jurists have specified.

Muwāṭanah, on the other hand, is not a contract, rather it is a permanent status consisting of a relationship between a person and a place that gives rise to certain rights and obligations. *Muwāṭanah* inheres in a person by the fact of birth and residence which need not be created through an agreement with another party. It comes into being, in other words, when its grounds are present, without which it would not exist. *Muwāṭanah* in the sense of a legal relationship is not a new concept as its origins can be traced back to the time of the Prophet Muhammad when it was for the first time created under the constitution of Medina. The Prophet signed this document with the residents of Medina and those who migrated from Mecca to Medina. The non-Muslim parties who ratified this document consisted of Jews and pagans, and the document that was signed as a result was a constitutional instrument that articulated the rights and responsibilities of the citizens, or the *muwāṭins*, of Medina. The constitution of Medina regulated the relations between the newly created Islamic government under the Prophet's leadership and the citizens of that state, both Muslim and non-Muslim. 'The *muwāṭanah* that was created as a result was not based in any particular religion.'[69] For this was a constitution and not a bilateral contract which articulated the structure of relations in the Medinan society under the new government.

The contract of *dhimmah* that Muslim jurists later formalized was neither uniform nor well defined. The *dhimmah* contract that was defined and articulated in *fiqh* was basically a creation of necessity of the times of conquest. Each time the Muslim rulers conquered a territory, they had to deal with two groups of people, one of whom accepted the new religion and acquired the same rights and duties as the Muslims enjoyed themselves. The second group was those who chose to retain their religion and the Muslim rulers acquired responsibility to adjudicate their disputes and protect their rights and properties. It was in response to this need that Muslim jurists constructed the contract of *dhimmah* in line, more or less, with the agreement that the Prophet had concluded with the Christians of Najrān and the people of Bahrain.[70] To these prototypes the Muslim rulers added provisions as they deemed necessary in the light of circumstances in each particular locality and case. Basically the Muslim rulers entered provisions that recognised the religious freedom of the conquered people and a certain protection of their rights. But they also imposed a poll-tax which was payable once a year at a rate similar to *zakāh*. But even these basic provisions were adjusted at times when such seemed appropriate under the circumstances.

There were *dhimmah* agreements which eliminated the *jizyah* altogether as in the agreement entered during the time of the second caliph 'Umar with the Jarajima Turkish tribe who welcomed the Muslim forces and declared their dislike of the Romans, but stipulated that they remained Christian and this was agreed. They also agreed to help the Muslims in the event of military engagement with the Romans. The Muslims agreed to protect them and also waived their *jizyah*.

A similar example of a variant *dhimmah* was the peace agreement that the Muslims signed with the people of Cyprus, who did not offer resistance and in return the Muslim party agreed not to levy the *jizyah* on them. Another example of this was the agreement that 'Amr b. al-'Āṣ, caliph 'Umar's governor signed with the Copts of Egypt when his forces besieged and eventually conquered Egypt. There was no mention of *jizyah* in the treaty that was signed.[71]

When the Muslim forces entered Jerusalem in the time of the caliph 'Umar, its Christian residents refused to surrender the key to its fortress except to the caliph himself on condition that no Jewish settlers were allowed to reside in their area. The caliph wrote them a letter and agreed to their conditions and granted them safe conduct without imposing any *jizyah*.[72]

It is to be noted that *dhimmah* provided a formula by which the Muslim conquerors established a pattern of relations with the people they ruled but there was considerable variation in the terms of the particular agreements that were concluded.[73]

Then came the era of struggle for independence from western colonialism and the many long years of confrontation that followed. The anti-colonialist campaign was conducted with the participation of all the *muwāṭin*s in the former colonies; Muslims and non-Muslims struggled side by side and all made sacrifices. When they won that campaign and gained independence for their homelands, they sought to regulate their national life through a national charter and constitution. One of the major gains of this struggle that was articulated in many of their constitutions was equality before the law for all the citizens.

The *dhimmah* as a contract and a legal instrument came to an end with the colonial domination of the Muslim lands. After the collapse of colonialism a new state was formed which was not a successor to any of the previous regimes—neither to the colonial state, nor to the Islamic state that might have existed preceding it. The *dhimmī* status also terminated as a result. The non-Muslims that live in Muslim communities today are people who have fought for their country and continue to defend it through participation in the army and security forces. There is consequently no *dhimmah* in the Muslim state of today, as it has to all intents and purposes been replaced by *muwāṭanah* (citizenship) and the entitlement as a result of all to equal rights and obligations without any discrimination.

With reference to Egypt, Ṭāriq al-Bishrī has underscored the common cause of the Egyptian nation by recounting the events of the liberation movement in the late 19th century. Slogans such as 'Egypt for the Egyptians' and 'brotherhood of compatriots' came out of the pens of al-Ṭahtāwī and others. In 1879, when the National Homeland Party (*al-ḥizb al-waṭanī al-ahlī*) was formed on the eve of the ʿUrābiyyah revolution, it was stipulated in section five of its manifesto that 'Christians and Jews and everyone who protects Egypt and speaks its language may join this party, which shall not look at their differences of creed, knowing that they are all brethren and have equal rights in politics and legislation.'[74]

This was an eminently egalitarian call, one that united all Egyptians for the defence and liberation of their homeland, charting out the formation of a national society based on the historical experience of its people. This was not a sudden development but an historical pattern which was put to the test once again by developments in post WWI years where two types of identity for Egypt was commonly debated. People talked of an Islamic community within the framework of the Ottoman Caliphate just as they talked about the Egyptian society and nation as a smaller unit in its own right. The question typically posed was whether the one took priority over the other. The answer clearly emerged in favour of the Egyptian nation and society due in large measure to the national campaign against British colonialism.[75]

Situations in Egypt and elsewhere in the Muslim world were also influenced by developments in the Ottoman Empire. Legal reforms under the Ottomans were first introduced under the Tanzīmāt which culminated in the two imperial edicts of 1839 and 1856 as discussed earlier. Promulgated under European pressure, they established equality before the law for all the Sultan's subjects. In Egypt, the *jizyah* was abolished by the Khedive Sa'īd in 1855, followed in 1856 by a large scale recruitment of Copts into military service. Fifty years later, the 'Revolution of 1919' seemed to signal the victory of equality and national unity over religious segregation and communalism.

The principle of equality was soon after enshrined in the Egyptian Constitution of 1923 which proclaimed Islam as the official religion, but which stopped short of establishing the rule of *Sharī'ah*. Nor did this constitution provide for a system of proportional representation for non-Muslim minorities. This was the opposite of the Lebanese experience where the administrative system was based on proportional representation, which had the negative effect, however, of boosting communalism (*tā'ifiyyah*) that led to a civil war in the 1950s. Although right up to the time of Egypt's formal independence in 1922, Copts continued to fulfil important functions in the administration and economy as well as in the cultural sphere, they had either been discredited because of their association with the occupying power, or else brought into controversy with the new Egyptian Islamic middle class.[76]

I conclude this discussion by quoting Muhammad al-Ṭālibī who criticized the late Iranian leader, Ayatollah Khomeini's treatise, *al-Ḥukūmah al-Islāmiyyah* (Islamic government) where the latter advocated the return of *dhimmah* and *kharāj* to be imposed on the non-Muslims. Ṭālibī posed the question: which *dhimmah* is it that one can talk about in today's conditions? What about the forty per cent of the world Muslims who live under the rule of non-Islamic governments? Should they also be given a reciprocal treatment and considered as *dhimmīs* under the non-Muslim rule? And then the question over the factual determination of this status—as to who is under whose protection—arises in countries such as Lebanon and Israel. 'It is an irony of our time that in today's world and in the context of the balance of economic and military power the Muslims are the real *dhimmīs*.'[77] To talk therefore of *dhimmah*, *jizyah* and *kharāj* is to turn away from reality. We now live in the era of human rights and it is in this context that the Muslims should see themselves in their own societies and regulate their relations with the non-Muslims on precisely the same basis.

VI. Second Class Citizens Among Arabs—the *Mawāli*

The pre-Islamic system of patronage (*walā'*) survived and presented a problem vis-à-vis the Islamic teachings on equality within the Muslim community and those who joined the new religion. *Walā'* entrenched itself as a basis of superiority of the Arabs over non-Arabs and also slaves who remained under the patronage of their former masters even after their release from slavery. Tribalism and *walā'* became obstacles to social cohesion and development of citizenship along the lines of the egalitarian teachings of Islam. As one commentator noted with reference to *walā'*, the prevalence of *walā'* among the Arab warrior tribes and then the Arab Islamic Empire increasingly rendered the concept of citizenship into a function mainly of the logic of power rather than that of religion.[78] What it meant was that religion translated itself into a basis of discrimination between Muslims and *dhimmīs*, but there was no religious basis for discriminating against the *mawāli* who were Muslims, albeit of non-Arab origin. This level of discrimination was a function of power and domination of a kind that eventually destroyed the social equilibrium of the Arab society of the dynastic period. Our reading of history also needs to be adjusted due to historical changes.

The *mawāli* included, in addition to former slaves, foreigners of non-Arab origin who embraced Islam and resided among the Arabs. They included Persians, Turks, Greek, Berbers, Slavs, Sudanese, Armenians and Transoxanians. Al-Sayed took a different view of *walā'* when he wrote 'the system of *mawāli*, or dependents, was a practical way to ameliorate the conditions of foreigners in order to integrate them in the society, and to gain their confidence and support toward the state.'[79] One may or may not agree with this view, but what seems fairly obvious is that the concept as a whole was rooted in inequality. A considerable portion of the *mawāli* were persons who were released from slavery but still remained under the patronage of their former masters. They were expected to help their former masters, and the latter were entitled to inheritance from their former slaves. Two other types of *mawāli* were known as *jār* and *ḥalīf* (neighbour, and covenanted person) respectively.

The neighbour was basically a refugee into a neighbouring tribe and referred to a person who was ousted from his own tribe for a crime or misconduct. Since it was difficult for such persons to lead a life of seclusion, they took refuge with another tribe by way of *jiwār* and became one of the *mawāli* of that tribe with certain customary rights and obligations.[80]

The *ḥalīf*, or covenantee, was a 'neighbour' who had permanently resided in his new Muslim habitat. He was treated like a 'neighbour' but could be deprived of the protected status in accordance with the terms of protection, known as *walā' al-ḥilf*.

Most of the war prisoners from Persia who embraced Islam became the *mawāli* of the Arab warlords. There were instances when some of them regained their status as equal citizens through agreement on exchange of war prisoners, or personal prominence, but most of the *mawāli* were treated like second-class citizens. The typical Arabian tribe thus consisted of three classes of persons, namely the *mawāli*, the Arabs themselves, and the slaves. Only the Arab Muslims enjoyed full civilian rights and took upon themselves the warrior duties of defence against external aggression, and 'none but an Arab was eligible for judgeship.'[81]

The second caliph ʿUmar who instituted a pension register and an army register actually departed from the more egalitarian stance of his predecessor when he entitled different classes of people to differential allowances. Muslim armies in their camps and new locations were organized along tribal lines and the *mawāli* were accorded an inferior status compared to Arab Muslims. The *mawāli* were naturally angered with their lot, and it was one of the *mawāli*, Abū Luʾluʾah, the slave of Mughīrah b. Shuʿbah, who assassinated the caliph ʿUmar. One of their grievances was that they were not given equal shares from the funds of *bayt al-māl*.[82] This situation was further exacerbated during the time of Caliph ʿUthmān when tribal and family ties verging on nepotism became a feature of his government and a further cause of instability that was partly accountable for his assassination.

The Umayyad caliphs followed the precedent and differentiated the Arabs from the *mawāli* and went to excess by imposing the poll tax on the latter even after they had professed Islam. They were also precluded from appointment to political and administrative positions in the government, which were reserved for Arab nobility, and from participation in state affairs. An Arab would not agree to his daughter's marriage to one of the *mawāli*, and although they served in the army, they were not given the same allowances, and were assigned to infantry divisions 'and other such treatments that the Arabs would not like to have for themselves.'[83]

The Umayyad caliph ʿUmar b. ʿAbd al-ʿAzīz (99–101 AH) attempted certain improvements in the conditions of the *mawāli*. Those who had embraced Islam were exempted from *jizyah* and he granted non-Arab Muslim warriors the same privileges as those enjoyed by their Arab counterparts. But that did not last for long and most of the reforms were reversed after his death.

Many historians have held the view that the Arab discrimination against the *mawāli* was a major incentive for their persistent rebellion that led to the collapse of the Umayyad state. During Muʿāwiyah's time, the *mawāli* joined the rebel faction of Mukhtār b. Abī ʿUbayd, then they joined hands with the Kharijites whose egalitarian views on many contentious issues appealed to the *mawāli*, and then they also took part in the rebellion of ʿAbd al-Raḥmān b. al-Ashʿath.[84]

Following the collapse of the Umayyads and the establishment of the Abbassid rule, there was an almost total reversal of the previous status quo. The Abbassid rulers relied on the *mawāli* and entrusted them with high positions in government and many other privileges in preference even to the native Arabs. The Abbasid movement is often characterized as 'a movement of *mawālis* to exact revenge on Arabs and demolish their state.' The violent anti-Arab Shuʿūbiyah (lit. popular, or people's) movement that spread widely among the *mawāli*, especially the Persians, with the aim of combating Arab superiority, seems to have largely succeeded in its objectives. The *mawāli* became powerful both under the Abbasids as well as in the Fatimid state of Egypt. As in the Abbasid state, the *mawāli* under the Fatimids were of different races, but 'the bulk of them were black Sudanese' and they played a major role in state policy and administration.[85]

The *mawāli* success was partly due to their superiority in literary pursuits. During the Umayyad rule when the *mawāli* were excluded from leading government positions, they occupied themselves with acquisition of knowledge in various fields including literature, history and Islamic sciences. Most of the Abbassid rulers took wives from among the *mawāli*—some were the released slaves of their predecessors. Apart from what was said of the beauty of non-Arab women, it was easier for the rulers to know these women through personal contact—unlike the Arab women who were customarily not allowed to interact with men. Thus it is known that the caliph Ma'mūn's (d. 198/813) mother was a Persian, that of Muʿtaṣim (d. 218/833) a Turk, and the mother of al-Mutawakkil (232/847) was a Roman. Al-Muqtadir's (295/908) mother was also a Roman. A similar account is given of the Fatimid rulers and those of the Mamluks in Egypt—one of the Mamluk Sultans, Najm al-Dīn Ayyūb (684/1250) married a former slave and most of his army consisted of slaves of non-Arab origin.[86]

VII. *Dār al-Islām* and *Dār al-Ḥarb* Revisited

The advent of the nation state has had the effect of making citizenship a more definitive concept compared to what it was conceived of in earlier times. Citizenship today is essentially a politico-legal relationship between the individual and the state without any obvious grounding in religion. But in the works of early Muslim jurists, this relationship has been inextricably tied up to the dichotomous division of the world into *dār al-Islām* and *dār al-ḥarb*. This division takes for granted the existence of a permanent state of war between its two component parts, itself a questionable premise to say the least. To determine the citizenship status of the individual in this context, reference was made not only to the religious following of the individual but also to the religious following of the ruler or the government of the territory in which the individual resided. Another consideration was whether Islamic law was the applied law of the land in which the individual resided. There was in principle no issue over determining the citizenship status of an individual when both of these criteria, namely professing Islam, and domicile in *dār al-Islām*, were met. A Muslim who took domicile in a territory that was ruled by a Muslim state was, in other words, a full-fledged citizen of that state. Questions did arise, however, about the citizenship status of those individuals who met only one of those two criteria. To pose the same question in a contemporary context, suppose that a Muslim minority group resides in a non-Muslim country where the *Sharīʿah* is not applied, yet the Muslims residing there are not prevented from practicing their religion. In response to this question, a Ḥanafī jurist might be inclined to identify the non-Muslim territory as *dār al-ḥarb*, simply because for the Hanafis the most important indicator of determining a territory as a part of *dār al-Islām* is the sovereignty of *Sharīʿah* as the law of the land, and not necessarily the religious following of the individual inhabitants thereof. But suppose that the Muslim minority in this example is permitted to apply the *Sharīʿah* and have Muslim judges who adjudicate their disputes in accordance with Islamic law, the question would obviously become complex. Examples of this kind could be found in India under the British rule, and in earlier times in a part of al-Andalus, namely in Aragon. Those territories were ruled by Christian rulers, but they allowed the Muslims to apply their own laws. Is it right then to designate such a territory as a part of *dār al-Islām*, or that of *dār al-ḥarb*? The Ḥanafī jurists would find it difficult to label this as *dār al-ḥarb*, whereas their Shāfiʿī and Ḥanbalī counterparts would most likely classify it as *dār al-Islām*. This is because the Shāfiʿīs and Ḥanbalīs view *dār al-Islām* as any place where a Muslim can perform the obligatory duties of Islam, especially pertaining to devotion and worship, without any fear.

Dār al-Islām thus includes, according to the Ḥanafīs, all territories that are under the sovereignty of Muslim government and ruled by the *Sharīʿah* even if some or most of their inhabitants are not Muslim. The majority would on the other hand qualify as *dār al-Islām* all the territories that are inhabited either wholly or mostly by Muslims who are in the meantime free to practice their faith.

In their description of *dār al-Islām* many commentators have referred to the following two Qurʾānic passages which refer to the community of believers:

(1) (They are) Those who, if we establish them in the land, offer regular prayer and give regular charity, enjoin right and forbid wrong. (22:41)

الذين إن مكّناهم فى الأرض أقاموا الصلوة وآتوا الزكوة

وأمروا بالمعروف ونهوا عن المنكر

This verse was revealed concerning the early migrants from Mecca to Medina who were consequently authorized to establish a government of their own. It is implied in this verse that those who establish the regular prayers and charity, promote good and prevent evil—they are the ones who are entitled to govern.[87]

(2) The second verse quoted in this connection provides:

وعد الله الذين آمنوا منكم وعملوا الصالحات ليستخلفنهم
في الأرض كما استخلف الذين من قبلهم

God has promised those of you who profess the faith and do
good work that He will surely make them succeed (the present
rulers) on earth even as He caused those who were before them
to succeed (others) (24:55).

Neither of the two verses are explicit on *dar al-Islām* or *dar al-
ḥarb*, yet it has been said that doing good work while having faith
in God is the key description of those who are entitled to rule the
House of Islam. Al-Qurṭubī noted that God has granted the privilege
of succession to the rule to Muslims who work sincerely and have
faith in God.[88] *Dār al-Islām* is thus focused on the maintenance of
the ritual duties of Islam including the obligatory prayers, collection
and distribution of *zakāh* charity to the poor, promotion of good and
prevention of evil, and establishment of a peaceful and orderly life for
the people.

Dār al-ḥarb includes all territories which are not governed by the
laws of Islam nor is there freedom for Muslims to practice their
religion. Those territories may be under the sovereignty of one or
more states. The native inhabitants of such territories may be Muslim
or non-Muslim but the territory remains *dar al-ḥarb* if the Muslims
are not free to publicly practice their religion. The inhabitants of *dar
al-ḥarb* may thus be either belligerents (*ḥarbī*) or Muslim, neither of
whom is protected under Islamic law and the fact of being a Muslim is
not enough to give them such protection. Such people are viewed as
enemies and their lives and properties are not protected. This would
mean that a Muslim who permanently resides in *dar al-ḥarb* and does
not migrate to *dar al-Islām* is not a protected person according to the
Ḥanafī school, whereas according to the other three Imams, Mālik,
Shāfiʿī, and Aḥmad b. Ḥanbal, he is protected by the fact of being
a Muslim, even if he resides in *dar al-ḥarb*. If such a person wishes
to enter and travel in *dar al-Islām*, he will not be obstructed. Just as
the belligerent (*ḥarbī*) has no protection in *dar al-Islām*, the Muslims
and *dhimmī* resident of the *dar al-Islām* are likewise unprotected in *dar
al-ḥarb* without obtaining permission or grant of safe conduct; when
they obtain safe conduct, they too become *musta'min* in *dar al-ḥarb*.[89]

Does the dichotomy in question originate in the Qur'ān? Or is
it based on juristic opinion? In a reference to migration of the early

Muslims to Medina, the Qur'ān refers to Medina by the word '*al-dār*' (the abode) which might suggest that the expression '*dār al-Islām*' may have been taken from there. But the reference here occurs in the sense of having a home and clearly refers to the *Anṣār* (Helpers) who lived in and had Medina as their home. The text thus provides:

والذين تبوّءو الدار والإيمان من قبلهم يحبون من هاجر
إليهم ولا يجدون فى صدورهم حاجة مما أوتوا

> And those who had home (*al-dār*—in Medina) before, and embraced the faith, show affection to such as came to them for refuge, and find in their hearts no need of what they are given... (59:9)

'*Al-dār*' is used here literally as it refers to the home of the *Anṣār*, that is, people who lived in Medina before the arrival of the Immigrants. They had their homes in Medina before the event of the migration at a time when Medina could hardly be described as *dār al-Islām*. Neither the Prophet, nor the Companions are known to have used that phrase '*dār al-Islām*', even after the revelation of this verse, which leaves little doubt that the term has been coined and given currency by the jurists of later centuries.

The division in question also contemplated the *dār al-Islām* as a major player on the world scene, one that only saw itself as the more dominant of the duo. This is precisely where its relevance to the power balance of the colonial and post-colonial world has become increasingly questionable.[90] The three distinctive features of *dār al-ḥarb* are thus described as follows: 1) it is governed by a law other than the *Sharī'ah*; 2) it is adjacent to *dār al-Islām*; and 3) the Muslim does not feel secure for his life, honour, property and religion. The last two of these three conditions are now very much in doubt as most Muslims may be said to be living in the abode of treaty (*dār al-'ahd*) where international relations are regulated by treaties. 'The dichotomy under discussion,' according to al-Ḥuṣarī, 'does not affect the normative validity of peace as the basic foundation of international relations (under the *Sharī'ah*).'[91] If security of life and property were to be the test of a place becoming *dār al-Islām*, a totally different conclusion can be drawn in light of the fact that Muslims are sometimes safer in the West—regarding the free practice of their religion—than they are in some Islamic countries. Imagine the sectarian violence between the Sunni and Shi'ite communities in Karachi or Iraq under the

American military occupation and compare that with the safety and freedom that the Muslims enjoy in the West.[92]

Since the Muslim jurists 'could not agree on a definition of *dar al-Islam*,'[93] the juristic notion of *dar al-Islam* and *dar al-harb* cannot provide an adequate basis on which to determine the question of citizenship. It is also difficult to agree with al-Nabhānī's categorical statement that 'it is the domicile of a person in *dar al-Islam* or *dar al-kufr* which determines his citizenship (*al-tabiʿiyyah*). The citizenship of a person is, in other words, anchored in the place which he has chosen to reside.'[94] Domicile is undoubtedly the principal, even determinative, factor in citizenship, and one would not wish to dispute this part of al-Nabhānī's statement. What is disputable is the second limb of his observation to the effect that when a person, Muslim or non-Muslim, resides in *dar al-Islam* he is a citizen of *dar al-Islam* and when he resides in *dar al-kufr*, he is a citizen of *dar al-kufr*. The ambiguity thus sets in when citizenship is linked to a concept that is inherently unstable and does not admit a clear definition.

In the Indian sub-continent, Chiragh Ali, a contemporary of Sir Sayyid Ahmad Khan (d. 1898) addressed the question whether India was, at the dawn of the twentieth century, a *dar al-harb* or *dar al-Islam*, and the response he gave was premised on the concept of safety (*al-amn*).

According to Chiragh Ali, it was useless to discuss the question because British India was not ruled by an Islamic ruler and there were no Islamic courts. Chiragh Ali added that Islamic jurisprudence was formulated for the Muslims and it was based on the idea that the Muslims are the rulers, not the ruled. Therefore, India was neither *dar al-Islam* nor *dar al-harb*. India was not ruled by a Muslim ruler; it was British in the sense that the Muslims of India were 'the subjects of the British government which protects them. Therefore an intelligent *mujtahid* can say that British India is a *dar al-amān* (abode of peace) or *dar al-dhimmah* (abode of protection).'[95]

There is no objection to using '*dar al-Islam*' for what it literally means as a place of unity and solidarity of Muslims. This is how the Islamic Council of Europe has referred to it in the Universal Islamic Declaration of Human Rights, which reads in Article (23) that '*Dar al-Islam* is united; it is the homeland of every Muslim ...'. Since this declaration only dates back to 1981, when there was no 'United *Dar al-Islam*,' but over forty independent Muslim states, '*dar al-Islam*' had no juristic reality and it was only employed to convey the unity of Muslims in faith, and may therefore be indicative only of a statement of principle or of a hope, one might say, for their greater unity in the future.

The second half of the twentieth century witnessed unprecedented movement of migrant workers into Europe. The reconstruction of Europe after long years of war required cheap labour force, which, in turn, brought the first wave of Muslim migrant workers especially to Britain and France, and then to Germany and other European countries. In less than fifteen years (between 1945 and 1960) Muslim Asians, North Africans and Turks had emerged in large numbers and established immigrant communities in Britain, France and Germany respectively. Between 1950 and 1970, the number of Muslim residents in European countries trebled. This so-called economic migration was not to stop until the beginning of the 1970s when the need for additional workers dwindled to almost nothing and the European economy showed its first signs of weakness. But by then hundreds of thousands of Muslims had been living in Europe. Families were established, children were born and for many the intention of going back home had already been giving place to permanent residence.[96]

During the 1970s and 1980s increasing numbers of Muslims considered the west as their home and began to organise themselves toward that end. In order to protect their identity, some Muslims began to organise their communities through the creation of community centres, associations, private tutoring in their languages and religion. Mosques were built and Islamic organisations were created where community members gathered for worship, socialising, and communal activities.

In the 1990s there were between twelve to fifteen million Muslims in Western Europe alone and they were 'very much a part of society'—many have taken a European nationality, and have become more and more visible in the public sphere due to their diverse organisations and activities. Added to this is the fact that there are numerous converts to Islam who have, together with the young generations of Muslims, formed a unique identity of European Muslims.

Muslims in Europe are generally 'allowed to practice their religion in peace, to build mosques... and found Islamic organisations... European constitutions, and laws respect Islam as a Religion.'[97]

'Alwānī has noted that the *dār al-Islām–dār al-ḥarb* dichotomy is controversial and anachronistic, and suggested that it should be abandoned and replaced by the more appropriate terms, *dār al-daʿwah* and *dār al-ijābah*:

> We must identify with Fakhr al-Dīn al-Rāzī, who divided the world into two realms: *dār al-ijābah* (the land of acceptance, where people accepted Islam and Islamic values are practiced) and *dār al-daʿwah* (the land of invitation, to which *daʿwah* is presented and its people are invited to Islamic values and practices). This view of the world removes the potential for conflict…[98]

Qaraḍāwī has similarly noted that the conventional division of the world into *dār al-Islām* and *dār al-ḥarb* is no longer in harmony with the realities of contemporary times and no longer serves the best interests of Muslims. To say that war is the norm that determines the basic pattern of Muslim non-Muslim relations is, in any case, indefensible and no clear evidence is found in its support in the sources. On the contrary, the Qur'ān encourages amicable relations in a number of places, including the declaration 'We have made you into tribes and nations so that you may know one another' (49:13). Countries that accept religious pluralism also enable Muslims to engage themselves in *daʿwah* activities through the mass media and other methods of propagation. Peace and amicable relations must therefore be the norm and objective of Muslim non-Muslim relations.[99]

Thus it would be sensible to say that the earlier dichotomy should be set aside and the nation state should instead be taken as the basic framework together with domicile as the basic determinant of citizenship. This may, however, be seen as a temporary phase and a response that is dictated by the attending realities of the world today. Muslim countries and nations should in the meantime engage themselves in promoting the awareness of their common values and heritage as members of the wider *ummah*, and work toward the idea of building a commonwealth of nations on that basis.

Various levels of cooperation may be considered and developed, which may eventually provide a new framework for a formal definition of citizenship. The renewed emphasis on closer ties will hopefully be inspired not by a divisive and conflicting bifurcation of interests that characterised the hallowed notions of *dār al-Islām* and *dār al-ḥarb* but by the higher objectives of beneficial exchange that contemplates the common destiny of man and nurtures genuine awareness of the need for wider cooperation among nations. Yet the nation state itself seems to be changing and can only provide a temporary framework. Economic realities of the contemporary world have already made the nation state in many ways marginalised and point to the desirability of wider geographical alignments of nation states.[100]

The nation state idea has in any case its roots in the European political thought of the pre- and post-industrial revolution which did not prove to be good for the former colonies and emerging developing nations as it might have for the colonial powers themselves. Rapid advances in communication, science and technology and globalisation of the market place might be leading the world of the 21st century to a new phase of history where fresh levels of cooperation and alliances among them mark a departure from the nation state phenomenon to new forms of political organisation. Indications are that the Muslim *ummah*, which happens to combine most of the underdeveloped countries of the world, have little choice but to move closer to the idea of a larger, more effective and economically viable forms of organisation among themselves. This might also encourage, very gradually perhaps, a revision of the formal framework for citizenship and wider prospects for defining the political relationship of the individual with the ruling authorities and perhaps also a wider framework for his civic and humanitarian rights and obligations.

VIII. *Ummah*, Nation-State and Citizenship: A Round-up of Modern Opinion

Prior to 1258 (collapse of Baghdad at the hands of Mongols), Muslim societies had been built around a central ideological framework, where the concept of *ummah*, the community of believers, held a prime position. The common belief in one God and shared religious practices such as prayer, fasting and pilgrimage signified the core of that unity. Within this unity there was considerable divergence of custom and culture as well as scriptural and scholastic interpretation. Additionally, there was the development of a cosmopolitan society in the centre of the Caliphate. Yet the era of dynastic rule and the imperial system of medieval times were showing signs of inner weakness, which had yet to find outward expression. At the dawn of 18th century the Ottoman Empire still controlled much of the Balkan Peninsula, most of the Mediterranean coast of Africa, and virtually all of the Arab lands. The Mughal Empire continued to be the largest political unity in South Asia and the Safavid empire ruled Persia. There were also long established Muslim Khanates in Central Asia which stretched from Eastern Europe to China. In Southeast Asia and West Africa new Caliphates and Sultanates were emerging due to the influence of Muslim teachers and merchants and inner changes in the tribal structure of local societies.

By the end of the 18th century, the European Renaissance and technological advance marked the onset of colonialism and the eventual domination of almost the whole of the Muslim *ummah* which culminated in the formal abolition of the Ottoman caliphate in 1924. Following their military subjugation, Muslim societies were transformed through replacement of their basic institutions, educational system, law and even language of learning. One major political transformation that colonialism brought along with it was the emergence of the nation state which then itself became the rallying point of the independence movement of 20th century.[101]

The word 'nation' lay at the foundation of the historical era that came to be called the age of nationalism and nation state. Its allied concept 'nationality' is the politically concretised expression of a juridical status that distinguishes the 'national' from the foreign. The Arabic word *al-jinsiyyah* is a close, though not exact, translation of this status.

Expressions such as '*ummah*' and '*qawm*' which are sometimes used as equivalent to 'nation' occur in the Qur'ān, both simply referring to a group of people. Other equivalent expressions are also found in the Qur'ān for tribe, sub-tribe and clan, but there is no precise expression in the Qur'ān for nation, nationality or nation state.[102]

The nation-state is both the creation and creator of modern Europe. The Catholic Reconquista of Muslim Andalusia favoured the development of the Hispanic nation state and the state that emerged was linked simultaneously with the territory, history, political, religious, and cultural characteristics of the nation. The nation state is a multi-dimensional reality that is composed of diverse elements ensembled together in one unit. The emergence of nation states in Europe and America signified a sense of regeneration of the self that was a necessary development of a certain pattern of triumphalist history. The relative absence of this element of self-definition and renewal in the former colonies explained the fragility of these nation-states. Due partly to colonialists who drew the borders of the post-colonial states in violation of local identities, developing countries are sometimes described as 'forms of government' rather than nation-states. The national identity of the modern state is grounded not only in language and religion but in national sovereignty which acts as a connective force to bind the disparate parts of a state and weld them together—if necessary by force. Consolidation of sovereignty in turn requires significant economic and military power that enhances the capabilities of the state, which plays in turn an important role in the lives of its citizens and also encourage a sense of loyalty and belonging among them.[103]

The emergence of nation states and nationalism as the driving force of the post-colonial liberation movements also served to show how Islamic doctrines can be used for or against nationalism. Commentators have spoken against nationalism and its divisive impact on the unity of the *ummah*, just as there were those who considered nationalism a worthy cause and appealed to the masses to support it. Some even made it a part of their religious struggle in the name of *jihād*. The opponents of nationalism held that the nation state did not merit loyalty nor had the authority to confer or deny citizenship to a Muslim. The whole *ummah* was deemed as one monolithic citizenry and the idea of divided loyalties within *ummah* in the name of citizenship meant loyalty to one unit at the expense of alienation from the rest.

Mawdūdī compared nationalism (*qawmiyyah*) to tribal fanaticism (*ʿaṣabiyyah*) of earlier times that was clearly condemned in the *Sunnah* and was therefore to be shunned and abandoned. Mawdūdī considered the nationalist movements as 'a great calamity that had befallen the humanity, dividing them into hundreds and thousands of disparate sections.'[104] The nationalist movements appeal to unity on the basis of blood tie or place of birth and rely on such other factors as language, race, economic and political factors. The end result of this nationalism is disunity and divisiveness.

Qaraḍāwī believed that nationalism among the Muslim masses was an epiphenomenon of colonialism and its concomitant secularism (*ʿalmāniyyah*) which was characteristic of western approach to law and government. Yet Qaraḍāwī also observed that nationalism combined the love of homelands, which is not only considered a natural human characteristic but also praiseworthy in Islam. The Islamic approach to unity is not focused on race, language and geography but on unity in faith. If nationalism discourages wider unity among Muslims and advocates parochialist and divisive tendencies, then it would obviously go against the Qur'ānic dictum of fraternity among the believers.[105]

Muḥammad al-Ghazālī considered the heydays of nationalism of the early twentieth century as blind ignorance and contrary to the unitarian impulse of Islam. Muḥammad al-Ghazālī denounced the ardent protagonists of nationalism in Turkey, Iran, Egypt, Iraq etc., who only spoke for their own nations and states whereas Islam could not benefit from such tendencies. Prior to the colonial onslaught the

Arabs used to live a life of dignity under the banner of Islam but became enmeshed in controversy when they attached themselves to fanatic Arabism. Then the Arabs sided with the British in order to fight the Turks. This was contrary to the notion of fraternity among Muslims, and had adverse consequences for the Muslim community. The nation state idea was therefore repugnant to Islamic teachings.[106]

Ghazālī also noted that Islam's principles of morality and justice were addressed not just to the Arabs but to all believers, and even though Islam originated in the Arabian society, its teachings were not confined to that framework. He then added that nationalism was not necessarily objectionable in a system of government which conformed to the basic principles of Islam.[107]

This view also found support in the writings of Ḥasan Duh and Ḥasan ʿAshmāwī, Khālid Muḥammad Khālid, Shaykh ʿAbd al-Muttaʿāl al-Saʿīdī and others who thought that nationalism manifested a natural tendency of love among people of their home, language, and heritage and was not therefore another form of blind fanaticism. According to Ḥasan Duh, 'Arab nationalism is not necessarily a manifestation of racial fanaticism, but expressive instead of the real and natural belonging of a people to a territory and language.' In this sense the religion of Islam incorporated the values of Arab history and heritage, and Arab nationalism rose to defend these same values against the onslaught of colonialism.[108]

Khālid Muḥammad Khālid's renowned work *Min Hunā Nabda'* (From Here We Begin) spearheaded the attack on theocracy and advocated the nationalist system of rule. Muḥammad al-Ghazālī's book *Min Hunā Naʿlam* (From Here We Learn) was in fact written in response to Khālid's ultra-nationalist bias and in defence of the universality of Islamic teachings. This was also followed by a rejoinder entitled *Min Ayn Nabda'?* (Where Do We Begin?) by Shaykh ʿAbd al-Muttaʿāl al-Saʿīdī who refuted both of these claims and stated instead that 'every Muslim has a dual citizenship, one of which is a general one, shared with the wider community of all Muslims, and the other a specific citizenship which may be shared with both Muslims and non-Muslims.'[109] Every Muslim has similarly two homelands (*waṭanān*), one of which he shares with all the Muslims of the world. In reference to this wider entity, the whole of the Muslim world is a single homeland—even though it combines smaller units within itself. The other homeland is the one that he shares with his non-Muslim compatriots. Membership of each of these two circles of citizenship confers upon a Muslim certain rights and obligations which are neither contradictory nor competing. For a Muslim shares his homeland with his non-Muslim compatriot just as he does so with other Muslims. Saʿīdī thus observed that an Egyptian Muslim takes pride in his Egyptian heritage as well as his Islamic heritage. The Prophet himself is in this connection quoted to have said: 'I am the most articulate of the Arabs and I am from the Quraysh.' Saʿīdī is critical of both Khālid and Ghazālī for confounding the Islamic caliphate with Islamic government, as if the latter could not exist without the former. It is not correct to confine the Islamic system of rule to only the historical caliphate. The electoral system of government is also a modern equivalent of the caliphate.[110]

The former President of Egypt, Jamal ʿAbd al-Nasser, and also ʿAbd al-Raḥman al-Bazzāz, the former Prime Minister of Iraq, saw Islam as an expression of Arabism. Nasser visualized three circles in which Egypt must operate, namely Egypt, the Arab world, and the Muslim world. Nasser was not relegating 'Islam to a third place, rather he placed Islam in a universal perspective.'[111]

Sāṭiʿ al-Ḥuṣrī observed that the Islamic affinity among the Egyptian Muslims was more prominent than their shared history in the Pharaonic or other parts of Egyptian heritage. Yet it is not right for Egypt to make Islam the sole criterion of its domestic and foreign policy. For Islam is not the religion of all Egyptians. There is therefore a need for a new framework and relationship that can unite all Egyptians, Muslims and Christians alike, and that is their relationship to one another as compatriots, one which should precede, in this regard and in respect of civilian affairs, their religious affinity.[112] Yūsuf Khalīl drew attention to the changes that have brought about a situation whereby it is now hard to find any one nation that follows a single religion. A religious system of government and citizenship that is premised on that basis is thus bound to lead to the domination of one religious group over the others.[113]

Islam is an important component of Arab nationalism in that none of the advocates of nationalism have actually sought to isolate Islam but tried to find a formula that would integrate Islam into the fabric of nationalism. The formula that is often proposed for citizenship is thus *muwaṭanah* which is premised on respect for the religious identity of all of its participants. The fact that the Qur'ān is in the Arabic language and has played a significant role in the preservation and advancement of Arab heritage also makes Islam a component part of the Arab heritage, not just for Muslim Arabs but Christian Arabs as well. In Abd al-Malik al-Sayed's phrase 'Arab nationalism operates within the Islamic religious and cultural organism.' Many have acknowledged that 'the Arab society lacked cultural vitality until Islam provided it . . . Islam is the embodiment of the spirit of the Arab nation.'[114]

Islam has also been a force behind the advancement of Arab culture in that a great deal of Arab intellectual heritage comes from religious personalities and movements such as that of the Wahhābiyyah in the Arabian peninsula, Sanūssiyyah of north Africa, Mahdiyyah of Sudan and many others. Islam is the main frame of reference whether one speaks of the Arabian philosopher al-Kindi, or of Farabi of Turkish origin, or of Ibn Sina of Persian origin. Islam and Arabism combine themselves as the two most important components of the Arabian psyche. Thus it is not surprising when Qustantin Zarīq, himself a Christian, wrote in his book *al-Waʿy al-Qawmī* (*National Awareness*, 1938) that 'it is therefore a duty of every Arab, regardless of which religion he professes, to study Islam and the Prophet Muhammad as the principal bases of Arab unity . . . true nationalism can under no circumstances be said to conflict with true religion. Arab nationalism is therefore not in conflict with any of the religions of the Arabs.'[115]

Islam is also not against the basic idea of a nation state. For after all the Prophet Muhammad established the first Arabian state in Medina which then became a vehicle and carrier of the teachings of Islam—unlike Christianity which sought to isolate itself from the state. Ever since its early beginnings, Islam and state have operated together. Provided that the nation state upholds the basic Islamic principles of good government, equality and justice, there should be no necessary conflict. Islam and the nation state can thus be expected to be supportive of one another, not the opposite.

Developments in Turkey have traversed a different course in that the Turkish nation state is more western than Islamic in orientation. In March 1924, Turkey abolished the caliphate and all members of the Ottoman dynasty were banished from the country. The Constitution of April 1924 stated that sovereignty belonged to the nation. The same constitution originally stated that the religion of the nation was Islam, but this clause was struck out in 1928. The progressive secularisation of its institutions also implied a profound change in both the social identity and political legitimacy of the nation state in Turkey. As a result of the Kemalist revolution, the Turkish state is generally said to have been transformed from an Islamic state to a nation state, and its legitimising ideology from Islam to Turkish nationalism.[116]

Patriotism in the sense of emotional attachment to one's country is natural. However, when patriotism feeds on hatred and mistrust of outsiders and becomes xenophobic and intolerant it ceases to be rational. Islam is not against patriotism provided it is not in conflict with the cherished principles of the equality and brotherhood of mankind, justice and compassion. Aggressive and chauvenistic nationalism tends to conflict with Islamic values. This is the ethnic nationalism that is analogous to ʿaṣabiyyah which the Prophet saw among the tribes of Arabia and resolutely denounced.

Arab nationalism is a composite which has exhibited facets of approved patriotism and disapproved ʿaṣabiyyah, but seems to have moderated its unacceptable manifestations in recent times. Arab nationalism that was advocated by Jamal Abd al-Nasser in Egypt, the Baʿth party in Iraq, and Colonel Qadhdhafi in Libya suffered a setback when Syria, Libya and Algeria sided with Iran in the Iran-Iraq war in 1980-1988. Iraq's invasion of Kuwait and Saudi Arabia's military alliance with the United States exposed the fragile edifice of Arab nationalism further. Arabs are said to be 'no longer a cohesive ethnic group.' There are significant political, economic and sectarian divisions among them which prevent them from emerging as an 'effective political block or even as an international pressure group.'[117]

The events of the 20th century and radicalisation of Islam seem to have exposed some of the weaknesses of nationalism and nation state. This is because Islamic resurgence is linked with the failure of the nationalist promises of progress and westernisation and it is seen to be in many ways representing a post-nationalist ideology.

Toward the end of 20th century, it is noted that radical Islamic tendencies made their presence felt even in Turkey. Far from being eradicated by modernisation and nationalism 'Islamism has thrived in the current period of Turkey's deepened integration with global capitalism.' The erosion of confidence in the nation state has also caused its supporting ideology, Kemalism, to be perceived primarily in terms of its oppressive aspects.[118] The Islamic radicals have gone so far as to say: just as the Ottoman empire disintegrated due to nationalism, so the current situation may lead to the disintegration of the Turkish Republic.[119]

The Refah party consequently put forward a proposal for a political system with 'multiple legal orders' advocating freedom of the individuals to live by that legal order which corresponds with their beliefs. Refah considered this an appropriate constitutional amendment to the principle of secularism. The proposal derived from the argument that in Islam the community takes priority over the state. Hence 'democracy', the rule of the majority over the minority should be replaced with 'pluralism' whereby each community is governed by its own belief system. In a given society, several different legal systems may thus coexist. The role of the state would be to guarantee the autonomy of each community, and the laws and conventions of each community would be binding on all of its members.[120]

In conclusion, it may be said that Muslims today tend to have three bases of identity, and they do not live in a dichotomous world of *dār al-Islām* and *dār al-ḥarb*, but in the world of the *ummah*, the nation state, and their natural homeland respectively. The first is basically founded in the idea of unity in religion, whereas the second is a political framework, and the third is rooted in custom. Muslims today find themselves in these three circles of which the *ummah* is the outer circle, whereas the natural birthplace, whether a village or town is the inner circle. In between lies the nation state. These three circles represent three levels of loyalty which need not be seen to be necessarily divisive and conflicting, for they have the potential no less to be complementary and integral. People can naturally belong to a plurality of circles and have multiple layers of loyalty. The village and family home often remains as much of a reality today as it might have been in the past.

The nation state is the political home and the wider framework where individuals realise their aims and objectives in life and utilise opportunities that can exist at this level, not only for personal growth but also for greater and more effective cooperation with other communities and states. If the Muslim countries of today decide to take up a plan to have greater levels of interaction and cooperation, the nation state can well provide a valuable instrument and vehicle for it. This remains to be largely a prospect, at present, but there is greater awareness of the need for wider cooperation in economic, political and other spheres that can substantiate the essence of ideological unity within the *ummah*.[121]

IX. Unity and Equality: A Re-Examination of the *Fiqh* Rules

There is conclusive evidence in the Qur'ān on the unity of the *ummah* as an ideological entity beyond and above divisions on the bases of class, race and language. The Qur'ān thus declares:

Verily this nation of yours constitutes one nation and I am your Lord, therefore worship Me (alone). (21:92)

إن هذه أمتكم أمة واحدة وأنا ربكم فاعبدون

Verily this nation of yours constitutes one nation, and I am your Lord, be mindful of Me. (23:52)

وإن هذه أمتكم أمة واحدة وأنا ربكم فاتقون

There is little doubt that the basic criterion of membership of the *ummah* is unity in faith, yet there is evidence to suggest that *ummah* also implies political unity and, as such, includes in its ranks, non-Muslims, who declare allegiance to the Islamic government. This is borne out by the fact that the *ummah* came into being after the Prophet's migration to Medina when the nascent community of believers, who were a religious *ummah* in Mecca, formed a government under the leadership of the Prophet in Medina. The *ummah* that was formed in Medina was both religious and political as it was open to including non-Muslims within its fold. The constitution of Medina thus provided 'The Jews of Banī 'Awf constitute a community (*ummah*) with the believers' (Art. 26). The succeeding eight articles of this constitution gave other Jewish tribes the same status as that of Banī 'Awf. This obviously meant that the Jews constituted a part of the one and the same community and were integrated into the political fabric of the *ummah*. As for their choice of religion, the same document provided in another clause: 'For the Jews is their religion and for the believers their religion.'[122]

Despite its relative openness to diversity, the *ummah* remains basically unitarian in character. Commenting on the two verses quoted above, al-Kurdi noted that the phrase 'one *ummah*—*ummatan wāḥidatan*' has been repeated in the Qur'ān to signify a basic attribute of the *ummah*.[123] A question has nevertheless arisen whether this only refers to unity in religion, or does it also imply political unity. Said Ramadan noted that the *ummah*'s concept of community is such that no prejudice and no considerations other than 'common ideals and moral values are allowed to distinguish man from man or group from group.' *Ummah* as a concept is not amenable to the creation of barriers and borders between human beings nor does it imply the narrow conception of nationalism that may be based on some alleged supremacy of linguistic or ethnological kind.[124]

Equality is the basic norm of *Sharīʿah* that must apply to all citizens, Muslims and non-Muslims alike. The caliph ʿAlī clearly confirmed this in his renowned statement concerning the non-Muslim citizens that 'they have the same rights and the same obligations as we have.'[125] This statement of principle finds support in the Qur'ānic proclamation, 'We have bestowed dignity on the progeny of Adam' (17:70)

ولقد كرّمنا بنى آدم

And the *ḥadīth* of the Prophet which declared that 'people are as equal as the teeth of a comb.'[126]

الناس سواسية كأسنان المشط

The Prophet-cum-head-of-state declared his commitment clearly to the fair treatment of *dhimmīs* when he said 'whoever annoys a *dhimmī*, I shall be his opponent in this world and his opponent on the Day of Resurrection.'[127]

من أذى ذمّيا فأنا خصمه ومن كنت خصمه خصمته يوم القيامة

The Qur'ānic provisions of equality also consist of general (ʿāmm) proclamations for the most part and make no exception for any class or group of individuals. The *Sunnah* has more specifically confirmed the general character of these proclamations with reference to the *dhimmīs* and *muwāṭinūn*. Similarly, the Qur'ānic injunctions on justice are all conveyed in the spirit of objectivity to benefit the whole of mankind regardless of the particularities of race and creed. ʿAbd al-Qādir ʿAwdah was by no means an exception when he wrote that the *nuṣūṣ* (textual rulings) of the Qur'ān and *Sunnah* are premised on equality in its absolute and unqualified sense which encompass the whole of mankind without 'any exception or recognition of superiority in favour of any individual, group, nationality and race.'[128] When one reads in the Qur'ān, for instance, that 'God commands justice and fair dealing' إنّ الله يأمر بالعدل والإحسان or the injunction 'when you judge among people, you judge with justice' (4:58)

وإذا حكمتم بين الناس أن تحكموا بالعدل

or the Prophetic *ḥadīth* that 'both of the litigating parties must present themselves before the judge' and be granted equal opportunity to present their case; or the *ḥadīth* that 'the Imam is like a shepherd and he is responsible for his subjects,'

فالأمير الذى على الناس راع وهو مسؤول عن رعيته

all of these are general principles and comprise Muslim and non-Muslim citizens alike. Commenting on the universality of Qur'ānic justice, al-Nabhānī wrote 'It is not permissible for the government to discriminate between the various strata of its citizens in the adjudication and management of their affairs. It is on the contrary imperative to treat them all equally regardless of their race, colour and religion.'[129]

The detailed evidence of the Qur'ān and *Sunnah* on equality has been examined in a separate volume of this series.[130] The main reason they are referred to here is to call attention to a certain tendency both in the scholastic works of the *madhāhib*, and works even of more recent origin, which stand in contrast to the normative teachings of the Qur'ān and *Sunnah* on the status of non-Muslim citizens. Some writers have thus been persuaded to take discriminatory positions that do not correspond with the preponderance of evidence in the sources. Historical aberration from the norms of equality are also noted in the treatment of non-Arabs Muslims, the *mawāli*, as already discussed. Some of the earlier conclusions of *fiqh* regarding the *dhimmīs*, *dār al-Islām* and *dār al-ḥarb* were influenced by the then prevailing circumstances and reflected the vicissitudes of power politics, hostile situations and shifting positions of international relations. Thus according to one observer, the somewhat unrealistic traditional dichotomy between the *dār al-Islām* and *dār al-ḥarb* was a response to the Mongol invasion of the Muslim heartland in the 7th/13th century. Many Muslim jurists, especially of the Ḥanafī school, insisted that territories conquered by Mongols remained a part of the *dār al-Islām*.[131] Some of the juristic conclusions that were consequently drawn were less than egalitarian, as they advanced a certain viewpoint and purpose that could not be said to be a matter of axiomatic knowledge nor could they be said to be based on any obvious reading of the text. I have elsewhere examined some of the *fiqh* rulings in relationship to the status of *dhimmī*s, on such subjects as testimony and retaliation. It will suffice to say here that the basic idea of creating different types of unequal citizenships in an Islamic polity is repugnant to the uncompromising calibre of justice in the Qur'ān.

A reference may be made here to Mawdūdī's views on citizenship, and the unhesitating style of his writing where he observed: 'Since Islam is a system of both thought and conduct and since it aims at creating a state on the basis of its ideology, it prescribes two types of citizenship... The two kinds of citizenship that Islam envisages are the following: 1) The Muslims; and 2) The Zimmis.'[132] Mawdūdī has not referred to any authoritative source or precedent in making these observations. Instead he refers to the unity of thought and conduct in Islam and the ideological orientations of the Islamic state as the basic premises of his views, which, it is submitted, are far from self-evident and can hardly justify the conclusion that Islam actually 'prescribed two types of citizenship.' If unity of thought were to be the main concern, then would it not be more appropriate to say that social unity and cohesion can hardly be realised through establishing separate classes of citizens? The present writer has nowhere seen such an explicit and categorical classification of citizenship in the works of Muslim jurists of any school or period. Mawdūdī was himself unable to find a precedent and as it is, his conclusion is unprecedented and weak. The early jurists who wrote on *dār al-Islām* and *dār al-ḥarb* also spoke of *dhimmī*s and *musta'min*s, terms which are sometimes perceived to be less than egalitarian, but which are not necessarily premised on discrimination. In deference evidently to the egalitarian outlook of the Qur'ān and *Sunnah*, Muslim jurists have nowhere attempted a division of citizens into classes or types that could so obviously be seen to be discriminatory and unjust.

In his book, *The Muslim Conduct of State*, Muhammad Hamidullah has, much to his credit, discussed the *dhimmī* and *musta'min* but has nowhere attempted a classification of ranks among the citizens of an Islamic state. In a similar vein, in his 1993 publication entitled *Ḥuqūq al-Muwāṭanah* (citizenship rights) Rashīd al-Ghannūshī has rightly observed that 'the citizens of *dār al-Islām*, whether Muslim or non-Muslim, that is, regardless of their creed, bear the one and the same nationality.'[133] There is obviously only one type of citizenship which constitutes the basis of equal rights and duties. Absolute equality in all rights and obligations is not a necessary corollary of this. What it basically means is that the unitary concept of citizenship does not admit of any direct or implied superiority of some of its bearers over others. But when it comes to certain rights and privileges there are admittedly some differences which may be said to be justified because of the difference of religion. The *Sharīʿah* thus exempts the *dhimmīs* from certain obligations in the areas of personal law, criminal law, military service and *zakāh*.[134] The *dhimmīs* are on the other hand required to pay a poll-tax (*jizyah*) which is equivalent to *zakāh* and imposed in return for security and protection that the Muslim state offers. *Jizyah* is only imposed on able-bodied individuals and precludes children, women, the elderly, the invalid and even the monks.[135] But I attempt a brief analysis on the subject of *jizyah* as follows:

The Qur'ānic text that validates *jizyah* specifically reads in part that no war should be waged if the non-Muslims agree to pay the *jizyah* but that it must be paid 'by (a capable) hand that submits to authority (of the Muslim state).' (9: 29)

عن يد وهم صاغرون

Two points may be noted here, one of which is that *jizyah* is paid from a capable hand (*ʿan yadin*), thereby exempting the poor, women, children, the elderly and those who cannot afford to pay it. The second point in this text is that *jizyah* is payable by those who are basically affluent but they must nevertheless submit to the authority of the Muslim state, and not, as it were, to buy their way from a position of superiority. This may be said to be precluding payment of money, which is not accompanied by submission to the authority of the state. For it is possible that powerful tribes, groups and business concerns pay money and literally dictate their wishes to the state.[136] The Qur'ānic phrase *wa-hum ṣaghirūn* is often misunderstood to mean 'so that they will be humiliated.' Ibn Qayyim al-Jawziyyah, who has extensively written on the subject, has rightly stated that *wa-hum ṣaghirūn* implies that all subjects should obey the law and submit to the authority of the state.

The *dhimmīs* are exempted from the payment of *zakāh* simply because *zakāh* is a pillar of the faith and partakes in worship. They were also exempted from military service as this too partook in *jihād*, which is a religious duty and may be deemed inappropriate to impose on non-Muslims. However, if the *dhimmīs* volunteer to take part in the defence of the homeland, they are allowed to do so and are consequently exempted from the payment of *jizyah*. There were, in fact, many instances of this in the past, as discussed earlier, when non-Muslims were exempted from payment of *jizyah*.[137] There were instances on the other hand of *jizyah* being levied on Muslim farmers in Egypt when they were exempted from military service. The basic norm of *Sharīʿah* concerning non-Muslim citizens is a substantive equality of rights and obligations, and not an exact quantitative equivalence, as it were, to those of their Muslim compatriots.[138]

In his commentary on the Qurʾānic verse of *jizyah*, Sayyid Quṭb writes that Muslim jurists have held different views on it; some would still apply the *jizyah* whereas others do not. Quṭb then observes that *jizyah* is an historical issue which applied at a certain time but which is not applicable today. This is because 'the Muslims today are not involved in *jihād* and those who took up *jihād* are no longer with us. The issue today is also not the same.' Muslims are faced with bigger issues and a whole array of other challenges. The challenges are such, that if any *jihād* were needed it would probably not be *jihād* in the military sense but *jihād* that involved the Muslims to restore and revitalise Islam among themselves first.[139]

In view of the fact that the laws pertaining conscription and military service in many of the present-day Muslim countries apply to all citizens regardless of their religious following, there remains no basis for *jizyah* to be separately imposed on the *dhimmīs*. Since the effective cause (*ʿillah*), namely differential status in respect of rendering military service, on which the *jizyah* was originally founded, is no longer applicable, the requirement of *jizyah* may accordingly be set aside. Qaraḍāwī has made a slightly different observation where he writes that 'there is no objection for *zakāh* to be imposed on the *dhimmīs*, though not as a religious duty but as a simple tax when the government or the *ʿulū al-amr* should decide to do so.' In that eventuality, Muslim citizens will be paying the *zakāh* as a religious duty whereas non-Muslims would pay it only as a tax and a contribution to the community. This would not only eliminate the differences between fellow citizens and compatriots, but also prove to be administratively more convenient. To have a similar regime of taxation and military service for all citizens is bound to be more efficient.[140]

Ghannūshī added his voice to that of Qaraḍāwī and wrote that 'this would help eliminate the doubt that the *jizyah* penalises the non-Muslim citizen for not embracing Islam which made them feel humiliated as a result—while the truth of the matter is that Islam does not permit any form of compulsion and humiliation in one's choice of religion.'[141] Tawfīq al-Shāwī has also spoken in support of Qaraḍāwī's *fatwā* which he found to be consistent with the egalitarian position that was taken by the Caliph ʿUmar b. al-Khaṭṭāb in the treatment of *dhimmīs*. The *dhimmīs* and non-Muslim minorities were accordingly entitled to welfare assistance from the revenues of *zakāh*. It would be a logical extension of that position that they also pay the *zakāh* as a social welfare tax on an equal basis.[142]

ʿAbd al-Ḥamīd Mutawallī has drawn attention to the fact that unlike the Islamic state of Medina, which derived its *raison d'être* and identity from Islam, the nation state of today has departed from that paradigm. This is reflected, Mutawallī adds, in the adoption of formal nationalist constitutions and application of uniform laws to all citizens. Under these conditions, to insist on applying the rules of *jizyah* to non-Muslim citizens might be less than egalitarian and just.[143]

X. *Dār al-Ḥarb*: An Unwarranted Designation!

Muslim jurists are admittedly in disagreement over the basic definitions of the binary division of *dār al-Islām* and *dār al-ḥarb*. What is even more questionable is the assumption that the two are in a perpetual state of war. The Qur'ān, as earlier reviewed, validates fighting against the aggressor and fighting for justice but it does not advocate fighting those who have not waged war against Muslims.

Islam validates other revealed religions and accords their followers a recognised status, which the jurists have extended to Sabeans, Zoroastrians and to all non-Muslims living in Islamic lands. Non-Muslims are not prohibited from practicing their own ways of living, and may not be forced to embrace Islam. The Qur'ān recognises the validity of other revealed religions and speaks in their praise: 'Not all of them are alike: of the People of the Book are a portion that stand for [what is right]; they recite the verses of God all night long and then prostrate themselves in adoration' (3:113).

$$\text{ليسوا سواء من أهل الكتاب أمة قائمة يتلون آيات الله}$$
$$\text{أناء الليل وهم يسجدون}$$

In the face of these and similar other verses in the Qur'ān which advocate peace and equanimity even with the enemy, it is difficult to see how war rather than peace could be said to be the norm of relations among Muslims and non-Muslims. Islamic warfare is basically directed 'to the securing of essential human liberties.' Some people think that Islam only validated defensive war, meaning one would obviously need to wait until one is actually attacked. This would be inaccurate because 'War must be' waged in defence of human liberties.'[144] The Qur'ān conveys this purpose in such terms: 'Fight with them until there is no persecution and religion should only be for God.' (2:193)

وقاتلوهم حتى لا تكون فتنة ويكون الدين لله

Fighting for the sake of God also means fighting for social justice, 'it does not mean fighting for the spread of the dogma.' The Qur'ān confirms in several places that warfare in Islam is meant to eliminate tyranny and suppression of liberties:

ما لكم لا تقاتلون فى سبيل الله والمستضعفين من الرجال والنساء والولدان الذين يقولون ربنا أخرجنا من هذه القرية الظالم أهلها واجعل لنا من لدنك وليا

And what reason have you that you shall not fight in the way of God and (for the sake) of the weak among men, women and children and those who say: Our Lord! Cause us to go forth from this town whose people are oppressors and give us from Thee a helper.' (4:75)

This verse explains the purpose of waging war in the way of God for social justice. It is not a fight for a theological victory. 'Fighting for justice only is enjoined by Islam, a war for any other purpose is un-Islamic.'[145]

Maḥmūd Shaltūt maintains that the strongest emphasis of Islamic teachings is on the unity and equality of all people in respect of rights and obligations. The basic norm of *Sharī'ah* in the sphere of international relations is peace that is founded in cooperation and friendship.[146] Several Qur'ānic verses are quoted in support:

يآيها الناس إنا خلقناكم من ذكر وأنثى وجعلناكم شعوبا وقبائل لتعارفوا إن أكرمكم عند الله اتقاكم

O people! We created you from a male and a female and made you into tribes and nations so that you may know one another. Truly the most noble of you before God is the most righteous of you. (49:13)

يَٰٓأَيُّهَا ٱلنَّاسُ ٱتَّقُوا۟ رَبَّكُمُ ٱلَّذِى خَلَقَكُم مِّن نَّفْسٍ وَٰحِدَةٍ وَخَلَقَ مِنْهَا زَوْجَهَا وَبَثَّ مِنْهُمَا رِجَالًا كَثِيرًا وَنِسَاءً وَٱتَّقُوا۟ ٱللَّهَ ٱلَّذِى تَسَآءَلُونَ بِهِۦ وَٱلْأَرْحَامَ

O people! Be mindful of your Lord who created you from a single soul and created its mate of the same (kind) and created from them multitudes of men and women. And keep your duty to your Lord by whom you demand your rights from one another, and (observe) ties of kinship. (4:1)

These verses are explicit on the unity in origin and creation of mankind who live in multitudes scattered on the face of the earth. They are entitled to rights and obligations from one another by the fact of their kinship as members of one large family, and by the grace of their Creator who created them in that order. It is of interest to note, in the second verse above, that it begins with a note on unity and ends by reference to *al-arḥām* (ties of kinship), an expression which derives from *raḥim* (womb). '*Al-arḥām*' is usually employed in the Qur'an and *Sunnah* in the context of family relations and inheritance.

The unity of mankind that the Qur'ān has declared is also substantiated by its appeals to equality and justice. For unity without respect for each other's rights would lack foundation. Justice is a requirement even among close relatives in the family, in the society at large, and also in relations among communities and nations. Hence the Qur'ānic address to the believers:

وَلَا يَجْرِمَنَّكُمْ شَنَآنُ قَوْمٍ عَلَىٰٓ أَلَّا تَعْدِلُوا۟ ٱعْدِلُوا۟ هُوَ أَقْرَبُ لِلتَّقْوَىٰ

Let not the hatred of a people swerve you away from justice. Be just. For it is closest to righteousness. (5:8)

The right course is not to perpetuate hatred but to stall it with being just. This is the basic pattern of relations that Islam has envisaged among Muslims as well as their relations with other communities and nations. Peace is therefore the norm of Islam and it should nurture friendship and cooperation among people. Shaltūt put it succinctly as follows: 'When the non-Muslims observe peace, they and the Muslims are brethren in humanity, expected to cooperate for their common good. Each side is entitled to follow its own religion and also to advise and invite one another with wisdom and exhortation without prejudice to anyone or disrespect of anyone's rights.'[147]

Waḥbah al-Zuḥaylī also noted that 'peace, not war, is the norm of relationship with non-Muslims and those who have held otherwise have maintained a superficial position which was influenced by hostile relations between Muslim and non-Muslim powers.'[148] Zuḥaylī goes on to point out that the word *al-silm*—'peace' occurs in the Qur'ān on more than a hundred occasions whereas *al-ḥarb* (war) is mentioned only in six places. The Qur'ānic references to war are concerned mainly with encouragement to fight when war is waged against Muslims, preparation for war, and reciprocal treatment. The Qur'ān then addresses the believers. 'And if anyone attacked you, attack him in the like manner as he attacked you. Observe your duty to God and know that God is with those who are righteous.' (*al-Baqarah*, 2:194)

فمن اعتدى عليكم فاعتدوا عليه بمثل ما اعتدى عليكم
واتقوا الله واعلموا أن الله مع المتقين

Thus it is clear that the text validates war not because of disbelief, but in order to defend oneself against hostility and violence. Note also the following two verses:

And wage war on all of the idolaters as they wage war on all of you. (9:36)

وقاتلوا المشركين كآفة كما يقاتلونكم كآفة

Fight in the way of God against those who fight against you, but begin not hostilities. Lo! God loves not the aggressors. (2:190)

وقاتلوا في سبيل الله الذين يقاتلونكم ولا تعتدوا إن الله
لا يحب المعتدين

Jihād is validated in Islam in order to repel aggression and also to help the weak and the helpless against tyranny. Islam does not validate recourse to violence as a means of its own propagation and *daʿwah*.[149]

Fathī Osmān has read in the Qur'ānic verses cited above a certain diversity within unity when he says that divisions of different kind will naturally continue to exist among people. Such divisions are acknowledged in the Qur'ān (49:13) and 'there is nothing wrong with it so long as such divisions do not hinder universal human relations and cooperation, and are not abused through chauvinistic arrogance and aggression.'[150] Osmān went on to say that God and his teachings should be put above any allegiance to a particular group or land, and so long as this principle is observed, allegiance to one's family, to one's homeland and other human relations is recognized in the Qur'ān.

In his *The Children of Adam*, Fathī Osmān advances the theme that diversity is a part of God's plan and must be recognized as such. Thus he concludes:

> Muslims, like adherents of other religions of the world, have to live with non-Muslims within a given country. Muslim citizens of a country can have their ethnic or doctrinal differences within themselves or with other Muslims in the world. Muslim unity does not require that Muslims form a single state.[151]

Islam has in other words embraced pluralism within the Islamic majority societies. Religious freedom is recognized in the Qur'ān and by the *Sunnah* of the Prophet. As noted earlier, the Constitution of Medina which the Prophet signed with the Jews of Medina in 622 AD declared: 'The Jews . . . are a community along with the believers. For the Jews is their religion and for the Muslims theirs.' (Art. 25)[152]

XI. What of *Dār al-ʿAhd* (Abode of Treaty)?

The intermediate category of *dār al-ʿahd* (abode of treaty) that is attributed to al-Shāfiʿī but which many have cited ever since as a more relevant concept to the realities of the world of nation-states may not be as adequate as it may seem at first glance. *Dār al-ʿahd* is often seen as a framework within which Muslim and non-Muslim states can regulate their relations through agreement whether bilateral, multilateral or regional, such as the United Nations, the OIC, the OAU, ASEAN and so forth. Yet a closer examination reveals that the *dār al-ʿahd* is not an independent category in that it tends to acquire its meaning in conjunction with the two other concepts that we have discussed so far. This is because *dār al-ʿahd* is premised on the existence of two hostile abodes. When it is acknowledged that these two abodes do not have a real and well-defined existence, *dār al-ʿahd* also tends to become a doubtful concept. *Dār al-ʿahd* may in the context of contemporary world offer a situation without war but whether it can also provide a reasonable alternative and framework for relations among states is not without ambiguity. Apart from the absence of the context in which *dār al-ʿahd* acquired its original meaning and purpose, the geo-political and power dynamics of the world have brought about a different scenario where there are fundamental imbalances and where the concept of *dār al-ʿahd* may not offer a feasible alternative and framework for cooperation.

As for the view that regards supremacy of the *Sharīʿah* as a defining feature of *dār al-Islām*, it will be noted that Western domination of the Muslim world for about two centuries provoked many changes in Muslim countries. The alliance of many Muslim countries and leaders with the west and the introduction, step by step, of an alien and legal system has led to a large-scale modification of the *Sharīʿah* within Muslim societies.

An era of complexity and mix has marked the contemporary realities of both the western and Islamic societies such that it is no longer sufficient or appropriate to focus on the nature of the law that a government applies, or indeed to identify the nature of the government that applies it. The question as to whether a particular Muslim country or population is ruled by the *Sharīʿah* can hardly receive a clear answer. The criterion of religious freedom and the question whether a Muslim has the freedom to practice his religion cannot be taken as a basis of division either, as freedom of religion is now respected in the west where Muslims are able to practice their faith.[153]

About forty per cent of the world Muslims are at present living amidst non-Muslim countries spread in various proportions in Russia, India, China, Yugoslavia, Albania, France, Britain, Germany and the United States etc. Non-Muslims also live in various combinations among the Muslim majority countries of Egypt, Syria, Iran, Iraq and Sudan etc. Under these circumstances, al-Ṭālibī thought it would be unrealistic to imagine that these communities would join together, whether through massive migration (*hijrah*) or through other forms of political unity to live under one Islamic government and the rule of the *Sharīʿah*.[154] In the face of all this, there is no realistic alternative to pluralism and a genuine commitment to human rights, equality and justice everywhere. What is important is not the form of government and the system of rule, but the substance of its commitment to basic rights. 'The best system of government is one that respects human dignity and human rights, and that is also in conformity with Islam.'[155]

XII. Rights of Citizens

The relevant literature in *fiqh* hardly addresses the rights of citizens in the manner that is now familiar to the students of constitutional law. Mawdūdī's book, *Islamic Law and Constitution*, departs from the earlier pattern by devoting a brief section to the rights of citizens where he specifies four rights, namely the right to protection of life and property, right to safety against unlawful arrest, freedom of opinion, and right to the provision of the basic necessities of life.[156] This may be said to be somewhat inaccurate as the first two of these are basic human rights in Islam and not particularly associated with citizenship as such. Only the last of the four rights may properly be said to be related to citizenship. The present treatment of this subject attempts to identify six rights, namely the right to vote and nomination for political office, the right to consultation, right to express an opinion on political matters, the citizen's right not to obey a deviant ruler, and the right to welfare and education, which are separately addressed in the following pages. A more detailed presentation of the right to education, work and welfare can be found in a separate volume of this series. It will be noted at the outset that my treatment of the rights and duties of citizens includes both Muslims and non-Muslims alike and unless there is a specific divergence from this premise, the basic principle of equality prevails. But before I address the specifics of rights and duties of citizens, some observations need to be made on historical developments.

During the post-colonial period, citizenship rights have on the whole been poorly observed in the Muslim countries due to the prevalence of dictatorship, military coup d'etat and a certain disregard of the basic rights and liberties. Progress in this area has also been impeded to some extent by the complexity of issues especially in countries with religious minorities that had conflicting interests and demands. One may be able to find some exceptions to this otherwise poor record in some Muslim countries or certain periods, but the general pattern still remains that despite elaborate constitutional clauses on basic rights and liberties, these have largely remained theoretical—even after decades of the promulgation of those constitutions. This general pattern also extends to countries such as Saudi Arabia, Iran, Sudan and Pakistan which have proclaimed themselves as Islamic states.

Saudi Arabia has upheld traditional interpretations of Islam and it seems that the promulgation of its first constitution in 1992 has had little impact on the basic rights of citizens. *Muwāṭanah* and citizenship have, in any case, not received much attention in this constitution and it has done little to change the conventional practice whereby 'citizenship is accorded in the kingdom on the basis of birth from Saudi parents. Some civil and political rights such as right to life, work, and ownership have been granted and the ruling authorities see this position in full accord with the *Sharīʿah*.'[157]

The Iranian revolution of 1979 marked a political milestone in that country where an *ʿulamāʾ*-led Islamic revolution toppled a despotic monarchy and promulgated a new constitution. The constitution envisaged a democratic government with an elected president and parliament. The fact that citizenship in this constitution is confined to Iranians only invoked some criticism that it was 'un-Islamic' as it precluded other non-Iranian Muslims. Yet in the meantime this constitution recognized non-Muslim Iranians including the Jews and other minorities as part of the political community with rights to participate in parliament and other electoral offices in accordance with certain procedures. Yet the constitution also adopted a number of other provisions that tended to water down or create difficulty toward a fuller realisation of its earlier provisions. The fact that the Constitution singled out the Shīʿī Jaʿfarī school/*madhhab* and proclaimed it as the basis of statutory legislation, and the fact also that the religious leaders dominated government hierarchy tended to have negative consequences for citizen's equality under the law. Then the Constitution tended to compromise itself by subjugating the decisions of parliament and government to the supreme leader in accordance with the Shīʿī doctrine of *vilayat-e faqih*, which was also deemed to have had consequences for the non-Muslim minorities of Iran. Only after the 1997 election of President Khatami, steps were taken toward pluralism and openness, yet 'the basic foundations and principles of government have not changed' even under President Khatami.[158]

Developments in the Sudan following the military coup of 1989 have been variable. Following that event restrictions were imposed on constitutional rights and liberties of all citizens. Political parties were banned as were all political activity by the citizenry. New restrictions were imposed on freedom of expression, assembly and asso ciation. A new constitution was promulgated in 1998 that granted full citizenship rights for all Sudanese regardless of their religious following. All are to enjoy equality in rights and obligations. Yet somewhat similar to the Iranian situation, the rest of the constitution is not entirely free of clauses that can very well compromise the integrity of its egalitarian clauses. The military has remained dominant and political participation of the citizen in the government has also achieved limited success.[159]

Pakistan has hardly seen a normal constitutional order ever since its inception as an Islamic state. Although the effort to maintain a constitutional order has been persistent, its continuity has been disrupted by frequent military intervention, and the wholesale abandonment of constitutional order under President Musharraf.

One of the reasons that citizenship rights of non-Muslims, especially Christian minorities in the Muslim lands, were not addressed during the colonial period was their privileged status and the protection they had from European powers. The situation continued even after the colonial rule under the regime of capitulations whereby the non-Muslim settlers were not even subject to the jurisdiction of the national courts in the newly emerging states. The privileged status that European residents of those countries enjoyed apparently turned out disadvantageous for them over a longer term as it impeded their integration into the local communities and issues pertaining to their status were not addressed by the legislative and judicial institutions of the host countries. A certain imbalance was also noted in the writings of such influential figures as Sayyid Quṭb and Mawdūdī who sought to make exclusivity and religious discrimination the basic principle of social and political organisation within the Islamic state.[160] In their writings, non-Muslim citizens were treated as second-class citizens who were not entitled to be employed in 'key government positions,' nor to participate in legislative assemblies. They were treated as *dhimmī*s and protected groups of people who need not be integrated in the body politique that was created by Muslims for Muslims. In el-Affendi's assessment, these writers were at the other extreme of the fifth/eleventh century writer, Abū'l Ḥasan al-Māwardī, who held that a non-Muslim could be appointed to ministerial posts. A corrective was then called for and it was provided in the writings of Fathī Osmān, Salim el-ʿAwa, Fahmi Huwaydi, ʿAbd al-Wahhāb el-Affendi, Tawfīq al-Shāwī, Rashīd Ghannūshī, etc., (including my own writings), all of which have advocated total equality for all citizens.[161]

ʿAbd al-Ḥamīd Mutawallī and Ṭāriq al-Bishrī are of the view that Islam advocated equality between Muslims and non-Muslims in most of their rights and duties. The sources of *Sharīʿah* contain a number of general principles that could provide the basis of an egalitarian regime of rights and duties for non-Muslims. Yet the early jurists have not treaded that path and did not aim to establish total equality between Muslims and non-Muslims. Since the introduction of a series of modern constitutions, Muslim countries have undergone a transition toward national unity rather than unity in faith. Under these conditions, equality of rights and obligations for different religious denominations is a realistic prospect. ʿAbd al-Wahhāb Khallāf similarly noted that the status of non-Muslims in the midst of the larger Muslim community in earlier times was affected, not only by the religious factor but also by political considerations. It is now important that the Christians of Egypt are no longer made to suffer inequalities but that a spirit of fraternity and trust should usher a regime of equality in rights and obligations.[162]

It is important also to note that the rules of *fiqh* on the status of non-Muslims and *dhimmī*s were a creation not so much of a central government or of state functionaries but mainly of individual jurists and *fuqahāʾ*. The rules of *fiqh* were thus developed by men of religion and scholars of *Sharīʿah* in accordance with the methodology of *uṣul al-fiqh* and *ijtihād*. The modern nation state has departed from that premise and exercises its authority on the basis of a constitution. There is in addition an attempt in many of the applied constitutions of Muslim countries to separate religion from politics and base the laws of administration and government not on the religious but on the nationalist identities of the state.[163] Based on this analysis, some commentators such as Fatḥī Osmān, Salim el-Awa, Ṭāriq al-Bishrī, and el-Affendi have even held it permissible for a non-Muslim to be elected as the head of state. They explain that this is now primarily a political position, not a religious one. This is also, broadly speaking, an elected office, which means that the people would vote for a candidate whom they consider to be suitable. It might have been natural in earlier times to assign the office of the head of state and government to Muslims only, but modern constitutions usually regulate this matter in the light of the prevailing realities of each community which would imply that no prior stipulations are called for.[164] In my own view, public opinion in many present day majority Muslim countries of the Arab world and Asia would hesitate to support the idea of a non-Muslim head of state, although one may be able to see a different prospect in Muslim countries with sizeable non–Muslim minorities.

I now turn to the basic rights of citizens.

THE FRANCHISE

The citizen is entitled to participate in the election of the head of state and other representative government bodies. Ibn Qudāmah (d. 620/1223) has recorded the majority position here when he wrote: 'whoever Muslims agree upon as their leader and Imam and pledge their oath of allegiance (*bayʿah*) to is designated as Imam and must be assisted and obeyed (by everyone).'[165] The Imam is elected into office in two stages, one of which is nomination (*al-tarshīḥ*), and the other the pledging of allegiance (*mubāyaʿah*). A person may be nominated for leadership by a college of electors known as the *ahl al-ḥall wa'l-ʿaqd* (those who loosen and bind), or by the outgoing Imam. This latter procedure is known as *istikhlāf* (also *al-ʿahd*). Both of these methods were applied in the designation of the early four caliphs (i.e. *Khulafāʾ Rashīdūn*). It is the *bayʿah* of the community at large, or their vote in other words, which completes and brings to fruition the initial nomination of the *ahl al-ḥall wa'l-ʿaqd*. Nomination alone which is not followed by *bayʿah*, in other words, is of no consequence in the designation of the head of state into office.[166]

A certain amount of confusion has arisen, however, between nomination and *bayʿah* and many prominent jurists have gone on record to say that nomination in both cases, that is, by the *ahl al-ḥall wa'l-ʿaqd*, and by the outgoing Imam transfers power to the nominee. The *bayʿah* that is subsequently given has a declaratory (*kāshif*) rather than a creative (*munshiʾ*) role in the election of the Imam. Al–Sanhūrī has drawn attention to this and stated that this view, attributed mainly to the *ʿulamāʾ* of Basra, has confounded nomination (*al-tarshīḥ*) with the assignment of authority (*al-wilāyah*), a confusion which is so misleading as to amount to distortion. Nomination simply identifies a qualified candidate but power is vested in the nominee by virtue of a valid *bayʿah*.[167] A number of prominent *ʿulamāʾ* including Abū Yaʿlā al-Farrāʾ (d. 1066 AD), Ibn Taymiyyah (d. 1328) and more recently Abu Zahrah, ʿAbd al-Wahhāb Khallāf, Muḥammad Yūsuf Mūsā and many others have subscribed to this view and held that nomination whether by the *ahl al-ḥall wa'l-ʿaqd* or by the outgoing Imam has no independent value of its own simply because the community of believers have the choice whether or not to grant their *bayʿah* to the nominee, and nomination alone does not create an obligation for them to be complied with.[168]

The Qur'ān encourages the community's active participation in its own government. This is understood from the numerous verses which are addressed directly to the community of believers. Being the direct audience of the revelation, manifested, for example, in the familiar Qur'ānic phrase *yā ayyuhā 'lladhīna āmanū*—'O ye who believe'—the Muslim community is entrusted with the responsibility of implementing the *Sharī'ah*.[169]

Since the community cannot always discharge its responsibility directly, it has the power to appoint representatives to act on its behalf. The head of state is thus a representative (*wakīl*) of the community elected and entrusted to administer its affairs in accordance with the *Sharī'ah*.[170] As for the method in which the community organises elections, whether direct or indirect (i.e. through a college of electors), or a combination of both, this is a matter that may be determined through consultation. Since election is a right of the community, it is for the community to determine the method of exercising that right. The Qur'ānic verse that 'their affairs are a matter of consultation between them' (42:38) is a clear text on direct participation. There is, however, authority for indirect elections in the precedent of the Pious Caliphs. The first Caliph Abū Bakr was elected by nomination and *bay'ah* of the people of Medina, wherein the rest of the community did not participate directly. Yet there has been no objection to the manner in which he was elected. This may be seen, if translated into modern terms, equivalent to indirect election.[171]

The basic principles of representation, consultation and election that the jurists have stated in regard to the designation of the Imam also apply, *mutatis mutandis*, to the election of other officers and representative organs of government. It seems desirable and in harmony with the Qur'ānic guidance to widen the scope of consultation in political matters as effectively as possible.

Traditionally only the Muslim citizens participated in *bay'ah* concerning the election of the head of state. This was due to the prevailing view among the early jurists that entitled only the Muslims to participation in *bay'ah*, and also due to the fact that non-Muslims did not participate in the election of any of the Pious Caliphs. A rule of convention thus came into being to allow only the Muslims a say in the election of the head of state. Notwithstanding this, 'Abd al-Karīm Zaydān has observed, and rightly so, that under the present circumstances the non-Muslim citizens may participate in the election of the head of state just as they are permitted generally to participate in the affairs of government and its representative organs. They are accordingly entitled to nomination for membership of the representative assemblies and also have the right to vote. They may also initiate an opinion in political matters, offer advice to the government and make complaints on behalf of the electorate. Hence there is neither an objection to the participation of non-Muslim citizens in the election of the head of state nor to their membership and election to the representative assemblies.[172] Al-Ghannūshī has discussed Zaydān's views on this and expressed unqualified support for them.[173] Said Ramadan likewise upholds the 'right of non-Muslim subjects to both voting and membership of the parliament.'[174] Ramadan adds that the legislative powers of the Muslim parliament should be subservient to the injunctions of Islamic law in which non-Muslim members may or may not believe. 'This problem could be resolved' writes Ramadan 'by stipulating a provision in the constitution that makes it *ultra vires* of the parliament to enact any law which is repugnant to the Qur'ān and *Sunnah*'.[175] I may conclude to say that equal treatment in the political sphere of all citizens would naturally require that they are duly represented in the designation and election of the head of state and members of representative assemblies. Muslim and non-Muslim citizens, men and women, should naturally be entitled to participate in general elections on an equal footing to ensure credibility and confidence in the representative substance and foundation of the nation state.

RIGHT TO NOMINATION (*ḤAQQ AL-TARSHĪḤ*)

There is evidence in the *Sunnah* to suggest that the individual, be he a Muslim or otherwise, may not nominate himself for a public office. Self-canvassing is, in other words, discouraged. It is accordingly reported that the Prophet instructed ʿAbd al-Raḥmān b. Samurah that 'you may not ask for government office (*amārah*). If you are given it at your request it will amount to (a contract of) agency but if you are given it without your asking, you would be given assistance over it.'[176]

يا عبد الرحمن بن سمرة: لا تسأل الإمارة فإن أعطيتها عن مسألة وكلت إليها، وإن أعطيتها عن غير مسألة أعنت عليها

It is reported in another *ḥadīth* that Abū Dhar al-Ghaffārī asked the Prophet if he could be appointed to a government post, to which the Prophet responded as follows:

يا أبا ذر إنك ضعيف، إنها أمانة وإنها يوم القيامة خزي وندامة إلا من أخذها بحقها وأدى الذى عليه فيها

O Abū Dhar, you are weak; this is a trust (position of responsibility) and (brings nothing but) accountability and regret on the Day of Judgment, except for those who take it rightly and duly discharge the duty they have undertaken.[177]

This does not, of course, apply to nomination of one person by another person or a group of persons. For nomination by others implies invitation by the community and assurance over the competence of the person for the task.

Modern writers have held, however, that due to the change of circumstances, it may now be difficult to locate suitable candidates for public office if they did not come forward to declare themselves. The instruction conveyed in the foregoing *ḥadīth* may thus be seen as a temporary legislation (*al-tashrīʿ al-zamanī*) which was suitable at the time it was given but may not be in harmony with the *maṣlaḥah* of the community now. Zaydān has even gone so far as to say that self-candidacy on the part of the competent individual under the present conditions is an act of merit as it helps the community to make the right choice in the selection of officials.[178] Further to substantiate this view, Zaydān has referred to the Qurʾānic example in which the Prophet Yūsuf (Joseph) is quoted for his invocation when he said: 'Place me (in authority) over the treasures of the land; surely I am a good and knowledgeable keeper' (12:55).

قال اجعلنى على خزائن الأرض إني حفيظ عليم

Al-Māwardī has held that the *dhimmīs* may hold the post of a minister (i.e. *wazīr al-tanfīdh*), but that the post of prime minister (*wazīr al-tafwīḍ*) and that of the Imam must be reserved for Muslims. More recently, many Muslim scholars including al-Nabhānī, Muhammad Hamidullah, Aḥmad Yusrī and Ghannūshī have spoken in support of the participation, candidacy and nomination of non–Muslims in the consultative assemblies. In this connection, Ghannūshī has also referred to the provisions of the constitution of the Islamic Republic of Iran that reserve a number of seats in the Majlis for the Jewish and Zoroastrian citizens of Iran.[179] The matter thus remains open to *ijtihād* and consultative decision-making by the community to determine the best manner in which the non-Muslim citizens can participate in government at all levels, especially in areas where they can best represent and serve their own respective communities.

Muḥammad al-Ghazālī wrote that the basic guideline of *Sharīʿah* in respect of the rights and obligations of non-Muslim citizens is that 'they have rights and obligations similar to our rights and our obligations.' When a non-Muslim, Jew or Christian, becomes citizen of a Muslim state, he becomes 'a Muslim from the political and citizenship viewpoints, someone who has the same rights and obligations as we have,' although they retain their own identity in personal matters and religion. The basic principle in the sphere of social relations is participation and involvement. This is especially so in the area of economic activity and employment. There is no objection therefore for a Muslim to enter employment with the *Ahl al-Kitāb* nor is there an objection for the latter to enter employment with the Muslim. Appointment of Jews and Christians in the high positions and in lower government posts has, in any case, become widespread in Muslim lands in both earlier and modern times.[180]

Al-Ghazālī also noted that Islam recognises Christianity and Judaism as valid religions and its perspective toward the followers of these faiths is also not premised on fanaticism. Those of the Qurʾānic verses which advised the Muslims against friendship with the Jews, Christians and disbelievers were, all of them, revealed concerning 'the aggressors against Islam and belligerent *muḥaribīn* toward Muslims.' Those verses were revealed with the purpose of cleansing the Muslim community from the mischief of the hypocrites (*munāfiqūn*) who helped certain groups among the *Ahl al-Kitāb* in security matters against Muslims. These verses were concerned with belligerent Jews and Christians who threatened the security and social order of the Muslim community and Muslims were consequently ordered not to befriend them.[181]

With reference to the employment of non-Muslim citizens in public services, Qaraḍāwī wrote in a 1977 publication that 'the *ahl al-dhimmah* are entitled to be employed in government positions as are the Muslims,' except for certain religious posts such as that of the head of state, army commander, judgeship over Muslims and administration of religious charities. Qaraḍāwī explained this by saying that the Imamate, that is, the office of the head of state, combines both religious and secular duties and it combines 'successorship to the Prophet, peace be on him.' The army leadership is also not purely secular as it involves *jihād* which is an act of worship (*ʿibādah*), and so is being a judge which involves enforcement of the rulings of *Sharīʿah*, and a non-Muslim is not required to issue judgment on the basis of what he does not believe in. In saying this Qaraḍāwī also referred to what al-Māwardī wrote so long ago on the distinction between the two types of vizierates, namely, *wizārat al-tafwīḍ*, and *wizārat al-tanfīdh*. The *dhimmī* may be appointed to the latter but not to the former.[182]

Most other commentators including Fatḥī Osmān, Muḥammad al-Ghazālī, el-Awa, Fahmi Huwaydi among others, do not specify these limitations on employment. This is partly due to the fact that the institutions of modern government are bound by laws and procedures, which seek propriety and fairness. We also have constitutional limitations on state powers which must be observed by the individuals in charge, be they Muslim or non-Muslim. I also concur with the view that equality and fair treatment of all citizens is the preferable approach, one that realises the public interest and *maṣlaḥah* of the people in pursuit of greater harmony among them.

In his 1977 publication in Egypt, Fatḥī Osmān calls for clear and unambiguous legislation on the rights and duties of non-Muslim citizens in Muslim territories where the *Sharīʿah* applies. He poses the question: is it at all clear whether total equality among all citizens is the accepted norm, and whether the non-Muslims are equally treated under the law? Osmān similarly raises the question whether the law permits the non-Muslims to be members of parliament, ministers, judges, army commanders and the like. What are the rights of non-Muslims in respect of building new places of worship? These and similar other questions have arisen before but the responses given have not been devoid of ambiguity. What is now needed, Fatḥī Osmān urges, is to depart from the language of ambiguity and take clear stance on issues that would help build a climate of understanding and confidence in the community.

The need for clarity becomes all the more evident in view of the confusion that the non-Muslims of Egypt have experienced. Osmān then added: 'It is a right of these non-Muslim *muwāṭins* (compatriots) to know their legal status and their rights so as to give them confidence over their future.'[183] The *muwāṭins* should also know their standing vis-à-vis the *Sharīʿah* with a degree of clarity whereby they know the difference between its basic and decisive provisions and those that are interpretation-based and optional. They should also clearly know the rules that are changeable with the change of circumstances. The issues involved are also not entirely of a legal nature but include political and economic questions that need to be addressed. To do this, it is necessary, Osmān adds, to set up a combined committee of the scholars of *Sharīʿah*, non-Muslim religious leaders and prominent thinkers in various fields who should investigate and then publish the results of their findings.[184]

RIGHT TO CONSULTATION (*SHŪRĀ*)

Once the head of state is lawfully elected, he is under an obligation to consult the community in government affairs. Thus it may be stated that after the right to vote, the second political right the citizen enjoys in an Islamic polity is that he or she should be consulted in the affairs of government. It is a collective right of the community and those members of the community who are competent to give advice and counsel can exercise it. There is evidence in the Qur'ān and *Sunnah* on the subject of consultation which need not be elaborated here. According to the author of *Tafsīr al-Qurṭubī*, in the event where the head of state refuses to fulfil this obligation and refuses to consult the community in government affairs, he may be deposed.[185] Ibn Taymiyyah has also observed that the government in power and the *ʿulū al-amr*, indeed all Muslim rulers and officials, must be diligent in consultation. For God Most High enjoined it upon His Messenger to consult the community even though the Prophet was recipient of divine revelation. It is all the more advisable for the Muslim ruler to do the same.[186]

According to Rashīd Riḍā, consultation is an emphatic duty of the Islamic government and a right therefore of the citizen and the community as a whole. It should be solicited in all matters of public concern which have not been regulated by decisive textual injunctions. The Prophet himself and the Pious Caliphs after him were diligent in consulting the community, hence it became a distinctive feature of Islamic government which must never be neglected.[187] Sayyid Quṭb has concurred and added that no particular method need be followed as the *Sharīʿah* does not specify any particular procedure for the implementation of *shūrā*. It is thus left for the community to devise suitable methods in the light of its prevailing conditions and public interest.[188] As discussed earlier, the methods may require direct participation, such as consultation in local affairs, or may provide for representative assemblies. The community may determine them as they deem fit. It would also appear from this analysis that the consultative substance of the Islamic government and its organisational matters need to be addressed by the constitution. Some constitutional guidelines would, in other words, be necessary to specify the citizen's right to consultation and identify the institutional framework and methods by which this right may find its proper role and application in the various spheres of community affairs.

Non-Muslim citizens are also eligible to give advice and counsel when they are competent to give it and government leaders may solicit their counsel in community affairs. This is the purport of the Qur'ānic directive to the believers to 'ask those who have knowledge if you do not know (yourselves)' (16:43).

فسئلوا أهل الذكر إن كنتم لا تعلمون

Commentators have stated that this verse was in fact revealed concerning the Jews and Christians and consequently permitted the Muslims to seek their advice and opinion. Recourse may thus be had to expert opinion in matters of specialised nature and the expert opinion, whether given by Muslims or non-Muslims, may be followed. Non-Muslim citizens are also eligible for membership of the Consultative Assembly (*Majlis al-Shūrā*), especially in their capacity to represent their own communities, but also to participate in the general deliberations of the *Majlis al-Shūrā*. The only point of reservation that some commentators have recorded in this connection is that they may not initiate an opinion in matters that concern the dogma of Islam and legislation on purely religious matters.[189] This and similar other matters of concern can be addressed perhaps in the bye laws and governing procedures of the representative assemblies in the spirit of efficiency and cooperation among the various strata of the community.

RIGHT TO CRITICISE

Islamic government is participatory and consultative and it contemplates an active role for the citizens in all affairs of concern to them, including government policy and administration. This is evident from the Qur'ānic mandate on *hisbah*, that is, promotion of good and prevention of evil (*amr bi'l-maʿrūf wa-nahy ʿan al-munkar*) which is a broad yet a basic right of all citizens. For no one can be disallowed to promote a good cause or to put a stop to an evil one. The details of *hisbah* need not be elaborated here.[190] Suffice it to say that *hisbah* is a prominent Qur'ānic principle which entitles the citizen to express an opinion on the conduct of government. This may be said to be of concern also to *shūrā*, but since the right to *shūrā* is normally exercised when an advice or counsel is solicited by the leaders and the *ulū al-amr*, it may be subjected to some limitation in the event the authorities do not take the initiative to ask for it. The citizen's right to *hisbah* is, on the other hand, an inherent right which does not depend on solicitation by the government. Yet it may be noted that at least one of the two aspects of *hisbah*, that is, *nahy ʿan al-munkar* (prevention of evil) is limited to situations where the citizen is a direct witness of an evil that occurs before his or her eyes, which might also prove to be a limiting factor. When *hisbah* and *shūrā* both fall short of enabling the citizen to express an opinion on political matters, he or she may resort to his parallel right of criticising the ruling authorities within the limits of propriety and public interest. This is known as *hurriyyat al-muʿāraḍah* (the freedom to criticise); some writers refer to it as *hurriyyat naqd al-ḥākim*, which is perhaps more specific as it literally means 'the freedom to criticise the ruler'.

'*Muʿāraḍah* is a fundamental principle of the Islamic system of government,' writes ʿAfīfī, 'which entitles the individual to tell the truth and expose transgression even when this entails exposing the ruling authorities.'[191] The textual authority for this in the Qur'ān and *Sunnah* is the same as can be cited in support of *hisbah*, which is the central theme of a number of verses in the Qur'ān. *Muʿāraḍah* is also upheld in the *Sunnah* of the Prophet and the precedent of the early caliphs. Thus it is provided in a *hadīth* that 'the best form of *jihād* is to speak a word of truth to a tyrannical ruler.'[192]

أفضل الجهاد كلمة عدل عند سلطان جائر

It was in line with the basic message of this *hadīth* when the first caliph Abū Bakr addressed the people in his inaugural speech upon taking office in the following terms: 'O people, I have been entrusted with authority over you, but I am not the best of you. Assist me if I am right and rectify me when I am wrong.'[193] Abū Bakr's successor, ʿUmar b. al-Khaṭṭāb also asked the people in his inaugural speech to 'rectify any aberration you might see on my part.'[194]

The citizen is thus entitled to speak out against transgression and criticise the authorities from a position of conviction and in the true spirit of sincere advice or *naṣīḥah*. The criticism must be based on truth; it should be courteous and suitable to the occasion in that it is neither excessive nor ineffective and feeble.[195]

Both Mawdūdī and Ghannūshī have spoken in support of the freedom of opinion, expression, and association for non-Muslim citizens in government affairs in the same way as is recognized for their Muslim fellow citizens. If there are limitations on the exercise of these rights, they apply equally to the Muslims and non-Muslims; both are expected to observe the limits of the law and within those limits, there are no special disabilities nor privileges for either.[196]

THE RIGHT TO DISOBEY THE DEVIANT RULER

The citizen is normally under duty to obey and assist the lawful authorities, except when they violate the law. The duty of obedience thus collapses when obeying a command amounts to a clear transgression. In all other instances of lesser violation and also occasions when the citizen doubts the legality of a command issued by the lawful government, his or her duty of obedience is not affected, but he or she may voice an opinion through normal methods. The principle here is established in the authority both of the Qur'ān and *Sunnah*. The Qur'ān demands obedience to the lawful government when it addresses the believers with 'Obey God and obey the Messenger and those who are in charge of the affairs among you. If you dispute over a matter, refer it to God and to the Messenger, if you believe in God' (4:59).

يَآيِها الذين آمنوا أطيعوا الله وأطيعوا الرسول وأولى الأمر منكم فإن تنازعتم فى شيئ فردوه إلى الله والرسول إن كنتم تؤمنون بالله واليوم الآخر

The citizen must therefore obey the government provided that the latter conforms to the injunctions of the Qur'ān and *Sunnah*. The text here has invoked much elaboration from commentators in that it lays down a number of important principles.[197] I have reviewed some of these commentaries elsewhere,[198] and I shall here refer only to some of the basic directives on the subject of obedience that need to be read together with the above verse. Thus it is provided in another Qur'ānic verse that not everyone in position of power is entitled to obedience: 'And obey not a person whose heart We have permitted to become negligent of Our remembrance, one who is following the dictates of his own desire, and whose case has gone beyond all bounds' (18:28).

ولا تطع من أغفلنا قلبه عن ذكرنا واتبع هواه وكان أمره فرطا

It is further provided in a *ḥadīth*:

> A Muslim is under duty to listen and to obey in what he likes or dislikes unless he is commanded to commit a transgression. When he is so commanded, he is not required to listen nor to obey.[199]

السمع والطاعة على المرء المسلم فيما أحب وكره ما لم يؤمر بمعصية فإذا أمر بمعصية فلا سمع ولا طاعة

The same message is conveyed in two other *ḥadīths*, one of which simply declares that 'there is no obedience to a creature in disobedience of the Creator.'[200]

لا طاعة لمخلوق في معصية الخالق

The other affirms that 'no obedience is due in transgression, behold, obedience is due only in righteousness'.[201]

Some of the implications of these declarations will be discussed below in the context of the duties of the citizens. It should suffice here to note that an unlawful command may not be obeyed only when it is explicit and self-evident and not based on individual understanding and interpretation. Al-Sibāʿī has summed up the substance of these directives: 'Put in contemporary parlance, the message here would be that a government order is not enforceable when it violates the constitution and other laws.'[202]

The *Sharīʿah* takes a direct approach to the principle of individual responsibility in that anyone who follows a command which is against the clear injunctions of *Sharīʿah* shall have no excuse and will be held accountable for it himself. The Qur'ān has thus clearly denounced as feeble excuses the plea of those who persisted in transgression and blamed their ancestors and superiors for it:

وقالوا ربنا إنا أطعنا سادتنا وكبراءنا فأضلونا السبيلا ربنا

آتهم ضعفين من العذاب والعنهم لعنا كبيرا

And they say: Our Lord, we only obeyed our leaders and our great men, so they led us astray from (the true) path. Our Lord, give them a double chastisement and curse them with a great curse. (33:67–68)

This is confirmed in another verse:

وقال الذين اتبعوا لو أن لنا كرّة فنتبرأ منهم كما تبرءوا منا

كذلك يريهم الله أعمالهم حسرات عليهم

And those who followed (others in transgression) will say: if we could only return, we would renounce them as they renounced us. Thus will God show them (the result of) their deeds... (2:167)

It is stated in a report that the Prophet sent a military expedition outside Medina under the leadership of a man from the Helpers (*Anṣār*) and ordered that he should be obeyed. Then it so happened that the commander became unreasonable and ordered his men to gather wood which was then set ablaze and he asked the soldiers to enter the fire, but they refused to comply. When the episode was reported to the Prophet, he said: 'If they had entered, they would have remained in it for ever: obedience is only required in righteousness.'[203]

لو دخلوها ماخرجوا منها أبدا، إنما الطاعة فى المعروف

The textual evidence reviewed above leads to the conclusion that one who knowingly obeys an unlawful command is personally responsible and guilty of unlawful obedience (*al-ṭāʿah al-muḥarramah*). He or she is responsible for its consequences and may also be punished for it. The only avenue that such a person can be relieved of punitive consequences would be for him or her to show that the command in question was carried out under duress (*ikrāh*) which could not be avoided.[204]

RIGHT TO BASIC NECESSITIES

I shall not elaborate much on this as I have addressed the subject elsewhere in a separate volume of this series.[205] It may briefly be stated here that Islam entitles the citizens to the provision of basic necessities of life without any distinction of caste or creed.[206] The legal alms (*zakāh*), which is a Qur'ānic duty and one of the five pillars of Islam, was made compulsory on Muslims for this very purpose. The Qur'ān also speaks unequivocally of a basic right of the poor in the wealth of the affluent (70:25) and promises with distinction those who 'feed for the love of God the indigent, the orphan and the captive' (76:8).

ويطعمون الطعام على حبه مسكينا ويتيما وأسيرا

The reports incidentally suggest that this latter passage was revealed at a time when the captives and war prisoners in Medina were all non-Muslims.[207] To ensure a decent living for the people and fulfil their needs is also considered to be in the nature of *amr bi'l-maʿrūf wa-nahy ʿan al-munkar*, that is promoting good and preventing evil, which is firmly rooted in the Qur'ān and is in so many ways characteristic of Islam itself.[208]

The *Sunnah* has taken the Qur'ānic guidance a step further to enunciate assistance to the poor and the needy as a principle duty of the government. Thus it is provided:

السلطان ولي من لا وليّ له

The government is the guardian (helper) of one who has no guardian.[209]

And again:

فمن توفي وعليه دين فعليّ قضاؤه، ومن ترك مالا فلورثته

Whoever leaves behind property, it shall belong to his heirs, but whoever leaves a debt or dependants in need, they shall be my responsibility.[210]

The Prophet is also reported to have said:

من ولاه الله عز وجل شيئا من أمر المسلمين ماحتجب
دون حاجتهم وخلقهم وفقرهم احتجب الله عنه دون
حاجته وخلقه وفقره

He whom God has made an administrator over the affairs of
Muslims but remains indifferent to their needs and their poverty,
God will also be indifferent to his needs and poverty on the Day
of Judgment.[211]

The caliphs Abū Bakr and ʿUmar b. al-Khaṭṭāb are reported to
have disagreed concerning the entitlement to equal assistance of
the citizens from the funds of the *Bayt al-Māl.* Whereas Abū Bakr
entitled everyone to an equal share without any distinction on the
basis of seniority or service to Islam, ʿUmar took these factors
into consideration. Abū Bakr considered equal treatment as a basic
guideline for government policy leaving the differences in piety and
service to Islam a matter between man and his Creator.

During the two years of his rule (June 632 to August 634 AD) the
caliph Abū Bakr fought the wars of apostasy against the refusers of
zakāh, on which occasion the caliph decided to distribute the war
booty equally among the Muslims, regardless of early conversion to
Islam, kinship ties with the Prophet, or bravery in championing the
cause of Islam. This manner of treatment is reported to have encouraged many Arabs to join the Muslim army. Abū Bakr divided the
booty equally among the warriors and assigned to the state treasury
the one-fifth portion that was formerly given to the Prophet.[212]

Right to basic necessities subsumes the right to employment and
assistance to find a suitable occupation especially for those who are
able to work. This is because the *Sharīʿah* does not entitle support
for an able-bodied man who does not apply himself in order to earn
his living. The only right that such a person has is to be provided
with an employment opportunity, or the basic means, that would
enable him to work. This may mean purchase of equipment, a loan,
or a small investment capital that facilitates engagement in productive
work.[213] The fourth caliph ʿAlī has been quoted to have said in this
connection that poverty and affluence make all the difference to one's
belonging to a homeland—*waṭan*: 'Affluence, even if it is away from
one's homeland, turns that place into a homeland, and poverty in
one's homeland (can easily) turn one into a stranger.'[214]

When ʿUmar became caliph, he introduced a system of benefits and pensions as well as an army register (*Dīwān*) which was used as a basis for the determination of benefits. ʿUmar's system of distribution took certain factors into account: Those who had embraced Islam before the conquest of Mecca were favoured to those who converted afterwards. Service to Islam and affinity to the Prophet were also considered. ʿUmar has thus been quoted to have said that he could not treat equally those who fought with the Prophet and those who fought against him.

A side effect of instituting the *Dīwān* for army and pensions register might have been to concretise some of these divisions. Divisions based on blood ties were clearly recognised. Three genealogists were appointed to establish a hierarchy of pensions in basically two categories, one general and one particular. In the general category, the Arabs were divided into tribes and clans and their members were identified. The criteria applied in this category were early Islam, distinguished service to Islam, age and affinity to the Prophet. People were thus classified between the 'old' citizen and the 'new' citizen, both ranking higher than the non-Muslims.[215]

Muslim armies, camps, new cities and the army registers were organised along tribal lines, a factor that was reflected in turn in the relationship with non-Arab Muslims who accepted to become protected subjects (*mawālī*). This also meant another form of inter-Muslim differentiation. The population within the Muslim society before ʿUmar's death was thus classified into: Muslims from Muhājirūn, Muslims from the Anṣār, Meccan Muslims, Arab Muslims in general, non-Arab Muslims (*mawālī*), people of the Book (Jews and Christians), and those belonging to other creeds.[216] Commentators seem to be divided on the merits and demerits of these early distinctions and I do not propose to engage into further details. From the viewpoint of the material aspects of citizen's entitlement to welfare assistance, these developments did not change the basic principles which even the Caliph ʿUmar himself had recognized.

All citizens of an Islamic state are thus entitled to the basic necessities of life from the public treasury, which it must strive to provide to the extent of its capability. In the event where the public treasury runs out of funds, the state may impose additional taxes on the rich in order to provide the poor with the basic necessities and it becomes the duty of the rich to give it.[217]

It is certainly remarkable to note in this connection the report that toward the end of his ten years in office, the caliph ʿUmar b. al-

Khaṭṭāb had to make a special effort to find poor people to receive the *zakāh*. Later during the reign of the Umayyad caliph ʿUmar b. ʿAbd al-ʿAzīz (99–101 AH) it is reported that his officer in charge of *zakāh* in Africa informed him that the public treasury remained in surplus but there were no poor people in Africa that needed support. The caliph then ordered him to relieve the debtors of their debts, and this was done until there was no debtor left, and when the caliph was informed that there were still funds available, he ordered that they should be used for buying the slaves and setting them free.[218]

XIII. Duties of Citizens

Textbook writers on government and caliphate have spoken of two principal duties of the citizen namely obedience (*ṭāʿah*), and assistance (*naṣrah*), both of which are primarily political and relate to trust and loyalty between the ruler and ruled. Obedience alone can be non-committal and passive, but rendering assistance and support requires active involvement and good will. Each of these are discussed separately as follows:

(1) Obedience to the lawful government and *ulū al-amr* is a Qurʾānic duty (4:59) and a religious obligation which is primarily addressed to the believers. The *aḥādīth* on the subject of *ṭāʿah*, some of which we have already reviewed, are also conveyed in a language that takes the Muslims as their principal audience. The substance of this obligation is extended by analogy to non-Muslim citizens in all civic matters, which do not compromise their freedom to adhere to the religion of their choice. The analogy that is drawn between Muslims and non-Muslims in respect of obedience to the government remains valid to this day and is in harmony with the constitutional norm of equality that is now generally upheld under the constitutions and laws of Muslim countries. The head of state and the *ulū al-amr* that are elected by universal franchise and *bayʿah* of the citizens, both Muslims and non-Muslims, are consequently entitled to the obedience of the latter.[219] The basic evidence of the Qurʾān and *Sunnah* on obedience has already been reviewed and it will suffice merely to give some of the main points that are derived from that evidence. These are as follows:

(a) As it is a duty of the citizen, obedience is expected in all lawful matters. This is understood from the clear terms of the *ḥadīth* earlier quoted which requires obedience to the leader regardless as to the personal inclination, liking or disliking of the one to whom it is addressed. The only qualification to be noted is that the person in question must be in possession of his faculties and there be no lawful impediment to exonerate him from the duty of obedience.[220]

(b) When the government issues a law or command which involves a clear violation and sin under the *Sharīʿah*, the citizen is not under duty to obey it. The violation in question must, however, be self-evident and certain and not a result of interpretation or juristic *ijtihād*.[221]

(c) If the government sets itself openly and deliberately against the clear text of the Qur'ān and commits a flagrant transgression, it becomes guilty of infidelity whereupon it loses the right to rule and may be deposed by the electorate and all those who pledged allegiance to it. Further details on this issue can be found in chapter three of this volume on 'Accountability of Government in Islam'.

(d) In situations other than a clear declaration of unbelief (*kufr*) and renunciation of Islam, defiance of lawful authority must never be brought about by armed rebellion on the part of a minority within the community. For the Prophet has warned that 'He who raises arms against us ceases to be one of us,'[222]

من حمل علينا السلاح فليس منا

and another *ḥadīth* conveying the same message has it: 'He who unleashes his sword against us ceases to be one of us'. [223]

من سلّ علينا السيف فليس منا

Both of these *ḥadīths* are concerned with rebels and mutineers who challenge the authority of the lawful government without a valid cause.[224] Further detail on the community's right to depose a government that is guilty of a clear violation of the *Sharīʿah* are discussed below under accountability and impeachment. It may be noted in passing, however, that no such clear case of deposition of the ruler on grounds of *kufr* has been recorded in the history of Islamic government, although failed attempts of mutiny and rebellion, espoused with charges of transgression and even *kufr* against government leaders have been frequently encountered.

(2) The citizen's duty of giving assistance (*naṣrah*) to the lawful government is not altogether a formal requirement but one which is essentially inspired by loyalty and affection on the part of the populace. This is also to a large extent a matter of propriety and uprightness of leadership and its dedication to the service of the community. Since the citizen pledges *bayʿah* to the elected ruler, it becomes a duty to assist and support him to the best of his or her ability. This may take a variety of forms depending on the role that a citizen can play and the extent to which he or she can assist the leaders. Civil servants and members of the army or indeed those who are involved in development and welfare activities and enforcement may all be able to assist the leaders each in their own capacities. Muslim jurists have particularly emphasised two themes in relationship to *naṣrah*, one of which is sincere advice (*naṣīḥah*) which the citizen should generously give, as a matter of his or her own initiative, in all matters that promote peace, affection, cooperation and good work for the benefit of the community. *Naṣīḥah* should be given in the most discreet and tactful manner.[225]

Basic authority for assistance (*naṣrah*) is also found in the Qur'ān where the text enjoins cooperation (*taʿāwun*) (5:1) in good and beneficial works. Although the Qur'ānic text on *taʿāwun* applies to the ruler-and-ruled relationship, it is not confined to this context alone as cooperation in good works is also required at all levels among the believers and indeed all citizens, within and outside the framework of government. The constitution of Medina may be said to be the earliest authority on this. The Prophet admitted the Jews as full citizens of Medina and entitled them to assistance and protection, just as they were required also to contribute to the defence expenditures incurred by the state of Medina. All the signatories of this document were thus required to assist the government and one another in pursuit of the stated objectives of defending Medina against outside aggression and help with administering justice among its citizens.[226]

Assistance and cooperation (*naṣrah wa-taʿāwun*) also extends among the citizens and manifests an aspect of community relations in the context, for example, of neighbourhood (*jiwār*), something that is emphasized in the Qur'ān and *Sunnah*. There is much instruction in these sources on neighbourhood rights, which can be partly understood through the reading of the early history of Islam, especially in conjunction with the migration of the Prophet and his Companions to Medina. Those who came from Mecca to Medina, namely the *Muhājirūn* (migrants) took residence in Medina basically as guests and neighbours of the Madinan Muslims, the *Anṣār*. Later the Prophet added a new dimension to this by establishing the covenant of fraternity (*mu'ākhāt*) between the Migrants and Helpers. To refer to but one *ḥadīth* on the subject: 'Whoever believes in God and the Last Day, let him say something good or else remain silent; whoever believes in God and the Last Day, let him not annoy his neighbour; whoever believes in God and the Last Day, let him honour his guest.'[227]

من كـان يؤمن بالله واليوم الآخر فليقل خيرا أو ليصمت ومن كان يؤمن بالله واليوم الآخر فلا يؤذ جاره، ومن كان يؤمن بالله واليوم الآخر فليكرم ضيفه

The relationship of *jiwār* went beyond the barriers of religion especially with reference to the Muslims and Jews of Medina. Thus it is reported that when a servant of the renowned Companion Ibn ʿAbbās slaughtered a sheep, Ibn ʿAbbās told him to give some of the meat to their Jewish neighbour. Ibn ʿAbbās repeated this more than once until the servant turned around and said to Ibn ʿAbbās that he had said that several times, to which Ibn ʿAbbās replied that it was due to the fact that the Prophet himself had emphasised the neighbour's rights so much that 'we thought as if he was going to make him into an heir.'[228]

ما زال جبريل يوصيني بالجار حتى ظننت أنه سيورثه

Neighbours whether Muslim or non-Muslim are therefore entitled to the same rights and have the same obligation toward one another. This is especially relevant to the present day context, where Muslims often find themselves living in pluralist societies side by side with people from other faiths and cultures, both as fellow citizens and neighbours. Although the concept of neighbourhood is especially meaningful among fellow citizens, it is of wider application in that a neighbour may not even be a citizen, yet be entitled to the same special treatment that Islam has required for all neighbours.

The next context in which assistance is required is participation in *ḥisbah*, that is *amr bi'l-maʿrūf wa-nahy ʿan al-munkar* (promotion of good and prevention of evil). This is a broad Qur'ānic principle which in its general outline and purpose can relate to a variety of themes. What needs to be specified here perhaps is that *hisbah* requires the citizen to be vigilant and alert in promoting beneficial objectives, peace and justice in the community. The citizen is thus required to prevent, as far as he or she can, evil conduct, hostility and oppression wherever he or she sees it and whenever he or she is convinced that a certain initiative on his or her part, whether in words on in action, can prevent an imminent evil. When the citizen has taken that initiative and acted or spoken in support of a good cause, he would have fulfilled his civic and religious duty of giving assistance to the lawful government. By the same token the citizen is under duty to promote loyalty and affection toward the government and alert the latter of any immediate threat, attack, or act of treason that he or she might know about. Apart from the many Qur'ānic verses and *aḥādīth* on *hisbah*, the essence of *naṣrah* is also conveyed in the following *hadīth*.

ألا كلكم راع وكلكم مسؤل عن رعيته، فالأمام الذى على الناس راع وهو مسؤل عن رعيته، والرجل راع على أهل بيته وهو مسؤل عن رعيته

Everyone of you is like a shepherd and everyone of you is responsible for what is under his custody. The Imam is a custodian and he is responsible for his subjects, and a man is responsible for his family and what is in his custody, and every (married) woman is responsible for her husband's household and what is under her custody.[229]

XIV. Women and Citizenship

The *fiqh* literature does not articulate the position of women regarding citizenship and the issue is consequently dealt with, almost entirely, under statutory legislation. Immigration and citizenship laws in most Muslim countries are, on the whole, based on their western antecedents that also fall short of treating women equally in respect of citizenship rights. A question thus arises whether a woman can pass on her nationality and citizenship to her husband and child in the same way that the law entitles the husband and father to these privileges. The basic issue here is one of equality before the law, and the laws that currently prevail in most Muslim as well as non-Muslim countries do not offer equal citizenship rights to women. A woman under the prevailing laws is usually not entitled to pass on citizenship to her child nor to her husband.

Many commentators, including Salim el-Awa and Muḥammad Shahrūr, have spoken critically of this and called for a reform of the personal status laws of the Arab and Islamic countries wherein it is urged that women should be entitled to confer citizenship on her alien husband as well as her offspring. For as long as the law continues as it is without the necessary reform, according to Shahrūr, 'the male domination of the Arab societies will perpetuate itself and women will remain second class citizens.'[230] Shahrūr has also called for necessary legal reform that would entitle women to nomination and election to all government positions and full participation in the civic life of modern society. Salim el-Awa has drawn attention to the underdeveloped state of *fiqh* on citizenship especially with reference to women, and has himself attempted to discuss certain issues in the light of the textual guidelines of the Qur'ān and also the legal maxims of *fiqh*. I have referred to his work in the following paragraphs.

Looking at the issues from the *Sharīʿah* perspective, one would need to refer to the general norms of equality in the sources of *Sharīʿah*, simply because the issue has not been specifically addressed in the *fiqh* literature. The following Qur'ānic verses provide basic guidelines on equal rights for women:

> And they (women) have rights similar to those (of men) over them in an equitable manner. (2:228)

This is evidently a general declaration that entitles women to an equal regime of rights and obligations to those of men, particularly their husbands—as this is the immediate context of the verse—and other members of the community. Equality and similarity of rights and obligations to which men and women are entitled is the principal theme of this Qur'ānic declaration, and citizenship is naturally no exception. The reference to considerations of equity and kindness (*bi'l-maʿrūf*) in this verse probably means that the Qur'ān does not necessarily call for a mechanical regime of equality but equality that is fair and meaningful and in keeping with the spirit, if not the letter, of that approach.

The Qur'ān also provides:

للرجال نصيب مما اكتسبوا وللنساء نصيب مما اكتسبن

Men are entitled to what they earn and women are entitled to what they earn. (4:32)

Although the reference to earning/acquisition (*al-kasb*) is commonly seen to be inclusive of all earning, whether material or spiritual, what is not commonly seen, however, is that one's offspring is also a part of one's *kasb*, or what a person has acquired and begotten. If the father is entitled to the transfer of his nationality through the blood tie to his child, then the mother stands in precisely the same position and her blood tie to her offspring is at least as strong as that of the father. The mother should therefore be entitled to the same right in respect of citizenship. This is also Salim el-Awa's reading of the verse under review. Statutory legislation in Muslim countries should therefore observe this and ensure equal treatment for women in the matter of citizenship.[231]

With reference to the mother's relationship to her offspring, the Qur'ān further provides the following guideline:

لاتضارّ والدة بولدها ولا مولود له بولده

The mother may not be made to suffer (nor be treated unfairly) on account of her child, nor should he to whom the child is born (be made to suffer) because of his child. (2:233)

The underlying tone of this verse is also one of equality since the kinship tie (*al-ṣilah*) of each of the parents to their child is one and equal in every respect, the law should therefore treat it as such. Notwithstanding the fact that the verse occurs in the context of matrimony and financial support for the child, the concern for fair and equal treatment of both of the parents is clearly upheld therein. 'It is obligatory that any legislation that proceeds from here and regulates the consequences of this relationship treat the man and woman from the position of equality, for it would otherwise stand in violation of the essence of Qur'ānic equality between them.'[232]

In yet another verse the Qur'ān speaks the same language of equality. This is with reference, in particular, to the weaning of the child where the text recommends that this should be determined by the parents' joint decision:

فإن أرادا فصالا عن تراض منهما وتشاور فلا جناح عليهما
وإن أردتم أن تسترضعوا أولادكم فلا جناح عليكم

If they decide to wean the child by mutual consent after consultation, it is no sin for them to do so. And if you wish to give your children out to a wet nurse, that is also not a transgression. (2:233)

It was customary among the Arabs, especially the affluent among them, to have a wet nurse to take care of the child as from early age. This had sometimes meant, as in the case of the young Muhammad himself, for the child to be taken away from the parental home and be brought up by a foster mother. The point here is that the text permitted taking these decisions on the basis of mutual agreement and consultation between the parents. The question then arises as to why should the same participatory manner of decision-making not apply in other family matters. Citizenship laws that currently prevail treat the parents differently in respect of nationality and citizenship they might be able to pass on to their offspring, and our argument here is that both the parents should enjoy equal rights in this respect.[233]

Based on the assumption that the *Sharīʿah* norms of equality and justice permit the mother to enjoy equal rights in citizenship matters, a number of legal maxims of *fiqh* can also be brought in to substantiate the tenor of that call. The legal maxims (*qawāʿid kulliyyah*) that are discussed in this connection appear in the *Mujallat al-Aḥkām al-ʿAdliyyah*, which is an influential source of Ḥanafī law that was until recently the applied law of many Muslim countries of the Middle East. A select number of these maxims are reviewed in the following paragraphs:

(1) When the original is nullified, recourse may be had to the substitute (*idhā baṭal al-aṣl yuṣāru ilā 'l-badal*).[234] The mother may, in other words, be seen as the nearest substitute of the father: The *Sharīʿah* often assigns a ruling to a certain issue and incident that is duly applied to them. Should there be a case, however, when the ruling in question cannot be applied, the jurist may apply that ruling to the next nearest situation. Here it is assumed that both the *fiqh* rules and statutory legislation entitle only the father to pass his identity to his child. The *fiqh* rules generally proceed on the assumption that the child takes his identity and lineage through the male link primarily from the father. This is also upheld in the *Sharīʿah* law of inheritance wherein the father-child relationship is the strongest tie in the entire network of family relations.

With reference to citizenship, the original ruling here entitles the father to pass on his nationality to his offspring. But if this becomes unfeasible for some reason such as uncertainty or ignorance about the father's nationality or when the father happens to have no nationality, then a transfer is due to the nearest substitute, which would be to allow the mother's nationality be passed on to the child.[235]

(2) Recourse may also be had to the rules of necessity and hardship: In the event where the child of a mixed marriage cannot inherit the citizenship of the father nor can the native mother pass her status to the child, hardship and loss of rights would be the likely result. A way out must therefore be found by recourse to the relevant maxims of *fiqh* which pertain to necessity (*ḍarūrah*), or hardship (*ḥājah*).

According to a leading maxim of *fiqh* 'necessity makes the unlawful lawful (*al-ḍarūrāt tubīḥ al-maḥzūrāt*).'[236] The obvious meaning of this maxim is in need of no analysis, but the circumstances of its application may need to be carefully evaluated. In individual cases of personal distress, for example, where the normal rules do not offer a fair solution, the law permits relief on grounds of necessity. In the case of a child who cannot inherit the nationality either of his father or mother the desired solution might require for the child to be allowed to acquire his mother's nationality.

Moreover, the law itself gives rise to problems by disallowing the mother's nationality to inhere in her offspring. Given the basic permissibility of marriage over and above the barrier of nationality, the likelihood is that over a period of time there will be a large number of children that face problems over nationality and citizenship. This is the case under both the *Sharī'ah* and modern law which allow inter-marriage among individuals of different nationalities, and if the law does not in the meantime allow the mother to transfer her nationality to her offspring, the seeds of a problem situation are sown by the law itself, which must mean that a way out of the problem must be found. The following two maxims of *fiqh* would once again be relevant in this situation: (1) 'hardship begets facility' (*al-mashaqqatu tujlab al-taysīr*); and (2) 'when rigidity sets in, a way out of it must be found' (*idhā ḍāq al-amr ittasa'a*).[237]

(3) According to yet another legal maxim 'the affairs of government are judged by reference to benefit and *maṣlaḥah*'.[238] Public good or *maṣlaḥah* is thus the criterion of legitimacy in the governance of public affairs. Government decisions in the sphere of administration and decisions that affect the rights and duties of the people must refer to the public interest. A law that fails this test must therefore be amended to the extent that it realises the people's *maṣlaḥah*. El-Awa

has aptly observed in reference primarily to Egypt that all legislation which differentiates between men and women in respect of citizenship, entitling one and disentitling the other, to pass on citizenship to their offspring, actually fail the test of *maṣlaḥah*. They are 'prejudicial laws—*nuṣūṣ ḍārrah*—which do not secure any benefit and must therefore be nullified.'[239] Contemporary *ijtihād* in *fiqh* must seek to establish equality between men and women and entitle both to the right to transfer citizenship to their offspring.

XV. Conclusion And Reform Proposals

Citizenship is an evidently important and yet problematic area in the general scheme of fundamental rights and liberties. It has gained greater significance since the advent of the nation-state in Europe and its eventual acceptance by the Muslim countries. One of the problematics to note at the outset is that immigration and nationality laws that are now in force generally fail to address issues of citizenship in the spirit of harmony and cooperation among people. General custom, or *ʿurf*, which is a recognised proof of Islamic law, can now be said to have accepted the nation-state, just as it has also been ratified by the constitutions and national charters of these countries. Yet neither in European thought nor in the works of Muslim jurists can one find a clear recognition of citizenship as a fundamental right in itself. This may be due partly to the fact that citizenship is not a monolithic concept, for it tends to comprise and subsume a number of other rights such as the right to domicile, work, education, welfare, and so forth. Juristic discourse on fundamental rights and liberties has tended to address some of the rights that are conferred as a result of citizenship, but citizenship itself has not been identified as a basic right of the individual. Notwithstanding the fact that modern constitutions tend to provide guidelines on citizenship, they still fall short of recognising it as a basic right as such. Since citizenship concerns not only the citizens but also the aliens, it has been treated primarily as a privilege and a political subject more than a fundamental right. We call for an adjustment and recognition of citizenship as a basic right.

At the dawn of the twenty-first century one can observe three phenomena that bring into question the basic notion of nation-state and its historical significance. Firstly the crisis of the post-colonial states in the South, secondly the disintegration of the Soviet Union and Yugoslavia, and thirdly, the emergence of a supranational entity in the countries of the European Union. These three sets of facts are not always in harmony with one another, yet they all point to certain fault lines in the nation-state idea and its failure to accommodate the desire for greater cooperation and unity among people.

The anachronistic, and sometimes, discriminatory content of nationality laws of our time call for reappraisal and adjustment in favour of a real affinity between 'human rights' and 'citizens rights'. For it is doubtful whether a meaningful affinity of the kind can be established in the face of a continued adherence to the hollow notion of national sovereignty over and above the stressing humanitarian call of respect for human rights.

The distinction between the citizen and non-citizen, the national and the alien is the contemporary form of discrimination in rights between individuals within the borders of national states. What we witness today is a new era of exclusivist nationalism in Europe that expresses itself in local rhetoric and relies on ethnicity, culture and religion which present a serious setback to human progress.

The present study assumes nevertheless the validity, on an *ad hoc* basis, at least, of the nation-state as a substitute to the earlier notions of *dār al-Islām* and *dār al-ḥarb*, which seems to have historically dominated Islamic thought on the subject. But the assumption here has been invoked more by necessity rather than choice, simply because the nation-state formula itself is problematic as it tends to clash with many of the recognised rights of the individual in *Sharīʿah* as well as the wider levels of unity and cooperation among people. The right to work, for example, is recognised in *Sharīʿah* for every Muslim, indeed every individual, but the nation-state tends to confine it only to its own nationals. Does it at all sound right to disallow a Muslim, or anyone for that matter, of the right to earn a living, or to deny him or her the right to continued residence in a country or place, even after having lived there for many years? This is merely to point out that a certain tension remains between the relatively more open approach of *Sharīʿah* and the more restrictive attitude that underlines the nation-state. More research effort needs to be undertaken to address these and other relevant issues on citizenship from both the *Sharīʿah* and nationalist perspectives.

As noted earlier, the *dār al-Islām–dār al-ḥarb* concept has no clear origin and the contemporary generation of Muslims is not necessarily bound by it. Today the world is home to over fifty independent Muslim states, not just one big political entity that could, in political terms, be described as *dār al-Islām*. The complex network of international treaties and bilateral agreements that now exist between Muslim and non–Muslim countries cannot accommodate the existence in concept or in reality of *dār al-ḥarb* which is rooted in the dubious idea of accepting war as a normal state of relations with the rest of the world.

Yet there is cause for further reflection as to how nationalism is reasserting itself as a result of advancements in globalisation, and the European Union at the expense often of cultural minorities. With reference to globalisation, Zainab Badawi noted that globalisation blurs national boundaries, but in the meantime impresses upon people the need to retreat into their own sense of self and look for past assurances in order to validate themselves. Racist groups, with names such as racial harmony, and First Amendment Purists, One Nation Party, National Front etc., are making skilful use of the internet to propagate their exclusivist views and prejudices all over again.[240]

With regard to the European Union, one hears of enlargement of this Union toward the development of a super state in Europe. This too is evoking the reaction 'I want to be French, German, British, etc.,' rather than European and 'a crude sense of nationalism' is again reasserting itself. A somewhat aggressive feature of this kind of nationalism is manifested in its demand for cultural assimilation as a basis of social bond: power should only be in the hands of this national culture.

Badawi urges that the EU countries must move on from a definition of national identity which is based on mainstream culture and relegates minorities to junior partners. The idea of multiple identities is gaining acceptance. A national identity which appeals to constitutional patriotism based on values rather than culture or ethnicity could solve many problems. A person can be British or French as long as they accept a constitution which is based on 'human rights and democratic values.' Questions of culture, ethnicity, descent and race are here to stay and they are not neutral ideas. Turning these into a pluralistic identity is a challenge, not only for governments but for all members of society, who must all be involved, if the challenge were to be successfully met.[241]

Having discarded the idea of *dār al-ḥarb* that had been a stumbling block in the way of constructing a sound theoretical approach to citizenship in Islamic law, I believe that Islamic law provides a set of general principles relating to citizenship that encourage flexibility and openness. I attribute this mainly to the humanitarian outlook of the Qur'ān and *Sunnah* that designate mankind as God's vicegerent and custodian of the earth who should establish a just order and advance harmony among people. The Islamic ideals of human dignity, equality, justice and cooperation in good works tend to view the *homo sapiens* as a single entity without recognition of nationality and race or of divisive factors that would obstruct these values or decry the natural freedom of the individual regarding his choice of residence. Having said this, however, considerations of a judicious policy within the general framework of *siyāsah sharʿiyyah* may still be utilised to determine a policy framework that is beneficial to all concerned, without however, violating the basic ideals of equality and justice as are expounded in the sources of Islam.

I now proceed to discuss a reform proposal that seeks to advance the prospects of unity and closer cooperation among Muslim countries.

In an Epilogue to his 1926 Sorbonne doctoral dissertation, *Le Califat*, an Arabic edition of which appeared under the title *Fiqh al-Khilāfah*,[242] ʿAbd al-Razzāq al-Sanhūrī (d. 1971) wrote about the future developments of the Muslim world in the light of his understanding of the historical caliphate. Sanhūrī distinguished two types of caliphates, namely *al-khilāfah al-ṣaḥīḥah*, the valid caliphate, which lasted only about three decades following the demise of the Prophet, and al-*khilāfah al-nāqiṣah*, or deficient caliphate, which continued in one form or other until its final abolition in Turkey in 1924. Sanhūrī's distinction was a reflection of the disunity that befell the *ummah* and its consequent division into a number of political entities following the collapse of the caliphate. It is in this framework that Sanhūrī discussed the prospects of reunification of the Muslim world within the rubric of what he called *Munaẓẓamat al-Jāmiʿah al-Sharqiyyah*, Organization of Oriental Society (OOS), which sought to establish greater cooperation among its member states.

Sanhūrī explained the choice of this name and its deliberate exclusion of any religious designations, such as 'Islamic' or 'Islamiyyah' in that the OOS represented not only the Muslim but also non-Muslim communities and individuals. Sanhūrī did not propose a departure from the *Sharīʿah*, yet he suggested that 'implementation of the *Sharīʿah* at the present time must be such that it ensures complete equality for non-Muslim compatriots (*al-muwāṭinīn ghayr al-muslimīn*) with their Muslim counterparts, while in the meantime, nothing is taken away from their freedom to practice the religion of their choice.'[243]

With regard to the Muslims themselves, Sanhūrī wrote that here too 'it is not feasible to enforce the *Sharīʿah* without some necessary adjustments of its rules concerning economic and property matters as well as those that may seem at odds with the demands of modern civilisation . . . The *fiqh* needs to be adjusted in two stages, preparatory, and legislative.'

Some aspects of Sanhūrī's detailed proposal that he articulated in no less than 70 pages, now seem to be dated, in which case I have suggested suitable alternatives while pursuing basically the same objectives which prompted Sanhūrī to write his blueprint of an organizational structure for the Muslim world. I do this with a limited purpose, however, which is to suggest prospective solutions to some difficult citizenship-related issues. Sanhūrī's main framework was political organisation and unity without specifying citizenship as such, but since my more specific theme also necessitates a reference to the wider framework, I shall refer to some of his ideas.

Sanhūrī states that political unity of the Muslim world in a centralised authority or *khilāfah* was no longer feasible in view of the multiplicity of nation-states. To this he adds that there was in any case no juristic requirement from the *fiqh* perspective for a caliphate as such. Yet he is convinced, nevertheless, of the need for some form of unity of Muslim states while acknowledging their autonomous status therein.

Sanhūrī emphasises a graduated and piecemeal approach to unity, with which I also concur. A piecemeal approach might suggest that one should specify a few basic themes for unity and policy coordination, and use them as stepping stones toward wider coordination in other areas. I propose to take up labour relations and employment of workers as one such theme to be followed by policy coordination in other areas. Citizenship is not an easy topic for initial cooperation but some suggestions may be advanced for Muslim countries to create a category of citizenship, or of recognition of residency rights, for individuals from the OOS member states to enjoy certain benefits within the laws and territories of its member countries.

Sanhūrī's overall proposal aims at the creation of a deficient caliphate that puts in place only certain elements of a unified government, the elements that are reflective of the current needs and realities of the Muslim societies. This is seen as a temporary and transitional phase toward political unity and the ultimate purpose is the development of a supranational government that may evolve through greater cooperation and desire for unity.[244]

Sanhūrī also suggests that representative bodies should be created and entrusted with powers to develop cooperation in political and religious matters while recommending that political and religious affairs should be dealt with by separate forums. This is because history has shown that concentration of political and religious authority in one hand or organisation leads to domination of politics over religion. Sanhūrī thus proposes the creation of a Religious Affairs Committee (*Hay'at al-shu'ūn al-dīniyyah*), a General Assembly (*al-Jam'iyyah al-'āmmah li'l-hay'ah*), and a Supreme Council (*al-majlis al-a'lā li'l-hay'ah*).

Members and representatives to each of these are to be selected by the member states and by organisations for Muslim minorities. The General assembly members are selected by their governments on an annual basis. Whereas the General Assembly is proposed to be a permanent body, the Supreme Council sits periodically on a number of occasions in a year at the headquarters of the Organisation of Oriental Society. The Supreme Council may have a lesser number of members compared to that of the General Assembly, but it should have various committees on financial affairs, the *hajj* committee, education and *da'wah* (religious affairs) committee, foreign relations committee, and internal affairs committee.

The president of the religious affairs committee is to be nominated by the Supreme Council and approved by the General Assembly. He should have no political functions and his role should be confined to religious matters until there is greater political coordination and unity among members, in which case, matters of legal concern and *Sharī'ah* related matters may also be entrusted to him. The President of Supreme Council is a *de facto* Caliph who only exercises jurisdiction in religious affairs and takes decisions on the advice of the Supreme Council. This is the basic outline of Sanhūrī's plan.

The whole of the OOS is designed to promote cooperation among Muslims and act as a liaison among them, and pave the way toward their greater unity.[245] It is then added that the OOS should be accorded a juridical status and a corporate personality in the capacity of a state which is enabled to conduct its own international and diplomatic relations. Sanhūrī adds that the proposed organisation might function better if it has a parallel national organisation that is set up for the purpose of liaison and preparatory work at the national level.

Sanhūrī has much to say concerning the type of response that his proposed organisation might invoke from western countries of

Europe and beyond. The general pattern that he anticipated is one of cooperation for mutual benefit. He recommends that the OOS should also be a member of the UN (League of Nations in Sanhūrī's time) and should liaise with the world body and see it as a parent organization.[246]

I do not propose to engage in further details, but it is important to note that from cooperation in religious and *Sharīʿah* matters, the OOS should aim at wider levels of economic and political integration. Careful preparatory work would be needed to facilitate this. To this end, Sanhūrī has suggested the creation, in every member state, of a political party to promote political unity and prepare a detailed agenda on the steps that may need to be taken. Formal and informal consultation between the national parliaments as well as conferences and discussion groups should be set up for the purpose.[247]

It is now in order to mention briefly that a number of new organisations have come about since Sanhūrī made these proposals. The Organisation of Islamic Conference (OIC) is perhaps the most extensive in terms of membership as virtually every Muslim country is currently a member of it. The OIC has admittedly not become as prominent and efficient as per expectation, yet it is fully aware of this and may regenerate itself so as to face the challenges of greater cooperation among its member states. The OIC has an Islamic Fiqh Academy in Jeddah which organises periodical meetings of *Sharīʿah* experts from member countries and pass verdicts on issues of common interest. The OIC foreign ministers also meet periodically, often preceding the OIC summit in which deliberations are conducted at the level of heads of states.

It is perhaps possible to work within this framework but to suggest certain changes along the lines that Sanhūrī had envisaged. The necessary organisational structure and reform is a matter of agreement by the OIC summit. But a three-tiered plan of cooperation in religio-legal, economic and political matters may be taken up and planned such that one phase of cooperation leads to the next, eventually culminating into a greater unity of the kind perhaps that is currently underway within the framework of European Union.

Although the OIC shares within itself much similarity in culture and socio-economic econditions, in contrast to EU, it is a more het-erogenous mix of countries that includes categories of low, medium and high-income groups and diverse political structures. The one common denominator that can bring the OIC member countries under one umbrella is the factor of religious unity. Religion as a force of cohesion also derives much of its strength from common social and cultural patterns. Yet the various integration schemes among the OIC have met with difficulties due to divergent interests and membership of regional organisations. More than two-thirds of the OIC countries are associated with some form of regional and sub-regional economic cooperation pacts. The African and Arab groups of the OIC have co-operation units of their own. The OIC charter of 1972 emphasises economic cooperation to help individual members accelerate their productive capacities. Much work needs to be undertaken to promote greater coordination and cohesion. This would, however, require 'a firm political commitment on the part of the member states of the OIC, expressing their political will and a common understanding on the coverage, extent, mechanism and stages of implementation...'[248]

Tawfīq al-Shāwī wrote in his 2001 publication:

> I earnestly hope that cancellation of visa requirements among the OIC member countries becomes a priority agenda and objective of this organisation. It is necessary in my view that the OIC member countries do not consider Muslim individuals as aliens regardless of their country of origin or nationality. The OIC should facilitate for Muslims entering these countries all the opportunities they extend to their own citizens.

Al-Shāwī also quotes ʿAbd al-Qādir ʿAwdah with whom he concurs in saying that Islam entitles the Muslims to enter and reside freely in the Muslim territories.[249] These views are in consonance also with the Universal Islamic Declaration of Human Rights (1981) which provided the following in its section on 'Right to Freedom of Movement and Residence':

> a) In view of the fact that the World of Islam is veritably *Ummah Islamia*, every Muslim shall have the right to freely move in and out of any Muslim country (Art. XXIII).

Al-Shāwī is under no illusion as to the current state of the *ummah*. Citizenship in the world we live, he says, is a state matter that is regulated by political rather than religious considerations. The state is the unit of organisation at present and the *dār al-Islām* of the past has been dismembered and replaced by territorial units. The basic problem in all of this stemmed, al-Shāwī adds, from the fact that citizenship as a concept was unfamiliar to our *fiqh* scholars and the notions of *dār al-Islām* and *dār al-ḥarb* seemed suitable, even convenient at a time when the Islamic empire was a dominant world power. The nation state as a unit of organisation, and citizenship as a basic framework of identity and relationships have replaced those earlier concepts. The *ummah* remains nevertheless to be a wider framework of religious fraternity among Muslims regardless of their nationality and place of residence.[250]

The nation state is evidently here to stay for the foreseeable future. If progress were to be projected along the three-tiered structure as mentioned in al-Sanhūrī's proposals, matters pertaining to rights of residence and citizenship would be considered at any stage of cooperation among the member states. The project on migration and citizenship would need to be carefully drafted and prepared with a specified framework. This should preferably be based not only on the religious following of individuals, but on a set of attributes that observe the criteria of equality and justice as well as due regard for socio-economic conditions of each member community and state.

Due to a variety of new developments, including the aftermath of September 11, 2001, Muslim unitarian sentiment has gained ground and the belief that they need to be united if they are to influence world events in their favour has strengthened. At a time when the harsh realities of disunity, diversity and differential interests still seem to be predominant among the Muslim countries, the sentiment of unity and affiliation to the wider *ummah* remains nevertheless as an ideal that cannot be ignored.

NOTES

1. Cf. Taqī al-Dīn al-Nabhānī, *Muqaddimāt al-Dustūr*, 23–26.

2. Cf. Muhammad Hamidullah, *The Muslim Conduct of State*, 111ff.

3. Mawdūdī, *The Islamic Law and Constitution*, 245–253.

4. Haitham Manna, *Citizenship in Arab Islamic History*, 10.

5. Id.

6. Cf. Manna, *Citizenship*, 92.

7. Ibid., 82.

8. Alwani, 'Naturalization and the Rights of Citizens,' *AJISS* ii (1994), 73.

9. Cf. Nawaf Salam, 'The Emergence of Citizenship,' 125–126.

10. Cf. Partington, 'Citizenship and Housing,' in Robert Blackburn, ed., *Rights of Citizenship*, London: Mansell, 1993, 124; Haitham Manna, *Citizenship in Arab Islamic History*, 18.

11. Keith Ewing, 'Citizenship and Employment,' in Blackburn, ed. , *Rights of Citizenship*, 99.

12. Waqar Ahmad and Charles Husband, 'Religious Identity, Citizenship and Welfare. The Case of Muslims in Britain,' *AJISS*, vol. 10 (1993), 216.

13. Cf. Nawaf Salam, 'The Emergence of Citizenship,' 127–128 referring to the views of T.H. Marshal, and Bryan Turner among others.

14. Oppenheim, *International Law*, 645.

15. Id., vol. I, 642. See also Haitham Manna, *Citizenship*, 82.

16. Waqar Ahmad and Charles Husband, 'Religious Identity,' 218.

17. Id., 217.

18. Id.

19. Cf. Manna, *Citizenship*, 92.

20. Id., 91.

21. Ahmad and Husband, 'Religious Identity', 218.

22. Id., 219.

23. 'Abd Allāh al-Basyūnī, *Naẓariyyat al-Dawlah*, 25–26.

24. Manna, *Citizenship*, 83.

25. As quoted in Salam, 'The Emergence of Citizenship,' 138–139.

26. Quoted in Id., 140.

27. Cf. Haitham Manna, *Citizenship*, 8–9.

28. Id., 11.

29. Ibn Mājah, *Sunan Ibn Mājah*, *ḥadīth* no. 3108.

30. Enayat, *Modern Islamic Political Thought*, 128.

31. Id.

32. Enayat, *Modern Islamic Political Thought*, 127.

33. Mawdūdī, *Islamic Law and Constitution*, 246.

34. Bukhārī, *Ṣaḥīḥ* (Khan's tr.), v, 155, *ḥadīth* 239.

35. Rosenthal, 'I am you': Individual piety and society in Islam' in Amin Banani and Speros Vryonis, *Individualism and Conformity in Classical Islam*, 53.

36. S.D. Goitien as quoted in Salam, 'The Emergence of Citizenship,' 13.

37. Cf. Salam, 'The Emergence of Citizenship,' 131.

38. Joseph Schacht, 'Islamic Law in Contemporary States,' *The American Journal of Comparative Law*, 19, also quoted in Salam 'The Emergence of Citizenship,' 131.

39. Hamidullah, *Muslim Conduct of State*, 111.

40. Id., 111.

41. Id., 130.

42. Al-Sayed, *The Social Ethics*, 220; Mūsā, *al-Islām wa'l-Ḥayāt*, 177.

43. El-Affendi, *'I'ādat al-Naẓar fi'l-Mafhūm al-Taqlīdī li'l-Jamā'ah al-Siyāsiyyah fi'l-Islām: Muslim am Muwāṭin?*, 144.

44. Bukhārī, *Ṣaḥīḥ al-Bukhārī* (Khan's tr.), iv, 102.

45. al-Saffār, 'al-Waṭan wa'l-Muwāṭanah,' 19.

46. Id., 111.

47. Id., 130.

48. For a discussion of the business laws of Saudi Arabia see Nabil Saleh, 'Company Legislation in the Gulf: Recent Developments,' in ed. H.L. Ruttley and Chibli Mallat, *Commercial Law in the Middle East*, 92–103.

49. In all appearance, the Nationality Ordinance (*Niẓām al-Jinsiyyah*) of Saudi Arabia 1974 contains (under Article (9)) terms which are not very different from its parallel regulations in other Muslim countries. Saudi nationality may thus be conferred on a person who is adult and sane, and a person of good character, who has no record of criminal conviction for six years at least prior to his application and 'has obtained a permanent resident status in the Kingdom of Saudi Arabia for a minimum of five years in accordance with the special regulations that lay down certain requirements.' It seems that official policy makes fulfilment of this last condition considerably more restrictive than the legal text would appear to suggest.

50. See for the text and summary of the nationality laws of a number of Muslim countries Aḥmad Ḥamad, *Fiqh al-Jinsiyyah*, 280ff.

51. Hamidullah, *Muslim Conduct of State*, 129–130.

52. Zuḥaylī, *Ḥuqūq al-Insān*, 338.

53. Id., 130.

54. Id., 131.

55. Cf. Basyūnī, 'Abd Allāh, *Naẓariyyāt al-Dawlah*, 28; Ramadan, *Islamic Law*, 165; Zuḥaylī, *al-Fiqh al-Islāmī*, VI, 447.

56. Zaydān, *Aḥkām Ahl al-Dhimmah wa'l-Musta'minīn*, 27; al-Ghannūshī, *Ḥuqūq al-Muwāṭanah*, 57; Hamidullah, *The Muslim Conduct of State*, 118.

57. See for details on *siyāsah shar'iyyah* my article 'Siyāsah Shar'iyyah or The Policies of Islamic Government,' *AJISS*, 6 (1989), 59–81.

58. Ramadan, *Islamic Law*, 165–166.

59. Cf. Basyūnī, 'Abd Allāh, *Naẓariyyāt al-Dawlah*, 28–29; Hamidullah, *The Muslim Conduct of State*, 202; Zuḥaylī, *al-Fiqh al-Islāmī*, IV, 435.

60. Zuḥaylī, *al-Fiqh al-Islāmī*, VI, 434; 'Awdah, *al-Tashrī' al-Jinā'ī*, I, 277; Khadduri, *War and Peace*, 164.

61. Cf. Al-Ghannūshī, *Ḥuqūq al-Muwāṭanah,* 61; Fatḥī Osmān, *Al-Fikr al-Qānūnī al-Islāmī*, 270.

62. Bukhārī, *Ṣaḥīḥ al-Bukhārī*, IV, 102; Abū Dāwūd, *Mukhtaṣar Sunan Abī Dāwūd*, *ḥadīth* 195; Zuḥaylī, *al-Fiqh al-Islāmī*, VI, 432.

63. Abū Yūsuf, *Kitāb al-Kharāj*, 244; Zuḥaylī, *al-Fiqh al-Islāmī*, VI, 432.

64. Cf Zuḥaylī, *al-Fiqh al-Islāmī*, VI, 433; Khadduri, *War and Peace*, 168.

65. Cf. Mawdūdī, *Islamic Law and Constitution*, 181.

66. Zuḥaylī, *Ḥaqq al-Ḥurriyyah*, 147. See also Khallāf, *al-Siyāsah al-Shar'iyyah*, 35.

67. Al-Sarakhsī, *Sharḥ al-Siyar al-Kabīr*, IV, 115; Hamidullah, *The Muslim Conduct of State*, 119.

68. This was the subject of a lecture delivered in London by Salim el-Awa, 'al-Muwāṭanah Hiya Asās al-ʿIlāqa Bayn al-Muslimīn wa-Ghayrihim,' *Islam 21* (no. 20, Dec. 1999), 11.

69. Id., 11.

70. Cf. Balādhurī, *Futūḥ al-Buldān*; Zuhaylī, *Ḥaqq al-Ḥurriyyah*, 146.

71. Id., 12; Ṭabarī, *Tārīkh*, IV, 229.

72. Id., 12; Balādhurī, *Futūḥ al-Buldān*, 136.

73. Id., 12.

74. Quoted in al-Bishrī, *Bayn al-Islām wa'l-ʿUrūbah*, 92.

75. Id., 95.

76. Cf. Kramer 'Dhimmis or Citizens' in ed. Nielsen, *The Christian-Muslim Frontier*, 37–38.

77. Shukri Mabkhut & Hasan Osman, *Maʿ Muḥammad al-Ṭālibī: ʿAyāl Allāh*, 111–112. The book compiles a series of interviews with al-Ṭālibī. The reference to Khomeini's book is to page 31 of Khomeini's book.

78. Manna, *Citizenship in Arab Islamic History*, 55.

79. Abd al-Malik al-Sayed, *The Social Ethics of Islam*, 185.

80. Ḥasan Ibrāhīm Ḥasan, *al-Nuẓum al-Islāmiyyah*, 310.

81. Id., 311; Manna, *Citizenship*, 54.

82. Manna, *Citizenship*, 39.

83. Ḥasan Ibrāhīm Ḥasan, *al-Nuẓum al-Islāmiyyah*, 311; al-Sayyid, *The Social Ethics of Islam*, 184.

84. Ḥasan Ibrāhīm Ḥasan, *al-Nuẓum al-Islāmiyyah*, 312. The Kharijites considered Imamate the right of any Muslim Arab, non-Arab, black or white provided he obtained the homage or *bayʿah* of the populace. Some of them, especially the Shabibiyah, also sanctioned the Imamate of women. Many of the Kharijites betrothed their Arab women relatives to the non-Arab *mawāli*.

85. al-Sayed, *The Social Ethics*, 186.

86. See for detail Ḥasan Ibrāhīm Ḥasan, *al-Nuẓum al-Islāmiyyah*, 313–314.

87. Cf. al-Qurṭubī, *Tafsīr*, II, 548.

88. Id., II, 301.

89. Kāsānī, *Badāʾiʿ*, VI, 252; ʿAwdah, *al-Tashrīʿ al-Jināʾī*, I, 278.

90. Cf. Ramadan, *To Be a European Muslim*, 123.

91. Al-Ḥuṣarī, *al-Dawlah wa-Siyāsat al-Ḥukm*, 268–269.

92. Ramadan, *To Be a European Muslim*, 127.

93. Abou el-Fadl, 'Islamic Law and Muslim Minorities,' 161.

94. Al-Nabhānī, *Muqaddimāt al-Dustūr*, 23.

95. Quoted in Siddiqi, *Modern Reformist Thought*, 90–91.

96. Cf. Ramadan, *To Be a European Muslim*, 120.

97. Id., 121.

98. Ṭāhā Jābir al-ʿAlwānī, 'Globalisation: Centralisation not Globalism,' *AJISS*, 15 (1998), viii.

99. Al-Qaraḍāwī, *Fiqh al-Awlawiyyāt*, 91–92.

100. For detail see Kenichi Ohmae, *The End of the Nation State: The Rise of Regional Economics* (New York: The Free Press, 1995).

101. See for a general account Normal Daniel, *Islam and the West: The Making of an Image*; Ansari and Esposito eds, *Muslims and the West*, 250ff.

102. Cf. Sharaiyra, *Right and Freedom*, 208.

103. Cf. Manna, *Citizenship*, 81–85; Ibn ʿĀshūr, *Al-Ḍamīr waʾl-Tashrīʿ*, 89f.

104. Quoted in Ṭāriq al-Bishrī, *Bayn al-Jāmiʿah al-Dīniyyah waʾl-Jāmiʿah al-Waṭaniyyah fiʾl-Fikr al-Siyāsī*, 7.

105. Id., 8, quoting Qaraḍāwī, *Ḥatmiyyat al-Ḥall al-Islāmī*, 138.

106. al-Ghazālī, *Min Hunā Naʿlam*, 53.

107. Cf. Ghazālī, *Min Hunā Naʿlam*, 53, 106 and *passim*.

108. Al-Bishrī, *Bayn al-Jāmiʿah*, 15–16, summarising Ḥasan Duh, *Ḥiwār Maʿ al-Ajyāl*.

109. Id., 17, summarising ʿAbd al-Muttaʿāl al-Saʿīdī, *Min Ayna Nabda'?*

110. Id., 18.

111. Al-Sayed, *The Social Ethics of Islam*, 260.

112. Ṭāriq al-Bishrī, *Bayn al-Jāmiʿah*, 19.

113. Id., 21.

114. Al-Sayed, *Social Ethics of Islam*, 260.

115. Quoted in al-Bishrī, *Bayn al-Jāmiʿah*, 24.

116. Cf. Gulap, 'Islamism and Kurdish Nationalism,' in Tamara Sonn, ed., *Islam and the Question of Minorities*, 94.

117. Momin, 'Pluralism and Multiculturalism,' *AJISS* 18 (2001), 141.

118. Id., 102.

119. Id., 104.

120. Id., 103–104.

121. Cf. Ḥasan al-Saffār, 'al-Waṭan waʾl-Muwāṭanah,' 19; see also Mūsā, *al-Islām waʾl-Ḥayāt*, 175f.

122. Constitution of Medina (Art. 26); Ramadan, *Islamic Law*, 124–125.

123. Al-Kurdi, *The Islamic State*, 55.

124. Ramadan, *Islamic Law*, 113.

125. Dāraquṭnī, *Sunan Dāraquṭnī*, II, 350; al-Kāsānī, *Badāʾiʿ al-Ṣanāʾiʿ*, vol. VII, 100.

126. Al-Muttaqī al-Hindī, *Kanz al-ʿUmmāl*, ḥadīth 24822; Maḥmaṣṣānī, *Arkān*, 261.

127. Al-Muttaqī al-Hindī, *Kanz al-ʿUmmāl*, ḥadīth 10913.

128. ʿAbd al-Qādir ʿAwdah, *Al-Tashrīʿ al-Jināʾī*, I, 35.

129. Al-Nabhānī, *Muqaddimāt al-Dustūr*, 19.

130. Kamali, *Freedom, Equality and Justice in Islam*, see part III on Justice.

131. Khalid Abou el Fadl, 'Islamic Law and Muslim Minorities,' *Islamic Law and Society* 1, 2 (1994), 183.

132. Mawdūdī, *Islamic Law and Constitution*, 245.

133. Al-Ghannūshī, *Ḥuqūq al-Muwāṭanah*, 66. See also al-Nabhānī, *Muqaddimāt al-Dustūr*, 19 to the similar effect.

134. See for details al-Nabhānī, *Muqaddimāt al-Dustūr*, 27 & 31.

135. Cf. Ghazāwī, *Ḥurriyyah*, 90–91.

136. Ibn Qayyim al-Jawziyyah, *Aḥkām al-Dhimmah*, I: 24; see also Ramadan, *Islamic Law*, 131; Ghazāwī, *Ḥurriyyah*, 90–93.

137. Zaydān, *Aḥkām Ahl al-Dhimmah wa'l Musta'minīn*, 157; al-Ghannūshī, *Ḥuqūq al-Muwāṭanah*, 102.

138. Cf. Quṭb, *Shubhāt Ḥawl al-Islām*, 176.

139. Quṭb, *Fī Ẓilāl al-Qur'ān*, III, 1634 (8th edn., 179)—also quoted in al-Bishrī, *Bayn al-Jāmiʿah*, 26. Al-Bishrī adds that Quṭb voiced the same view in his other work, *Maʿālim fi'l-Ṭarīq*.

140. Al-Qaraḍāwī, *Fiqh al-Zakāh*, I, 98.

141. Al-Ghannūshī, *Ḥuqūq al-Muwāṭanah*, 102.

142. See Tawfīq al-Shāwī's Preface to al-Ghannūshī's book, *Ḥuqūq al-Muwāṭanah*, 26.

143. Mutawallī, *Mabādi' Niẓām al-Ḥukm*.

144. Khalifa Abdul Hakim as quoted in Siddiqi, *Modern Reformist Thought*, 91.

145. Id., 92.

146. Shaltūt, *al-Islām, ʿAqīdah wa-Sharīʿah*, 451–453.

147. Id., 453.

148. Zuḥaylī, *Ḥaqq al-Ḥurriyyah*, 217.

149. Id., 218.

150. Fatḥī Osmān, *The Children of Adam: An Islamic Perspective on Pluralism*, 3.

151. Id., 2–3.

152. The entire text of the Constitution of Medina appears in English translation in W. Montgomery Watt, *Islamic Political Thought*, 130–134.

153. Cf. Ramadan, *To Be a European Muslim*, 130.

154. Al-Ṭālibī, *ʿAyāl Allāh*, 99.

155. Id., 101.

156. Cf. Mawdūdī, *Islamic Law and Constitution*, 248–251.

157. Cf. el-Affendi, *Iʿādat al-Naẓar*, 151.

158. Id.

159. Id.

160. Kramer 'Dhimmi or Citizen,' 43.

161. El-Affendi, *Iʿādat al-Naẓar*, 147–149.

162. Views recorded in al-Bishrī, *Bayn al-Jāmiʿah al-Dīniyyah*, 36–37.

163. Cf. ʿAyyāḍ Ibn ʿĀshūr, *al-Ḍamīr wa'l-Tashrīʿ*, 138–139.

164. Cf. el-Affendi, *Iʿādat al-Naẓar*, 150.

165. Ibn Qudāmah, *Al-Mughnī*, VIII, 106.

166. Al-Sanhūrī, *Fiqh al-Khilāfah*, 139; Madkūr, *Maʿālim al-Dawlah*, 242; Samīr ʿĀliyah, *Naẓariyyāt al-Dawlah*, 47.

167. Al-Sanhūrī, *Fiqh al-Khilāfah*, 139.

168. Cf. Fu'ād ʿAbd al-Munʿim Aḥmad, *Uṣūl Niẓām al-Ḥukm* at page 174 where the author has quoted and given specific references to some of the views of the above-mentioned commentators. See also al-Khālidī, *Maʿālim*, 121 to the similar effect.

169. Zaydān, *Al-Fard wa'l-Dawlah fī'l-Sharīʿah al-Islāmiyyah*, 23–25.

170. Cf. Al-Māwardī, *Aḥkām*, 29; Zaydān, *Al-Fard wa'l-Dawlah*, 27.

171. Zaydān, *Al-Fard*, 30.

172. Zaydān, *Aḥkām Ahl al-Dhimmah wa'l-Musta'minīn*, 83–84.

173. Al-Ghannūshī, *Ḥuqūq al-Muwāṭanah*, 84.

174. Ramadan, *Islamic Law*, 145.

175. Id.

176. Al-Bukhārī, *Ṣaḥīḥ al-Bukhārī* (Muhsin Khan's trans.), IX, 195, *ḥadīth* 261; Ibn Taymiyyah, *Al-Siyāsah al-Sharʿiyyah fī Iṣlāḥ al-Rāʿī wa'l-Raʿiyyah*, 6.

177. Muslim, *Ṣaḥīḥ Muslim*, K. Al-Amārah, b. karāhah al-amārah bi-ghayr ḍarūrah.

178. Zaydān, *Al-Fard wa'l-Dawlah*, 53; see also Mutawallī, *Mabādi' Niẓām al-Ḥukm*, 43. Mutawallī also refers to Abū 'l-Aʿlā Mawdūdī's view in support of his own.

179. Al-Ghannūshī, *Ḥuqūq al-Muwaṭanah*, 80; al-Nabhānī, *al-Dustūr al-Islāmī*, 19; and Muhammad Hamidullah, *Nabī al-Islām*, 148; Aḥmad Yusrī, *Ḥuqūq al-Insān*, 148.

180. Ghazālī, *al-Taʿassub wa'l-Tasāmuḥ*, 72.

181. Id., 40.

182. Qaraḍāwī, *Ghayr al-Muslimīn*, 23; also quoted in al-Bishrī, *Bayn al-Jāmiʿah*, 33.

183. Fatḥī Osman, quoted in al-Bishrī, *Bayn al-Jāmiʿah*, 27.

184. Id., 87.

185. Al-Qurṭubī, *Tafsīr al-Qurṭubī*, IV, 250.

186. Ibn Taymiyyah, *al-Siyāsah al-Sharʿiyyah*, 169.

187. Muḥammad Rashīd Riḍa, *Al-Khilāfah aw al-Imāmah al-ʿUẓmah*, 30.

188. Sayyid Quṭb, *Al-ʿAdālah al-Ijtimāʿiyyah fī'l-Islām*, 99.

189. Cf. Al-Khālidī, *Niẓām al-Ḥukm fī'l-Islām*, 185.

190. There is a section on *ḥisbah* in vol. 4 of this series: Kamali, *Freedom of Expression in Islam*, 28–34.

191. Muḥammad Ṣādiq ʿAfīfī, *Al-Mujtamaʿ*, 93. See also al-Sibāʿī, *Ishtirākiyyah*, 50.

192. Ibn Mājah, *Sunan*, Kitāb al-fitan, b. amr bi'l-maʿrūf wa-nahy ʿan al-munkar.

193. Ibn Hishām, *Sīrah*, iv, 262.

194. Al-Khuḍarī, *Muḥāḍarāt*, ii, 17; Abū Ḥabīb, *Dirāsah*, 743.

195. For further details on *naṣīḥah* and *muʿāraḍah* see Kamali, *Freedom of Expression in Islam*, 34–40 and 49–61 respectively.

196. Mawdūdī, *Naẓariyyāt al-Islām wa-Hadyihi*, 307; al-Ghannūshī, *Ḥuqūq al-Muwāṭanah*, 73.

197. See for discussion Muhammad Asad, *State and Government*, p. 75, and Said Ramadan, *Islamic Law*, 143.

198. In chapter three of the present volume.

199. *Ḥadīth* reported by five of the six main collections. Cf. al-Bukhārī, *Ṣaḥīḥ al-Bukhārī*, (Muhsin Khan's trans.) ix, 193, *ḥadīth* 258.

200. Tabrīzī, *Mishkāt*, vol. ii, *ḥadīth* 3696.

201. Tabrīzī, *Mishkāt*, vol. ii, *ḥadīth* 3665.

202. Al-Sibāʿī, *Ishtirākiyyah*, 51.

203. Al-Bukhārī, *Ṣaḥīḥ*, (Muhsin Khan's trans.) ix, 193, *ḥadīth* 259.

204. Cf. Zaydān, *Al-Fard wa'l-Dawlah*, 96.

205. Cf. vol. 6 of the present work, entitled *Right to Education, Work and Welfare in Islam*, especially the chapter on welfare.

206. Cf. Mawdūdī, *The Islamic Law and Constitution*, 250.

207. Yūsuf al-Qaraḍāwī, *Ghayr al-Muslimīn fi'l-Mujtamaʿ al-Islāmī*, 45.

208. Cf. Al-ʿĪlī, *Ḥurriyyah*, 494; Fu'ād ʿAbd al-Munʿim Aḥmad, *Uṣūl Niẓām al-Ḥukm*, 286.

209. Abū Dāwūd, *Sunan Abū Dāwūd*, K. al-Nikāḥ, b. al-Walī.

210. Muslim, *Mukhtaṣar Ṣaḥīḥ Muslim*, p. 263, *ḥadīth* 999.

211. Abū Dāwūd, *Sunan Abū Dāwūd*, K. al-Kharāj wa'l-fay', b. fīmā yalzam al-imām min amr al-raʿiyyah.

212. Manna, *Citizenship*, 38.

213. Cf. Saffār, 'al-Waṭan wa'l-Muwāṭanah,' 25.

214. Ibn Abī 'l-Ḥadīd, *Sharḥ Nahj al-Balāghah*, section no. 56; see also Saffār, id., 25.

215. Cf. Manna, *Citizenship*, 38–39.

216. Manna, *Citizenship*, 39.

217. Abū ʿAbd Allāh Muḥammad al-Qurṭubī, *Al-Jāmiʿ li-Aḥkām al-Qur'ān* (also known as *Tafsīr al-Qurṭubī*), ii, 223; Ibn Ḥazm al-Ẓāhirī, *al-Muḥallā*, iii, 560.

218. Cf. Abū Zahrah, *Tanẓīm al-Islām*, 187; al-ʿĪli, *Ḥurriyyah*, 500.

219. Cf. Al-Zuḥaylī, *Al-Fiqh al-Islāmī*, vi, 707.

220. Cf. Al-Bukhārī, *Ṣaḥīḥ*, vol. 9, *ḥadīth* 258; al-Zuhaylī, *al-Fiqh al-Islāmī*, vi, 707; Asad, *Principles of State*, 79.

221. See for further details Asad, *Principles of State*, 76ff.

222. Muslim, *Mukhtaṣar Ṣaḥīḥ Muslim*, 334, *ḥadīth* 1235.

223. Tabrīzī, *Mishkāt*, vol. 2, *ḥadīth* 3521.

224. Al-Zuhaylī, *Al-Fiqh al-Islāmī*, vi, 708.

225. See for details on *naṣīḥah* vol. 4 of this work entitled *Freedom of Expression in Islam*, 34–40.

226. Cf. al-Saffār, 'al-Waṭan wa'l-Muwāṭanah,' al-Kalima, 10 (1996), 21.

227. Bukhārī, *Ṣaḥīḥ al-Bukhārī* (Muhsin Khan's tr.), viii, 321, *ḥadīth* 483.

228. Bukhārī, *Ṣaḥīḥ al-Bukhārī* (Muhsin Khan's tr.), viii, 27 *ḥadīth* 43; see also al-Saffār, 'al-Waṭan wa'l-Muwāṭanah,' 22.

229. Al-Bukhārī, *Ṣaḥīḥ*, (Muhsin Khan's tr.), vol. ix, 190, *ḥadīth* 252.

230. Shahrūr, *Naḥw Uṣūl Jadīdah li'l-Fiqh al-Islāmī: Fiqh al-Mar'ah* (Damascus, 2000), 382.

231. Cf. Salim el-Awa, *al-Fiqh al-Islāmī fī Ṭarīq al-Tajdīd*, 90.

232. Id.

233. Cf. Salim el-Awa, *al-Fiqh al-Islāmī fī Ṭarīq al-Tajdīd*, 91f.

234. The *Mejelle* (Art. 52). A similar legal maxim provides: When difficulty impedes the realisation of the original, its ruling attaches to its substitute—*al-badal ʿind al-ʿijz ʿan al-aṣl hukmuhu ḥukm al-aṣl*. Cf. Aḥmad al-Nadwī, *Mawsūʿat al-Qawāʿid wa'l-Ḍawābiṭ al-Fiqhiyyah*, 29.

235. Cf. el-Awa, *al-Fiqh al-Islāmī*, 92.

236. The *Mejelle* (Art. 20).

237. The *Mejelle* (Art. 18).

238. Id. (Art. 57): *al-taṣarruf ʿalā al-raʿiyyah manūṭ bi'l-maṣlaḥah*.

239. Al-Awa, *al-Fiqh al-Islāmī*, 98–99.

240. Zainab Badawi, 'The Dilemma of Identity in a Multicultural Europe,' *Islam 21* (no. 27, February 2001, 2).

241. Id., 3.

242. Edited with annotation by Sanhūrī's daughter Nadia al-Sanhūrī and her husband Tawfīq al-Shāwī, Cairo: al-Hay'ah al-Miṣriyyah li'l-Kitāb, 1989.

243. Sanhūrī, *Fiqh al-Khilāfah*, 348.

244. I have here amended Sanhūrī's proposal that leads ultimately to the return of *Khilāfah Ṣaḥīḥah*, or valid Caliphate, which is bound to be based on religion. For I believe a proposal of that kind is likely to be unrealistic now even more so than in the 1920s. Cf. *Fiqh al Khilāfah*, 339.

245. Id., 344–346.

246. Id., 368.

247. Id., 373.

248. Kabir Hassan and Faridul Islam 'Prospect and Problems of a Common Market: An Empirical Examination of the OIC Countries', *AJISS* 18, no. 4 (2001), 22.

249. Tawfīq al-Shāwī, *Al-Mawsūʿah al-ʿAṣriyyah fī'l-Fiqh al-Jinā'ī al-Islāmī*, Cairo: Dār al-Shuruq, 2001, vol. II, 412. Al-Shāwī adds with regret, however, that in some Muslim countries and organisations one notices the unpleasant reality that non-Muslims are given better treatment than that which the Muslims experience. This kind of discrimination is somewhat surprising and definitely unacceptable.

250. Id., 418–419.

CHAPTER THREE

Accountability of Government

I. Introductory Remarks

Muḥāsabah (lit. accounting) conveys two meanings, one of which refers to the individual's accounting of himself, that is, *muḥāsabat al-nafs* (also *al-muḥāsabat al-dhātiyyah*), and the other is accountability in public affairs. These two aspects of *muḥāsabah* are basically an extension of one another, and it is the former meaning that is the focus of attention in the writing of Muslim jurists and theologians. The concept is connected both with the Qur'ānic teachings on public and commercial matters and with that of the final end of man. Both of these occurred side by side, one might say, also in a correct order, in a recommendation attributed to the caliph ʿUmar b. al-Khaṭṭāb to 'take account of your souls yourselves (*ḥāsibū anfusakum*) before you are taken to account (*qabla an tuḥāsabū*) and weigh them (yourselves) before they are weighed (by others).'[1] The latter portion of this statement can also be read in two ways, one of which would be that one should weigh one's own conduct before it is weighed by God in the Day of Judgement, or alternatively that it is weighed by temporal authorities and the government.[2]

Al-Ghazālī's use of the allied term, *murāqabah*, in a chapter he devoted to '*al-murāqabah wa'l-muḥāsabah*' conveys the religious sense of 'spiritual surveillance', that involves examination of the motives of one's own action in order to reject everything that would serve egoism and passion and displeasing God Most High. The three typical questions that are addressed to the soul in this context are: Why?

How? For whom? This self-questioning is, according to al-Ghazālī, designed to chastise the soul for its inadequacies so that it does not persevere in them.[3]

Muḥāsabah has an equally long history in the practice of Islamic government, especially with reference to that of the caliph ʿUmar b. al-Khaṭṭāb to whom frequent references are made in the following pages. *Muḥāsabah* as a principle of government has thus been concerned with political and financial matters and abuse of public office for selfish purposes. *Muḥāsabah* in its literal sense of computation and preparation of accounts (also accountancy as a discipline of learning) has been a feature of the regulatory regime of Public Treasury in the collection of legal alms (*zakāh*) and other taxes. *Muḥāsabah* in this sense is of central importance to government and efficiency in *muḥāsabah* necessitates clear criteria and guidelines so that a reliable accounts sheet can be produced, and violators can also be taken to task for distortion and abuse.[4]

The discussion that follows is presented in three parts, the first of which addresses the basic postulates of accountability, which begin with highlighting the role and position respectively of the *ummah* and the head of state. This is followed by a review of some principles of *Sharīʿah* such as consultation (*shūrā*), *ḥisbah* (promotion of good and prevention of evil), *naṣīḥah* (sincere advice) and their relevance to accountability. The Islamic characterisation of government as a trust (*amānat al-ḥukm*) is also rooted in the notion of accountability, which is, in turn, related to selection and employment of officials, and responsible usage of public funds. A section is also devoted to personal and corporate aspects of accountability in reference especially to offences committed in the course of duty. This is followed by a brief account of the limits to the citizen's duty of obedience to authority in the event especially when the latter itself violates the law. The right to seek redress and judicial relief (*ḥaqq al-shakwā*) is the subject of another section. And then abuse of power and corruption feature in another section where the *Sharīʿah* prohibitions against bribery and corruption are expounded. The last two sections address the principles of *muḥāsabat al-nafs* to which a reference has already been made, and then the people's right to challenge the authority of deviant rulers. This last is expounded under the familiar *fiqhī* heading of *al-khurūj*, or civil disobedience to an unlawful government.

The second part of this chapter provides a brief account of deviation and departure from valid precedent by oppressive dynastic rulers among the Umayyads and Abbasids and draws attention to instances of political distortion, oppression and misuse of public fund by irresponsible rulers.

The last part of this chapter addresses the instruments of accountability with reference especially to the role of the judiciary, the *maẓālim* jurisdiction, the role of the ombudsman or *muḥtasib*, impeachment of the head of state and leading officials. This is followed by a brief discussion of audits and accounts and institutions that played a role in the implementation of *muḥāsabah*.

II. Basic Postulates of Accountability

The basic premises of accountability may be summarised under ten sub-headings as follows.

(1) Political authority in the Islamic system of rule belongs to the community as it is the community that elects the head of state and is ultimately entitled to depose him in the event of manifest abuse.

(2) Consultation and the right of the people to be consulted in government affairs is one of the principal means by which the community participates in government, voices its concerns over government policy, and takes the government to account.

(3) The Qur'ānic principle of promotion of good and prevention of evil (*amr bi'l-maʿrūf wa-nahy ʿan al-munkar*) and its allied concept of giving sincere advice (*naṣīhah*) also render the government accountable to the people and encourage public participation in its affairs.

(4) There is no recognition in *Sharīʿah* of any prerogative or exception to the rule of law. No one is above the law and this includes the head of state and all government officials including the administration and consultative assemblies.

(5) The community is vested with the right to depose (*ḥaqq al-ʿazl*) of a deviant ruler and government.

(6) The citizen's duty to obey the lawful government comes to an end when the government itself violates the law. A corollary of this is the recognition in *Sharīʿah* of the citizen's right, under certain circumstances, of disobedience and defiance (*ḥaqq al-khurūj*) against a deviant ruler.

(7) Accountability in the Islamic system of rule is also manifested in the selection and appointment of officials, the criteria of selection/and or dismissal of government employees.

(8) The trust of governance (*amānat al-ḥukm*) in Islam is predicated in accountability to God Most High and to the community. This is

also a consequence of the concept of vicegerency (*khilāfah*) which entrusts the community to establish a good government.

(7) The *Sharīʿah* also recognizes the right to complaint (*ḥaqq al-shakwā*) by one who is wronged or made a victim of official abuse.

(8) Everyone is accountable for what they do. This is the substance of the foundational principle of *muḥāsabat al-nafs*, which applies equally to the ruler and ruled.

(9) One of the consequences of accountability under the rule of law is that violators and those who are found guilty of misconduct are liable to the payment of damages, penal sanctions, or both.

(10) Bribery and corruption are punishable offences, and use of official position for personal advantage of any kind is not tolerated.

We now discuss each of these principles in the following pages.

UMMAH AS LOCUS OF AUTHORITY

In the Islamic constitutional theory, the community, or *ummah*,[5] is the locus of political authority and the head of state represents that authority in his capacity as representative (*wakīl*) of the community. In the theory of agency (*wakālah*), when the representative fails to fulfil the duty that is entrusted to him, the principal party (*muwakkil*) is entitled to depose him. Thus the community is entitled to question, take to account, and ultimately to depose the head of state when he deviates from the accepted norms of *Sharīʿah* and fails to fulfil his duties. The head of state, 'whether called *ḥākim,* Imam, or Caliph, is not the representative of God but the representative of *ummah*. For the *ummah* elects him, supervises him, taking him to account and eventually deposes him.'[6] The community's right to depose a ruler, known as *ḥaqq al-ʿazl*, naturally entitles it to question the conduct of its government. The representative capacity of the head of state is a corollary of the pledge of allegiance (*bayʿah*), which he receives from the electorate and which pledges him to the trust (*amānah*) of government and the enforcement of *Sharīʿah*. Muslim jurists have 'concurred in the view that the ruler derives his authority and power from the *ummah* which is also entitled to depose him when his condition changes and he fails to administer the affairs of religion and the temporal affairs of Muslims.'[7] Al-Māwardī wrote that when the head of state fulfils the trust of office and faithfully secures the rights of the people, he is entitled to their obedience and assistance (*ṭāʿah wa-naṣrah*) so long as there is no change in his condition in two respects: his uprightness of character (*ʿadālah*), and physical fitness; he may be deposed when he loses these capacities. In the event he later regains his uprightness, he may become leader again by virtue of a new contract.[8] Diyā' al-Dīn al-Rīs wrote that 'the *ummah* is the first party to the contract of *Imāmah* ... the authority to designate the Imam into office exclusively belongs to the *ummah*, and it is the *ummah* that is entitled to dissolve and terminate it.'[9]

With reference to *bayʿah* as the bedrock of accountability, al-Rīs quotes Ibn Khaldūn as saying that 'when the emir receives the pledge of *bayʿah* and concludes the contract with the people, they shake hands to signify the valid conclusion of contract similar to what the parties do in a contract of sale, which is why it is called *bayʿah*.' It is on this basis that the *ummah* becomes the principal party (i.e., the *muwakkil*) in that contract.[10] Al-Māwardī also wrote: 'The vast majority of jurists and theologians have held that the contract of imamate is not concluded except with the consent and choice of the electorate. If they agree, the contract is concluded.'[11]

Bayʿah connotes a contract between someone who makes an offer and another who accepts it, the latter being the one engaged in *bayʿah*. Historically, the *bayʿah* pledged to the caliph consisted of two stages, special *bayʿah*, and general *bayʿah*. In the former, a selected group of individuals, the *ahl al-ḥall waʾl-ʿaqd* (those who can enter into the contract or dissolve it) engaged in consultation to build a consensus and then gave *bayʿah* to a potential caliph. This choice was tantamount to nomination. In the second stage, the general public gave *bayʿah* to the chosen candidate, and it was by virtue of this general *bayʿah* that the candidate assumed office.[12] Since the Imam is 'the employee of the *ummah*, it is to the *ummah* that he submits his resignation. This is because the *ummah* is the locus of all authority (*maṣdar al-sulṭāt*). Upon his resignation, the Imam returns the authority back to the *ummah*.' The reason why the state officials, such as the army commanders remain in their posts, even when the head of state resigns, is because the latter appointed them on behalf of the *ummah*.[13] The community continues to exercise its supervisory authority on the head of state in respect of the following: (1) promotion of good and prevention of evil (*ḥisbah*) which is the collective duty of the community and the head of state conducts it on behalf the community; (2) to ensure that the head of state consults the community; (3) to give *naṣīḥah* (good advice) to the head of state when there is occasion for such; (4) to take him to task when he betrays the trust of the community and indulges in criminality or corruption; (5) to depose him when he loses his qualifications and is no longer fit to be leader.[14] Fu'ād Aḥmad has quoted al-Baghdādī to the effect: 'When the Imam deviates, the *ummah* decides on his position whether to confirm him in office or to depose and replace him. The community's relationship to the Imam on this resembles that of the Imam to his employees. When the latter deviate, the Imam takes them to task and decides on their case.'[15] No one may violate the authority of the *ummah* or violate its consent and form a government by coercive methods, and anyone who does so commits a crime.[16]

The community's right to take to account the head of state and other government officials is clearly reflected in the precedent of the Pious Caliphs and general consensus (*ijmāʿ*) of the *ʿulamāʾ*.[17] 'The leading jurists are in agreement,' wrote Wasfī, 'that the head of state and caliph derive their authority and power from the people who have pledged their fealty to him. Political authority entirely belongs to the community, there being no hereditary nor divine appointment for any person or office in the Islamic system of rule.'[18]

The *Sharīʿah* entitlement of the community to depose a deviant ruler involves a great deal of responsibility and a carefully regulated approach for its proper exercise. History has shown that the issue of deposition has been prone to abuse and it has actually remained one of the most problematic areas of Islamic constitutional law. This is because recourse to deposition and impeachment of the head of state becomes an option often at times of crises when matters are likely to have reached the point of controversy and confrontation. This issue will be addressed in further detail in a section on impeachment below. Suffice it here to note that an early instance of an unwarranted and abusive attempt at impeachment was that of the caliph ʿUthmān. The critics and detractors of the caliph took him severely to task for irregularities in the appointment of officials among other matters. Without even giving the caliph the opportunity to explain and defend himself, his assailants ruthlessly attacked and assassinated him. This was clearly an extremist act, abusive of the principle of accountability and proper exercise of the right of deposition.

ACCOUNTABILITY: THE EARLY PRECEDENT

The principle of accountability in *Sharīʿah* basically draws no distinction between government leaders and other members of the community and render them all accountable for their conduct. Everyone is in principle responsible for what they do regardless of his/her social or political status. This is because all the evidence that is found in the Qurʾān and *Sunnah* on personal accountability of individuals is conveyed in general (*ʿāmm*) terms which makes no exception in favour of anyone. Hence, personal accountability remains the basic and normative principle of *Sharīʿah*.

There is conclusive evidence in the precedent of the Pious Caliphs that they regarded themselves accountable to the people and were observant of the teachings of the Qurʾān and *Sunnah* in the conduct of duty. The first caliph Abū Bakr made a point of this in his inaugural speech upon taking office when he addressed the people in the following terms:

> O people, I have been entrusted with authority over you but I am not the best of you. Assist me when I am right but stop me (*fa-saddidūnī*) when I am wrong. The weak among you is strong in my eyes until I get him what is due to him, and the strong among you is weak in my eyes until I take from him what is due to others.

The caliph went on to ask the people 'Obey me for as long as I obey God but you have no duty to obey me if I disobey Him.'[19] The caliph Abū Bakr clearly conveyed his concern for accountability when he addressed Yazīd b. Abī Sufyān upon the latter's departure as governor to Sham: 'I appoint you to this office in order to test you and it is for you to assure me of your capability and competence. It is also a burden on you. If you do well, I shall reinstate you and enhance your standing, but I shall not hesitate to dismiss you for any miscarriage of duty.'[20] Abū Bakr's successor, ʿUmar b. al-Khaṭṭāb too addressed the people at his inaugural speech after receiving their pledge of allegiance, or *bayʿah*, and asked them in categorical terms 'rectify any deviation you might see in me.' A man from the audience tersely responded 'if we see deviation on your part, we shall rectify it by the sword,' which obviously meant killing. To this the caliph is reported to have conceded and praised God that there was someone among the Muslims who was prepared to go as far as that. Ṭalḥah b. ʿUbayd Allāh who was present told the caliph: 'Why did you not say that if you deviated, they should depose you?' To which the caliph apparently responded that: 'Killing is a greater deterrent for the one who succeeds to the rule.'[21] The caliph ʿUmar has also been quoted to have said: 'When one of my employees commits an act of injustice against someone and the latter complains to me but I fail to rectify it, it would be as if I had committed the act of injustice myself.'[22] The egalitarian sentiment of this precedent was also voiced by the Umayyad caliph ʿUmar b. ʿAbd al-ʿAzīz (d. 101/720) who has been quoted to have said in an address to the people: 'I am one of you except that God Most High has made my burden greater than yours.'[23]

The caliph ʿUmar I used to invite the people to monitor his activities and remind him of any shortfall they observed on his part. He is thus noted for having said 'may God be merciful on those who remind us of our faults.'[24] The caliph clearly saw himself accountable to the people just as he saw his officials accountable and frequently took them to task over the accomplishment of their duties. His confiscation of the personal properties of some of the office holders is highly instructive and is found in varying details in the historical accounts of that period. The Companion Abū Hurayrah, the collector of *zakāh* in ʿUmar's time and then governor of Bahrain, received a salary for his service. He also received a pension from *bayt al-māl* as was payable to his fellow leading Companions. However, Abū Hurayrah also engaged in horse-trading and his wealth was considerably increased as a result. The caliph ʿUmar took him to task for it and, as the reports indicate, took away a part of his wealth. For the caliph had instructed those with fixed salaries not to hoard wealth nor to invest their income in certain types of properties and businesses.[25]

According to another report, the caliph had heard of the riches that were accumulated by Nuʿmān b. ʿAdī, the officer of Emessa in the fertile Sawad lands of Iraq and two other officials, even though there was no clear proof against them. The caliph appointed Muḥammad b. Maslamah as inspector and magistrate and advised him to confiscate half of each officer's property.[26] Even the kinsmen of the office holders were taken to task. It is thus reported that the caliph took away a portion of the earnings of the brother of a tax collector of Uballa in Ahwaz (Persia) because this officer used to lend his brother public money which he invested in profitable business.[27]

The head of state is himself expected to supervise the conduct of his officials in his capacity as custodian (*rāʿī*) and trustee of the community. He is to employ to government posts only knowledge-able, competent and God-fearing individuals and then remain vigilant over their activities and look into complaints against them. He may remove from office anyone who is guilty of serious neglect of duty. It is reported that the Prophet himself sacked ʿAlā b. al-Ḥaḍramī, the governor of Bahrain, after he looked into certain complaints against him by a delegation from ʿAbd al-Qays tribe, and then appointed Abān b. Saʿīd to replace him.[28]

The caliph ʿUmar I warned his leading officials to avoid the temptation of indulging in a lifestyle that is discourteous to, and sets them apart from, the people. Thus he wrote to the governor of Egypt, ʿAmr b. al-ʿĀṣ:

> I have been informed that in your meetings (with people) you sit in a reclining position (*tattaki'*). Beware! When you sit with people, you must try to be like one of them.[29]

In a letter that the caliph ʿUmar wrote to the governor of Kufa, Saʿd b. Abī Waqqāṣ, the latter was warned:

> I was informed that you have built a mansion and have taken residence in it and named it as Bayt Saʿd (House of Saʿd) and that you have also installed a gate that separates you from the public. This mansion of yours is confounding (the people) ... Do not deny the people their right to approach you by building barriers and gates ....

The report adds that the caliph sent Muḥammad b. Maslamah together with this letter to Saʿd and ordered that the mansion should be burnt down.[30]

ʿUmar b. al-Khaṭṭāb also sent a warning letter to Abū Mūsā al-Ashʿarī, the governor of Basra, which reminded him of his responsibilities:

> The Commander of the Faithful has come to learn that you and members of your family have taken to a lifestyle in the clothes you wear, the food you eat and the animals you ride, the like of which other Muslims cannot have ... Know that officials are accountable to God. When there is deviation on the part of officials, it then spreads among the public, and the most wretched of officials are those who set a bad example for the people.[31]

According to another report, which also involved Abū Mūsā al-Ashʿarī, a man complained to the caliph ʿUmar that al-Ashʿarī had lashed him with a whip for no apparent reason. The Caliph sent al-Ashʿarī this message: 'If you lashed the plaintiff in the midst of a crowd, you would have to let him retaliate in the like manner.' When the man met with al-Ashʿarī, the latter surrendered to him for retaliation on which occasion the man forgave him and the matter was resolved.[32]

Abū Zahrah who recounted these episodes has also recorded the incident in which the leading Companion, ʿAmr b. al-ʿĀs, had called an Arab man 'O *munāfaq* (hypocrite),' apparently in the mosque in the presence of other worshippers. The man complained to the caliph ʿUmar that "ʿAmr called me *munāfiq*. No one had ever called me this since I embraced Islam.' The caliph sent a message to ʿAmr b. al-ʿĀs to the effect that if he had insulted the man in the presence of a congregation, he is liable to punishment by way of retaliation. The man then went to the mosque with the caliph's letter to that effect. When he showed the letter and asked members of the congregation 'Who heard ʿAmr calling me *munāfiq*?' They replied: 'All of us heard it.' Then when the letter was read out the people objected to the idea of retaliation, but the man insisted by saying that there was little sign of obedience to the command of the caliph. At this point, ʿAmr b. al-ʿĀs came forward and surrendered himself for retaliation. The plaintiff then said, 'Now I have forgiven you.'[33]

The caliph ʿUthmān continued ʿUmar's precedent of meeting the people during the hajj season and receiving public complaints against officials. He is also reported, for instance, to have sacked his secretary, Ḥamdān b. Abān, when he learned that he had taken bribes, lied and concealed information concerning the governor Walīd Ibn ʿUqbah who was accused of wine drinking. Ḥamdān was also asked to leave Medina and 'never to stay anywhere near me.'[34] Like his predecessor, the caliph ʿUthmān received delegations from the outlying areas and enquired about their conditions, the price of commodities in their respective localities, and the conduct of government officials.

The caliph ʿAlī also followed the precedent and enquired into the conduct of officials. In his renowned letter to the governor of Egypt, al-Ashtar al-Nakhaʿī, the caliph directed his governor:

> To look into the affairs of your employees to ensure that they are employed for their ability, experience, good character and background; that they are not people who are covetous of the nobility and wealth of others; that they have keen insight into the consequences of affairs and are not open to favour and influence. For these are akin to oppression and betrayal of trust. Then you ensure that they are adequately paid as this would serve as an incentive for them to be strong and you would have a good case to take them to task when they deviate and betray your trust. Then you should remain vigilant of their activities when they are employed...[35]

On another occasion, the caliph ʿAlī wrote a letter to Kaʿb b. Mālik whom the caliph appointed as his representative to look into the activities of officials in the region between Tigris (Dajlah) and al-ʿAdhib, to question them about their affairs and report to him. By this time the precedent of periodical inspection into the conduct of officials was well recognised and became an established practice. The caliph advised his tax officers not to sell the horses of the taxpayers nor their oxen nor cows, nor their summer nor winter clothing and insisted on their being kind and lenient in the collection of taxes.[36] On occasions, it is noted that the first Umayyad caliph Muʿāwiyah (41–60/661–679) continued this practice and later the caliph ʿUmar Ibn ʿAbd al-ʿAzīz is said to have shown the desire to reinvigorate the precedent of the Pious Caliphs. Thus it is reported that when Muʿāwiyah was informed of some injustices done by Muslim tax collectors in Iraq, he replaced them with the natives. Similar incidents are noted in the records of the Abbasid caliphs including Jaʿfar al-Manṣūr (136–158 AH/754–775) and Hārūn al-Rashīd (170–193 AH/786–809) who took their officials to task and penalised them for miscarriage of duty.

It is reported that the family of the Umayyad caliph Sulaymān b. ʿAbd al-Malik (d. 99/717) greeted the new caliph ʿUmar b. ʿAbd al-ʿAzīz with presents and perfumes and said: 'This is for you and this is for us.' The caliph asked: 'What are these?' and he was told that, 'Some of these were used by the previous caliph and the rest were not. The part that was used belongs to us and the rest belongs to you.' The caliph ʿUmar said: 'None of it belongs to either me, Sulaymān, or yourself,' and ordered the keeper of *bayt al-māl* to add them all to the public assets.[37]

ACCOUNTABILITY AND CONSULTATION

The Islamic government is under duty, during its tenure in office, to conduct the community affairs through consultation with the community and their representatives. By its very nature, consultation involves a certain degree of accountability to the public as well as their participation and involvement in decision-making. Consultation is meaningful when it facilitates unhindered exchange of views in which the parties communicate over matters of mutual concern.

The Qurʾān commentator al-Qurṭubī (d. 671/1273) is emphatic on consultation and considers it a criterion of accountability, 'for *shūrā* is one of the cardinal principles (*ʿazāʾim al-aḥkām*) of *Sharīʿah*. A ruler who fails to consult the learned and the pious must therefore be dismissed.'[38] Ibn Taymiyyah (d. 728/1328) has similarly observed that a leader who is entrusted with the community affairs must not turn away from consultation. For God Most High commanded the Prophet to consult the people, even though he was recipient of divine revelation. The requirement of consultation is therefore all the more emphatic with regard to governors and rulers who are not recipients of *wahy*. Ibn Taymiyyah added: if the result of consultation shows that people are divided in their opinions, the leader should endorse that which bears greater harmony with the Book of God and the *Sunnah* of His Messenger.[39] According to Maḥmūd Shaltūt (d. 1965): 'When the Qur'ān placed *shūrā* between *ṣalāh* and *zakāh* (in the verse of *shūrā*), it clearly did not envisage the empty *shūrā* practices of the subsequent ages where *shūrā* became a tool in the hands of despotic rulers.' *Shūrā* is a right of the community, a vehicle for the exercise of its authority, and a means therefore by which to fight despotism.[40]

Some commentators have confined *shūrā* to military affairs as this was the tendency during the Prophet's time, but there is no such particularisation of the subject matter of *shūrā* in the Qur'ān. Hence *shūrā* remains applicable to government affairs generally, and this actually became the practice of the heads of state in the Islamic lands following the demise of the Prophet. The Pious Caliphs resorted to consultation in all matters, within and outside the scope of the *Sharīʿah* rulings (*aḥkām*). The first issue of major significance they determined by consultation was the *khilāfah*.[41] The Companions also determined the punishment of *shurb* (wine drinking) through consultation and consensus, and there were issues in inheritance that were addressed and determined on the same basis.

No particular prototype or model has been determined for *shūrā*; it thus remains for the community itself to determine the form and method of *shūrā* in the light of their prevailing conditions and *maṣlaḥah*. What the *Sharīʿah* requires is that government should consult the community, especially the learned among them, in public affairs. Consultation may be through direct participation or through representation and it may take a variety of forms, some of which are nowadays regulated by law and constitution whereas others are determined in the light of prevailing conditions.[42] In modern times the elected assembly and parliament are the principal instruments of *shūrā* and the executive branch of government is, under the constitutions of many contemporary Muslim states, accountable to parliament. *Shūrā* thus functions as an instrument of accountability, a role which has found a more authoritative institutional expression in modern parliaments.[43]

In response to the question as to who actually represents the people, al-Māwardī (d. 450/1058), Ibn Taymiyyah and many others suggest that these are the *ʿulamā'* and community leaders, (*ʿulamā' wa-umarā'*, also known as *ahl al-ḥall wa'l-ʿaqd*, those who loosen and bind) who must be consulted in community affairs. Twentieth century writers on the subject of *shūrā*, including Maḥmūd Shaltūt, ʿAbd al-Razzāq al-Sanhūrī, Muḥammad Yūsuf Mūsā, ʿAbd al-Ḥamīd Mutawallī and others have spoken in support of an electoral process that enables the people to elect their representatives who may then be consulted in community affairs. Leading government officials, experts and members of representative assemblies are the present–day *ulū'l-amr*. The electoral process should naturally ensure that the candidates for such assemblies possess the qualifications of knowledge and just character and enjoy the trust of the community. Without a credible electoral process that institutionilises *shūrā* and enables the people to take government leaders to account, accountability and *muḥāsabah* in government are likely to remain ineffective.

Notwithstanding some reservations that have been expressed over the acceptability in principle of political parties within the body politique of Islam, many have seen political parties to serve as organised platforms where the views of the government in power and those outside the government are represented. The organisational structure of parties equip them with a degree of influence that tend to reinforce the role of consultation in public affairs. Political parties are naturally governed by a set of guidelines and procedures that regulate consultation within its ranks and they also give, to some extent, the Islamic concept of *muʿāradah* (constructive criticism) a role in the formulation of policies.[44] Political parties are also an integral part of democracy and the current constitutions of many Muslim countries have recognised this and consequently assigned a role for them. Opposition parties in modern democracies tend to play a moderating influence and act on the whole as protectors of people's rights.[45] Qaraḍāwī has forcefully spoken on the positive role that political parties play in support of *shūrā*, *ḥisbah*, and accountability and has consequently refuted the somewhat simplistic argument of the opponents of political parties in an Islamic state. He is right in saying that due to the absence of organised platform for opposition, those who opposed the ruling authorities in the past usually resorted to uprising and rebellion that often went out of control and became destructive.[46]

Critics have often said that *shūrā* is elitist and does not recognise the universal suffrage known by democracy. In response, it may be said that the Qur'ān lays down the requirement of *shūrā* in the broadest of terms. It should therefore be possible to design a procedure for it that relates it to the grassroot as well as to those who are competent to give a counsel. *Shūrā* should moreover, not be seen as a substitute to general election, but complementary to it. Election as such replaces the pledge of allegiance (*bay'ah*) but not the *shūrā*. Even if *shūrā* is made compulsory on the head of state, that by itself does not guarantee accountability and a separate procedure would still be needed to ensure accountability on his part. Having said this, Sanhūrī emphasised the role that an independent judiciary can play in holding to account a government leader who violates the law. The head of state in the Islamic system of rule does not enjoy any special immunities and is fully subject to the authority of the judiciary like any of his subjects.[47]

Said al-Najjar has rightly observed that 'public officials should be accountable, not only before God, but before other humans... and we should have freedom of choice through elections.'[48] People should thus be able not only to choose and elect their leaders but also to be able to depose them when they violate the trust of the electorate. Since the community is entitled to elect the leader, it is also entitled to remove him. The community and its representatives may resort to force if this is likely to achieve its desired purpose without causing civil strife. But if it is likely to lead to civil strife, use of force is not permitted (further details on this appear below under impeachment).[49] The theory of caliphate is however conspicuously silent in regard to laying down a procedure as to how a deviant ruler may be peacefully deposed without inciting civil strife and sedition. Modern constitutional law in many Muslim (and non-Muslim) countries has on the other hand overcome this hurdle by adopting an impeachment procedure, which specifies a method as to how the head of state and other government leaders can be taken to account, investigated and tried. A procedure of this kind was initially adopted in the US Constitution of 1776 and has ever since featured in an increasing number of the constitutions of other states, including those of Egypt, Pakistan, and Afghanistan. Although early Muslim jurists have not suggested a specific procedure for impeachment, the source evidence in *Sharī'ah* is supportive of it, as I shall later elaborate.

ḤISBAH AND NAṢĪḤAH

The Qur'ānic principle of *ḥisbah* (promotion of good and prevention of evil) (cf. 3:104 & 110; 9:71), to which a reference has already been made, is a broad principle of public law that entitles everyone to take a vigilant attitude toward criminality and evil. To quote but one of these verses, it is provided 'the believers, men and women, are friends and protectors of one another, they enjoin good and they forbid evil...' (9:71).

والمؤمنون والمؤمنات بعضهم أولياء بعض يأمرون بالمعروف وينهون عن المنكر

It seems that prevention of evil takes priority over the promotion of good. The *Sunnah* has provided further elaboration on this and has accordingly envisaged three stages in the implementation of *ḥisbah*, the first of which authorises the direct observer to take action against an evil that is committed before his/her eyes provided that he/she is actually able to do something about it. If this is not possible, one may verbally denounce and criticise evil conduct that one witnesses, and in cases where verbal denunciation is also unfeasible, one may silently denounce it as a part of *taqwā* and affirmation of one's conviction to reject evil and disassociate oneself from it. These three stages of *ḥisbah* are expounded in the following *ḥadīth*:

من رأى منكم منكرا فليغيره بيده، فإن لم يستطع فبلسانه فإن لم يستطع فبقلبه وذلك أضعف الإيمان

If any of you sees something evil, he should set it right by his hand; if he is unable to do so, then by his tongue, and if he is unable to do even that, then (let him denounce it) in his heart. But this is the weakest form of faith.[50]

The 'ulamā' have elaborated *ḥisbah* in great detail and it is not our purpose to delve into these details here. A brief reference may, however, be made to al-Ghazālī's characterisation of *ḥisbah* as 'the most important objective of all of God's revealed scriptures,'[51] and to Ibn Qayyim's assessment of it as 'the basic objective of all governmental authority (*jamīʿ al-wilāyah*) in Islam.' *Ḥisbah* is accordingly ranked as a collective obligation (*farḍ kifā'ī*) of the community in which everyone must participate to the extent of his or her ability.[52] *Ḥisbah* may be conducted either as a religious obligation, or indeed as a civic duty, by both Muslim and non-Muslim citizens. For there is nothing in the *Sharī'ah* to discourage anyone from promoting a good cause or from attempting to prevent a manifest evil. Since non-Muslims are required to be useful members of the community, they too cannot remain indifferent to the essence of *ḥisbah*, especially when *ḥisbah* involves something that is not necessarily religious in character.

Accountability is an integral part of *ḥisbah* and it is therefore a collective obligation of everyone to enjoin good and to suppress evil.[53] Khiḍr al-Ḥusayn has reached the conclusion that 'Islam has made it an obligation of the community' to monitor the conduct of the head of state and his officials and be alert to rectify those who are deviant.[54] The public is thus entitled to speak out and complain against the activities of government officials. The proper exercise of the right to complain is, however, subject to certain requirements that are specified in the Qur'ān and *Sunnah*. One should accordingly investigate first and avoid indulgence in suspicion and doubt that might lead to prejudice. Criticism and complaint must also be constructive and conveyed in the spirit of sincere advice that stays clear of indulgence in acrimony and foundless accusation.[55]

Naṣīḥah (sincere advice) is the focus of much attention in the *Sunnah*, so much so that the Prophet, peace be on him, addressed his Companions with the profound statement that 'religion is sincere advice.' And this invoked the inevitable question: 'To whom, O Messenger of God?' And the Prophet replied: 'To God, to His Book, to His Messenger, to community leaders, and to the generality of the believers.'[56]

الدين النصيحة، قلنا لمن يارسول الله؟ قال لله ولكتابه
ولرسوله ولأُمّة المسلمين وعامتهم

Naṣīḥah has thus been identified as a pillar of Islam. To give *naṣīḥah* to God, to His Book and His Messenger evidently means to have faith in them and to attempt *naṣīḥah* in full sincerity and devotion to their cause and their teachings.

Ḥisbah and *naṣīḥah* are among the fundamental postulates of Islam and its *Sharī'ah*, and I refer to them here with the purpose mainly to show that accountability in both its moral and legal senses is an inalienable part of these principles. They are foundational and pervasive which is why they can be traced in various degrees in almost every principle of public law in Islam. *Hisbah* and *naṣīḥah* nurture accountability and can have little meaning in the context of an absolutist system of government, nor indeed in a totally servile and conformist social environment. For they both encourage vigilance and involvement on the part of the individual, demanding the individual to be alert, participatory and sensitive to the conditions of the society in which he or she lives.

The third caliph ʿUthmān followed the precedent of his predecessors and readily acknowledged the people's right to remind and advice him of his shortcomings when a group of Muslims criticised him about his management of provincial affairs. In one of his statements, the caliph thus said: 'I shall refrain from what the Muslims see to be a fault on my part. For I heard the Messenger of God saying "One who slips should repent and one who errs should repent and let no one remain in falsehood. For any one who does that remains distant away from the right path." '[57]

The third caliph promoted the cause of good government through setting personal example for others, which may be said to be the most effective form of *hisbah* and *naṣīḥah*. He was one of the richest Companions who expended most of his wealth on charitable causes and also refused to receive a salary for his service. He was anxious to see that his officers were concerned more with discharging their duties to the people and giving them their due than with securing what was due to the government. 'Become supporters and protectors of the people rather than collectors of taxes,' thus he addressed what is described to be the first letter he issued to his officers after assuming his caliphal duties.[58]

One of the manifestations of assistance, which is a right of the leader over his people is for the latter to give sincere advice and courteously suggest any improvement he needs to make in the conduct of government. This was perhaps possible in earlier times when the community was small and personal contact was effective. Owing to the growth of bureaucracy and procedure, personal contact may now be neither feasible nor even effective. It seems that *naṣīḥah* under the present circumstances is given best within the framework of political parties, which are basically organised to pursue a programme and implement ideas that in the judgment of their advocates are beneficial. Political parties that pursue beneficial objectives that partake in *naṣīḥah* are acceptable, but the answer would be in the negative if the party in question committed itself to questionable and unlawful objectives.

Since *naṣīḥah* as well as *ḥisbah* are not to be monopolised by only some individuals or groups, it would follow that a wider level of participation and plurality of individuals and parties would be desirable. Qaraḍāwī has resembled political parties to the schools of law and theology (i.e. the *madhāhib*), the main difference between them being that the *madhāhib* were primarily concerned with juristic issues. Although a clear line of division between juristic and political matters would be difficult to draw, yet the leading schools of law that have survived have not laid claim to exclusivity and have not, on the whole, denied legitimacy to other similar schools and movements. What is clear in the history of the *madhāhib* is their acceptance of pluralism, which may by analogy be extended to political parties. For a political party that pursues a programme, method and philosophy is like a *madhhab*, albeit a political one, which also integrates consultation within its ranks. Provided that its objectives are not in conflict with the principles of Islam, a pluralist approach to *naṣīḥah* within the framework of political parties is perhaps a more effective and organised way of giving it.[59]

As for the question that political parties are a manifestation of western democracy which can claim no Islamic credentials, one might say that if one is convinced of the basic efficacy of political parties, rather than blindly following it for the sake of following, then there is no objection. Islam does not close the door to following ideas from other sources if it consists of good advice. At the Battle of the Ditch, the Prophet took the advice of a man of Persian stock, Salmān al-Fārisī, whose idea it was to dig a ditch around Medina, and the Prophet accepted it. On a similar note, the Caliph ʿUmar followed the tax system, and Muʿāwiyah borrowed the postal system, from foreign sources—hence there should be no objection to political parties merely because of their western origin.[60] If good advice can be sought in the teachings and doctrines of other traditions Muslim are not under any interdiction in regards to them.

GOVERNMENT AS A TRUST (*AMĀNAT AL-ḤUKM*)

The first manifestation of this is the trust of vicegerency (*khilāfah*) whereby humans are entrusted with the responsibility to establish justice and good governance. In an address to the Prophet-cum-King David, the Qurʾān spells out the requirement that the trust of vicegerency, or *khilāfah*, that was placed in him had to be faithfully discharged. To quote the text:

يا داود إنا جعلناك خليفة فى الأرض فاحكم بين الناس بالحقّ ولا تتبع الهوى فيضلك عن سبيل الله

> O David! Surely We have made you a vicegerent (*khalīfatan*) in the earth. So judge justly among people and follow not desire, lest it leads you astray from the path of God (38:26).

Prophet David thus became the carrier of the divine trust of vicegerency in order to establish justice and avoid the pursuit of desire (*hawā*). This last term in the terminology of the Qur'ān stands at the opposite pole of *Sharī'ah* in that the main purpose of *Sharī'ah* is to discipline the pursuit of untrammeled desire. David's exercise of power as a ruler and vicegerent was thus valid only if it conformed to correct guidance and avoided arbitrariness and indulgence in *hawā*. If the Prophet-cum-King was under duty to abide by the rule of law and refrain from *hawā*, then the demand here may be said to be even more emphatic with regard to ordinary rulers, men and women, who are entrusted with the responsibility of governance.

The head of state and government officials are under duty, as the Qur'ān provides in another verse, to faithfully discharge their trust:

إن الله يأمركم أن تؤدوا الأمانات إلى أهلها وإذا حكمتم بين الناس أن تحكموا بالعدل

> God commands you to render the trusts to whom that they belong and when you judge among people you judge with justice. (4:58)

Reports indicate that this verse was revealed concerning government officials and the fact that government office is designated as an *amānah* is indicative of accountability to God and to the community. This is also confirmed in a *ḥadīth*, which the Prophet is reported to have uttered in response to a request by the renowned Companion, Abū Dharr al-Ghaffārī who asked the Prophet if he could be employed to a government post. To this the Prophet replied: 'O Abū Dharr! This is a trust (*amānah*) and you are weak; it brings remorse in the Day of Judgment unless it is rightly undertaken and duly discharged.'[61]

يا أبا ذر إنك ضعيف إنها أمانة وإنها يوم القيامة خزي
وندامة إلا من أخذها بحقها وأدّى الذى عليه فيها

Commenting on this *ḥadīth* Muḥammad al-Ghazālī wrote that a man may be very learned, as was Abū Dharr himself, but may not possess technical and practical skills, administrative acumen and leadership qualities. Then al-Ghazālī also noted that the Prophet entrusted Khālid b. al-Walīd with leadership of the army at a very young age as he saw the potentials of leadership in him.[62]

The Qur'ān commentator, al-Qurṭubī, has noted that 'this verse [4:58] incorporates a cardinal ruling of the Qur'ān in that it embraces within its fold the whole of the religion and the *Sharīʿah*.' Al-Qurṭubī then refers to a certain disagreement that arose over the question whether the verse addressed only the rulers or other persons in position of trust and responsibility as well—he observed that 'it is most likely that the verse is addressed to all strata of the people including government officials, regarding their duties in the distribution of assets as well as administration of justice and adjudication of disputes. The verse also applies to all other varieties of trusts.'[63]

Elsewhere the Qur'ān praises 'those who observe their trusts and their promises' (23:8),

والذين هم لأماناتهم وعهدهم راعون

and then warns against betrayal of trust in the following terms: 'O believers, do not betray God and His Messenger by betraying your trust while you know it.' (8:27)

يا آيها الذين آمنوا لا تخونوا الله والرسول وتخونوا
أماناتكم وأنتم تعلمون

In a *ḥadīth* the Prophet has singled out three attributes of a *munāfiq* (transgressor, hypocrite), one of which is 'When he is entrusted, he betrays his trust.'[64]

One of the pitfalls of rulers and governors is when they create barriers between themselves and the people and choose to turn a blind eye to the people's needs. Thus according to a *ḥadīth*:

One whom God has entrusted with administering the affairs of the people, and then he distances himself from the people and refuses to be involved in their needs, their poverty and loneliness, God Most High will turn away from his needs, poverty and loneliness on the Day of Judgement.[65]

من ولاه شيئًا من أمور المسلمين فاحتجب دون حاجتهم وخلتهم وفقرهم، احتجب الله دون حاجته وخلته وفقره يوم القيامة

Accountability is seen as an integral part of trust in the following *ḥadīth* where the Prophet addressed the people in a language that virtually made no exception for anyone:

ألا كلكم راع، وكلكم مسؤل عن رعيته، فالإمام الذى على الناس راع وهو مسؤل عن رعيته، والرجل راع على أهل بيته وهو مسؤل عن رعيته، والمرأة راعية على بيت زوجها وولده وهي مسؤلة عنهم... ألا فكلكم راع وكلكم مسؤل عي رعيته

Beware that every one of you is a guardian and responsible for that which is in his custody. The imam is a guardian and he is responsible for his subjects, a man is a guardian and he is responsible for his family, a woman is guardian of her husband's home and children and she is responsible for them... Surely, everyone of you is a guardian and responsible for what is under his charge.[66]

Everyone is, in other words, accountable for what is in his or her custody and trust. Accountability thus becomes a general principle that applies to everyone within and even beyond the affairs of government. But since the head of state is the immediate audience of the *ḥadīth*, he becomes the most important bearer of accountability. The substance of this *ḥadīth* finds a more emphatic expression in yet another *ḥadīth*, which combines a warning to those who betray the trust of public office:

ما من عبد يسترعيه الله رعية يموت وهو غاش لرعيته، إلا

حرّم الله عليه الجنة

No servant of God, whom God has made custodian over others, dies while betraying those who were under his custody, but God will forbid him Paradise.[67]

This is matched by an equally rigorous attitude toward vindication of truth in government affairs whereby everyone is strongly encouraged to remind the deviant ruler of his responsibility and trust. The Prophet thus declared unequivocally that 'the best form of *jihād* is to utter a word of truth to an oppressive ruler.'[68]

أفضل الجهاد كلمة عدل عند سلطان جائر

This *hadīth* may be said to be a more concrete expression of the general Qur'ānic directive 'to advise one another to truth and advise one another to be patient' (103:3).

وتواصوا بالحق وتواصوا بالصبر

The immediately preceding verses of this short Qur'ānic *sūrah* also conveys the message that man is in a state of loss unless he remains alert to his responsibility to advocate the truth. The *sūrah* in which this passage occurs bears the title *al-ʿAṣr* (the Time), and, more specifically, the later segment of the time of day. This may be said to be endorsing the message that man is in a losing battle against time unless he uses it for a good purpose. When the time comes that one should stand for truth and justice, one should not procrastinate, but one should be equally steadfast and remain patient if more time and effort is required in order to discover and vindicate the truth.

In a letter that the caliph ʿUthmān sent to his governors shortly after his election into office, he wrote that 'God has commanded the leaders to act as custodians (*ruʿāt*) . . . the leaders of this *ummah* must always act as trustees and custodians and never allow themselves to become oppressors, mere tax collectors, and tyrants . . .' He also wrote to army commanders and tax collectors reminding them of their responsibilities and the trust of duty with which they were entrusted. Thus, he wrote to his tax officers confirming the directives they had earlier received from the caliph ʿUmar with the added instruction that 'truth and justice are the pillars of God's creation. God does not accept the opposite of truth (*al-ḥaqq*), so be steadfast in your duty to uphold it. Whatever you take and whatever you give (to the peoples) must be based on truth. You are also bearers of trust (*al-amānah*) which you must faithfully fulfil... Be mindful of justice with the orphans and the covenantees (*al-muʿāhidūn*), for God shall be opponent of the one who deals unjustly with them.'[69]

When the Umayyad caliph ʿUmar b. ʿAbd al-ʿAzīz (d. 101/720) assumed office, he assembled the Bani Marwān clan including the family of the previous caliph, Marwān Ibn al-Ḥakam and told them that the Prophet had assigned the land of Fadak for himself from which he drew his maintenance and it also supported some of the children of the Banu Hāshim clan. The caliph continued: On one occasion when Fāṭimah (the Prophet's daughter) asked the Prophet if she could be assigned that land, her request was not granted and Fadak remained as it used to be until the Prophet passed away. The caliph Abū Bakr simply continued the Prophet's precedent, and so did his successor the caliph ʿUmar. Then Muʿāwiyah assigned the Fadak land by way of assignment (*iqtāʿ*) to Marwān and Marwān had kept it as part of his private property.

Mughīrah b. Ḥakim al-Ṣanʿānī who transmitted this report then added that the caliph ʿUmar b. ʿAbd al-ʿAzīz ordered that the Fadak land be transferred back to the public assets. For this was what the Prophet had meant when he turned down Fāṭimah's request. The Fadak land was then taken away from the Marwān family and was joined to the assets of the *bayt al-māl*.[70]

In a letter sent to Zayd b. ʿAbd al-Raḥmān b. ʿUmar b. al-Khaṭṭāb, who was governor of Kufah under the caliph ʿUmar b. ʿAbd al-ʿAzīz, the governor was given the following instruction: 'I write this to mention that you have accumulated some left-over funds after disbursing payments to the army. You may now give of this fund to those among them who are indebted without any corruption, or those who wish to get married but cannot raise the necessary cash.'

According to another report, one ʿAnbasah b. Saʿīd asked the caliph ʿUmar b. ʿAbd al-ʿAzīz for some financial assistance. The caliph asked him in return: 'Tell me O ʿAnbasah, are you in need of help?' and he said: 'No.' He was then asked: 'Are you indebted?' to which he also said: 'No.' The caliph then told him: 'You are asking me to give you of public assets while you are not in need, and that I should prefer you to those who are in need? If you were indebted, I would have paid your debt for you, and if you were in need, I would have seen to your need. So take care of yourself and spend of your own property and fear God.'

Ibn Taymiyyah wrote concerning the *amānah* of rulers while narrating one of the last statements of the pious caliph ʿUmar b. ʿAbd al-ʿAzīz as follows:

> One who fulfils his *amānah* and subjugates his whim, God gives him strength and protection, and one who follows his whim contrary to his trust, God humiliates and punishes him. It is narrated that the caliph ʿUmar b. ʿAbd al-ʿAzīz, who left his family members less than 20 dirhams each to inherit, addressed his young family on his deathbed, while a large number of them were present, all of a tender age, none of whom had reached adulthood. The caliph addressed his family with tears welling up in his eyes: ' . . . by God I have not withheld any of your rights that are due to you, nor have I taken the peoples properties in order to enrich you with. You will be one of two types: either you are upright, and God will be your protector, or a transgressor, in which case I do not leave behind what might help the transgressor in his evil pursuits. You may go now.'

Ibn Taymiyyah continued the narrative to say that later it was noted that some of the caliphs' sons became wealthy and donated up to one hundred horses to charitable causes. Then it was also noted concerning some of the other Abbasid caliphs who died and left vast amounts of property to their children, some of whom inherited sums to the tune of six hundred thousand dinars, and yet they were later seen begging people for help.[71]

SELECTION OF OFFICIALS

One of the manifestations of *amānah* in government which commentators have highlighted is selection and appointment of officials. This must strictly be based on suitability and qualification. Anyone who betrays this trust calls upon himself condemnation and reprimand. It is betrayal of trust (*khiyānah*) in regard to the selection of officials to ignore a well-qualified and competent person who can be of great service to the people and assign him to a lowly task that is not in consonance with his ability. The opposite of this is even worse and that is when a person of little knowledge and capability is appointed to a responsible position merely because of friendship or ability to please his superiors.[72]

Māwardī has stipulated three conditions for a valid appointment to a government post, one is the terms of appointment, such as the limits of territorial jurisdiction, that must be clearly conveyed to the new recruit. He must also be informed of the general nature of his work, whether administrative, accounting, or executive etc. And lastly the person must be informed of his rights, such as salary and benefits, and his duties as to the rules and regulations he must observe. The information so conveyed, Māwardī added, must be sufficient so as to eliminate ignorance.[73] The three conditions that Māwardī stipulated are, in fact, prerequisites of accountability in that every employee is answerable in accordance with the contractual terms of his employment of which he must remain in no doubt.

With regard to remuneration for service, ʿIzz al-Dīn ʿAbd al-Salām al-Sulamī wrote that those who combine decision making and *fatwā* in their duties are to be paid more than those who are concerned mainly with the one and not the other. Both of these should, moreover, be paid more than those who merely execute orders. The head of state should be paid more than the judge and the *muftī*, not only because the former combines decision making and *fatwā* in his normal duties but also because he plays a more important role in realisation of benefit to the public and in protecting them against harm.[74]

Trustworthiness, responsibility and competence are naturally among the principal criteria by which a person is judged for eligibility to government office. The fact that the Prophet turned down Abū Dharr's request finds some explanation elsewhere in another *hadīth* addressed, this time, to another Companion, ʿAbd al-Raḥmān b. Ghanam, in which the Prophet discouraged people from actually asking for appointment to government positions. They may be selected to such positions on the basis of recognition and trust, but they may not actually ask for it nor engage in self-canvassing.[75] The message of this *hadīth* is about the same as the one addressed to Abū Dharr al-Ghaffārī. But if a person sees himself to be a suitable candidate for a task or a government position, he may apply for it. This is the conclusion Muḥammad al-Ghazālī has drawn from the Qurʾānic passage wherein the Prophet Yūsuf nominated himself to combine management of financial affairs with his prophetic office: 'Then he (Yūsuf) said (to the King): "Appoint me over the store-houses. I will indeed guard them, and I know how."' (12:55).

قال اجعلني على خزآئن الأرض إني حفيظ عليم

The Prophet Yūsuf was entrusted by the King with certain duties but he asked to be put in charge of the store-houses ad granaries, and the Qur'ān recounts this with implied approval.[76]

The salient qualifications that the Qur'ān stipulates in the selection of employees are knowledge, piety, ability and trustworthiness. This is concluded from the reading of the relevant passages of the Qur'ān. In one such passage, the daughter of the Prophet Shuʿayb (Jethro) recommended to her father to employ young Moses, as the text provides: 'O father! Hire him, for the best man you can hire is one who is strong and trustworthy.' (28:26)

يا أبت استأجره إن خير من استأجرت القوي الأمين

The substance of this verse is also supported in a *ḥadīth* wherein the Prophet has declared 'A believer who is strong is better and has a greater entitlement to God's love than a believer who is weak, but there is goodness in all of them.'[77] Another Qur'ānic verse, quoted in this connection, highlights the value of piety and knowledge:

يرفع الله الذين آمنوا منكم والذين أوتوا العلم درجات

God will raise in ranks those among you who have faith and those who have knowledge. (58:11)

The text here refers to knowledge and faith in the context of 'raising to high ranks,' which might imply that these should be considered as prerequisites of appointment to higher government positions. Whereas strength and honesty in the previous verse are more general, knowledge may be said to be a special requirement. The qualification of knowledge is thus suggested to be a requirement in the selection of the head of state and leading officials of government, for two main reasons, one of which is that knowledge enables the leader to understand and correctly apply the laws of *Sharīʿah* with a sense of purpose and vision. And secondly that a learned leader would inspire greater affection and respect from the community.[78] These qualifications should each be read in a comprehensive sense, but also in so far as they might relate more clearly to the nature of the task or jobs involved. Strength in reference to a particular position may mean physical strength but it can also mean intellectual strength as well as strong judgement. Knowledge too can be understood in a wider sense as well as in reference to skill and know–how relating to a particular task. Both the specific and the more general meanings are therefore relevant.

In a letter that the renowned Abū Yūsuf (d. 182/798), Chief Justice under the Abbasid caliph Hārūn al-Rashīd, sent to the caliph, he urged him to 'appoint as tax collectors upright people who are pious and trustworthy as well as knowledgeable. They should have a clean record such that the people have not known anything shameful about them. Those who are not upright and trustworthy should not be entrusted with financial responsibilities.'[79] Abū Yūsuf also advised the caliph not to entrust to public office again to anyone who has previously violated the trust and committed acts of injustice. He should make sure instead that such persons are reprimanded and punished.[80]

In the event where these conditions cannot be met and the government needs to fill up a number of posts, then it must select those who come close to meeting these requirements from among those who might be available. But anyone who attempts to select and appoint government officials on grounds of personal favour and friendship, or others who are unsuitable, would have failed the terms of his trust and would have betrayed his responsibility to the community.[81]

Al-Māwardī has also drawn a distinction between officials who are entrusted with general authority in decision-making and those who are appointed to administrative positions with the task mainly of executing decisions made by their superiors. The former involves *ijtihād*, and the person must therefore have that ability and also be a Muslim, but since the latter does not involve *ijtihād*, a non–Muslim may be appointed.[82]

Al-Māwardī wrote further that 'just character (*al-ʿadālah*) is a prerequisite of all appointments to government positions (*al-wilāyāt*)'. A just person is then described as one who is truthful and trustworthy and also refrains from indulgence in sin and activities which cast doubt on his uprightness. A just person is also observant of his honour and manliness (*murūʾah*) and acts in keeping with this image in all his affairs pertaining to this world and the next. When these qualities are obtained in a person, he qualifies as a person of just character; his testimony is admissible and he is eligible for appointment to government positions. But if he is lacking in these qualities, his uprightness collapses and he is not qualified to be either a witness or bearer of a government office.[83]

The head of state has the authority, in principle, to depose and dismiss an employee whom he suspects of corruption and abuse. For allowing a suspect to remain in office is not in the public interest. As for dismissal of officials who are not suspected of anything, three possibilities are envisaged:

(1) When a more qualified person is dismissed in order to be replaced by one who is less qualified. This is impermissible as it is not in the public interest and the head of state may not act contrary to the public interest.

(2) When a lesser-qualified official is dismissed in order to be replaced by a more qualified one. This is permissible as it is in harmony with public interest and *maslahah*.

(3) When someone is dismissed in order to be replaced by one who is his equal. There is disagreement over this. Some jurists have held this permissible saying that since the head of state has power to select between equally suitable options among his officials at the outset when he assumes office, then that option also remains open for him afterwards. The opposing view on this maintains that retaining and safeguarding of what is in existence takes priority over that which is unknown. The preferable view on this is to do what would realise the public interest best.[84]

In the event of shortage or lack of upright persons to be employed to government positions, al-Sulamī more or less provided the same response that Ibn Taymiyyah later gave in his *al-Siyāsah al-Sharʿiyyah*. Both authors take a pragmatic stance on this by saying that the best of what is available should be employed: One who might have a cleaner record or committed the lesser number of violations is to be given priority over the one who has committed more, for otherwise the people's lives and properties will be exposed to danger and loss. In support of this practical response, both al-Sulamī and Ibn Taymiyyah quoted the Qurʾānic directive to 'fear God to the extent of your ability' (64:16). Ibn Taymiyyah also quoted the *hadīth*: 'When I order you to do something do it to the extent of your ability.'[85]

Both of these quotations suggest acting on what is feasible and also taking the best option available under the circumstances.

It is reported that the caliph ʿUmar b. al-Khaṭṭāb appointed Sharaḥbīl b. Ḥasanah as Governor of Sham, but then he dismissed him and appointed Muʿāwiyah b. Abū Sufyān to that position. Sharaḥbīl then asked the caliph: 'Was it due to anger/displeasure that you dismissed me, O Commander of the faithful?' To this the caliph replied that it was not due to anger, for 'I hold you in affection now as I did before, but I wanted to employ a stronger man.' Sharaḥbīl then asked the caliph to make this known to the people, and the caliph consequently said it in a public address: 'I did not dismiss Sharaḥbīl because of anger or annoyance but I merely wanted to employ a man stronger than him.'[86]

It seems that Sharaḥbīl was dismissed prior to assuming office and the precedent that is set here probably validates just that. My understanding of the subject would otherwise tell me that once a person is duly selected and appointed, dismissal should then be based on performance. This is because appointment involves a degree of contractual commitment, and dismissal without cause in that situation tends to amount to harshness and possible *ḍarar*, which the *Sharīʿah* would not encourage. In modern times the practice of advertisement and procedural steps that are normally observed in the selection and employment of officials would appear to be in basic harmony with the substance of the *Sharīʿah* guidelines on the subject. If the absence of mass media in earlier times restricted the prospects of finding the best candidates for jobs, this has to a large extent been remedied by better means of advertisement. Once a suitable choice of candidate is made, dismissal should henceforth be based on performance and a cause that warrants dismissal. What follows next is a brief historical account of the employment policies of some Muslim rulers.

There was a tendency among the Umayyad rulers to appoint their relatives and individuals who enjoyed their trust to important government posts. The Abbasids also exhibited this tendency although the latter entrusted non-Arabs especially the Persians to leading positions in government. In a comment concerning these employment policies Abdul Malik al-Sayed has defended the policies of the Umayyad rulers to say that they were clear of 'religious or racial prejudice' in the employment of candidates to the state's bureaucracy. 'No qualified candidate was excluded on religious or racial bases...' It is further added that rulers of 'Muslim states were tolerant' and on numerous occasions appointed qualified Christians, Jews and Zoroastrians to high government posts 'without religious or denominational restrictions.'[87]

There is some evidence, however, to suggest that the Umayyad rulers did not treat the *mawālī* equally. ʿAbd al-Malik b. Marwān is noted, for example, to have actually barred the *mawālī* from employment to government posts. Philip Hitti commented that the *mawālī* under the Umayyads were reduced to 'the lowest stratum of Muslim society,' which they bitterly resented. This was why the *mawāli* often espoused hostile attitudes to the ruling authorities, and took common cause with the Shīʿites in Iraq or the Kharijite in Persia.[88] This policy was apparently reversed under the Abbasids.

Both the Abbasids and Fatimids employed non-Muslims to government posts 'in larger proportions than their percentage in the total population.' There were also several periods when Muslims were ruled by Christian viziers and both Christians and Jews held favourable positions throughout the Fatimid period in Egypt.[89] Jews are reported to have held important positions in both Egypt and Iraq. The first prime minister of the Fatimid state appointed by al-ʿAzīz (d. 365/975) was a former Baghdadi Jew, Yaʿqūb Ibn Killīs, who later converted to Islam. Several Fatimid viziers were Christians. Caliphs and governors also employed Jews and Christians as physicians, interpreters and scribes. Twice in the third/ninth century the defence ministers in Baghdad were Christians, and in one instance under the Fatimids of Egypt one Christian vizier, ʿĪsā Ibn Nastūrus, succeeded another Christian vizier, Mansūr Ibn ʿAbdun. Non-Muslim citizens were found 'in every *dīwān* of the state except those of purely religious function, such as *Diwān al-Qaḍā*'.'[90]

Both the Abbasid and Fatimid states paid attention to the education and training of officials before they entered government service. 'The Islamic Arab states devoted great effort to higher education establishing several institutions of higher learning.' One of the practical objectives of such institutions was to prepare potential candidates to enter the state bureaucracy. Institutions of higher learning were organised and supported by money from and the personal involvement of the caliphs, and pious and philanthropist individuals who drew inspiration from the Qur'ānic emphasis on education.[91] Women received their education at the same schools as men and were qualified to assume responsibilities in certain areas, such as teaching, medical services and law and literature. Imam Abū Hanīfah declared in the second/eight century that women were as entitled to be jurists and lawyers as men. Imām al-Shāfiʿī informs us that he studied theology with a renowned woman professor in the main mosque in Cairo.[92]

CRITERIA OF ACCOUNTABILITY: PERSONAL AND CORPORATE

The Qur'ān makes no exception whatsoever when it lays down the principle of individual responsibility in its declarations that 'whoever commits a transgression only commits it against his own soul,' and that 'No soul shall be burdened with the burden of another soul,' and 'man is only rewarded for what he strives (himself)' (*al-Nisā'*, 4:111, and *al-Najm*, 53:38 respectively). These are clear affirmations of the uncompromising character of individual accountability in Islam. Privileges of high office, including that of the head of state, presidency or parliament do not provide any basis of immunity in the general implementation of this principle.

Personal responsibility is also the basic theme of the *ḥadīth*, earlier quoted, which provides that 'every one of you is a guardian and is accountable for what is placed in his custody. The Imam is a guardian and he is responsible for his subjects . . .'[93]

Yet there is evidence to suggest that the state is responsible to compensate members of the public who might have been harmed by its employees in the performance of duty. The authority for this can be found in a long *ḥadīth*, reported by the Prophet's widow, ʿĀ'ishah, which may be summarised as follows:

> The Prophet (pbuh) sent Abū Jahm b. Ḥudhayfah for collection of *zakāh* and when a man quarreled with him in the matter of payment of his *zakāh*, Abū Jahm struck him and injured him in the head. Then his relatives came to the Prophet and demanded retaliation. The Prophet said 'you can have such and such' in compensation, but they did not agree. Then the Prophet raised the sums involved and they still disagreed, but when it was raised again, they agreed. The Prophet then said that he was addressing the people that evening and he will inform them that 'you have agreed to the settlement.' This was also agreed. Then the Prophet addressed the people that: 'These Laythiyyin [from al-Layth tribe] demanded retaliation and I offered them such and such in compensation and they finally agreed.' (The Prophet actually repeated the whole process of negotiation, which made the audience somewhat angry and aggressive toward the plaintiffs, but the Prophet said that they should not be harmed). The Prophet then asked both the plaintiffs and his audience if they were in agreement, and when he heard both sides that they were, then he stepped down.[94]

In his capacity as head of state the Prophet evidently took the sum he was giving away in compensation from public assets, but more importantly that he accepted responsibility to compensate the plaintiffs for the wrongful act of his official.

As already noted, the principle of personal accountability in *Sharīʿah* draws no distinction between the ruler and ruled. There is only a limited recognition of transfer of liability from employee to the government for damages in respect of acts and violations committed in the course of duty. The head of state and government officials are answerable not only for deliberate but also for their erroneous conduct and tortuous liability incurred in the course of duty, but the jurists have disagreed as to whether compensation for damage is payable from their personal assets or from the assets of *bayt al-māl*. Many have held that compensation for erroneous misconduct is payable from the *bayt al-māl*, for the head of state or his officials may not have sufficient personal assets for the purpose, or else that there may be too many claims for compensation than can be paid either by the head of state himself or the family and relatives of the offender. It is in any case argued that in the discharge of duty the head of state and state employees are normally engaged in work on behalf of the community and not for themselves.[95]

The Prophet-cum-head of state held himself personally accountable in regard to his conduct in office. Thus it is reported that al-Faḍl Ibn ʿAbbās visited the Prophet when he was unwell. The Prophet asked Ibn ʿAbbās to hold his hand and help him go to the mosque. When the Prophet entered the mosque he addressed the people in the following terms:

> If I have fallen short of fulfilling your rights, it is only because I am a human (and liable to error). If there be anyone among you whom I might have humiliated in any way, I stand here ready for him to retaliate. If I have physically hurt any of you, you may also retaliate. Should anyone among you have a financial claim against me, let him take what is due to him from my property. Know that I hold in esteem a man who has a claim against me and takes it from me or exonerates me. For I want to meet my Lord while I am clear of such claims.[96]

The principle of personal accountability of rulers has been confirmed in the words and conduct of the Pious Caliphs after the Prophet. The caliph ʿUmar has on more than one occasion actually cited the above *ḥadīth* to affirm that he himself and his officials are personally accountable for their conduct. He also held many of his leading officials to account on that basis.[97]

The Imams Abū Ḥanīfah, Mālik, and Aḥmad b. Ḥanbal have held concerning punishment for crime that if the person to whom punishment is applied suffers injury as a result or dies, the head of state and his officials are not responsible if they have not exceeded the normal and customary methods in which the punishment in question is administered. This is because the head of state is required in the normal conduct of duty to impose punishment by order of the court of justice and so long as he and his officials have not violated the legitimate bounds of their duty, and have not deliberately gone to excess, they are not to be held responsible.[98]

Imam Shāfiʿī has held, on the other hand, that the head of state (and presumably also his officials) is liable for the payment of blood money, or *diyyah*, for erroneous killing if the punishment that is lawfully imposed leads to the death of the convict, even if the punishment is death by execution but which is wrongfully administered. For the head of state has in principle powers to grant pardon, especially in cases of *taʿzīr*, or to authorise a lighter punishment instead. This would mean that every case of *taʿzīr* is potentially pardonable, and *taʿzīr* is in any case meant for correction and discipline, not destruction and death. When *taʿzīr* punishment leads to death, the head of state is responsible to pay the *diyyah* regardless as to whether the punishment was potentially lethal or light but was not to bring about the death of the convict. A clear case of excess that al-Shāfiʿī has given in illustration is when the convict for the offence of wine-drinking is lashed more than forty lashes and he dies as a result, the head of state is responsible to pay the *diyyah* to his next of kin for culpable homicide.[99]

The basic principle here is that the state bears responsibility for the harm that it causes when it exceeds the limits of its authority and violates the law. If a particular employee of the state acts on behalf of the administration and someone is harmed as a result, the administration is responsible to remove the injury (*ḍarar*) caused or compensate for it under the *ḥadīth* 'lā ḍarar wa-lā ḍirār' and the legal maxim that harm must be removed 'al-ḍarar yuzāl'.[100]

Juristic disagreements over the details may have to be resolved in the light of the general principle, which is that the head of state and government officials are not liable for the consequences of their conduct in office if they act within the limits of the law and do not act deliberately in order to punish to excess—only when they act in a way that violates the accepted standards of proper conduct, they become criminally responsible if they knew that they had no right to act in that way. But when the head of state and his official act in good faith and act while believing that they only discharge their duty, then they are not responsible for the adverse consequences that may materialise.

With regard to the administration of penalties, the government is normally under duty to apply them by virtue of final judicial orders, be they prescribed (*ḥudūd*) penalties, or deterrent (*taʿzīr*) penalties. Moreover, fulfilment of an obligation (*wājib*) is normally not contingent upon safety as no one can guarantee that punishments can all be carried out under that condition. Thus when a person is convicted for an offence to eighty or to one hundred lashes, and the convict dies as a result of their application, there is no criminal liability, if the lashing is carried out under normal conditions. But there is criminal liability in the event the person who administers them applies greater force such that it breaks the flesh, or that he exceeds the number of lashes as a result of forgetfulness. If there is no criminal intention involved on the part of the administrator of punishment and the harm that materialises is unintentional, the government would not be liable for payment of compensation, but if the harm inflicted is intentional and the person knew he was exceeding the limits, the person himself would be criminally responsible. This would normally be the case, for example, when in his personal capacity the head of state or a government official kills another person deliberately and he is subsequently convicted by the court of justice, he would be personally liable to *qiṣāṣ*. This may also be said with reference to all the prescribed (*ḥudūd*) offences committed by the head of state or government officials, for which they are personally responsible, and the law pertaining to *ḥudūd* would apply to them as it would to anyone else.[101]

Furthermore, there is no recognition in *Sharīʿah* of separate tribunals and jurisdictions for high ranking state officials, which means that the head of state and all leading officials can be tried by the courts of *Sharīʿah* for their crimes, be it within or outside the conduct of duty, and the *Sharīʿah* courts as courts of general jurisdiction apply the law equally to all. There is similarly no recognition in the *fiqh* manuals of a separate category of punishments outside the triple classification of penalties into *qiṣāṣ*, *ḥudūd* and *taʿzīr*. The *fiqh* discourse on crimes and punishments is not elaborate on administrative crimes as a separate category, nor does it expound separate sanctions that may be imposed for wrong-doing in the course of duty. The matter would consequently fall under *taʿzīr* for lack of any separate classification.

ʿAwdah's explanation for the absence of separate tribunals and punishments is focused on the prevention of double jeopardy as a state employee could be punished on disciplinary grounds and then be also held liable for trial before the *Sharīʿah* court. Tawfīq al-Shāwī has observed, and rightly so, that there is no necessary conflict in the recognition of separate tribunals, nor of punishment types, for administrative offences. The fact that the *fiqh* manuals do not recognise separate types of disciplinary punishments means that they all fall under *taʿzīr*.[102] To this may be added perhaps the point that neither of the two commentators have mentioned the *maẓālim* jurisdiction in this connection. From the analysis I have presented below, it would appear that the *maẓālim* was basically an administrative tribunal which made extensive use of discretionary and disciplinary punishments, within the rubric of *taʿzīr*.

The picture that is depicted here tends on the whole to manifest the unitarian view of justice to which Islam and its *Sharīʿah* subscribe. The basic attitude of uniformity in law and justice bears the imprint of *tawḥīd* that favours a holistic approach to justice. Having said this, it will be noted that the *Sharīʿah* also recognises specification and assignment of jurisdiction on such grounds as territory, subject matter and the like as the head of state may apply in the best interest of good government. Under the principle of *takhsīs al-qaḍā*, or specification of justice, the head of state may thus authorise separate tribunals for civil servants, commercial disputes and the like.[103]

THE LIMITS OF OBEDIENCE

The citizen's duty of obedience to the lawful government is not absolute in that he or she is entitled to dispute with the rulers when the latter fail to comply with the directives of the *Sharīʿah*. This is the subject of the Qurʾānic verse that follows:

$$\text{يَأَيُّها الذين آمنوا أطيعوا الله وأطيعوا الرسول وأولى الأمر}$$
$$\text{منكم فإن تنازعتم فى شيئ فردوه إلى الله والرسول}$$

> O you who believe! Obey God and obey the Messenger and those in authority from among you. Then if you dispute about a matter, refer it to God and the Messenger ... (4:59).

The believers are thus enjoined to obey the rulers, but only if the rulers are themselves committed to the rules of law and *Sharīʿah*. While obedience remains the principal theme of this verse, the latter portion of the text clearly allows disputation with the rulers. The text also makes clear that both parties to such disputes, that is, the ruler and ruled, must submit to God's law as the final arbiter of their differences. They are all accountable and their conduct is to be measured by reference to the same criteria that are expounded in the *Sharīʿah*. Two other Qur'ānic passages may be quoted in support:

> And obey not the command of those who are extravagant, who make mischief in the land and mend not (their ways). (26:151–152)

ولا تطيعوا أمر المسرفين الذين يفسدون فى الأرض ولا يصلحون

> And obey not one whose heart We have permitted to neglect the remembrance of Us; who follows his own desire and whose case has gone beyond all bounds. (18:28)

ولا تطع من أغفلنا قلبه عن ذكرنا وأتبع هواه وكان أمره فرطا

It is further provided in a *ḥadīth*:

السمع والطاعة على المرء المسلم فيما أحبّ وكره ما لم يؤمر بمعصية ، فإذا أمر بمعصية فلا سمع ولا طاعة

> A Muslim is under duty to listen and to obey in what he (or she) likes or dislikes unless he (or she) is commanded to commit a sin, but when he is commanded to commit a sin, he is under no obligation to listen nor obey.[104]

Obedience is thus required to responsible rulers who consider themselves accountable to God and the community and remain clear of violation and abuse. If a command is found to be manifestly unlawful, the person to whom it is addressed is entitled to disobey it even if it be a military order or issued in any other context. The ruling of this *ḥadīth* is in harmony also with the essence of *ḥisbah* in that every individual is directly responsible to enjoin good and to avoid and forbid what is manifestly unlawful.

Several *ḥadīth*s have been recorded on the subject of obedience, the most well-known of which is as follows:

لا طاعة فى معصية، إنما الطاعة فى المعروف

There is no obedience in transgression; obedience is required in what is lawful.[105]

The *Sunnah*, on the other hand, advises restraint and tolerance of the minor failures of leaders. Thus according to a *ḥadīth*:

من رأى من أميره شيئًا يكرهه فليصبر فإنه ليس لأحد
يفارق الجماعة شبرا

When you see something on the part of your leaders that you dislike, try to remain patient, for no one may split the community (through acts of defiance) as far as one can.[106]

And then it is further noted in another *ḥadīth*:

من رأى منكم منكرا فليغيره بيده فإن لم يستطع فبلسانه
فإن لم يستطع فبقلبه وذلك أضعف الإيمان

If any of you sees an evil, let him change it by his hand. If he is unable to do so, let him change it by his words; if he is unable to do even that, then let him denounce it in his heart, but this is the weakest form of *īmān* (faith).[107]

It is thus obvious that the *Sharī'ah* does not simply assign a role of passive subservience to any one, but entitles every one to exercise judgement and initiative to promote a good cause or act against what he or she considers to be prejudiced and harmful. Obedience is also due to leaders who are themselves diligent in the discharge of their own responsibilities. These guidelines are incorporated in the works of writers on the theory of caliphate who specify the following among the salient duties of the caliph, and the criteria therefore of his entitlement to obedience and the grounds also for his accountability.

(1) Protection of the religion and safeguarding its cardinal tenets against heresy and false doctrine through correct education and guidance.

(2) Administration of justice, resolution of disputes, and protection of the peoples rights.

(3) Maintenance of peace and security so as to enable the people to pursue their livelihood.

(4) Enforcement of the prescribed penalties (*ḥudūd*) and fighting criminality and aggression.

(5) Defence of the borders against threat of hostile attacks and preparation of adequate defense capabilities.

(6) Waging war against aggression and sedition (*fitnah*) that threaten the freedom of religion.

(7) Collection of taxes and efficient management of financial affairs.

(8) Selection and appointment of officials.

(9) Personal supervision and involvement in the affairs of the community so that neither pastime nor even worship separates the head of state from his basic duties.[108]

For as long as the ruler is assiduous in the execution of his duties while observant of the basic terms of the community's trust that is vested in him, he is entitled to the obedience (*ṭaʿah*) and support (*naṣrah*) of his people. He remains in office and no one is entitled to disobey him without cause. Unlawful disobedience is considered an act of rebellion (*bughā*) that is punishable under the law. ʿIzz al-Dīn al-Sulamī underlined the virtues of a just ruler when he wrote that 'rulers and government leaders who are just are among the most virtuous of all people and earn greatest rewards based on the unanimous agreement of all Muslims (*bi-ijmāʿ ahl al-Islām*). This is because they bring greatest benefit to the people and avert and prevent prejudice and corruption.' Their reward is consequently proportionate to the benefit they secure for the people through their persistent efforts.[109] This is also the clear purport of a *ḥadīth* wherein the Prophet is reported to have said 'A day that a righteous head of state spends in the service of his people is more meritorious than one hundred (or fifty) years (the transmitter is doubtful) that a worshipper spends with his family.'[110] To administer justice is clearly one of the most important duties of the head of state and other leading officials.

ʿAlī b. Abū Ṭālib is reported to have said:

> It is binding on the head of state (Imam) to rule in accordance with what God has revealed, to establish trust, and restore to the people what belongs to them. If he does so, then the people are under obligation to listen to him and follow his commands.[111]

As for the predicament of leaders who combine justice with injustice in their conduct, ʿIzz al-Dīn al-Sulamī has given an interesting answer as follows:

If people have lost their properties because of it, the leaders concerned must pay them back, failing which the latter are taken to task for it in the Day of Judgement and their good deeds will be reduced proportionately. In the event where all of their good deeds are exhausted, they will be burdened with the sins of those whom they had oppressed, and they will be thrown in Hell thereafter. The same applies to injustices committed about the lives and honour of the people, and in respect also of the rights that were unduly delayed after they were due, and rights that were precipitated before they were due.[112]

Al-Sulamī then quotes the Qur'ānic verse, which provides 'And We shall set up scales of justice for the Day of Judgment so that not a soul will be dealt with unjustly in the least.' (21:47)

ونضع الموازين القسط ليوم القيامة فلا تظلم نفس شيئًا

There is general agreement on the principle that the ruler is entitled to the obedience of citizens within the limits of the law and loses this right when he himself becomes a transgressor. The duty of obedience thus terminates when the ruler himself violates the *Sharī'ah* yet it is not every little violation that would qualify, but one which is self-evident, and according to a *ḥadīth*, that it amounts to disbelief. The limit of obedience is a complex subject that needs to be separately addressed. Suffice it here to say, however, that the ruler is accountable to the people under the law, but this can only be effective if he is supported and obeyed by the people in the first place. The relationship between accountability and obedience here may be said to resemble the interdependency of most other rights and obligations.[113]

Among the virtues of conduct one could expect to see in a leader, humility (*tawāduʿ*), forgiveness (*ʿafw*) and sincerity (*ikhlāṣ*) are particularly recommended. When a leader possesses them, he qualifies as upright and inspires loyalty and obedience on the part of his employees and the general public. With reference to humility the Qur'ān directed the Prophet repeatedly in such terms as to: 'Lower thy wing in tenderness to the believers (*wa'khfiḍ janāhaka li'l-mu'minīn*),' and 'Lower your wing (in tenderness) to the believers who follow you.' (*Al-Ḥijr*, 15:88; *al-Shuʿarāʾ*, 26:214). But more generally the Qur'ān praises: 'Those of God's servants who walk on the earth with humility and when they are addressed (with rudeness) by the uncouth, they meet them with a greeting.' (*Al-Furqān*, 25:63).

وعباد الرحمن الذين يمشون على الأرض هونا وإذا
خاطبهم الجاهلون قالوا سلاما

A leader should thus be endowed with humility and tolerance and be able to turn a blind eye to a thoughtless encounter of an ignorant individual. The Qur'ān thus required the Prophet to be tolerant to the people and to avoid alienating them through pomp and ceremony of the kind that was in vogue in the Roman and Persian courts at that time. It is all the more important that the same is observed by all government leaders who are entrusted with the affairs of Muslims. Humility is admittedly a moral virtue, yet its total neglect would mean a departure from the veritable ethos of Islam. Humility in a real sense means that the leader should make himself approachable to the people and act as their trustee and servant. Thus it is evident that obedience to rulers does not imply servitude as the leaders themselves are advised to excercise humility and avoid arrogance in his dealings with the people.

The Qur'ān is equally emphatic on the virtue of forgiveness (al-ʿafw) and refers to it in a variety of themes and contexts so much so that it becomes an important feature of Islamic ethos. Thus it is proclaimed: 'If you forgive, it is closest to righteousness,' (2:237)

وأن تعفوا أقرب للتقوى

which suggests that if one makes an error, it should be on be side of leniency and forgiveness, and ' . . . so that you forgive and tolerate. Would you not want God to be merciful to you?' (24:22).

وليعفوا وليصفحوا ألا تحبون أن يغفر الله لكم

In another Qur'ānic passage, God Most High praises those who: ' . . . Swallow their anger and forgive the people. And God truly loves those who trust others well.' (3:134)

والكاظمين الغيظ والعافين عن الناس والله يحب المحسنين

And then in a direct command, the Prophet has been ordered to: 'Take to forgiveness, enjoin ʿurf (social custom, or what is decent and fair) and turn away from the ignorant.' The substance of this address is confirmed in another verse that similarly instructed the Prophet, and therefore also the believers: '. . . So forgive them and seek God's forgiveness for them and consult them in affairs.' (7:199; 3:159).[114]

The typical phrase 'God loves those who are good to others—*inna 'Llāha yuḥibb al-muḥsinīn*' often occurs in the context of forgiveness in the Qur'ān. The *Sunnah* of the Prophet is equally explicit on the virtue of *ʿafw*. Thus it appears that leniency and forgiveness are desired qualities in everyone, especially in the head of state and other government leaders. Yet there is no indication in any of these that *ʿafw* should be indiscriminately applied, nor should *ʿafw* be confounded with weakness. For *ʿafw* can attain excellence and beauty in places where severity may generate the opposite results. It is to rulers who conform to the laws and moral teachings of Islam that obedience naturally complements the ruler-ruled relationship.

RIGHT OF COMPLAINT (*ḤAQQ AL-SHAKWAH*)

The *Sharīʿah* entitles all individuals to approach the government authorities for grievances they might have against another private party or the government itself. This is the substance of the Qur'ānic text which provides:

ولمن انتصر بعد ظلمه فأولئك ما عليهم من سبيل

One who seeks assistance after suffering oppression has nothing to be blamed for. (42:41)

There are over fifty Qur'ānic verses on justice (*ʿadl*) and many more on denunciation of oppression (*ẓulm*). The text speaks rigorously against discrimination and therefore entitles everyone to seek redress against oppression and injustice. Every individual is entitled to impartial justice. When a dispute is brought before the court it becomes the duty of the court to adjudicate under the rule of law without grant of favour or preference to any one. The principles of Islamic justice would not allow the judge, for example, to treat a man of piety and knowledge in any way different to a man of questionable piety—if they be involved in a litigation before it. A pious litigant would have his spiritual reward in the hereafter but he is not entitled to preferential treatment in the court of justice. Equality and impartial treatment before the courts of justice must also be observed throughout the evidence and trial procedures. This was indeed conveyed in the renowned letter that the second caliph ʿUmar b. al-Khaṭṭāb issued to his judges, in which he asked them to treat all litigants equally. To quote a portion of that letter: '. . . let all men be equal in your sight, in your court, and in your judgment, so that the strong may not hope to sway you into injustice, nor is the weak led to despair in your justice. The burden of proof lies on the shoulder of the plaintiff . . .'[115] Islamic history has recorded many examples in which the head of state either brought a private suit against another or sat as a defendant before the court and these examples also involve cases in which the court issued decisions against the head of state. The state itself and its administration stand in this regard on the same footing as the individual litigant. All are subject to the same rules and procedures in the course of trial and presentation of evidence.[116]

The *ḥadīth* which provides that 'harm may neither be inflicted nor reciprocated in Islam—*lā ḍarar wa-lā ḍirar fi'l-Islām*',[117] conveys essentially the same message of equality in regard to entitlement to redress of one who is the victim of aggression and prejudice. One who has suffered injury as a result of a criminal act or tort is consequently encouraged to seek redress and once the incident is reported to the authorities in the form of a petition or complaint, the latter must act to alleviate it and respond to the demand for justice. This is clear from the latter portion of the *ḥadīth* that harm is not to be reciprocated through personal vendetta by one who takes the law into his own hands, but that recourse should instead be to the authorities. A legal maxim that is derived from this *ḥadīth* also provided that 'harm must be eliminated—*al-ḍararu yuzāl*.' It was indeed due to the emphasis the *Sharīʿah* lays on the government's receptiveness to people's complaints that Abū Yūsuf, Chief Justice under Hārūn al-Rashīd (d. 193/809), asked the caliph to assign a day in which to hold open court for the purpose of receiving complaints from members of the public. The precedent was in fact set much earlier by the Prophet himself, and later by the Pious Caliphs who used to receive complaints from the public against leading officials. The *maẓālim* jurisdiction that is discussed in some detail below was originally based in the idea of receiving complaints against official abuse and that remains to this day to be the basic justification for such a jurisdiction.

The *Sunnah* provides details of instances and encounters in which the people complained to the Prophet-cum-head of state against some leading officials and the Prophet responded to their pleas. There were complaints, for instance, that the governor of Yemen, Muʿādh Ibn Jabal, was lengthening the Qurʾān recitation in congregational prayers and that this had put the worshippers in hardship. The Prophet then addressed Muʿādh 'Are you being an agent of sedition (*fitnah*), O Muʿādh?'[118]

يا معاذ أفتّان أنت؟

The Prophet then instructed, in the same *ḥadīth*, the prayer leaders as to the manner in which they should lead the congregation: 'When any of you lead the people in prayer, try to make it light on them.'[119]

إذا صلى أحدكم بالناس فليخفف

In another incident it is reported that the Prophet's minister and companion, Abū Bakr, spoke to a Jew named Fanḥāṣ, whom he invited to embrace Islam, but he refused and ridiculed the poverty of the Muslims and their borrowings from Jewish moneylenders. Fanḥāṣ went on to refer to the following Qurʾānic passage: 'Who is there to extend a benevolent loan to God so that He will multiply it for him by many folds?' (2:245). Fanḥāṣ then told Abū Bakr 'If your God were wealthy He would not ask the people for a loan.' Abū Bakr slapped him in the face and told him 'Had it not been for the covenant of *dhimmah* between us, I would have struck your neck, O enemy of God.' The man subsequently complained to the Prophet and the Prophet questioned Abū Bakr about the incident, but when Fanḥāṣ was asked, he changed his version of the event. The matter was resolved in a Qurʾānic verse that was revealed concerning the event (3:180) which confirmed that Abū Bakr was telling the truth and Fanḥāṣ was casting false aspersions on God. The point to note here is that the Prophet did not simply dismiss the Jew's complaint against a prominent Companion but questioned the latter to verify if he had in fact been a transgressor in the incident.[120]

This narrative also serves to illustrate the generally accepted principle of *Sharīʿah* which entitles the citizens, both Muslim and non-Muslim, to lodge a complaint against government officials regardless of their rank and title.[121] Many scholars have thus concluded that accountability of the rulers (*muḥāsabat al-ḥukkām*) for their activities in office embodies both a right and a collective duty of the community to take appropriate measures to make this a reality of political life. Such measures may include instituting adequate rules and procedures to promote a responsible government that is dedicated to the rule of law and service to the community.[122]

After the conquest of Khaybar cultivated land was divided among groups of Muslims on condition of sharecropping and it is reported that the Muslims treated the land as their own property and began to use its produce without the permission of its Jewish owners. When the Prophet learned of this, he assembled the Muslims and addressed them in the following terms: 'We have given protection to the lives and properties of these Jews and appointed them as our workers. They are now in a treaty relationship with us. Eating out of their property without fair return for it is unlawful.' The report adds that after these instructions, there arose no further complaints against the Muslim residents.[123] This instruction laid down the basic principle of non-exploitation of a weaker party. It was this sense of justice that the custodian of the Khaybar properties, ʿAbd Allāh b. Rawāḥah, displayed when he went to share the crops with the Jews. He piled up the total produce in two equal heaps and gave them the option to take either, lest they felt critical of any injustice or exploitation in the proposed distribution.[124]

Upon receiving a complaint, the caliph ʿUmar would summon both parties and ask them questions in front of one another before taking any disciplinary measures. He also held public gatherings, especially during the *hajj* season, with his officials and members of the public on which occasion he solicited complaints against official abuse. The caliph also used to receive delegations from the tribes and outlying communities whom he enquired about their well-being and about the conduct of officials in charge of their affairs. He would ask them questions whether the governor on duty allowed the poor and weak to visit him, and whether or not he visited the sick. The caliph also wrote frequently to his governors and summoned them for consultation to Medina.[125] The caliph ʿUmar had envisaged a plan for himself as he once said:

> God willing if I lived long enough I shall travel for a year to enquire into the conditions of the people myself, as officials do not always keep me informed. I shall go to Al-Jazīrah (Algiers) and stay there for two months, and then stay for two months in Egypt, and then spend two months in Bahrain, and then travel and stay for two months in Basra. This would be a year well spent.[126]

The Umayyad caliph Umar b. ʿAbd al-ʿAzīz sent a letter to his officials in which he openly encouraged members of the public to voice their grievances:

> Anyone who comes to us and draws our attention to an act of transgression or a matter wherein God may bring benefit to all or some of the people, he will be given a grant of between one hundred and three hundred dinars, depending on the amount of hardship and *ḥisbah* he might have undertaken. May God bless the person who is not prevented by the hardship of travel, and may God enable us, as a result, to vindicate a right or put an end to a wrong, or open the door to a benefit.[127]

This heightened sense of accountability was inspired by personal piety and the desire to gain the pleasure of God. It is perhaps of interest to note here that ʿUmar b. al-Khaṭṭāb, who acted as a *Qāḍī* (judge) under the caliph Abū Bakr, was kept idle for months for lack of any dispute to be referred to him. When caliph Abū Bakr went to Mecca and assembled the people to inquire if they had any grievances against government officials, there was no report of any grievances either.[128]

HOLDING ONESELF TO ACCOUNT (*MUḤĀSABAT AL-NAFS*)

As noted earlier, Muslim jurists have emphasised the personal aspect of accountability in Islam with special emphasis on accountability to God and to one's own conscience. This is a part of the general concept of *taqwā* (piety) of the individual, but given the fact that the *Sharīʿah* draws no clear distinction between the public and private aspects of accountability, *muḥāsabat al-nafs* may be seen as an integral part of accountability. This aspect of accountability features prominently in the teachings of the Qurʾān and *Sunnah*. Accountability to God and appeal to the religious and moral self of the individual constitutes an integral part of the religion, especially its teachings concerning the Day of Judgement. Accountability accordingly begins with self-discipline and the purpose is ultimately to prevent deviation through nurturing an upright personality and outlook in personal matters as well as conduct in public office. The main difference being that *muḥāsabat al-nafs* is basically self-induced, whereas *muḥāsabat al-ḥukkām* is enforced as a principle of public law. The essence of *muḥāsabat al-nafs* can be seen in the following Qurʾānic directives, which are addressed to the individual:

أقرأ كتابك كفى بنفسك اليوم عليك حسيبا

Read your book and your own soul is sufficient as a reckoner against you on this Day. (17:14)

The individual is thus sensitised to be the first inspector and police of his own conduct. Elsewhere the holy Book confirms the natural inclination of man to be a critic of his own deeds:

بل الإنسان على نفسه بصيرة

Nay, (but every) man is a witness over himself. (75:14)

The message here is addressed to the enlightened conscience of man. The reward of those who feel the presence of God and discipline themselves for His sake is, as the text further proclaims, God's pleasure and great spiritual achievement:

وأما من خاف مقام ربه ونهى النفس عن الهوى فإن الجنة هي المأوى

And one who fears the countenance of his Lord and guards himself against (the dictates of untrammelled) desire—shall reside happily in Paradise. (79:40-41)

The scope of *muḥāsabah* in the hereafter is all-inclusive as the text provides in the following two passages:

يوم يبعثهم الله جميعا فينبئهم بما عملوا أحصه الله ونسوه والله على كل شيئ شهيد

On the Day when God will raise them (the people) all together and inform them of what they did. God has kept account of it while they forget. And God is Witness over all things. (58:6)

يومئذ يصدر الناس أشتاتا ليروا أعمالهم فمن يعمل مثقال ذرة خيرا يره ومن يعمل مثقال ذرة شرا يره

The Day (of judgement) when people will issue forth in scattered groups to be shown their deeds. Whoever does good an atom's weight will see it then, and whoever does ill an atom's weight will also see it. (99:6–8)

And then the constant reminders in the Qur'ān that 'God sees whatever you do,' that 'God is aware of your actions,' and 'God is watchful over you,' (3:156; 2:234; 4:1) instill fear of God in the believer and the notion of accountability to Him. 'Their final recourse is to Us and We shall take account of what they have done.' (88:25–26)

إن إلينا إيّابهم ثم إن علينا حسابهم

This is taken a step further in the verse where the individual is reminded of his accountability to the community of believers: 'God, His Messenger and the believers will take note and see the result of your actions' (9:12). The text here is so worded as to imply that the individual enjoys freedom of action but then it is the result of his conduct for which the community will take him to account. Then it is stated that the individuals 'may hide (what they do) from the people, but they cannot hide it from God . . . His knowledge encompasses all that they do.' (4:108)

يستخفون من الناس ولايستخفون من الله . . . وكان الله
بما يعملون محيطا

Accountability of the self is vividly shown in the personal records of the caliphs Abū Bakr and 'Umar who took from the *bayt al-māl* only subsistence salaries and even then on their deathbeds they expressed the wish to reimburse their receipts and return what they had received back to the public treasury. The caliph 'Uthmān did not even take a salary.[129]

Reports indicate that the caliph 'Umar continued with his own trade during the early days of his caliphate, and at one point when he needed money to finance his business he asked 'Abd al-Raḥmān b. 'Awf for a loan. The latter was surprised with the caliph's request and simply retorted 'why don't you borrow it from the *bayt al-māl*?' knowing that one of the functions of the *bayt al-māl* was to advance loans to individuals. 'No!' remarked 'Umar, 'if I die before repayment, you will propose to write it off as a bad debt and the *bayt al-māl* will suffer, but if I borrow it from you, you will arrange to receive it from my estate.' To cite another example, ʿUtbah b. Farqad, an army general who conquered Azerbaijan sent some sweets to the caliph ʿUmar, which he declined and returned with a letter and the stern remark that what he had sent was not the fruit of his own effort and that he would not eat something which was not available to all Muslims. It is further reported that a man came to the caliph ʿUmar and addressed him somewhat impudently over the distribution of the spoils of war saying 'fear God O ʿUmar.' Someone who was present volunteered to put this man in his place, but the caliph declined the offer and said 'It will be no good if they (the people) did not remind us so, and no good if we did not listen.'[130]

Caliph ʿAlī b. Abū Ṭālib, whose heightened sense of accountability and devotion to the cause of justice is a familiar theme of the early history of Islam was strict both with himself and his officials and in this he resembled the caliph ʿUmar. His ascetic attitude to personal expenditure even excelled that of his predecessors. He was not unaware of the caliph's right to subsistence from the *bayt al-māl* but he voluntarily deprived himself of it. One report thus has it that he took his sword to the market to sell, as he needed money to buy a shirt. When some of his friends found him shivering in the cold, they advised him to get himself a woolen mantle from the *bayt al-māl*, but he chose to forego that right. Reports also indicated that the Umayyad caliph, ʿUmar b. ʿAbd al-ʿAzīz gave away all of his assets estimated at over 23,000 dinars when he assumed office. He took from the *bayt al-māl* only two dirhams (about one-fifth of a dinar) for his living expenses a day. He lived a life of abnegation and self-denial leaving a large family but virtually no assets behind.

It is further reported that upon assuming office, one of the first things that the caliph ʿUmar b. ʿAbd al-ʿAzīz encountered was a gift of fine riding animals that no one had ridden before from courtiers and officials to welcome the new caliph. The caliph ordered the officer of *bayt al-māl* to 'add this to the public assets.' The caliph did the same to the large tents and canopies that were presented as a welcome gift to him. He walked on them until he reached the end, and then asked the officer in charge to 'add this to the *bayt al-māl* of the Muslims.'[131]

Abū Ḥāmid al-Ghazālī quotes most of these passages and follows them with a comment that God Most High has informed His servants that He is watchful over them and will be taking them to account. 'This is a certain prospect and the warning that these messages contain makes *muḥāsabah*, truthful *murāqabah* and self questioning (in this life) all the more advisable. Those who do it will be lightening their burden on the Day of Judgement... and those who neglect it shall be regretful.'[132]

The Qur'ānic teachings are addressed mainly to the individual, so much so that it makes the pursuit of justice a duty not only of the judges and governors but also of every conscientious man and woman. Everyone is accountable without any considerations of fear and favour and nothing must obstruct the course of justice. The believers are thus enjoined in the Qur'ān to be maintainers of justice 'as witnesses before God even if it be against yourselves, your parents and relatives' (4:135). To be a witness for truth and maintainer of impartial justice can hardly materialise without a high level of accountability to God, to one's own conscience, and to one's fellow humans.

CORRUPTION AND BRIBERY (*FASĀD WA-RASHWAH*)

A distinction is sometimes drawn between *fasād* and *rashwah*. *Fasād* is more general and encompasses dishonesty, betrayal of trust, abuse of power, inequity and deceipt in both private and public dealings. *Rashwah* is more specific and refers to private gain from public office or seeking recompense for rendering duties ordinarily considered as non-compensatory.

Because of the numerous forms it can take, corruption escapes the idea of a comprehensive definition. It knows no boundaries, applies to rich and poor individuals and countries, and it is as old as human history itself. In common usage, the word corruption (*fasād*) is associated with a range of acts, such as bribery, extortion, buying influence, nepotism, favouratism, fraud and embezzlement, and it is always rooted in moral failure. Unlike many other offences, corruption is invasive in that no clear distinction can exist between its perpetrator and victim.

Corruption also tends to have a cultural dimension. Whereas conduct such as officials demanding bribe is considered corrupt in virtually all societies, attitudes vary to gift giving and cronyism between countries and cultures. Alatas distinguishes between transactive corruption that is mutually arranged and agreed, and extortive corruption that involves some kind of compulsion. Investive corruption is, on the other hand, not linked to an immediate transaction but is instead investment for obtaining favour in the future. Autogenic corruption refers to benefits obtained from pre-knowledge of policy outcomes whereas supportive corruption protects and strengthens existing corruption.[133]

The *Sharīʿah* perspective on corruption is generic and objective. It is generic in that it encompasses almost all varieties of corruption from abuse of judicial and administrative power to political and financial corruption, and the scope extends both to private and public affairs. It is also objective as it is linked to values rather than circumstances of society and culture. In evaluating corruption, the Islamic perspective attaches considerable weight to events that took place in the early years of Islam during the life of the Prophet and the early caliphs. The basic criteria of distinguishing the corrupt from appropriate behaviour are derived from the Qur'ān. The text condemns those in authority who spread corruption and mischief (*fasād*) in the land by promoting racial divisions among people, bestowing favours on some and oppressing others (28:4; 89: 10–12). Also the rich are advised to seek with their wealth lawful gains and avoid conduct that spreads corruption in the land (28:77). Corruption is also understood as abuse of trust through abuse of judicial and administrative power, political authority and wealth (4:58).

It is forbidden for government officials to accept bribe of any kind, whether in the name of gift, donation or contribution from anyone in the course and conduct of duty. The gift may be specified or unspecified and it may benefit the official directly or in some other way, indeed any gift that is given because of the official position that is held would amount to a bribe, which is forbidden. Any other form of enrichment that materialises through misuse or manipulation of public assets also amounts to a breach of trust (*khiyānah*) and embezzlement (*ikhtilās*) all of which are forbidden. The clear Qur'ānic mandate on these is as follows:

ولا تأكلوا أموالكم بينكم بالباطل وتدلوا بها إلى الحكام

لتأكلوا فريقا من أموال الناس بالإثم وأنتم تعلمون

And eat not up your properties wrongfully among yourselves nor influence the rulers with the intention that one party transgresses over the property of another while you know it (being sinful). (2:188)

Ibn Kathīr commented on the authority of ʿAlī b. Abū Ṭālib, ʿAbd Allāh b. ʿAbbās and Ṭalḥah that this verse contemplated the position of a debtor who knowingly denies his debt and tries to influence, in response to his creditor's demand, the rulers in his favour. The person in this case knows that he is a transgressor and devours that which is *ḥarām* for him.[134] The text here is, however, not confined to any particular form of bribery or gift to officials, but comprises a general declaration addressed to the believers, within or outside government, to avoid indulgence in activities that lead to miscarriage of justice while knowing that what they are doing amounts to transgression.[135]

The Prophet has ruled that *rashwah* is forbidden and that all parties to *rashwah* invoke God Almighty's wrath and condemnation upon themselves. Abū Hurayrah thus reported the *ḥadīth* that: 'The Messenger of God, peace be on him, cursed the donor of *rashwah* and its recipient in all matters that involve a judgement or ruling.'[136]

لعن رسول الله صلى الله عليه وسلم الراشى والمرتشى

Al-Māwardī also wrote that 'one who is appointed to a judicial office may not accept a gift from a litigant nor from any one associated with the latter even if this latter is not involved in any litigation.' In support of this statement, Māwardī quotes the *ḥadīth* which declared that 'gifts given to officials are fraudulent and deceitful.'

Gift that has not yet been received by the official should be returned to the donor and if this cannot be done, then it is payable to the public treasury (*bayt al-māl*).[137]

If an official takes bribes or unjustly appropriates the property of another it is the duty of the ruler to return the assets to its true owner and to punish the offender accordingly. Government officials are under duty to honour the person and property of the citizens. ʿUmar Ibn al-Khaṭṭāb is thus reported to have said to an audience:

> By God I do not send my officials in order to slap you on your faces nor to devour your property. Whoever transgresses the limits of his duty, report him to me and I shall effect just retaliation. ʿAmr b. al-ʿĀṣ rose and asked, 'O Commander of the Faithful! If a man is in charge of the affairs of Muslims and he disciplines someone in his custody, will you then retaliate?' ʿUmar replied, 'Indeed I will. How can I not retaliate while you saw the Messenger of God who would retaliate upon himself?'[138]

According to a *ḥadīth* recorded by Imam Aḥmad and al-Bayhaqī, the Prophet is reported to have said:

Gifts given to (government) employees partake in betrayal (*ghulul, khiyānah*).[139]

هدايا العمال غلول أي خيانة

A similar *ḥadīth* has been recorded by Abū Dāwūd, on the authority of Abū Umāmah that the Prophet, peace be on him, said:

من شفع لأخيه شفاعة فأهدى له هدية عليها فقبلها فقد
أتى بابا عظيما من أبواب الربا

One who intercedes (to officials) on behalf of his brother and accepts a gift from him because of it has truly opened a door to *ribā* (usury).[140]

Ibn Taymiyyah concludes from his reading of these *ḥadīth* texts that it is the duty of the ruler (*wāli al-amr*) to return to the owner any gift a government employee has taken because of the work he has done.[141] Ibn Taymiyyah has also quoted the *ḥadīth* that accepting a gift by an official is tantamount to usury (*ribā*). The renowned Companion ʿAbd Allāh Ibn Masʿūd went on record to say 'When a man removes hardship from another and then receives a gift from him, large or small, (he) has taken something, which is *ḥarām* for him.'[142]

The scope of *rashwah* is extended, according to Ibn Taymiyyah, to financial transactions between members of the public and government officials, which are manifestly favourable to the latter. In this way sale, lease and hire, *muḍārabah* and trade partnership that are so concluded fall under bribery and the officials are taken to task for them. This is how the caliph ʿUmar b. al-Khaṭṭāb treated some of his officials who had accumulated wealth due to favours they had received. The caliph divided the assets in question and surrendered a portion thereof to the public treasury.[143] The caliph ʿUmar b. ʿAbd al-ʿAzīz went on record to say: 'I am of the view that the ruler should not trade. It is also not lawful for an officer to trade in the area of his office ... because when he involves himself in trade, he inadvertently misuses his office in his own interest often to the detriment of others, even if he does not like to do so.'[144]

In the event where someone in charge of government affairs extracts money and gift from his employees, both of them are wrongdoers, like one thief robbing another thief, or like two warring parties who fight for superiority and self-seeking purposes, neither of whom deserves any sympathy or support. Anyone who supports the wrongdoer falls foul of the Qur'ānic directive, which forbids cooperation in hostility and sin. (*al-Mā'idah*, 5:2).[145]

The *Sharī'ah* forbids bribery and its prohibition applies to everyone who facilitates it even if he does not gain anything from it. The actual sums, goods or presents that change hands are *ḥarām* to the recipient. In a *ḥadīth* recorded by both al-Bukhārī and Muslim, it is reported:

أن النبي صلى الله عليه وسلم استعمل رجلا من الأزد يقال له ابن اللتبية على الصدقة، فجاء فقال: هذا لكم وهذا أهدى لى، فقام النبى صلى الله عليه وسلم على المنبر فحمد الله وأثنى عليه وقال: ما بال العامل نبعثه فيجئ، فيقول: هذا لكم وهذا أهدى لى، ألا جلس فى بيت أمه أو أبيه فينظر هل تأتيه هدية أم لا، والذي نفس محمد بيده لا يأتي أحد منكم منها بشيء سرا إلا جاء به يوم القيامة على رقبته...

The Prophet, peace be on him, employed a man from (the tribe of) al-Azd by the name Ibn al-Lutbiyyah as collector of *zakāh*, and when he brought the assets he had collected, he told the Prophet that this (portion) is for you and this (other portion) has been gifted to me. The Prophet then addressed the people from the pulpit... and said: It is wrong for an official that I appoint to tell me that a portion of the collection had been gifted to him. Let the one who says this sit in his father or his mother's house and see if he would receive any gifts! By the One in whose hands the life of Muhammad rests that any of you who take anything from such assets, it will become a yoke on his neck on the Day of Judgement...[146]

The prohibitive rulings of both the Qur'ān and *Sunnah* on bribery are in no further need of elaboration and should not, therefore, be confused with the report that is attributed to the Prophet's widow,

'Ā'ishah, to the effect that: 'The Prophet, peace be on him, used to accept gifts and also reciprocated them.'[147]

Gifts of this kind are not forbidden and have, in fact, been commended as means of enhancing affection and fraternity among people. The Prophet used to receive gifts and often reciprocated them or gave something better from his own personal assets. Only in the event of reciprocating gifts from foreign dignitaries did he pay from the assets of *bayt al-māl*. Reports indicate that by the time of his demise, the Prophet had no assets and what he left behind, such as a mule, weapons and a plot of land, he had already given in charity. His widow 'Ā'ishah reported that the Prophet died and his garment was left as pawn with a Jew for thirty *sāʿ* (c. 30 kilos) of barley.[148]

Gifts that are given to government officials are usually not reciprocated as they are motivated by corrupt intention and given in anticipation of favour and procurement of an unlawful ruling that may be advantageous to the donor, but harmful to his opponent, or to the public at large. This is the subject of another *hadīth* as follows:

من استعملناه على عمل فرزقناه رزقا فما أخذ بعد ذلك فهو غلول

Those whom we employ to a particular work we assign to them a livelihood and what they take beyond that is fraudulent.[149]

Government employees are entitled to fair pay that is proportionate to the work they do and their earning should be sufficient for their needs. Government employees are not allowed, therefore, to indulge in unlawful self-enrichment activities. This is the purport of the following *hadīth* reported by Mustawrid b. Shaddād from the Prophet:

من كان عاملا فليكتسب زوجة فإن لم يكن له خادم فليكتسب خادما فإن لم يكن له مسكن فليكتسب مسكنا؛ وفى رواية من اتخذ غير ذلك فهو غال

One who is employed by us, let him get married if he has no wife, and let him hire a servant, if he has none; he is also entitled to a dwelling, should he be in need of one. Abū Bakr who narrated the *hadīth* then said that the Prophet added: one who takes more than this is either fraudulent or a thief.[150]

Al-Māwardī has emphasised that remunerations and salaries should be adequate so that government employees are not compelled to resort to bribery in order to meet their personal needs. A salary is not adequate if it falls short of enabling the employee to fulfil his own basic needs and those of his family in accordance with his standing. The key term al-Māwardī uses is sufficiency level (*al-kifāyah*) such that the employee would not need to ask others for help. Two other points that al-Māwardī added are that the employee should be paid for actual expenses incurred in the fulfilment of duty and this includes the cost of transportation or upkeep of a riding beast. The other point made is that salaries and wages should be reviewed in line with changes in the price of basic commodities or the cost of living. A similar view on this last point had been expressed earlier by Imam Abū Ḥanīfah.[151]

Accountability in government positions is non-transferable in that an office-holder cannot evade responsibility by assigning it to someone else. While elaborating on this, al-Māwardī points out that even when a government officer asks someone to replace him, the principal party remains accountable and not his replacement. Substitution and replacement would be invalid in the event where the substitute is granted total independence in the conduct of duty.[152]

It may thus be concluded that the *Sharīʿah* takes a resolute stand on official corruption, such as bribery and unlawful gifts and donations that exchange hands in the course of duty. The result of what bribery leads to is deemed to be immaterial and it is in any case presumed that bribery seeks to distort the course of justice or bring about an unlawful ruling that is prejudicial to one of the parties and also to the public interest. The criteria of evaluation in Islam are drawn not solely from the existential realities nor the attending circumstance on the ground but also from the objective principles of the *Sharīʿah*.[153] Many forms of corruption are also explained with concrete examples leaving little room for ambiguity.[154] In a section of their work bearing the title 'The Islamic Attack on Corruption' Iqbal and Lewis wrote that 'on the moral plane, there is zero tolerance for bribery in Islam,' and Islam rejects any idea that bribery serves as 'the grease that oils the economic wheels.' Furthermore, there is no scope for legalising corruption in the name of commission, gift, donation, advances, soft loan, loan write-offs and whatsoever. The touchstone of differentiation revolves around the question if these payments and favours would accrue had the suspect stayed at home and had no official position or profile.

Bribery and administrative corruption carry no fixed penalties under the *Sharīʿah* and the matter therefore falls under the general category of *ta'zīr* for which the head of state and judge may determine a suitable punishment and may also enact legislation to that effect. Thus according to Ibn Taymiyyah: 'One who breaches his trust, such as the administrator of public funds, or the administrator of *waqf* (charitable) properties, and guardians of the property of orphans ... and those who indulge in bribery, or issue judgements contrary to the Book of God, those who oppress the citizens or become the means of propagating misguidance among them' and such other offences for which the *Sharī'ah* has not specified a punishment but provides indications of illegality—these are punishable by a deterrent (*ta'zīr*) punishment. The punishment is determined by the ruler in conformity with the gravity of the offence and whether it is a manifest mischief or one of rare occurrence. Punishing such activities should follow the twin objectives of reformation and deterrence. In determining the punishment the ruler also considers the condition of the offender: If he is known for corruption and evil, his punishment should be greater than the first time offender or one who has no criminal record.[155]

Ibn Taymiyyah elaborates that there is no minimum limit to *ta'zīr* punishment, which includes all that inflict pain by words, by action, or by omission of a certain act. A man may thus be punished by a verbal rebuke or by severance of communication and boycott until he repents. The Prophet, peace be on him, thus punished the three individuals who stayed behind from participation in the battle of Tabuk by means of a social boycott and isolation but pardoned them afterwards.[156] *Ta'zīr* punishment for an official may consist of dismissal from office, or in some cases by refusal to employ him to a certain post, or by reduction of his allowances such as discontinuation of food supplements and so on, all of which find a precedent in the *Sunnah* of the Prophet.

Ta'zīr punishment may also consist of imprisonment or beating, or of blackening of the face of the offender and taking him on a ride in town on a donkey back to front, such as the caliph 'Umar b. al-Khaṭṭāb applied to a false witness who was convicted of perjury; this was done on the analysis that he had blackened the face of truth and had turned it to its opposite, hence the choice of the punishment.[157]

As for the maximum punishment of *ta'zīr*, some *'ulamā'* have stated that it should not exceed ten lashes, whereas others have held that it should not reach the level of a *ḥadd* punishment, which in terms of lashing would mean anything less than forty lashes of the whip. There are, however, reports that the Caliph 'Umar b. al-Khaṭṭāb punished a man with 300 lashes, applied in three consecutive days, for having forged his official seal. There are similar reports that have led to differences of opinion among jurists on the maximum limit of *taʿzīr* punishment. I do not propose to elaborate on *taʿzīr* any further, as details on this are available. It may be relevant to add, however briefly, that the Mālikīs and some Ḥanbalīs have validated death penalty for a Muslim spy who spies for the enemy. Then there is the *ḥadīth*, which evidently validates death for one who seeks to split asunder the unity of the community and causes sedition in conjunction with the selection of a leader. The *ḥadīth* thus proclaims: 'When consensus has been reached to entrust your affairs to one person and then another seeks to cause a split and separates the community—you may kill him.'[158]

The practice of expropriation of assets of corrupt officials was eventually institutionalised under the Abbasid caliph, Jaʿfar al-Manṣūr, when a department of government, known as *Diwān al-Muṣādirīn* was established for handling expropriation matters in cases of unwarranted enrichment. It was also known as *Bayt Māl al-Maẓālim*, a branch of the *Bayt al-Māl*, which specialised in expropriation matters and in looking into complaints pertaining to them. Reports indicate that vast amounts of properties were retrieved. The Abbasid caliph al-Qāhir (d. 320 AH) is thus reported to have expropriated the properties of the mother of his predecessor, al-Muqtadir, which raised the assets of *Bayt Māl al-Maẓālim* by a substantial amount.[159]

As already noted, one of the manifestations of accountability of government officials which became a well-known feature of ʿUmar b. al-Khaṭṭāb's period was expropriation of property accumulated during office. This was done to prominent figures including Abū Hurayrah, ʿAmr Ibn al-ʿĀṣ, Nāfiʿ Ibn ʿAmr, Saʿd Ibn Abī Waqāṣ, and Khālid Ibn al-Walīd, the governors respectively of Bahrain, Egypt, Makkah, Kufa and Sham, among others, who were found to have accumulated wealth which they did not have prior to their employment. Some of them indulged in trading activities and careless handling of public funds. The caliph is noted to have ordered Abū Hurayrah to 'take your own property and what is necessary for your living and surrender the rest to the *Bayt al-Mal*.' ʿAmr Ibn al-ʿĀṣ was simply ordered to hand over one half of his wealth to the *Bayt al-Māl* as he had acquired goods, slaves, livestock, and artifacts which he did not have before he was appointed as governor of Egypt.[160]

Expropriation was not confined to government officials but was also extended to merchants, contractors and dignitaries who con-

ducted business with the government and accumulated disproportion-
ate amounts of wealth. An interesting incident of this involved the two
sons of the caliph ʿUmar b. al-Khaṭṭāb, ʿAbd Allāh and ʿUbayd Allāh,
who accompanied, as the reports indicate, an army contingent to Iraq.
They were welcomed by the then governor of Basra, Abū Mūsā al-
Ashʿarī, whose eagerness to be of service prompted him into saying
'If I could do anything that would be of benefit to you, I'll be pleased
to do so.' Then he made this offer: 'Here is some money which I was
going to send to the Commander of the Faithful. May be I can advance them to you to buy some goods from Iraq and then sell them in
Medina. Give the capital to the Commander of the Faithful and keep
the profit for yourselves.' This was agreed and al-Ashʿarī wrote and
informed the caliph on the matter. Having made a profit out of the
transaction, the caliph's sons brought the capital to hand over to the
caliph, to which the latter responded: 'Does he give similar advances
to everyone in the army?' The answer to this was 'No,' and the caliph
continued, 'The two sons of the Commander of the Faithful were
given an advance and they made a profit.' ʿAbd Allāh remained silent,
but ʿUbayd Allāh said: 'Supposing we had made a loss or something
happened to the funds, it would have been our liability.' The caliph
asked them to pay both the capital and the profit. A man who was
present, said: 'O Commander of the Faithful, perhaps you could treat
this as an instance of *qirād* (or *muḍārabah*).' The Caliph agreed and
asked his sons to deliver the capital and only half of the profit to the
bayt al-māl.[161]

DISOBEDIENCE AND DEFIANCE (*AL-KHURŪJ*)

Disobedience and uprising against a lawful government is a serious
offence in *Sharīʿah* and may only be considered as the last resort by
which to depose a deviant ruler. Such an eventuality should preferably
be avoided in cases of minor violations and errors, in which the
citizens are entitled to draw the attention of their leaders by recourse
to *naṣīhah* (sincere advice) and consultation (*shūrā*) directly or through
their representatives.[162] Rebellion (*al-bughā*) that lacks a valid cause
and one which is supported by a large number of followers is a
punishable offence and may amount to *hirābah* if it resorts to violence
and spreads corruption. An important condition of rebellion is that it
incites a revolution and civil strife failing which it would not amount
to a rebellion and may qualify as a lighter offence punishable under
taʿzīr. Oral rebellion does not qualify until the rebels resort to the
use of force. The recommended course in these circumstances is for

the ruler to engage in a dialogue and try to pacify the rebels through reasonable persuasion.[163]

In the event when there is a decision to depose the head of state but he refuses to step down in defiance of the decision of the community representatives, the community is entitled to resort to forcible means and uprising against the deviant ruler. This is known in the *fiqh* terminology as *al-khurūj*, or refusal to obey the government in power. *Khurūj* differs from *bughā* and *ḥirābah* in that in *khurūj* it is the leader who violates the *Sharīʿah* whereas in *bughā* and *ḥirābah* criminality and lawlessness is committed by others.

The issue of *khurūj* and boycott of the normal constitutional order arose at an early stage in history and became the focus of attention in the rise of the early politico-theological groups, the Kharijites, Shīʿites and Muʿtazilah. The question posed then was not simply over a right or power to depose a deviant ruler who violated the *Sharīʿah* but also whether it was a religious duty of the people to attempt it. A full treatment of this issue falls beyond our scope here but an outline of some of the views may be given as follows:

Briefly, the Kharijites held that fighting a deviant ruler and deposing him is an obligation, which they held to be one of the basic principles of their movement. The Kharijites (lit. outsiders) boycotted the mainstream community over the outcome of the arbitration (*tahkīm*) between the caliph ʿAlī and the then governor of Sham Muʿāwiyah. The Kharijites did not agree with the idea of arbitration in the first place and boycotted the community because of it.

The Muʿtazilah subscribed to the view that a deviant (*fāsiq*) Imam must be challenged and deposed even if it necessitates asking the aliens for help. This is based on their understanding of the following Qurʾānic verse: 'My covenant is not within the reach of the oppressors—*lā yanālu ʿahdī al-ẓālimīn*' (2:124), and another verse that enjoins the Muslim community to 'fight the faction that transgresses until it complies with the command of God' (49:9).

The Shīʿites have in turn validated rebellion and *khurūj* against any ruler who challenges the standing Imam of the time. The Shīʿī sub-groups have differed over the question as to whether *khurūj* against the *Imam* actually amounts to an act of disbelief (*kufr*). The Shīʿa Imamiyyah have held that *khurūj* against the imam of the time is forbidden (*harām*) as he is in theory infallible and must at all times be obeyed.[164]

The mainstream communities (*ahl al-sunna wa'l-jamāʿah*) have also differed among themselves between basically two views, one of which advises patience (*al-ṣabr*) and the other recourse to the sword against a deviant ruler. Ḥasan al-Baṣrī (d. 110/728 AH) has been quoted to the effect that when the people remain patient vis-à-vis a deviant ruler, God Most High will reward them and raise them in ranks for their restraint in not resorting to the sword. Al-Baṣrī cited in this connection the Qur'ānic verse: 'The fair promise of the Lord was fulfilled for the children of Israel because they had patience . . .' (7:137). The Imams Aḥmad b. Ḥanbal, al-Ghazālī and others have concurred in this view. The renowned Companion, Ibn 'Abbās, is quoted to have said concerning the above-mentioned verse: 'There is no covenant for the oppressor, if you have promised them something, you may break it.' In support is also quoted a statement of the Companion, Ḥudhayfah al-Yamānī, who was asked a question: 'Do you not enjoin good and forbid evil?' And he replied: 'Enjoining good and forbidding evil is fine, but it is not the *Sunnah* to raise the sword against your leader.' Ḥudhayfah then cited these two *ḥadīths*: 'One who sees his *amīr* (ruler) doing what he dislikes, he should remain patient;'[165] من رأى من أميره شيئا يكرهه فليصبر and 'One who takes up the sword against us is not one of us.'[166]

من سلّ علينا السيف فليس منا

This ruling is then qualified by the ruling of another *ḥadīth* which provides in part 'unless what you see amounts to indisputable *kufr—illā an tarā kufran bawāhan.*'[167]

The second view on this, which is upheld by the majority, including Imāms Abū Ḥanīfah and Mālik, maintains that *khurūj* is permissible, but not obligatory, against a leader who becomes a transgressor provided that deposing him is feasible and does not lead to civil strife and *fitnah*. Imām Mālik went on record to say concerning the *bay'ah* (pledge of allegiance) to the Abbasid caliph, Ja'far al-Manṣūr (r.136–158/754–775) that his *bay'ah* was obtained under duress, and a person in those conditions can give no valid *bay'ah*. This he said despite the fact that al-Manṣūr had made known his intention to promulgate the *Muwaṭṭa* of Imām Mālik as binding law in the Abbasid Empire.[168]

The Shāfi'īs are divided between the two views, one for and the other against the permissibility of *khurūj*, but Imām Shāfi'ī himself has discouraged it. The Ḥanbalīs have considered *khurūj* permissible if it would prevent a civil strife and *fitnah*. To this effect Ibn Taymiyyah has quoted the Companion Jābir b. ʿAbd Allāh to have said: 'The Prophet, peace be on him, ordered us to strike with this (i.e. sword) one who violates this (i.e. the Qurʾān).'[169]

The Ẓāhiris have strongly advocated *khurūj* against a deviant ruler which they consider to be a part of the *Sharīʿah* duty of 'enjoining good and forbidding evil.' They have also quoted the aforementioned Qurʾānic verses in support of their position.[170]

From this brief review of juristic positions, it would appear that the basic issue over *khurūj* and its efficacy or otherwise was over the defence of religion. *Khurūj* was held permissible, even obligatory, in order to defend the faith. In the event where the faith was not under imminent danger, patience was advised. *Khurūj* would not be an option, as Waṣfī has rightly observed, in order to defend economic interests. *Khurūj* is a serious matter as it threatens *fitnah* and endangers peace and tranquillity in the community. The *Sharīʿah* also takes a serious view of declaring any Muslim as an infidel, let alone the head of state, unless he is guilty of indisputable apostasy, which would be highly unlikely. Outside that eventuality the issue before us would remain to be over the constitutional validity of impeachment as a last resort in situations that are most likely to lead to *fitnah* and widespread tumult in the community. The *Sharīʿah* validates this in principle and permits deposition and removal of a leader who becomes an instrument of lawlessness, disorder and sedition. A peaceful formula and procedure of impeachment that is determined through consultation and then stipulated in the constitution would clearly be a preferable alternative to *khurūj*. It would indeed be the only valid constitutional alternative in our times.

III. Deviation and Departure from Precedent: An Historical Narrative

This section is presented in two segments, the first of which addresses political aberrations and despotism, and the second discusses financial mismanagement and abuse of public assets in the hands of some Umayyad and Abbasid rulers.

DESPOTISM AND DYNASTIC MISRULE

Government during the time of the Pious Caliphs (10–41/630–661) was predicated on the principle that political authority belonged to the community and that government was accountable to the people.

This early period is in many ways seen to represent authoritative precedent. 'As for the dynastic systems of rule under the Umayyads and Abbasids, Ottomans, Persians and Berber, etc,' as Zuḥaylī pointed out, 'they were not sound Islamic governments as they became despotic and the *ummah* was no longer the locus of political authority under them.'[171] They lost much of their Islamic credentials simply because the Islamic system of government is fully accountable to the people and is duty bound to protect the people's rights, establish equality and justice and repel oppression.[172]

The first act of disloyalty and defiance was Muʿāwiyah's challenge of the leadership of the reigning caliph ʿAlī b. Abū Ṭālib that wreaked havoc on the nascent community and its government, and led to the military confrontation at Ṣiffīn. When Muʿāwiyah's forces were on the verge of defeat at Ṣiffīn he urged for arbitration to which the caliph ʿAlī begrudgingly agreed, and then came Muʿāwiyah's next act of political manipulation. He allowed himself and his representative at arbitration, Amr b. al-ʿĀṣ, to twist the facts of the agreement with ʿAlī's representative, Abū Mūsā al-Ashʿarī, and declare Muʿāwiyah as caliph.[173] This was a departure from the teachings of Islam on the unity of *ummah* and accountability of its leaders. Leaders were to be elected on the basis of consultation and *bayʿah* that allowed genuine participation. Then came, of course, the conversion of *khilāfah* to monarchy and dynastic rule, again at the hands of Muʿāwiyah. When the time came for him to nominate his son Yazīd as his heir apparent and successor, Muʿāwiyah was once again responsible for manipulation of *bayʿah* in favour of Yazīd.[174] Compare this with the earlier precedent when the second caliph ʿUmar nominated the council of six leading Companions, he included his pious son, ʿAbd Allāh b.ʿUmar, but issued instruction that he was to act as umpire in the event only of a split but was himself not entitled to nomination for leadership. Muʿāwiyah's nomination of his son Yazīd, not only departed from that precedent but also divested the *bayʿah* of its meaning. *Bayʿah* was preserved as a matter of ceremony in which the people pledged allegiance to the new leader 'only in name but was robbed of all substance.'[175]

The distance between people and their rulers grew wider under the Umayyads ʿAbd al-Malik b. Marwān (r.65–86 AH) who is otherwise known for his knowledge and effective policies but is said to have indulged in pomp and ceremony and made himself increasingly inaccessible. He eventually succeeded to pacify the al-Ashʿath rebellion and also defeated the Kharijites, yet he is accused of denying the non-Arabs (*mawāli*) right to equal treatment in employment to government office.[176]

Walīd b. ʿAbd al-Malik who ruled for ten years (86–96/705–715) apparently did not follow hereditary succession and did not appoint any of his son as heir to the throne. He simply nominated ʿUmar b. ʿAbd al-ʿAzīz who was the most eligible person available at the time.[177]

The governors of the Umayyad period were prone to despotism. This is evident in recorded speeches, for example, of Ḥajjāj b. Yūsuf, Ziyād b. Ubayh, and Mūsā b. Nuṣayr. Ḥajjāj was in office for twenty years or more and did not even heed the Caliph in Damascus. The Umayyad rule is also characterised as an Arab aristocracy that availed little opportunity of participation for non-Arabs. State power remained in the hands of the nobility and distrust between the public and government as well as between the sections of the bureaucracy developed due to these and also due to problems of succession. The Caliph was often kept in the dark over the course of events. There were additional problems over extended delays in the payment of stipends to the soldiers.[178]

The Abbasid period, especially during what is known as the early period (131–232/750–850), saw the return of administrative centralism and a marked reduction of the powers of governors. Provincial governors in this period continued also to act as army commanders and prayer leaders, but most of their other important functions were taken over by other officials such as the head of finance, postmaster and the *qāḍī*. Unlike the Umayyad rule that was characteristically Arab, the Abbasids relied on non-Arabs and adhered to ancient oppressive methods of the Sassanians and the Byzantines. Most of the important state positions were entrusted to non-Arabs, including Muslims, Jews and Christians, and ministers often wielded greater power in the name only of the Caliph.[179]

Al-Ghazālī has recounted the following episode of an encounter between a learned man among the *tābiʿūn* and the Umayyad ruler, Hishām b. ʿAbd al-Malik.[180] When Hishām b. ʿAbd al-Malik (105–125 AH/724–743) was about to enter Mecca to perform the *hajj*, he asked to meet with a man from the Companions of the Prophet but was informed that they had all passed away. When he asked for one of the *tābiʿun* (Followers) they brought Ṭāwūs al-Yamanī. When Ṭāwūs entered, he took off his shoes only when he sat next to the caliph; he did not greet nor address him by his title, Commander of the Faithful, but simply said '*al-salāmu ʿalaykum* O Hishām!' and said 'How are you O Hishām?' Hishām was overtaken by anger so much so that he wanted to kill Ṭāwūs, but was informed that this was not possible in the precincts of the Kaʿbah. Then he addressed Ṭāwūs and asked him what was the reason for what he did, Ṭāwūs replied: 'What did I do?' Hishām became more irritable and told him: 'You took off your shoes next to where I sat; you did not kiss my hand, nor did you greet me by my title, 'Amīr al-Mu'minīn', nor did you call me by my appellation; you sat next to me without my permission and told me "How are you Hishām?"' Ṭāwūs replied: 'As for my taking off my shoes next to you, I do this five times before God Most High (in the mosque) and He neither rebukes me nor shows anger. As for what you say that I did not kiss your hand, I heard the Commander of the Faithful, ʿAlī b. Abī Ṭālib, saying that it was not permissible for a man to kiss anyone else's hand except that of his wife or son for desire and compassion. As for what you said that I did not greet you by your title, Amīr al-Mu'minīn, this is because not all people are happy with your leadership and I disliked telling a lie. You say I did not address you by your appellation (*kunniyah*), I may remind you that God Most High called his Prophets and friends by their first names, like Yaḥyā and ʿĪsā, but called his foes by their appellation, such as Abī Lahab. As for your saying that I sat next to you, I have heard the Commander of the Faithful, ʿAlī b. Abī Ṭālib, saying: when you want to see a companion of the fire, then look at the man who likes crowds to stand around him and wait on him while he is seated himself.' On hearing this, Hishām told him: 'Advise me!' To which Ṭāwūs said: 'I heard the Commander of the Faithful ʿAlī, saying: "In Hell there are snakes and scorpions the size of mules ready to attack every *amīr* who fails to administer justice among his subjects."' Then he got up and left.

The hereditary system of succession was also retained by the Fatimids of Egypt (909–1170) and the Ottoman Turks (1517–1924) until the abolition of the Caliphate in Turkey. The reigning caliphs sometimes nominated two or even three successors to follow one another and occasionally caused tumult by deposing one in favour of another, often leading to assassination and revolt. The Caliph would proclaim as his successor the one among his sons or kinsmen whom he favoured most and would exact for him an anticipatory oath of fealty, first from the capital and then from the other principal towns of the empire.[181]

The Abbasid excesses with hereditary rule were evident from the outset. The founder of this dynasty, ʿAbbās al-Saffāḥ (132–

136 AH/750–754), nominated his brother Ja'far al-Manṣūr to be followed by his nephew 'Īsā Ibn Mūsā. When Manṣūr became Caliph (136–156 AH), he defrocked 'Īsā b. Mūsā and appointed his son al-Mahdī as his successor to be then followed by 'Īsā b. Mūsā. When al-Mahdī acceded to the Caliphate (r. 158–169), he divested 'Īsā b. Mūsā and instead nominated his own son al-Hādī to be followed subsequently by his brother Hārūn al-Rashīd. Al-Hādī became caliph (r. 169–170) and wasted no time to divest his brother Hārūn al-Rashīd and take *bay'ah* for his son Ja'far. Then came Hārūn al-Rashīd (r. 170–193) and he nominated three of his sons, Amīn, Ma'mūn and Mu'tamin which sowed the seeds of dissension between the three brothers, and the narrative of conspiracy and conflict continued at the leadership level.[182]

The Abbasids also arrogated to themselves divine authority, somewhat like the Shahs of Persia, and went far in that direction by issuing such announcements as made by Ja'far al-Manṣūr, 'I am the God-appointed Sultan on earth.' The Abbasid rulers no longer considered themselves bound by the authority of the people.[183]

The dictatorial methods of Abbasid rulers were significantly influenced by the fact that 'the Abbasid state was largely carried on Persian shoulders who had a different view of the caliphate. The Arab view of the caliphate was founded on *bay'ah*, consultation and justice whereas the Persians endowed the Shahs with sanctity and absolutism.'[184]

Next to the caliph stood his vizier who acted as the caliph's alter ego and himself wielded autocratic powers. In the decree appointing his vizier, the Abbasid caliph al-Nāṣir (r. 1180–1225) provides an example of his arrogation to the 'divine right' of kingship working by proxy when he said:

> Muḥammad Ibn Barz al-Qummī is our representative throughout the land and amongst our subjects. Therefore he who obeys him, obeys us and he who obeys us obeys God... As for one who disobeys our vizier, he disobeys us, and he who disobeys us disobeys God.[185]

From the beginning the Abbasid caliphs cultivated the notion that authority should forever remain in Abbasid hands 'to be finally delivered to Jesus, the Messiah.' Later the theory was promulgated that if this caliphate were destroyed the whole universe would be disorganised. 'As a matter of fact, the turn to religiosity was more apparent than real,' and the Baghdad caliph 'proved as worldly-minded' as that of Damascus.[186]

MISUSE OF PUBLIC FUNDS

The pious caliphs of the early decades of Islam set an example of clean personal record in regard to their own financial affairs. They treated the *Bayt al-Māl* as community's property and saw themselves as trustees and guardians thereof. But the situation changed under the Umayyad rulers at a time when almost all the leading Companions had passed away. The first blow was dealt, as Hasanuz Zaman pointed out, at the concept of justice. Formerly it was regarded as a requirement of justice, for example, to receive from the *dhimmīs* (non-Muslim citizens) only the amount of poll-tax (*jizyah*) as was pre-assessed and mutually agreed upon. Now the Umayyad rulers did not hesitate to claim more than what was due. The caliph Mu'āwiyah wrote to Wardān, his officer in Egypt to 'increase on Copts (their *jizyah*) by one carat per annum.' To this letter Wardān replied: 'How can I do this while the treaty with them stipulates that it will not be increased?'[187]

During the Umayyad rule (41–123/661–750), the threefold governmental functions of political administration, tax collection, and religious leadership were conducted by three different officials. The governor (*amīr, ṣāḥib*) would appoint his own '*āmil* (agent, prefect), over any particular district and simply forward the name to the caliph. Under Hishām b. 'Abd al-Malik (724–43) the newly appointed governor of Armenia and Azerbaijan often remained in Damascus and sent an accredited deputy (*nā'ib*) in his stead. The governor had full charge of political and military administration in his province, but quite often the revenues were under a special officer, *ṣāḥib al-kharāj*, responsible directly to the caliph. Mu'āwiyah was apparently the first to appoint such an officer, whom he sent to Kufa. Previously the government of a province in the Muslim territories had chiefly meant financial administration, but this had now been largely controlled by the centre. The revenues were basically derived from the same sources as under the orthodox caliphate, chief among which were land tax and poll tax (*kharāj, jizyah*). In the provinces all expenses of local administration, state annuities, soldier's stipends and miscellaneous services were met from the local income, and only the balance went to the caliphal treasury.[188]

During the reign of 'Abd al-Malik b. Marwān, a fresh survey was carried out of the population of Khurasan. Everyone was asked to pay their unpaid taxes and the *jizyah* was increased by three dinars per annum. The situation in Iraq was similar in that new taxes were imposed on the populace who were already burdened with taxes. Later the Caliph ʿUmar b. ʿAbd al-ʿAzīz (r. 99–101 AH) tried to remedy this situation and reinstated in many cases the rates that were enacted under the caliph ʿUmar b. al-Khaṭṭāb.[189] ʿAbd al-Malik b. Marwān is reported to have taken to task and dismissed some of his tax collectors for abusive practices. There are also reports that the revenue officers of Iraq demanded of the people of Sawad lands all the presents on the festivals of Nowruz and Mehrjān which were presented to the Sassanian rulers in the pre-Islamic period. There is reason to believe that the Umayyad Caliphs were not unaware of this excess but often turned a blind eye to it. The same practice is noted to have been later adopted in Khurasan. According to another report, the central mosque of Wāsiṭ in Iraq was built with materials brought from other cities, and although the people there protested against it, their protest did not move the rulers enough to pay for the materials as was done in the time of caliph ʿUmar b. ʿAbd al-ʿAzīz.[190]

It is further reported that under the reign of Umayyad caliph Hishām b. ʿAbd al-Malik, his governor of Iraq, Khālid b. ʿAbd Allāh al-Qasrī, supervised the engineering and drainage works of Iraq by Hassān al-Nabatī. The governor is said to have appropriated for himself a surplus of 13,000,000 dirhams after squandering revenues to nearly three times that sum. The governor was taken to task and 'met the same fate that befell others like him.' He was jailed, tortured and required to give an account of the state moneys and make repayments. Most of his assets were expropriated to the state treasury. 'His case is only one illustration of that maladministration and corruption in the body politic' that undermined the throne and rendered its occupants an easy prey for their Abbasid rivals.[191] Incidents of this kind were inevitably dealt with in a coercive manner which became a cause of instability and tension between the caliphs and their leading officials.

Misappropriation of the funds of *bayt al-māl* was, however, tolerated among the ruling family who were often given special grants and large plots of agricultural land. A ruler could now dispense any amount of money to poets in appreciation of their panegyrics, or to his own son to appease him. Many governors were near relatives of the rulers and were exempt from submitting accounts or sending any portion of revenues to the *bayt al-māl*.[192]

Another instance of abuse was a certain re-interpretation of the concept of chosen property (*amwāl ṣafiyyah*), which was revived for the first time since the Prophet's demise. The Pious Caliphs had treated this as the privilege of the Prophet, as it was a part of the one-fifth (*khums*) of booty that the Qur'ān assigned to the Prophet. It is thus reported that: 'The Prophet, peace be on him, took his chosen portion (*sahm ṣāf*) when he took part in a battle, and this portion was reserved for him even if he did not participate in the battle himself.'[193] But then the Umayyad rulers extended the concept and could pick any public property as their own in the name of chosen property, and even private property was not safe from the rulers' excesses. It was presumably through such official excesses that the ruling class became the richest class. Although deviant officers were occasionally brought to book and were made to relinquish their assets, corruption had infiltrated the highest echelons of government.[194]

The practice of generous allotment of land began with Muʿāwiyah himself whose name appears most frequently in this respect. First of all, he took over Fadak as his chosen property (*ṣafī*) and bestowed it upon Marwān, the Governor of Medina. He also added to his properties by purchase, sale and gifts. This was the first time that the ruler himself became interested in adding extensively to his fiefs and personal assets.[195]

In the midst of an otherwise bleak picture, history also recorded some honourable exceptions among Umayyad rulers, some of whom took corrective measures, and some were also known as upright and pious. When the self-same Muʿāwiyah was approaching his death, he offered half of his property to the *bayt al-māl*. Earlier he had wanted to extend the central mosque in Damascus, which was only possible through annexing a portion of the courtyard of the church of St. John. However the Bishop refused either to forego or sell this portion and Muʿāwiyah acceded and did not insist. Yazīd's son, Muʿāwiyah II (64/683) actually abdicated the throne in protest to the abandonment of consultative government that respected the people's free choice. He convened the people and addressed them in such terms that: 'My grandfather Muʿāwiyah extorted the leadership from ʿAlī b. Abī Ṭālib who had a greater entitlement to it due to his closeness to the Messenger of God and his record of service to Islam. He then installed my father, Yazīd, who was unsuitable and indulgent in pursuit of his desires...' He stepped down and asked the people to 'choose for yourselves whom you wish to be your leader.'[196]

A variant version of this sermon which some historians have recorded omits the derogatory references to Muʿāwiyah and Yazīd. According to this version, Muʿāwiyah II who was suffering from illness at the prime of his youth simply said '...I find myself too weak to shoulder this responsibility. I tried to find a man the like of ʿUmar b. al-Khaṭṭāb, but I could not find one. I also tried to find six counsellors, the like of those whom ʿUmar selected; but I could also not find any. So you are yourselves entitled to choose anyone for your leader that may appeal to you...'[197] ʿAbd al-Malik b. Marwān (d. 86/705) offered a large sum for annexing part of the church in Damascus, to which the response was still negative but then he insisted and annexed a part of the church to the mosque. When ʿUmar b. ʿAbd al-ʿAzīz became caliph, the Christians complained to him concerning what ʿAbd al-Malik had done to their church. The caliph wrote to his official and ordered that the annex should be returned back to the church. He issued this order despite the protest from the people of Damascus. But then the Christians preferred a monetary compensation and the matter was amicably settled.

Reports also show that ʿAbd al-Malik b. Marwān was averse to bribery and on occasions dismissed his officers for having received presents from the people.[198] ʿAbd al-Malik is quoted to have addressed one such official in the following terms:

> If you accepted the present without intending to reward its donor, then you are ignoble and base (*laʿīn, danīʾ*). If you accepted the gift with the intention to reward the donor and you did not so reward him then you are treacherous (*khāʾin*). If you had intended to reciprocate by giving an equivalent gift to the donor and you have not done so, you are indebted to him and his associates and you stand divested of the authority that you could otherwise be expected to have.[199]

During the early years of Umayyad rule, it seems that senior officials could argue against the orders of the caliph if they judged that the caliph was violating the law. When Muʿāwiyah advised his officers to raise the rate of the poll tax in some parts of Egypt, the officers refused and reasoned that it was a violation of the treaty with the Copts. Similar other instances are also noted. But by the time of Muʿāwiyah's death, most of the senior Companions had passed away and resistance against official abuse had weakened. The evolutionary changes that were brought by the caliph ʿUmar b. ʿAbd al-ʿAzīz were an extraordinary endeavour to revive the early tradition. ʿUmar II, as he is known, addressed himself to the task of reform and combat against corruption, but the two years and few months of his reign were not long enough to carry these through. The decline in standards of accountability that had started under Muʿāwiyah might have been arrested even before ʿUmar II by an otherwise upright prince, ʿAbd al-Malik b. Marwān, who unfortunately became involved in chaotic political situations due to the revolt of ʿAbd al-Raḥmān Ibn Ashʿath in Basra. His frequent attempts to improve the situation were frustrated and he had to condone official ruthlessness when the divisive forces grew stronger. He seems to have diverted himself from negative activities to positive works after suppressing Ibn Ashʿath's revolt (82 AH), but this left only a short period of peaceful rule before his death in 86 AH.[200]

It may be concluded that the Islamic principles of accountability and awareness of duty to implement justice under the *Sharīʿah* underwent steady decline following the period of the Pious Caliphs, and despite some lucid intervals, it is unfortunately marked by deviation and disregard of the norms of accountability.

IV. Institutional Developments

Judicial supervision over the conduct of government is an important aspect of accountability in public affairs. Some of the manifestation of this in reference to misconduct in the course of duty by high ranking officials can be found under impeachment of the head of state, the *maẓālim* jurisdiction, as well as the semi-judicial functions of *ḥisbah* in this volume. These may be regarded as the basic pillars of accountability and *muḥāsabah* in government. Between them, they incorporate substantive principles and methods that help to draw attention to official abuse, and they all promote accountability in public affairs.

The discussion that follows is presented in four sections beginning with a note on the role of the judiciary as the main instrument of *muḥāsabah*. This is followed by a discussion of the *maẓālim* jurisdiction, and then an overview of the role of *ḥisbah* in accountability. The succeeding section on impeachment discusses the right of the community to depose a deviant leader (*ḥaqq al-ʿazl*) and its ultimate resource to civil disobedience and forcible ousting (*al-khurūj*) in the event of resistance and refusal. There is some discussion also of how these principles can be practised under present conditions in the Muslim countries. The discussion continues with a brief account of two other institutions, namely the audits and accounts department (*dīwān al-azimmah*) and the expropriated assets department (*dīwān al-muṣādirīn*) both of which played a role in accountability of government office holders. The last section provides an overview of the constitutional reforms under Ottoman Turkey which had a bearing on accountability.

THE OVERRIDING ROLE OF THE JUDICIARY

The discussion in this section accentuates the role and importance of the judiciary as the bulwark of accountability in almost any legal tradition including the *Sharī'ah*. One of the more specific manifestations of accountability within the Islamic judiciary was the *mazālim* jurisdiction, which will be discussed separately in the next section. Some writers have treated the *mazālim* as a totally separate entity outside the Islamic judiciary, a view that I do not share with them. The *mazālim* may have remained in some ways outside the regular judiciary, yet it was essentially a judicial tribunal as will later be explained.

Traditionally the *Sharī'ah* courts were courts of general jurisdiction that were also authorised to receive and adjudicate all types of disputes. This was a manifestation largely of the unitarian conception of justice and judicial organisation in Islam that visualized an essentially monolithic judiciary whose powers extended to all types of disputes. That judiciary was basically not amenable to the idea of having specialised courts and jurisdictions within its ranks. The courts of justice were thus authorised to look into cases that were brought before them regardless as to whether the disputing parties therein were ordinary people or office holders in the government, tradesmen or soldiers, etc. All were subject to the *Sharī'ah* and therefore to the authority of the *Sharī'ah* courts. There is also no recognition in *Sharī'ah* of any differential treatment for ministers and state dignitaries including the head of state himself. A shopkeeper, a farmer, or labourer may bring a case before the *Sharī'ah* court against a minister or the head of state and demand judicial redress. It is incumbent on the judge to adjudicate the case in accordance with the norms and principles of justice while treating everyone equally without any discrimination. Maḥmaṣṣānī has quoted al-Māwardī to the effect that government administration and officials as well as ordinary members of the public are equally covered by the principle of 'equal treatment of the litigating parties before the courts of justice as of the moment they enter the court, the manner they are seated in the court, spoken to and treated in words and in deeds without discrimination between the noble and commoner, freeman and slave, Muslim and non-Muslim.'[201] This principle was manifested in the early precedent of the Companions and as it was also articulated in the renowned letter of the caliph ʿUmar I to his judges. Writers have frequently referred to one particular case wherein the caliph ʿUmar was himself involved in a dispute with Ubay b. Kaʿb which was adjudicated by Zayd b. Thābit. In another case, the fourth caliph ʿAlī brought a dispute against a Jew before the *qāḍī*. The principle that was followed in both cases was one of equal treatment and impartiality even when the head of state himself was one of the litigants. These cases also endorse what we stated earlier regarding the unrestricted jurisdiction of the *Sharīʿah* courts and their competency to adjudicate all types of disputes. This has basically remained valid ever since in that the *Sharīʿah* courts are courts of general jurisdiction, although the head of state is authorised to introduce special tribunals when this is deemed to be in the best interest of justice—as I shall presently explain.

If there is a recognition in *Sharīʿah*, as indeed there is, at the level of court organisation, of particularisation of justice (*takhṣīṣ al-qaḍāʾ*) and the formation of specialised tribunals as a result, it is subject to the requirement that it does not derogate from the overriding position of the regular judiciary as the mainstay of judicial power and accountability in government. The *maẓālim* jurisdiction should also be seen in this light, as it was basically a branch of the Islamic judiciary. It was due mainly to the fact that the *maẓālim* exercised adjudicatory powers over high ranking officials and the *qāḍīs* themselves that it was increasingly seen as an autonomous jurisdiction. There is no objection, in principle, to any of these developments, nor indeed to the fact that the *maẓālim*, a version of which currently operates in Saudi Arabia, has also acquired the attributes of an administrative court. All of this is acceptable if it would serve the cause of a more refined approach to accountability under the law. Yet the basic position still remains that the regular judiciary is the main instrument of accountability in an Islamic government.

Historically, the judges enjoyed independence in their capacity as the enforcers of *Sharīʿah* who were guided in their activities by a sense of devotion to a cause. They were often selected from among the religious leaders and *ʿulamāʾ* who commanded respect in their communities. People looked up to the *ʿulamāʾ* and judges and they were consequently influential with both the people and the government. In theory the judges were expected to engage in original interpretation and *ijtihād* especially in the event where the dispute before them was not regulated by the existing law. In their capacity as enforcers of *Sharīʿah* and carriers of *ijtihād*, they were to be guided by their sense of conviction to principles and their own understanding of the law and the issues before them, and were not subject to anyone's superior authority in this. This is confirmed by the recognition in *Sharī'ah* of the inviolability of *ijtihād*, the belief that the judge and *mujtahid* must be able to carry out *ijtihād* in the light only of their knowledge and personal conviction, which also meant the the judges must act independently of the other organs of state, especially the executive branch. It is also due mainly to this that the legal theory of *uṣūl al-fiqh* is reticent on the recognition of judicial precedent as a source of law lest it compromise the unfettered exercise of *ijtihād* and the independence of its carriers, including of course the judges.

The caliphs and governors respected judges with sound reputation for piety and scholarship and normally refrained from interference in their affairs. People were often so supportive of these learned figures that it 'made many a governor of the Abbasid period think deeply of the consequences of attempting to dismiss a judge and indeed it was under the Abbasids that the powers to dismiss the judges were taken away from the governors and decisions of this nature were then made in Baghdad. Judicial appointments and determination of the salaries of judges were also personally overseen by the Caliph.'[202]

During the early caliphate, and also under the Umayyad rule, the available information suggests that judges were independent in their professional capacities. Al-Ṭamāwī has thus concluded that under the Umayyad rule the judges remained to be independent in the exercise of duties due to the overall respect for the independence of *ijtihād*.[203] Whereas the caliphal office had hitherto combined judicial functions, the founder of the Umayyad dynasty, Mu'āwiyah, was the first to relinquish his judicial functions to appointed judges.[204] Another observer has qualified this conclusion by saying that during the Umayyads the judiciary was fully independent from the executive but that this independence was confined only to civil cases and private wrongs thereby excluding issues pertaining to constitutional law and politics.[205]

The emergence and gradual crystallization of the four schools of law during the early Abbasid period tended to impose more restrictions on the independence of judges. The establishment of these schools conveyed the impression that the law had already been expounded in a digested form and the judges were consequently expected to follow and apply it. Plurality of schools and doctrines had also brought with it a measure of disparity and confusion in court decisions, which is why it soon became official policy of the Abbasid state, beginning with Abū Yūsuf (182/798), the disciple of Abū Ḥanīfah and the first chief justice under Hārūn al-Rashīd, to adopt the Ḥanafī school of law for purposes of enforcement. The tendency then continued and became a widespread practice for Muslim countries to adopt one or the other of the prevailing schools as their official *madhhab*.[206] Further limitations on the jurisdiction of *Sharīʿah* courts were imposed in the Ottoman state as a result of importation and borrowing of European laws in the spheres of commercial and criminal legislation. In the sphere of civil transactions and *muʿāmalāt*, the Ottoman Turkey promulgated the renowned *Mejelle* that codified the Ḥanafī *fiqh* for purposes of implementation.[207]

The Abbasid caliph, Hārūn al-Rashīd, was the first to appoint a chief justice (*qāḍī al-quḍāh*). In Andalus the equivalent post was known as (*qāḍī al-jamāʿah*). Reports indicate that Chief Justice Abū Yūsuf exercised full authority in the selection and appointment of judges as well as in matters of accountability and supervision in the conduct of judicial office.[208]

Since the judges are appointed by the head of state and generally represent his delegated authority, the latter has powers to specify their jurisdiction and impose limits as he may deem appropriate. But in the absence of such limitations the regular judiciary exercises unlimited jurisdiction over all disputes. The general jurisdiction of an Islamic judiciary also extends to the *ijtihād*-based laws and constitutionality of the decisions of the consultative assembly (*majlis al-shūrā*). This is because judges have powers to adjudicate all decisions that are not based on a clear text and consensus and therefore questions that arise over their legality and compliance with the clear injunctions of *Sharīʿah*. Hence the Islamic judiciary is in principle authorised to scrutinise statutory laws and decrees and declare them *ultra vires* if they contravene the clear injunctions of Islam.[209] But as already noted the head of state is entitled under the principle of particularisation of justice (*takhṣīṣ al-qaḍāʾ*) to set up a separate tribunal for this purpose, or indeed to entrust judicial supervision of statutory instruments in the Supreme Court, or a court of higher jurisdiction. This limitation and assignment of specialised judicial powers can now be seen in the Saudi Arabian model of *Dīwān al-Maẓālim*, which acts almost exclusively as an administrative tribunal. When the head of state sets up a specialised tribunal, it would, in the exercise of its powers be normally required to observe the principle that govern *ijtihād*. The head of state must also observe this and grant to judicial tribunals the latitude and discretion that is an integral part of the theory of *ijtihād* and the independence of judicial office.[210]

Muslim jurists are in agreement that the head of state may not dismiss nor terminate the services of a judge without a valid cause. For this is deemed to be contrary to *maslahah* (public interest) and it is also likely to amount to a breach of contract. Yet the judges too are accountable and may be taken to task, and even dismissed, in the event of deliberate miscarriage of justice, just as they may be held personally liable to compensate for any loss or damage that their decisions inflict on another person. In the event, however, when a judge falls into error and makes a wrong decision while believing that he had followed correct procedure and principle, his decision may be set aside but claims for compensation and damages would be payable from the public treasury. However, if the wrong judgment is issued based on distorted evidence and deliberate misrepresentation by one of the parties or witnesses, the party concerned may be held liable for payment of compensation.[211]

DĪWĀN AL-MAZ̄ĀLIM (COURT OF GRIEVANCES)

The *mazālim* jurisdiction, which has already been discussed to some extent, originated in the notion that the principle of the rule of law can be compromised if the judges themselves, princes, ministers and powerful members of the community tried to circumvent the law, or violate and defy it for their selfish ends, in which case the *Sharī'ah* courts may be powerless to bring them and their departments to book and enforce the court decisions on them. The need was therefore felt for the creation of a powerful jurisdiction that could apply more expedient procedures in the interest of accountability in government, especially with regard to disputes arising between the citizen and state. One of the basic objectives of the *mazālim* jurisdiction was to subjugate the government itself to the rule of law and ensure that state organisations and men of authority and influence did not compromise the objectivity of justice and accountability in governance.

Al-Rifāʿī has described the *mazālim* as 'a specialized jurisdiction that operates side by side, yet separately, from the regular judiciary in order to adjudicate disputes and grievances wherein one or both parties possesses influence and power that may arise from holding a government position or other sources of influence.'[212] According to Muhammad Salām Madkūr, the *mazālim* jurisdiction 'is a judicial office that ranks above those of the *qāḍī* and the *muhtasib* and combines a degree of executive power with judicial authority in order to settle grievances brought before it by members of the public against government officials, governors and rulers, princes, army commanders and the judges themselves.'[213]

The *mazālim* jurisdiction dates back to the early Abbasid period. The head of the *mazālim* court, known as *walī al-mazālim*, was selected from among outstanding individuals of knowledge and piety who possessed the qualifications of a *qāḍī* at least. The phrase *wilāyat al-mazālim* refers to the jurisdictional authority and powers of this organization, which was otherwise known as *dīwān al-mazālim*.[214] The sphere of authority and jurisdiction of *walī al-mazālim* exceeded that of the *qāḍī*. The general sessions of the *mazālim* court, which were held on certain appointed times, were attended by the disputing parties, deputies and assistants of the *walī al-mazālim*, judges and government officials concerned with the case, the jurists (*fuqahā'*) who could be consulted on the occasion, clerks, and witnesses. The procedure did not always necessitate an adversarial process and witnesses did not have to testify for or against a litigant but more so in order to vindicate the truth.

Al-Māwardī and al-Farrā have both listed about ten varieties of disputes, all of which fell under the *mazālim* jurisdiction. Of these certain types of disputes, namely those which consisted of complaints against corruption and abuse of power by provincial governors, tax disputes and excesses of tax collectors, and abusive practices of record keepers in government departments. These disputes did not depend on a private claim because they were public rights issues and affected general interest (*maslahah*) of the community as a whole. Yet private individuals could also lodge a complaint against official abuse: in pecuniary and property-related matters such as pay disputes, usurpation (*ghasb*) of private property, disputes over private endowments (*awqāf ahliyyah*), grievances over delay in the enforcement of court decisions, public morality offences, offences against religion and acts that obstructed due performance of ʿibādāt, as well as disputes arising between private parties, the *mazālim* proceedings usually began with a claim or complaint by the aggrieved party.[215]

Basic authority for the establishment of *wilāyat al-mazālim* could be found in the Qur'ān, and also the *Sunnah* of the Prophet, who is noted to have received complaints against officials, just as was the case under the Pious Caliphs after him, although no specific tribunal by this name existed at that time. Justice being the cardinal objective of Islam, the Qur'ān is effusive in its condemnation of injustice and oppression (*ẓulm*) just as it is overtly supportive of efforts that fight oppression in the quest for justice.[216] This can also be said of the *Sunnah* of the Prophet, who said, for example, in a renowned *ḥadīth*:

> When the people see an oppressor committing acts of injustice and they fail to take him by the hand (and stop him), they will all share the same predicament as God has enacted for the oppressor.[217]

The precedent of Companions, especially that of the caliph ʿUmar b. al-Khaṭṭāb is supportive of an uncompromising attitude that the Islamic government must take against official abuse wherein government employees violated the rights of the people. Numerous instances and cases of official malpractice wherein government officials were taken to task for their abusive practices were earlier discussed. The literature suggests, however, that fighting official abuse was seen as an integral part of the administration of justice, and no specialised jurisdiction had existed for this purpose in the early period of Islam.

The caliph ʿAlī b. Abū Ṭālib is noted for having entertained public grievances, but he too did not assign a particular day or venue for hearing cases. The Umayyad ruler, ʿAbd al-Malik b. Marwān (d. 86/705), was the first to assign a day of the week for the purpose of receiving complaints in matters which the courts of justice found difficult to deal with. When the caliph Marwān could not be present, he assigned Ibn Idrīs al-Awdī to sit for him. Later the caliph Umar b. ʿAbd al-ʿAzīz zealously followed that precedent. The Abbasid caliphs, al-Mahdī (780 AD), al-Hādī and Hārūn al-Rashīd followed suit. Al-Muhtadī was the last to keep up the precedent and, towards the end of the second century *hijrah*, he established for the first time a jurisdiction known as *Dīwān al-Maẓālim*. Viziers in the capital and governors in the provinces were occasionally authorised by the Caliph to sit in the *Dīwān al-Maẓālim*.

In the latter part of the Abbasid period, the caliph's authority to review the *maẓālim* grievances was exercised, in the outlying areas, by the Sultan, whether or not the power had been delegated to him by the caliph. The *maẓālim* became an important organ of the Abbasid state at around mid-third/ninth century. It was, according to al-Māwardī, an attempt to combine 'the legal authority of the judge with the political authority of the ruler.'[218] It was essentially a judicial authority that was above that of the *qāḍī* and the *muḥtasib* (officer in charge of *ḥisbah*) and could adjudicate in disputes by applying methods that the *qāḍī* could not apply due to the constraints of judicial procedure. The *maẓālim* was empowered to issue orders addressed either to the *qāḍī* or the *muḥtasib*, but neither of the latter two could issue orders on the *walī al-maẓālim*. The *qāḍī* was also authorised to issue orders on the *muḥtasib* but the latter did not possess judicial authority of the kind that would entitle him to issue binding orders.[219] The main functions of the *maẓālim* jurisdiction may be further elaborated as follows:

(1) To look into issues and grievances at its own initiative without there being a litigant to start a case. Powers of this type, which were not available to the regular judiciary, were effectively used to monitor oppressive conduct of governors, tax collectors and state officials. In the case of unwarranted levying of tax, extortion and usurpation of property by state officials, the *maẓālim* had powers to issue orders for their return directly to their lawful owners and take appropriate measures against the officials concerned.

(2) General inspection of official records and works of secretaries in charge of documentation.

(3) Grievances that could not be effectively addressed by the *qāḍī* or the *muḥtasib*, or where decisions made by the latter had failed to be implemented.

(4) To monitor profiteering and monopolistic activities by wealthy individuals who could distort the food supplies or prices in the market place. The regular judiciary was not best suited to direct supervision of this kind and due to procedural requirements could not take swift measures to counteract transgression and abuse at the time when they actually took place.[220]

(5) Supervision of religious endowments (*awqāf*), both public and private, to ensure that they operated in accordance with the stated objectives of the *waqf*.

Al-Māwardī has recorded the following illustrations of cases that fell within the ambit of *maẓālim* jurisdiction, even before the establishment of a separate jurisdiction by this name:

It is reported that a man from the Yemen approached the Caliph ʿUmar b. ʿAbd al-ʿAzīz with a complaint against Walīd b. ʿAbd al-Malik, the previous caliph (d. 86/705), that the latter had usurped his landed estate. The caliph heard the grievance and asked the registrar of land to check the register of the *ṣafī* (chosen) landed estates, and it turned out that the land in question was taken by the then caliph Walīd b. ʿAbd al-Malik. ʿUmar b. ʿAbd al-ʿAzīz consequently instructed the registrar to strike the name of the previous caliph and transfer the land to its owner and also to compensate the owner for expenses he had incurred as a result.[221]

In another case, it is reported that the Abbasid caliph al-Ma'mūn (d. 198/813) had assigned Sundays for the *mazālim* disputes, which he received himself. On one such occasion, a woman wearing shabby clothes approached him with a grievance. She began praising the caliph for his attention to the weak and the oppressed. The caliph turned to her and said (the exchange seems to have occurred in the form of a poignant poetical expression by the plaintiff and the caliph both—as Māwardī's record indicates) that it was time for prayer and asked her to return on the following Sunday. She did, and the caliph asked her if she had an opponent. To this the woman responded that indeed she had and it was the caliph's son, Al-ʿAbbās b. Amīr al-Mu'minīn. The caliph then instructed his *qāḍī*, Yaḥyā b. Aktham and his minister, Aḥmad b. Abī Khālid, to look into the case. Then a meeting followed in which the caliph himself and the plaintiff were present and the latter expressed herself forcefully that the prince al-ʿAbbās had wrongfully usurped her property. The caliph listened but did not adjudicate in the matter, as his own son was a party to the dispute. As to the suggestion by a courtier that the plaintiff should lower her tone of voice, the caliph said, 'Let her speak. The strength of her voice may be due to the truth of her grievance.' The caliph then issued order that her property be returned to her.

The fact that the caliph handed over the case initially to his judge and minister was due to the involvement of his son. He knew that he could not adjudicate in favour of his son but that it was permissible for him to adjudicate against him. This being the case, as Māwardī explained, the caliph issued the final judgment himself.[222]

Recourse to the *mazālim* jurisdiction in both of these cases was evidently due to the involvement of powerful figures that could evade enforcement of judgment by the regular judiciary. The case that follows below presented somewhat of a different situation, which is that the case was actually extra-judicial and as such did not formally fall within the jurisdiction of regular courts.

It is reported that a woman came to the caliph ʿUmar b. al-Khaṭṭāb and addressed him: 'O Commander of the Faithful! My husband fasts during the day and prays during the night, and I hate to complain to him as he engages himself in worshipping God Most High.' The caliph's response to this was simply to say: 'What a good husband you have—*niʿmah al-zawju zawjak!*' The woman repeated her case and the caliph also gave the same response until Kaʿb b. Sūr al-Asadī told the caliph that this woman had a grievance against her husband for neglecting her in regard to his marital obligations. The caliph then assigned Ka'b to adjudicate over the case on the basis of his own understanding of it. Ka'b then summoned the husband and informed him of his wife's complaint. The husband is reported to have said: 'Was it concerning food and maintenance?' The judge heard the parties and then addressed the husband: 'God Most High has permitted you to marry up to four wives simultaneously. So you may have three nights in which you worship your Lord and the fourth night for you to share with your wife.' Having heard of this, the caliph 'Umar was pleased and praised Ka'b's understanding of the case and his judgment. Ka'b was subsequently appointed as *qāḍī* of Basra.[223]

Māwardī commented that the judgment in this case was basically over a matter that did not necessarily call for a judicial decision, and the judgment that was in fact issued was in the nature of a permissible rather than imperative ruling (*ḥukman bi'l-jā'iz dūn al-wājib*). For division of time (*qasm*) is not applicable in a monogamous marriage, but the judge premised his decision on it nevertheless.[224]

The *maẓālim* jurisdiction acquired prestige and prominence during the second phase of the Abbasid rule around the early third/ninth century. Leading officials paid greater attention to petitions, and complaints from the people and exercised greater self-restraint in handling their rights and properties.[225]

In modern times, it seems that adoption of the principle of separation of powers in most of the constitutions that Muslim countries have promulgated favour the establishment of a powerful judiciary that operates independently from the other organs of state. This has effectively placed the Supreme Court at the helm of the judiciary, and all other tribunals are consequently made subservient to the supervising authority of the Supreme Court. The Supreme Court thus to all intents and purposes acquired the powers that were exercised by the *maẓālim* jurisdiction in earlier times. This should not mean, however, that there is no room for a *maẓālim* tribunal to ensure and enhance accountability in government. There are constitutions and laws as we know, but it would appear that most Muslim countries have fallen short on accountability and the principle of government under the rule of law. A powerful *maẓālim* jurisdiction with a clear constitutional mandate and role to promote accountability would therefore be advisable even if it were accountable to the Supreme Court. A basic line of jurisdictional division between the regular judiciary and the *maẓālim* may be drawn when the latter is envisaged as an administrative tribunal that is concerned primarily with official abuse and disputes brought by the people against the government.

They would leave the regular judiciary in charge mainly of disputes among people wherein the government itself is not a party to the litigation.

The only *mazālim* jurisdiction, or *Dīwān al-Mazālim*, that currently operates in Saudi Arabia where it functions concurrently with the *Sharīʿah* judicial system but in effect supersedes it. The Saudi *Dīwān al-Mazālim* is not required to decide in accordance with the *Sharīʿah*; its procedure is simple, and its judges include lawyers with a modern background, factors which ensure flexibility of the kind that is not available in the *Sharīʿah* court procedures of Saudi Arabia.[226] In many of the contemporary states of the Middle East the functions of *dīwān al-mazālim* have on the other hand been wholly or partially assumed by various other agencies such as the *Majlis al-Dawlah* (state council) in Egypt, *Majlis Shūrā al-Dawlah* in Syria and Lebanon, and *Maḥkamat al-Qaḍāʾ al-Idārī* in Iraq. Syria and Lebanon had in fact followed the Ottoman model where it used to be called *Shura-e-Devlat* (and occasionally as *Shūrā*). Only in Saudi Arabia the organisation continues to be known by its original nomenclature as *Dīwān al-Mazālim*.[227]

Dīwān al-Mazālim in Saudi Arabia operates as an administrative jurisdiction side by side with the *Sharīʿah* Courts which are courts of general jurisdiction in that country, both enjoying independent status in their respective spheres. Under the royal decree of 1373/1954, the head of *Dīwān al-Mazālim* who holds a ministerial rank is directly accountable to the King with a measure of supervision by the Cabinet. Under the royal decree of September 1974, *Dīwān al-Mazālim* was made independent of the Cabinet and has retained that status ever since. This decree also specified the basic procedure of *Dīwān al-Mazālim* in respect of complains that it receives over official abuse of power. Within two weeks of receiving a complaint the Head (*Raʾīs*) of *Dīwān al-Mazālim* submits a report on the case to the King and a copy to the Prime Minister.[228]

Several other decrees were issued since on the regulatory and procedural aspects of *Dīwān al-Mazālim* but a measure of uncertainty remained concerning its independent status as the highest administrative court in the land. This was eventually determined under the royal decree (no. 2918) of 1402/1983 which ensured its independence from the ubiquitous jurisdiction of the *Sharīʿah* Courts. The head of *Dīwān al-Mazālim* who is appointed by the King has powers to issue orders directed to government departments and he alone is the point of reference regarding the employees of *Dīwān al-Maẓālim* and the determination of its regulatory procedures.

The head of *Dīwān al-Maẓālim* is assisted by a number of deputies, an administrative affairs committee, an advisory committee, an enquiry board, a disciplinary committee and a general council. Under the 1982 regulations the professional cadre of *Dīwān al-Maẓālim* has been granted total security of office and its members cannot by deposed or dismissed, after confirmation into office, at any time during the entire length of their service.[229] Should there be a legitimate case of disability or abuse of power, the member concerned may be recommended by the Administrative Committee for early retirement to the King. Persons who fail on three consecutive occasions to achieve promotion to the next rank may likewise be subjected to the same procedure.

Being an administrative court, the *Dīwān al-Maẓālim* in Saudi Arabia acts only in cases where the state is a party to the dispute and claims that involve abuse of power against individuals. The Saudi system bears much similarity in this regard to the French administrative court. The *Dīwān al-Maẓālim* has no powers to act as an appeal jurisdiction against the decision of the *Sharīʿah* Courts, just as it has no powers to hear complaints in cases relating to the exercise the sovereign of power of the state. Cases of this nature also fall beyond the jurisdiction of the *Sharīʿah* Courts. The *Dīwān al-Maẓālim* may however, entertain cases referred to it by the Cabinet in the sphere, for example, of private international law that may involve judicial decision of a foreign court that is considered enforceable in Saudi Arabia.[230]

ACCOUNTABILITY AND THE *MUḤTASIB* (OFFICER IN CHARGE OF *ḤISBAH*)

Ḥisbah is a Qurʾānic principle and it is concerned mainly with the promotion of good and prevention of evil. It would as such entitle every citizen to draw attention to an evil which may consist of cases of corruption and official abuse. Muslim jurists have elaborated in much detail the manner in which it is conducted. In its general application, *hisbah* must begin by *taʿrīf*, that is, explaining and identifying the nature of the conduct that is the target of *hisbah* to its perpetrator. This is to be followed by a courteous reminder and advice (*waʿz*), then by expression of anger (*qahr*) that may involve the use of harsh words in order merely to stop an evil, but the advice should not be such as would itself amount to insult or abuse. The initial stages of *hisbah* are thus confined to the use of words and peaceful methods of promoting a good cause but if they all fail to be effective, the next stage is recourse to carefully measured action that may seem the only way of preventing an evil. All of this is, once again, subject to a general condition that the attempt to prevent an evil does not lead to a greater evil. Hence the individual who attempts *hisbah* needs to be convinced of his/her ability at all times to contain and avert, and not to exacerbate, an evil that is taking place. It is therefore essential that the person acts from a position of knowledge and conviction and avoids attempting *hisbah* in doubtful situations of which he or she may have little knowledge.[231]

Prevention of evil is only one of the two aspects of *hisbah*, the other being promotion of what is considered to be beneficial and good. In both of these capacities, *hisbah* entitles the individual to take intuitive in order to promote a good cause or to prevent a bad one. In the context of accountability, *hisbah* entitles every member of the community to bring to light, or possibly to prevent, official abuse, and play a proactive role toward the development of good standards of government, be it through speech, writing, demonstration or constructive action. Although in principle it is said that *hisbah* is guided by the *Sharī'ah* and should be attempted by a person who has knowledge of the *Sharī'ah* it would be an exaggeration to assume that the *Sharī'ah* regulates all aspects of *hisbah*. The *Sharī'ah* often provides a basic guideline but the precise judgment when and how to attempt *hisbah* is often a matter of personal insight and initiative of the individual concerned. *Hisbah* has not, in other words, been entirely regulated and leaves much, in the context of accountability, for the personal judgment and initiative of the citizen to remind, criticise and rectify abuse of official power.

Hisbah was institutionalised under the Abassid caliph al-Mahdī (d. 780 AD) and it became the chief responsibility of the *muhtasib* who was authorized, however, to supervise the market activities and price regulation of basic commodities. In the course of time, a department of *hisbah* (*Dīwān al-Hisbah*) developed as a quasi-judicial institution concerned with matters that were not strictly legal nor were included in the jurisdiction of *Sharī'ah* courts—nor were they totally secular to be put under jurisdiction of the police department. *Dīwan al-Hisbah* was thus created to supplement the functions of both the courts of justice and the police. Much of its activities were concerned with social ethics and moral standards of public behaviour. The *muhtasibs* who were representative of *Dīwān al-Hisbah* were the guardians of public morality and religious propriety. They were responsible for safeguarding cemeteries from being used as gathering places, and kept lascivious and deviant activities under check just as they disallowed Muslim women from entering unsuitable places. The *muhtasib* also supervised the building of houses to ensure they did not obstruct public amenities nor violated the privacy of neighbouring houses.

In some ways the *muhtasib*s were like the modern ombudsmen in Scandinavian countries, acting as defenders and censors of public interest. In large geographical areas the *muhtasib*s were assisted by deputies known as *amīn* and *ʿarīf* and a number of subordinate officials. In organisational terms, the department head, *Ṣāhib al-Hisbah*, stood between the Chief Justice (*Qāḍī al-Quḍāt*) and the Chief of Police (*Ṣāhib al-Shurṭah*). The *Ṣāhib al-Hisbah* usually acted under the direction of a vizier, but in the Fatimid state of Egypt, this department was directly subordinated to the *Qāḍī al-Quḍāt*. *Hisbah* acquired much prominence under the Fatimids and also under the Umayyad rule in Andalus.[232]

Among the historical incidents of *hisbah* that might be of interest is a report to the effect that the *muhtasib* of Baghdad, Ibrāhīm b. Bathā', noted a large crowed of litigants awaiting at the courthouse of the chief *qāḍī*, Abū ʿAmr Ibn Ḥammād. It was close to noontime and the heat of the blazing sun had evidently caused discomfort to the people. So the *muhtasib* said to the doorkeeper of the court: tell the *qāḍī* that the litigants are waiting at his door and suffering discomfort, either to start the court session or else inform the people of your reason so that they may go now and return when you are able to hold a session.[233]

Another report has it that the governor of Damascus, Atābeq Tuftakīn, summoned the *muhtasib* of the town and reminded him to be diligent in the conduct of his duty. To this the *muhtasib* replied: 'Well then, I might start right here. You should dispose of the garment that is covering your seat as it is made of silk, and also discard the gold ring that you are wearing.' The *muhtasib* recited a *hadīth* in support of his critique, and no sooner had he cited it than the governor disposed of both the items and gracefully thanked the *muhtasib* for his reminder.[234]

An even earlier instance of *hisbah* on record was that of the renowned Companion, Abū Dhar al-Ghaffarī, who criticised the then governor of Sham, Muʿāwiyah, during the reign of the caliph ʿUthmān Ibn ʿAffān for Muʿāwiyah's indulgence in the accumulation of wealth. Abū Dhar caused a stir for his advice that government officials should have enough for their needs and distribute the rest of the excessive wealth they had amassed among the community.[235]

Ḥisbah thus provided an important basis for the promotion of accountability in government, and one finds numerous instances of its application to that end in the historical records of Muslim governments. As already noted, *ḥisbah* enables the citizens to expose deviation and wrongful conduct on the part of one another and the government, and also to promote what is beneficial and good. This may be attempted when deemed feasible and effective under the circumstances.

The *'ulamā'* have unanimously held *ḥisbah* to be a collective duty (*fard kifā'ī*) that may never be totally abandoned. It may be practised by individuals, groups and associations and by the government agencies, but being a *fard kifā'ī*, no one may totally monopolise *ḥisbah*—as it is basically a right of every citizen. The government may assign some aspects of *ḥisbah* to a particular agency or institution and this is, in fact, generally the case with regard to the coercive aspects of *ḥisbah*, which have been almost exclusively assigned to the police. But the peaceable aspects of *ḥisbah*, namely the part which consists of identification (*ta'rīf*) and verbal advice (*wa'ẓ*) must remain a part of the basic rights and liberties of the individual which he or she may exercise at his or her initiative without any need for litigation or judicial action. This is not, however, to say that judicial action is not of concern to *ḥisbah*: one may, for example, act as a witness in the cause of justice, which also partakes in *ḥisbah*.

Ḥisbah is attempted as a result of direct observation and personal knowledge (*mushāhadah wa-'ilm*) and not in respect of what has been heard or reported by others. One who conducts *ḥisbah* must in other words be a direct witness. This is unlike litigation in the courts in that court actions are normally concerned with past events. *Ḥisbah*, therefore, does not involve postponement to a later time. Should there be only one person, be it a government officer, or a member of the public, who alone knows about an evil being committed and can exercise *ḥisbah* in that situation, then it becomes a personal duty (*fard 'ayn*) of that person to attempt it. The *muhtasib* has no powers to adjudicate disputes; he does not hold a trial nor calls for witnesses or other evidence. Yet unlike the courts of justice, the *muhtasib* is not entirely dependant on formal presentation of claims and evidence and may conduct his duties based on his own initiative without any formal claims. The *muhtasib*, moreover, has very limited powers in the imposition of punishment and he basically does not issue orders but proposes practical solutions to issues where the parties involved do not face nor deny any allegations but are ready to settle the issue.[236]

Apart from a recent experience under the Taliban in Afghanistan where a Department of Vice and Virtues, or *hisbah*, was established and soon became one of he most active branches of the Taliban government, there is, to the best of my knowledge, no organisation or department by that designation in any other Muslim country. With the collapse of the Taliban in Afghanistan in late 2001, the department of *hisbah* was also disbanded.[237] Commentators have drawn parallels between the *hisbah* and the ombudsmen in the kind of functions that the latter undertake. Be that as it may, the general functions of *hisbah* are at present divided between various government departments such as those responsible for trade, public health, social affairs, the municipalities and the police. *Hisbah* may serve a good purpose, if it were to be revived in a well regulated fashion to enhance the moral fabric of society as well as act in the capacity of ombudsmen to enhance accountability in government. It may also be able to take a practical and less formalized approach to social and ethical issues of public concern. A well-regulated system of *hisbah* could diffuse the somewhat excessive concentration of coercive power in the police. The *muhtasib* could also play the role of the ombudsman to act as an intermediary and facilitator on behalf of the citizen.

Hisbah is also subject to other restrictions. The general restraints, for instance, that the *Sharīʿah* has imposed in regard to espionage and respect for the privacy of the people apply equally to *hisbah*. This would mean that the *muhtasib*, whether a private individual or a government officer, is not entitled to enter private dwellings nor pry on personal privacy of people in the name of *hisbah*. Other relevant details of *hisbah* in so far as they relate to accountability may be summarised as follows:

The *muhtasib*'s duty pertaining to the promotion of good (*amr bi'l-maʿrūf*) may relate to the Right of God (*haqq Allāh*), to the Right of Man (*haqq al-ādamī*), or to what may fall in between the two (*mushtarak baynahumā*).

The *muhtasib*'s duty pertaining to the Rights of God consists mainly of religious observances such as that of the congregational prayer on Fridays, fasting during Ramadan and other duties. To ensure, for example, that the public paths to the mosque are not obstructed by traffic, and also that restaurants and eating places in Muslim towns and villages do not entertain customers during daytime in the fasting month. Pertaining to the Right of Man the duties of *muhtasib* are subdivided into the two types of general and specific. General duties are those that concern the community as a whole. When there is disruption in public services such as water and electricity or transportation, for example, the *muhtasib* ensures prompt restoration and repair and spends of the funds of *bayt al-māl* on such works. When no funds are available in the *bayt al-māl* the *muhtasib* may collect contributions from the wealthy residents of the locality for the purpose, and take all necessary measures to facilitate this. The specific aspects of the duties of the *muhtasib* concern the rights and interest of individuals such as repayment of debt by procrastinating debtors, and due enforcement of court orders regarding maintenance to relatives, enquiry into the welfare of children and treatment they receive within and outside the family. Duties that fall between the two classes of rights (i.e. of God and man) may be illustrated by supervision of the treatment of employees by their employers, welfare of workers, fair treatment of animals and upkeep of their grazing lands, etc.

The *muhtasib* duties that relate to the prevention of evil (*nahy ʿan al-munkar*) also occur in the three contexts, as noted above, of the Right of God, the Right of man, and that which partakes in both. With reference to the Right of God, to give an example, the *muhtasib* ensures due collection of *zakāh* (legal alms) from those who fall negligent, or negligence of duty by the collectors of such revenues. The *muhtasib* also apprehends beggars who are able to work to take employment, and reprimand them if they persist. Most of the duties of the *muhtasib* in reference to the market place tend to fall under the common category between the two classes of rights under review. This includes price regulation and supervision of measurements and weights as well as prevention of fraud, and indulgence, with reference to employment contracts, in unlawful contractual agreements. The *muhtasib* also supervises the quality of market supplies and irregularities concerning currency, parity, purity and fabrication thereof. Prevention of hoarding (*ihtikār*) and monopolistic practices, oppressive strikes and practice of usury also fall within the ambit of the wide-ranging duties of the *muhtasib*.

Prevention of *munkar* relating to the Right of Man concerns violation of the rights of neighbours and violation of the rights of workers as well as supervision of professional practices of physicians, lawyers, chemists, due fulfilment of trusts by guardians and the like, as well as keeping the market clear of unpleasant smells, noise and dust. Prevention of *munkar* that partakes in both the Right of God and the Right of Man includes, according to al-Māwardī, cases of transgression over the rights of the religious minorities, ill-treatment of servants and animals, etc.[238]

One of the principles of *hisbah* has it that when transgression cannot be eliminated altogether, one must try to curb it to the extent possible. It is also desirable to make decisions based on reconciliation and agreement in cases of actual or potential disputes among people. The lesser of two evils may need to be acted upon at times in order to prevent occurrence of a greater one. *Hisbah* may not be attempted in technical matters, especially by one who is ignorant of the relevant information and general guidelines of *Sharīʿah*. And lastly *hisbah* is forbidden if it is likely to lead to a greater evil than the one which is being prevented.[239]

IMPEACHMENT

The constitutional theory of caliphate is explicit on the recognition of the community's right to censure and depose a leader who is no longer capable of due discharge of duty, or when he violates the clear injunctions of *Sharīʿah*. This is because government in Islam is a trust (*amānah*) and the head of state is a representative (*wakīl*) of the electorate, entrusted with the exercise of power that belongs to the community. In a contract of *wakālah*, each of the contracting parties is entitled to terminate the contract unilaterally even without the consent of the other party. Thus the head of State is entitled to resign if he wishes and the community or its representatives, the *ahl al-ḥall wa'l-ʿaqd*, are entitled to impeach and depose him when he loses his uprightness of character (*ʿadālah*), becomes a transgressor (*fāsiq*) and indulgent in lasciviousness and corruption.[240] The community may exercise this right, as al-Bayātī noted, through a vote of non-confidence in parliament. Muhammad Asad has emphasized that the attempt to impeach and depose must be the last resort. An individual or group of individuals have, moreover, no right to rebellion as such. It is only by an open verdict of the majority within the community that an established Muslim government may be removed from power by peaceful means, if possible, and by force, if necessary. It is in legal terms, a right of the principal party (*muwakkil*) to investigate and look into the affairs of its representative (*wakīl*) so as to ensure that the terms of the agency are duly fulfilled. The head of state incurs a commitment through fealty (*bayʿah*) to enforce the *Sharīʿah* and his failure to do so entitles the community to depose him. This is, moreover, an extension of the community's basic mission to enjoin good and forbid evil. Two Qurʾānic passages quoted in this connection thus provide:

The believers, men and women, are friends and protectors of one another, they enjoin good and they forbid evil. (9:71)

والمؤمنون والمؤمنات بعضهم أولياء بعض يأمرون بالمعروف وينهون عن المنكر

And fear tumult (or oppression—*fitnah*) which affects not in particular only those of you who do wrong. (8:25)

واتقوا فتنة لاتصيبنّ الذين ظلموا منكم خاصة

The oppressive conduct of a few can affect the innocent and the guilty alike. Hence it is a responsibility of the community to take to task the oppressive few among them. They can in this way protect one another against the evil of civil strife and *fitnah*.

To quote but one of several related *hadīth*s on this theme, it is provided in a *hadīth*, cited above: 'When the people see a tyrant and do not grab him by the hand (alert him), God may afflict them all with the same punishment.'[241]

أن الناس إذا رأوا الظالم فلم يأخذوا على يديه أوشك من يعمهم الله بعقاب منه

The community's right to remind, rectify and eventually to disobey and depose an oppressive ruler has also been confirmed in the statements of the Pious caliphs Abū Bakr and ʿUmar as earlier quoted. But before the full exercise by the community of its rights, recourse had to be made to sincere advice (*nasīhah*), which, according to a *hadīth*, is the essence and pillar of religion. In the event where *nasīhah* fails, the community may disobey the transgressor and resort to impeachment.[242]

A somewhat abortive attempt to depose a ruler in the early history of Islam was the uprising which led to the tragic massacre of Karbala. When the community considered Yazīd b. Muʿāwiyah an usurper and *fāsiq*, the Shīʿite defenders of the household of the Prophet staged an uprising against him under the leadership of the Prophet's grandson, al-Husayn. Although it is generally believed that al-Husayn was right in his assessment of Yazīd having become a *fāsiq*, he made an error of judgment as to his ability to depose him by force. The military confrontation that followed as a result led to the massacre of al-Ḥusayn and all of his 70-odd supporters at Karbala.[243]

According to al-Baghdādī (d. 429/1045) when the head of state indulges in deviation, the community holds the authority either to exonerate and allow him to continue or to depose him and entrust someone else to replace him. The Community stands, in this regard, in the same relationship with the head of state as the latter does with his own employees and officials. When an official transgresses and deviates the terms of his office, the head of state may either leave him to continue or depose him.[244]

Fakhr al-Dīn al-Rāzī noted in his commentary on the Qur'ānic verse: 'My promise is not within the reach of evil-doers' (2:124) that tyrants and oppressors do not observe God's commands nor are they entrusted with enforcing God's laws. Hence they do not become leaders and this verse in effect declares that the leadership of a transgressor is invalid and *bāṭil* in the first place.[245] Al-Ghazālī wrote that the oppressive ruler (*al-sulṭān al-ẓālim*) is under a duty to withdraw and resign his position for he is either deposed automatically by the operation of the law or is liable to be deposed by the community. He is, in reality, not a (legitimate) ruler.[246]

As noted earlier, Al-Māwardī has discussed two main grounds of deposition of the ruler as being collapse of uprightness and just character, and physical or mental disability.[247]

An early incident of public outcry against a government leader occurred during the caliphate of ʿUthmān Ibn ʿAffān. This was staged against the foster brother of the caliph, Walīd b. ʿUqbah, who was governor of Kufa and was accused of wine drinking. The caliph verified the charge and dismissed him as a result.

The community's right to impeach and depose an oppressive leader is thus supported by indisputable evidence which has been widely endorsed by the *ʿulamā'* and jurists. Notwithstanding the clear evidence in support of impeachment, the theory of caliphate has not determined a definite procedure for deposition of the head of state and other leading officials. As far as one can tell the theory of caliphate was articulated by scholars of the Abbasid period like al-Baghdādi, al-Māwardī and al-Farrā at around the late fifth and early sixth century *hijrah*. The theory that was so articulated was to some extent influenced by the prevailing conditions and realities of the Abbasid rule. By then the *ʿulamā'* were increasingly inclined to lay emphasis on the citizen's duty of obedience to the authorities but did not give an equal degree of prominence to accountability of government leaders. Ibn Taymiyyah almost repeated what al-Ghazālī had said earlier that any government is better than anarchy and that 'sixty years of dictatorship is better than a single night with no leader.' His predecessor Ibn Jamāʿah held that if a ruler committed wrong he should not be deposed if this was likely to lead to disturbance and *fitnah*. The notion of absolute obedience thus gradually gained ground. Both Ahmad Hasan and Kakakhel have observed that during the period of absolutism of kings and caliphs the ʿulamā' began to speak in such terms as 'no rebellion is valid as it may lead to anarchy and disintegration.'[248]

To sum up, notwithstanding the absence of a clear method for impeachment of the head of state one may suggest that in its capacity as the principal party (*muwakkil*) the community is entitled to specify a procedure as a prior stipulation and an integral part of the terms of its agency. It may also specify and articulate the type of misconduct that renders the head of state liable to censure and deposition.

In response to the question as to who should be entrusted with the responsibility of setting in motion the impeachment procedure, once there is sufficient evidence for invoking it, I agree with Asad and Khālidī that the judiciary should be entrusted with the necessary powers. They have also stressed the need for an independent judiciary that can adjudicate on disputes arising between the citizen and state. Attention is drawn in this connection to the Qur'ānic verse (4:59), which has envisaged the possibility of disputes arising between the citizen and the state. A proper implementation of this verse would thus necessitate the existence of an impartial judiciary that can adjudicate a dispute between the two sides. An independent judiciary that is capable of discharging the most sensitive task of impeaching the head of state and declaring him disqualified would therefore seem indispensable. It is equally important to ensure immunity of the judicial office such that the head of state should have no powers to dismiss or replace, without cause, the leading judges in the land.[249]

To make the impeachment procedure an integrated function of the regular judiciary is one way of tackling the procedural issue, in which case necessary guidelines would need to be clearly spelled out in the constitution. Alternative procedures for impeachment of the head of state have appeared in the constitutions of some Muslim countries, which have either entrusted an *ad hoc* constitutional tribunal to this task or instituted a separate body to monitor proper implementation of the constitution and its violation by the government in power. Whereas Egypt has a permanent constitutional court, the 1973 Constitution of Pakistan and the 2004 Constitution of Afghanistan entrusted an *ad hoc* constitutional court, which combined representatives from both the judiciary and parliament with powers to impeach the head of State. The 1979 constitution of the Islamic Republic of Iran, and its 1989 amendments, entrusted the Supreme Leader with the power of dismissing the President upon receiving the verdict either of the Supreme Court impeaching the President for breach of duty or upon a vote of the *Majlis* as to his political inefficiency.[250]

Having said this, the present writer is inclined to agree with what al-Sanhūrī as well as Asad and Khālidī have observed that the *Sharīʿah* entitles the judiciary basically to adjudicate all disputes including those that may involve the head of state, be it criminal prosecution, civil litigation, or issues pertaining to violation of the basic rights of citizens. It would then be a mere extension of the same logic to entrust the judiciary with the power of impeachment of the head of state and his leading officials.[251] A constitutional court of a specialised and more distinctive type that operates within the framework of the judiciary may also be acceptable.

OTHER INSTITUTIONS OF ACCOUNTABILITY

This section discusses two separate institutions that historically played a role in advancing the cause of accountability in government. These are the auditing department, and the office of expropriated properties—both developed in the early Abbasid period. This is followed by a brief account of constitutional reforms under the Ottomans that also had a bearing on accountability.

(1) Audit and Accounts Departments (*Dīwān al-Azimmah, Dīwān al-Muṣādirīn*)

One of the more practical measures taken in pursuit of accountability was the introduction of the *Dīwān al-Azimmah* (also known as *Dīwān al-Zimam*—Auditing and Accounts Department) in the Abbasid caliphate of Baghdad. It was introduced by al-Mahdī, the third Abassid Caliph (r. 158–169/775–785). Initially he established smaller auditing bureaux in every *dīwān* or ministry and charged them with the duty of auditing the expenditures of their respective *dīwāns*. In 168/784 he reorganised these auditing bureaux into a central *dīwān*, named *Dīwān al-Azimmah* which was, in turn, charged with the duty of checking and auditing the accounts of all other *dīwāns*. The secretary of this *dīwān* supervised and controlled all the auditing bureaux in the various departments and the latter were directly accountable to *Dīwān al-Azimmah.*

A further step toward consolidation was taken when caliph al-Muʿtadid (d. 279/892) reorganized the administration and merged all the various *dīwāns* putting all the finance and auditing affairs under the *Dīwān al-Azimmah.* The basic idea of *zimam* (pl. *azimmah*) was to centralise control of the various departments under one person. ʿUmar b. Bazigh served as its head under the caliph al-Mahdī. The functions of this *dīwān* were taken over in the modern states of Iraq and Egypt by *Dīwān Murāqib al-Ḥisābāt al-ʿĀmmah,* or Auditor General's Department.[252]

Actual collection and disbursement of the state revenue was put in Baghdad under the Treasury Department, or *Bayt al-Māl,* headed by *Ṣāḥib Bayt al-Māl.* The *Bayt al-Māl* had branches in the provinces. Both in the centre and provinces, government departments were required to send the left over funds, after payment of salaries and other civil and military expenditures, to the state treasury in Baghdad. In 314/996 the Baghdad treasury itself was ordered to submit weekly accounts of all revenues and expenditure to the prime minister to be investigated by him. Prior to this directive a monthly account was submitted to the treasury minister.

One of the principles of fiscal policy that guided treasury affairs was that 'taxes coming from different sources could not be indiscriminately spent without restriction.' Items of revenues, whether from land tax (*kharāj*), the *zakāh* (legal alms), war booty, or confiscated property, etc., were initially to be expended in the locality where they were collected and realised. These procedures were also followed in the Fatimid Egypt, albeit with some organisational differences that reflected the needs and style of the Egyptian society.

The function of *Dīwān Bayt al-Māl* of the Abbasid and Fatimid states have been taken over in the modern states of the Middle East by *Wizārat al-Khizānah* and the *Mudiriyyat al-Khazīnah* in Egypt and Iraq respectively.[253]

(2) *Dīwān al-Muṣādirīn* (Expropriated Assets Department)

Dīwān al-Muṣādirīn (Expropriated Assets Department) was created when the Abbasid state became victorious and took over the caliphate from the Umayyad dynasty. It was established with the purpose basically to administer properties confiscated from the Umayyads and their supporters. High officials of state who enriched themselves through corruption initially fell under the jurisdiction of *Dīwān al-Zimam* or the Auditing and Accounts Department. Whenever *Dīwān al-Zimam* determined that an official had accumulated wealth illegally and a judgment to that effect was made to confiscate it, *Dīwān al-Muṣādirīn* would then step in to seize and acquire control of the property in question. *Dīwān al-Muṣādirīn* later established special sub-divisions, including a particular department known as *Dīwān al-Mukhālifīn* (for assets taken from deviant and corrupt administrators).[254]

Officials were required to give account of their wealth when first appointed and then again when they left office. Any wealth illegally acquired was confiscated and put aside. Each deposit was kept separately under the name of the individual from whom it was taken. Deposits were sometimes returned to the owner if he was found innocent.[255]

OTTOMAN CONSTITUTIONAL REFORMS

The Ottoman state was initially a Turkish principality within the perimeters of the Roman empire with its capital in Adriana. It was with the conquest of Constantinople by Muhammad II in 1453 that its expansionist tendency took a fresh momentum until it subjugated the Mamluks of Egypt and the Maghreb and gradually engulfed all the Arab territories including the Yemen and the Hijaz. Most of these territories remained under Ottoman rule until the end of WWI, which was soon followed by the collapse and disintegration of the Ottoman Empire.

The Ottoman state was a military power with oligarchic tendencies that upheld the superiority of a group or family over the community and a hereditary and absolutist sultanate at its helm. The numerous ethnic groups and nationalities that it dominated subscribed to diverse religious and cultural traditions and were kept together by military might of the sultan. The Ottoman state did not seek to integrate them and permitted them instead to follow their own laws and traditions. Islamic law and culture thus remained at the periphery of the system and the despotism of the Sultan was not significantly touched by the Islamic principles of government.[256] These were some of the weaknesses of Ottoman state that contributed to its eventual decline. But even if the Ottoman caliphate did not conform to the requirements of *bayʿah* and free election and did not fulfil the Islamic conditions of *khilāfah*, it did represent a symbol of Muslim unity and its military power enabled it to defend the Islamic lands against foreign aggression.[257] The reformist pressure from within and from the European powers eventually led to the introduction in mid–19th century of constitutional changes and the renowned *tanẕīmat* reforms.

The Ottoman *tanẕīmāt* reforms may be seen as a manifestation in recent Muslim history of a representative government. An early instrument of these reforms was the 1840 Firman calling on provincial officials to establish 'administrative councils' and the convocation in 1845 of an 'extraordinary assembly' in Istanbul. The representative principle was expounded in the 1856 *Hatti Humayun* which provided that measures be taken to reform the 'provincial and administrative councils' in order to ensure fairness in the choice of the deputies of the Muslim, Christian and other communities and ensure freedom of voting. It was further provided that the temporal administration of the non–Muslim communities is placed under the supervision of an assembly to be chosen from among the members, both ecclesiastical and laymen, of the said communities.[258] The Vilayat Law of 1864 confirmed the adoption of the representative principle. But this was still an indirect and a *mellat*-based system of representation. With the expansion of the reform movement, the reformists were no longer content with the mere establishment of representative organs, they now sought the creation of a parliament and the adoption of a constitutional form of government.

Also worthy of mention in this connection is the reformist movement of the Tunisian Khayr al-Dīn, who played a prominent role in drafting the Tunisian constitution of 1861, the first modern constitution to be promulgated under Islamic rule.

Namik Kemal, a prominent Ottoman ideologue, assimilated western ideas within the rubric of traditional Islamic principles of *shūrā*, *siyāsah* and *bayʿah* (consultation, discretionary policy, and homage). He also held that the Islamic system of rule vested the people with sovereignty over their own governments. To quote Namik Kemal:

> The sovereignty of the people *(kahimiyyet-i ahali)* which means that the power of the government derives from the people and which in the language of the *Sharīʿah* is called *bayʿah* is the right necessarily arising from the personal independence *(istiklal-i dhati)* that each individual by nature possesses.[259]

The reformist voice in Ottoman Turkey was reinforced by European political pressure on the Sultan that led to the promulgation of the 1876 Constitution and its provisions for an elected parliament. Yet the Ottoman constitutional experience was short–lived. The Sultan suspended the constitution in 1878 for 30 years and did not promulgate the new electoral law. The constitution was later restored in 1908 and soon after the electoral law was also resurrected.

NOTES

1. *Encyclopedia of Islam*, vol. VII, 465; and *Mawsūʿat al-Mafāhīm al-Islāmiyyah*, 490.

2. The Arabic version reads: *ḥāsibū anfusakum qabla an tuḥāsabū wa-zinūhā qabla an tuzānū*. See al-Ghazālī, *Iḥyāʾ* (1939 edn.), IV, 384.

3. Ghazālī, *Iḥyāʾ*, IV, 336ff. (book 38); *Encyclopedia of Islam*, vol. VII, 465.

4. A brief account of the role and practice of *muḥāsabah* in the Ottoman Empire appears in *Encyclopedia of Islam*, vol. VII, 465–466.

5. The word 'ummah' is here used for the Muslim community as a whole and also the smaller units thereof that may be confined within geographical boundaries of a state or an autonomous Muslim community. This is dictated by necessity (*darūrah*) since the larger *ummah* no longer functions as a unit after the abolition of the Ottoman caliphate in 1924.

6. Al-Qaraḍāwī, *Min Fiqh al-Dawlah fiʾl-Islām*, 59.

7. Cf. Abū ʿId, *Waẓīfah al-Ḥakīm*, 250.

8. Māwardī, *al-Aḥkām*, 17.

9. Al-Rīs, *al-Naẓariyyāt al-Siyāsiyyah*, 216–217.

10. Al-Rīs, *al-Naẓariyyāt al-Siyāsiyyah*, 215—quoting Ibn Khaldūn's *The Muqaddima*, 174 (Chapter 29). See also al-Shāwī, *al-Mawsūʿah al-ʿAṣriyyah*, vol. I, 213.

11. Mawārdī, *al-Aḥkām al-Sulṭāniyyah*, 8.

12. Cf. Azizah Al-Hibri, 'Democratic Principles: An Islamic Point of View,' *Islam* 21 (December 1999), 8; al-Rīs, *al-Naẓariyyāt al-Islāmiyyah*, 215.

13. Al-Rīs, *al-Naẓariyyāt*, 219.

14. Cf. Fuʾād Aḥmad, *Uṣūl Niẓām al-Ḥukm*, 237.

15. Fuʾād Aḥmad, *Uṣūl Niẓām al-Ḥukm*, 238—quoting al-Baghdādī, *Uṣūl al-Dīn* (Beirut: al-Afaq edn., at 278).

16. Al-Shāwī, *al-Mawsūʿah al-ʿAṣriyyah*, vol. I, 115.

17. ʿAbūdī, *Raʾīs al-Dawlah*, 251.

18. Waṣfī, *Mabdaʾ al-Mashrūʿiyyah*, 239–240.

19. Ibn Hishām, *Sīrah*, IV, 611; al-ʿĪlī, *Ḥurriyyah*, 234.

20. ʿAbd Allāh al-Basyūnī, *Naẓariyyāt al-Dawlah*, 265.

21. Ibn al-Jawzī, *Sīrat ʿUmar*, 109; Abū Zahrah, *Al-Jarīmah*, 160; al-Sibāʿī, *Ishtirākiyyah*, 50.

22. Wahbah al-Zuḥaylī, *Ḥaqq al-Ḥurriyyah*, 63.

23. Al-Qaraḍāwī, in ed. Yāsīn, *Al-Qaḍāyā al-Muʿāṣirah*, 89.

24. Ibn Saʿd, *Ṭabaqāt*, III, 293.

25. Balādhurī, *Futūḥ al-Buldān*, 93; Zaman, *Economic Functions*, 107; ʿAbd Allāh al-Basyūnī, *Naẓariyyāt al-Dawlah*, 266. Reports indicate that Abū Hurayrah objected to ʿUmar's action and explained his condition and that the Caliph asked him to take up a government position again, after he was dismissed from his post in Bahrain, but that Abū Hurayrah declined the offer.

26. Id., 377. Balādhurī has given the names of nine officers half of whose property was taken away.

27. Id., 377. The name of the tax collector is given as Nāfiʿ Abū Bakra.

28. Ibn Saʿd, *Ṭabaqāt*, IV, 77; al-Badawī, *Daʿāʾim*, 415.

29. Id., 64.

30. Id., 63.

31. Id., 63–64.

32. Abū Zahrah, *al-Mujtamaʿ al-Insānī*, 173.

33. Id.

34. Cf. ʿAlī Kurd, *al-Islām waʾl-Haḍārah*, II, 139.

35. *Nahj al-Balāghah*, vol. III, 95–96; Basyūnī, *Naẓariyyāt al-Dawlah*, 267.

36. Abū ʿUbayd, *Kitāb al-Amwāl*, 40, s. 116; Hasanuz Zaman, *Economic Functions*, 203.

37. Ṭabarī, *Tārīkh*, vol. II, 181, 198; Badawī, *Daʿāʾim*, 419.

38. Al-Qurṭubī, *al-Jāmiʿ li-Aḥkām al-Qurʾān* (Beirut edn.), vol. IV, 249; see also El-Awa, *al-Fiqh al-Islāmī*, 61.

39. Ibn Taymiyyah, *al-Siyāsah al-Sharʿiyyah*, 156–57.

40. Maḥmūd Shaltūt, *al-Islām, ʿAqīdah wa-Sharīʿah*, 441–42.

41. Cf. Badawī, *Ikhtiṣāṣāt*, 246.

42. Cf. Shaltūt, *Min Tawjihāt al-Islām*, 35.

43. Cf. ʿAbūdī, *Raʾīs al-Dawlah*, 169.

44. Cf. ʿAbūdī, *Raʾīs al-Dawlah*, 227.

45. Cf. ʿImārah, *al-Islām wa-Ḥuqūq al-Insān*, 196.

46. Qaraḍāwī, *Min Fiqh al-Dawlah*, 158f.

47. Sanhūrī, *Fiqh al-Khilāfah*, 228.

48. Said al-Najjar in ed., Essam Hassan, *Revitalisation of Political Thought*, 14.

49. Cf. Zaydān, *al-Fard waʾl-Dawlah*, 51; al-Bayātī, *al-Niẓām al-Dustūrī*, 258f.

50. Muslim, *Mukhtaṣar Ṣaḥīḥ Muslim*, edr. Al-Albānī, p. 16, ḥadīth no. 34.

51. Al-Ghazālī, *Iḥyāʾ*, II, 310.

52. Ibn Qayyim al-Jawziyyah, *Al-Ṭuruq*, 278.

53. Cf. al-ʿĪlī, *Ḥurriyyat*, 235.

54. Khiḍr al-Ḥusayn, *Naqd*, 89.

55. See for further detail Kamali, *Freedom of Expression in Islam*, 54ff.

56. Muslim, *Ṣaḥīḥ Muslim*, K. al-Īmān, b. al-dīn al-naṣīḥah.

57. Ibn Saʿd, *Ṭabaqāt*, III, 67; al-ʿĪlī, *Ḥurriyyah*, 234.

58. Ṭabarī, *Tārīkh*, I, 280; Zaman, *Economic Functions*, 109.

59. Cf. Qaraḍāwī, *Min Fiqh al-Dawlah*, 150–155.

60. Id., 138.

61. Muslim, *Ṣaḥīḥ Muslim*, K. al-Imārah, b. karahiyyat al-imārah bi-ghayr ḍarūrah.

62. Muḥammad al-Ghazālī, *Mushkilāt fī Ṭarīq al-Ḥayāt al-Islāmiyyah*, 139–140.

63. Al-Qurṭubī, *al-Jāmiʿ li-Aḥkām al-Qurʾān*, vol. v, 255; for a discussion see also Qādirī, *al-Kifāʾah al-Idāriyyah fiʾl-Siyāsah al-Sharʿiyyah*, 12.

64. Tabrīzī, *Mishkāt*, vol. I, ḥadīth 55.

65. Abū Dāwūd, *Mukhtaṣar Sunan Abī Dāwūd*, ed., Muṣṭafā al-Bughah, 420, ḥadīth 2948; also discussed by Wahbah al-Zuḥaylī, *Ḥaqq al-Ḥurriyyah*, 17.

66. *Ṣaḥīḥ al-Bukhārī* (Muhsin Khan tr.), vol. IX, ḥadīth 252.

67. Muslim, *Mukhtaṣar Ṣaḥīḥ Muslim*, p. 329, ḥadīth 1211.

68. Ibn Mājah, *Sunan*, K. al-Fitan, b. al-amr biʾl-maʿrūf wa-nahy ʿan al-munkar, ḥadīth no. 4011.

69. Ṭabarī, *Tārīkh*, IV, 244; also quoted in Abū Ḥabīb, *Dirāsah*, 144 and Badawī, *Ikhtiṣāṣāt*, 231.

70. Cf. Abū Dāwūd, *Sunan Abī Dāwūd*, ed. Al-Bughah, 425, ḥadīth 2972.

71. Ibn Taymiyyah, *Majmūʿ Fatāwā*, vol. 28, 249–50.

72. Cf. Qādirī, *al-Kifāʾah al-Idāriyyah*, 151.

73. Māwardī, *al-Aḥkām al-Sulṭāniyyah*, 209.

74. Id.

75. Tabrīzī, *Mishkāt*, vol. II, ḥadīth 3683.

76. Cf. Muḥammad al-Ghazālī, *Khuluq al-Muslim*, 42.

77. Muslim, *Ṣaḥīḥ Muslim*, ḥadīth 2054.

78. Qādirī, *al-Kifāʾah al-Idāriyyah*, 25.

79. Abū Yūsuf, *al-Kharāj*, 106.

80. Id., 117; see also Jaʿfar, *Wilāyat al-Maẓālim*, 25.

81. Ibn Taymiyyah, *al-Siyāsah al-Sharʿiyyah*, 9; see also Bayātī, *al-Niẓām*, 97.

82. Māwardī, *al-Aḥkām al-Sulṭāniyyah*, 209.

83. Id., 66.

84. ʿIzz al-Dīn ʿAbd Al-Salām al-Sulamī, *Qawāʿid al-Aḥkām* (Muʾassasah al-Rayyān's edn.), 63.

85. Id., 66–67; Ibn Taymiyyah, *al-Siyāsah al-Sharʿiyyah*, 16.

86. al-Ṭamāwī, *ʿUmar b. al-Khaṭṭāb*, 273; Qādirī, *al-Kifāʾah al-Idāriyyah*, 37.

87. Abdul Malik al-Sayed, *Social Ethics of Islam*, 225; Badawī, *Ikhtiṣāṣāt*, 383.

88. Cf. ʿAlī, *Mabdaʾ al-Mashrūʿiyyah*, 307; Hitti, *History of the Arabs*, 232.

89. Id., 226-227.

90. Id., 226; Badawī, *Ikhtiṣāṣāt*, 385.

91. Id., 229.

92. Id., 231.

93. Bukhārī, *Saḥīḥ al-Bukhārī* (Muhsin Khan's tr.), vol. ix, *ḥadīth* 252.

94. Abū Dāwūd, *Mukhtaṣar Sunan Abū Dāwūd*, 650, *ḥadīth* 4534.

95. ʿAwdah, *al-Tashrīʿ al-Jināʾī*, i, 559; also referring to Ibn Qudāmah, *Mughnī*, x, 334; Shīrāzī, *Muhadhdhab*, ii, 228.

96. Ibn Saʿd, *Ṭabaqāt*, ii, 255; Ibn al-Athīr, *Tārīkh*, ii, 154; also quoted in al-Shāwī, *al-Mawsūʿah*, vol. i, 427; al-Bayātī, *al-Niẓām al-Siyāsī*, 254.

97. See for detail al-Shawī, *al-Mawsūʿah*, i, 428–430; Bayātī, *al-Niẓām*, 256.

98. ʿAwdah, *al-Tashrīʿ*, i, 559.

99. This is notwithstanding the fact that the majority of schools have validated 80 lashes of the whip for wine- drinking to which Shāfiʿī takes an exception and holds it to be 40 lashes. See for detail ʿAwdah, *al-Tashrīʿ*, i, 560.

100. Al-Bayātī, *al-Niẓām al-Siyāsī al-Islāmī*, 103.

101. ʿAwdah, *al-Tashrīʿ*, i, 558; al-Shāwī, *al-Mawsūʿah*, vol. ii, 426.

102. Cf. al-Shāwī, *al-Mawsūʿah al-ʿAṣriyyah*, vol. i, 208–210.

103. Cf. al-Bayātī, *al-Niẓām al-Dustūrī*, p. 279; al-Shāwī, *al-Mawsūʿah*, vol. i, 430.

104. Muslim, *Mukhtaṣar Ṣaḥīḥ Muslim*, 332, *ḥadīth* 1226.

105. Tabrīzī, *Mishkāt*, vol. ii, *ḥadīth* 3665.

106. Tabrīzī, *Mishkāt*, vol. i, *ḥadīth* 3668.

107. Al-Nawawī, *Riyāḍ al-Saliḥīn*, *ḥadīth* 189.

108. Cf. al-Māwardī, *al-Aḥkām al-Sulṭāniyyah*, 15f.

109. ʿIzz al-Dīn ʿAbd al-Salām al-Sulamī, *Qawāʿid al-Aḥkām* (Rayyān edn.), 105.

110. Abū ʿUbayd, *The Book of Finance* (Kitāb al-Amwāl), English trans. (no Arabic text provided) by Ghifarī, 5, *ḥadīth* 14.

111. Id., 5, *ḥadīth* 11.

112. Al-Sulamī, *Qawāʿid*, 105.

113. Cf. al-Shīshānī, *Ḥuqūq al-Insān wa-Ḥurriyātuh*, 633–634.

114. See also *al-Shūrā*, 38:42.

115. A fuller version of this letter appears in vol. ii of this work, *Freedom, Equality and Justice in Islam*, 123. Further details on justice can also be found in idem, 103–155.

116. Cf. Munīr al-Bayātī, *al-Niẓām al-Siyāsī*, 279–280.

117. Ibn Mājah, *Sunan*, ii, 784, *ḥadīth* 2340; Al-Shāṭibī, *Muwāfaqāt* (Dirāz edn), iii, 17.

118. Muslim; *Mukhtaṣar Ṣaḥīḥ Muslim*, 82, *ḥadīth* 289. The narrator of this *ḥadīth*, Jābir b. ʿAbd Allāh added that Muʿādh had recited the *sūrah al-Baqarah* and the Prophet suggested instead some of shorter *sūrahs*, which appear toward the end of the Qurʾān, for recitation in congregational prayers, so that 'the elderly, the weak and the one in need would all be able to pray behind you'.

119. Muslim, *Ṣaḥīḥ Muslim*, K. al-Ṣalāh; b. amr al-aʾimmah bi-takhfīf al-ṣalāh.

120. Cf. Al-Khālidī, *Qawāʿid Niẓām al-Ḥukm*, 202.

121. Ibid., 357.

122. Cf. ʿAbd Allāh al-ʿArabī, *Niẓām al-Ḥukm*, 92; Madkūr, *Maʿālim*, 178; al-Khālidī, *Maʿālim*, 349.

123. al-Maqrīzī, *Imtāʿ al-Asmāʿ*, 328; as quoted in Zaman, *Economic Functions*, 105.

124. Al-Balādhurī, *Futūḥ al-Buldān*, 41.

125. See for details, Al-Badawī, *Daʿāʾim al-Ḥukm*, 416f.

126. Al-Ṭabarī, *Tārīkh*, iv, 201; Abū Ḥabīb, *Dirāsah*, 144.

127. Ibn ʿAbd al-Ḥakam, *Sīrat ʿUmar b. ʿAbd al-ʿAzīz* as quoted in Sibāʿī, *al-Takāful al-Ijtimāʿī*, 352.

128. Ibn Saʿd, *Ṭabaqāt*, iii, 133; Zaman, *Economic Functions*, 106f.

129. Ibn Saʿd, *Ṭabaqāt*, iii, 137; Ibn Kathīr, *al-Bidāyah waʾl-Nihāyah*, 8.

130. Balādhurī, *Futūḥ al-Buldān*, 323f; Abū Yūsuf, *Kitāb al-Kharāj*, 13; Zaman, *Economic Functions*, 106.

131. Ṭabarī, *Tārīkh*, ii, 181; al-Badawī, *Daʿāʾim*, 419.

132. Ghazālī, *Iḥyāʾ ʿUlūm al-Dīn*, vol. iv, 381.

133. Sayyid Hussein Alatas, *Corruption, Its Nature, Causes and Consequences*, Avebury: Aldershot, 1990, as quoted in Iqbal and Lewis 'Governance,' 3.

134. Ibn Kathīr, *Tafsīr al-Qurʾān al-ʿAzīm*, vol. i, 225.

135. Cf. Basyūnī, *Naẓariyyāt al-Dawlah*, 263.

136. Tabrīzī, *Mishkāt*, vol. ii, *ḥadīth* no. 3753. A variant version of this *ḥadīth* includes also the middleman or facilitator in the act of bribery. This version appears in Māwardī, *al-Aḥkām al-Sulṭāniyyah*, 75.

137. Māwardī, *al-Aḥkām al-Sulṭāniyyah*, 75.

138. Abū Dāwūd, *Sunan Abū Dāwūd*, ed. Al-Bughah, 651, *ḥadīth* 4537; Ibn Taymiyyah, *al-Siyāsah*, 161.

139. Al-Albānī, *Ṣaḥīḥ al-Jāmiʿ al-Ṣaghīr*, *ḥadīth* no. 7021.

140. Abū Dāwūd, *Mukhtaṣar Sunan Abī Dāwūd*, ed. Al-Bughah, 504, *ḥadīth* 3541.

141. Ibn Taymiyyah, *al-Siyāsah*, 46.

142. Ibid., 44, 48.

143. Id., 42–43.

144. Ibn ʿAbd al-Ḥakīm, *Sīrat ʿUmar b. ʿAbd al-ʿAzīz*, 98, also quoted in Zaman, *Economic Functions*, 128.

145. Id., p. 44.

146. Abū Dāwūd, *Mukhtaṣar Sunan Abī Dāwūd*, ed., Muṣṭafā al-Bughah, 419, *ḥadīth* 2946; Ibn Taymiyyah, *al-Siyāsah*, 42.

147. Ibn Faraj al-Mālikī al-Qurṭubī, *Aqdiya Rasūl Allāh*, 82.

148. Id., 83.

149. Tabrīzī, *Mishkāt*, vol. ii, *ḥadīth* no. 3748.

150. Id., vol. II, *ḥadīth* no. 3751.

151. Māwardī, *al-Aḥkām al-Sulṭāniyyah*, 177; see also Hammād Satā, *al-Uṣūl al-Islāmiyyah li'l-Qānūn al-Idārī*, 516.

152. Māwardī, *al-Aḥkām al-Sulṭāniyyah*, 213.

153. Cf., Iqbal and Lewis, 'Governance and Corruption,' *AJISS* 19 (2002), 10.

154. Id., 15.

155. Ibn Taymiyyah, *al-Siyāsah*, 107–108.

156. These were Companions: Kaʿb b. Mālik, Mirārah b. al-Rabīʿ, and Hilāl b. Umayyah.

157. Ibn Taymiyyah, *al-Siyāsah*, 108–109.

158. Id., 111.

159. Ibn Taymiyyah, *al-Siyāsah*, 111.

160. Zaydān, *Tārīkh*, II, 13; ʿAlī Kurd, *Al-Islām wa'l-Ḥaḍārah*, II, 122; al-Badawī, *Daʿā'im*, 424.

161. Abū Yūsuf, *Kitāb al-Kharāj*, 35.

162. Cf.Munīr al-Bayātī, *al-Niẓām al-Siyāsī*, 336.

163. Ibn Qudāmah, *Mughnī*, vol. x, 48–49. See also Anwarullah, *The Criminal Law of Islam*, 199ff.

164. Cf. Waṣfī, *al-Niẓām al-Dustūrī*, 155f; Abū ʿId, *Waẓīfat al-Ḥākim*, 252.

165. Tabrīzī, *Mishkāt*, vol. II, *ḥadīth* 3668.

166. Tabrīzī, *Mishkāt*, vol. II, *ḥadīth* 3520.

167. Quoted in Waṣfī, *al-Niẓām*, 157.

168. Id., 156.

169. Ibn Taymiyyah, *al-Siyāsah*, 24.

170. Ibn Ḥazm, *al-Muḥallāh*, IX, 362.

171. Wahbah al-Zuhaylī, *Ḥaqq al-Ḥurriyyah fi'l-ʿĀlam*, 173.

172. Id., 174.

173. See for details ʿAlī, *Mabda' al-Mashrūʿiyyah*, 297–98.

174. Id. 299.

175. Philip Hitti, *History of the Arabs*, 196; ʿAlī, *Mabda' al-Mashrūʿiyyah*, 302.

176. ʿAlī, *Mabda' al-Mashrūʿiyyah*, 307; al-Rīs, *al-Naẓariyyāt*, 20f.

177. Al-Rīs, *al-Naẓariyyāt*, 206.

178. Ḥasan Ibrāhīm Ḥasan, *al-Nuẓum al-Islāmiyyah*, 161–62.

179. Id., 163.

180. Al-Ghazālī, *Iḥyā' ʿUlūm al-Dīn*, vol. II, 146.

181. Hitti, *History of the Arabs*, 196.

182. Ḥasan Ibrāhīm Ḥasan, *al-Nuẓum al-Islāmiyyah*, 51–52.

183. Cf. id., 49; ʿAlī, *Mabda' al-Mashrūʿiyyah*.

184. ʿAlī, *Mabda' al-Mashrūʿiyyah*, 308.

185. Philip Hitti, *History of the Arabs*, 288–89, 319.

186. Id., 288–89.

187. Balādhurī, *Futūḥ*, 73; Hasanus Zaman, *Economic Functions of the Islamic state*, 111.

188. Cf. Hitti, *History of the Arabs*, 225.

189. Abū Yūsuf, *Kitāb al-Kharāj*, 23; Ḥasan Ibrāhīm Ḥasan, *al-Nuẓum al-Islāmiyyah*, 240.

190. Hasanuz Zaman, *Economic Functions of the Islamic State*.

191. Phillip Hitti, *History of the Arabs*, 10th ed., 223; Jaʿfar, *Wilāyat al-Maẓālim*, 27.

192. Ibn Kathīr, *al-Bidāyah wa'l-Nihāyah*, vol. 9, 85.

193. Abū Dāwūd, *Mukhtaṣar Sunan Abī Dāwūd*, K. al-Kharāj wa'l-Imārah wa'l-fay', b. mā jā'a fī sahm al-ṣafī.

194. Hasanuz Zaman, *Economic Functions*, 123, 151.

195. Balādhurī, *Futūḥ*, 48 and 49; Hasanuz Zaman, *Economic Functions*, 123.

196. Quoted in Ḥasan Ibrāhīm Ḥasan, *al-Nuẓum al-Islāmiyyah*, 40.

197. Cf. al-Rīs, *al-Naẓariyyāt*, 201. Al-Rīs indicates that al-Ṭabarī and Ibn al-Athīr have preferred this version of the reports.

198. Balādhurī, *Futūḥ al-Buldān*, 131 and 132; Hasanuz Zaman, *Economic Functions*, 113.

199. Ḥasan Ibrāhīm Ḥasan, *al-Nuẓum al-Islāmiyyah*, 162.

200. Balādhurī, *Futūḥ al-Buldān*, 391.

201. Cf. Maḥmaṣṣānī, 'al-Qaḍā' ʿInd al-Māwardī,' a 1975 conference paper presented in Cairo—as quoted in al-Bayātī, al-*Niẓām al-Siyāsī*, 279.

202. Cf. al-Rifāʿī, *al-Qaḍā' al-Idārī*, 64–65.

203. al-Ṭamāwī, *al-Sulṭah al-Thālath fī al-Dasātīr*, 401.

204. Munīr al-ʿAjlānī, *ʿAbqariyyat al-Islām*, 343.

205. Azad, *Judicial System*, 50.

206. See for further detail Kamali, 'Appellate Review and Judicial Independence,' *Islamic Studies* 29 (1990), 220f.

207. See for details al-Rifāʿī, *al-Qaḍā' al-Idārī*, 69.

208. Munīr al-ʿAjlānī, *ʿAbqariyyat al-Islām*, 343; al-Ṭamāwī, *al-Sulṭah*, 402.

209. Cf. al-Bayātī, *al-Niẓām al-Siyāsī*, 281.

210. Id., p. 282; al-Rifāʿī, *al-Qaḍā' al-Idārī*, 326.

211. Al-Qurṭubī, *Bidāyat al-Mujtahid*, II, 514; Madkūr, *al-Qaḍā' fī'l-Islām*, 61; al-Bayātī, *al-Niẓām al-Siyāsī*, 302; see for further detail Kamali, 'Appellate Review', *Islamic Studies*, 29 (1990) 242f.

212. Al-Rifāʿī, *al-Qaḍā' al-Idārī*, 85.

213. Muḥammad Salām Madkūr, *al-Qaḍā' fī'l-Islām*, I, 141–also quoted in Bayātī, *al-Niẓām al-Siyāsī*, 286.

214. Unlike the other courts which were usually called *maḥkamah*, this was designated as a *dīwān*, which literally signifies a prominent organisation or office.

215. Māwardī, *al-Aḥkām al-Sulṭāniyyah*, 81; Abū Yaʿlā al-Farrā, *al-Aḥkām al-Sulṭāniyyah*, 77.

216. Cf. Qur'ān, 7:44; 3:182; 16:118, and 21:47.

217. Abū Dāwūd, *Sunan Abū Dāwūd*. Eng. Tr. Ahmad Hasan, K. al-Malāḥim, no. 17.

218. Al-Māwardī, *al-Aḥkām*, 77–80; al-Qarāfī, *al-Iḥkām*, 167; Ḥasan Ibrāhīm Hasan, *al-Nuẓum al-Islāmiyyah*, 295; al-Sayed, *Social Ethics of Islam*, 157; Hitti, *History of the Arabs*, 10th edn., 322; Jaʿfar, *Wilāyat al-Maẓālim*, 19f; Badawī, *Ikhtiṣāṣāt*, 545.

219. Māwardī, *Aḥkām*, 243.

220. For fuller detail, of the functions of *dīwān al-maẓālim* see al-Ṭamāwī, *al-Sulṭat al-Thālath*, 320ff; al-ʿĪlī, *Ḥurriyyat*, 630ff; al-Sayed, *Social Ethics of Islam*, 156; Jaʿfar, *Wilāyat al-Maẓālim*, 23f.

221. Māwardī, *Aḥkām*, 82.

222. Id., 84–85.

223. Id., 92.

224. Id., 93.

225. Jaʿfar, *Wilāyat al-Maẓālim*, 22.

226. Layish, 'Saudi Arabian legal Reform,' *The American Journal of Oriental Studies*, 1987, 290; al-Sayed, *Social Ethics*, 156.

227. Cf. al-Rifāʿī, *al-Qaḍā' al-Idārī*, p. 87.

228. Cf. Jaʿfar, *Wilāyat al-Maẓālim*, 57f.

229. Id., 84.

230. Id., 100; Satā, *al-Uṣūl al-Islāmiyyah li'l-Qānūn al-Idārī*, 190.

231. Cf. Al-Māwardī, *Al-Aḥkām*, p. 257. Some writers, including al-Ghazālī, have recorded seven, instead of four, steps for *ḥisbah*, adding such things as beating, seeking other people's help, and even killing. Cf. al-Ghazālī, *Iḥyā'*, vol. II, p. 34. See also ʿAwdah, *al-Tashrīʿ al-Jinā'ī*, I, 506f.

232. Badawī, *Ikhtiṣāṣāt*, 405 ft.; al-Sayed, *Social Ethics*, 161; Hitti, *History of the Arabs*, 10th ed., 322.

233. al-Māwardī, *al-Aḥkām*. Māwardī relates among other interesting duties of the *muḥtasib* the chastisement of those who dyed their grey beards black with a view to gaining favour with women.

234. Cf. Al-ʿĪlī, *Ḥurriyyat*, 645.

235. Ibid., 563.

236. Cf. al-Rifāʿī, *al-Qaḍā' al-Idārī*, p. 87.

237. In my visit to Kabul in August 2006, I had occasion to engage in conversation with the Chief Justice Azimi and some government ministers. I asked them whether the recently rumoured revival of the Department of Vice and Virtue was a likely prospect. I was given the impression that people had different views about it but that it was not likely to be revived as the whole

concept was closely aligned with the Taliban and had not made a favourable impression on the general public.

238. Māwardī, *Al-Aḥkām al-Sulṭāniyyah*, 247–257; see also al-Sibāʿī, *al-Takāful al-Ijtimāʿī*, 239–40.

239. Cf. Sibāʿī, *al-Takāful al-Ijtimāʿī*, 243–45.

240. See for details Māwardī, *Aḥkām*, 17; al-Sanhūrī, *Fiqh al-Khilāfah*, 243ff; Ḥilmī, *Niẓām*, 103; al-Khālidī, *Maʿālim al-Khilāfah*, 305; Shīshānī, *Ḥuqūq al-Insān*, 633.

241. Al-Nawawī, *Riyāḍ al-Ṣaliḥīn*, 113; see for a discussion also al-Bayātī, *al-Niẓām al-Siyāsī*, 332–34.

242. Cf. Zaydān, *Al-Fard waʾl-Dawlah*, 48–49; Fatḥī Osmān, *Al Fikr al-Qānūnī*, 143; Munīr al-Bayātī, *al-Niẓām al-Siyāsī*, 262; Asad, *The Principles of State*, 80.

243. Cf. Ḥilmī, *Niẓām*, 104.

244. Baghdādī, *Uṣūl al-Dīn*, 278; also quote din Bayātī, *al-Niẓām al-Siyāsī*, 259.

245. Rāzī, *al-Tafsīr al-Kabīr*, IV, 47.

246. Ghazālī, *Iḥyāʾ ʿUlūm al-Dīn*, II, 111.

247. Māwardī, *Aḥkām*, 17; see also al-Farrā, *Aḥkām al-Sulṭāniyyah*, 12.

248. Ibn Taymiyyah, *al-Siyāsah al-Sharʿiyyah*, 161; Ahmad Hasan, 'The Political Role of *Ijmāʿ*', 144; Kakakhel, 'Theory of Impeachment,' 9–96.

249. Cf., Al-Khālidī, *Qawāʿid*, p. 211; Asad *The Principles of State and Government*, p. 66.

250. Cf. Kamali, 'Appellate Review and Judicial Independence,' *Islamic Studies*, 29 (1990), 222; Owsia, *Formation of Contract*, 39.

251. Cf. Al-Sanhūrī, *Fiqh al-Khilāfah*, 226.

252. Al-Sayed, *Social Ethics of Islam*, 199–200; Ḥasan Ibrāhīm Ḥasan, *al-Nuzum al-Islāmiyyah*, 177; Hitti, *History of the Arabs*, 10th ed., 321; Badawī, *Ikhtiṣāṣāt*, 363.

253. Al-Sayed, *Social Ethics of Islam*, 188–191.

254. Al-Sayed, *Social Ethics of Islam*, 201; Badawī, *Ikhtiṣāṣāt*, 361.

255. Ṭabarī, *Tārīkh*, III, 415; Al-Sayed, *Social Ethics*, 201.

256. Cf. ʿAlī, *Mabdaʾ al-Mashrūʿiyyah*, 314; al-Rifāʿī, *al-Qaḍāʾ al-Idārī*, 68.

257. Cf. al-Rīs, *al-Naẓariyyāt al-Siyāsiyyah*, 207.

258. As quoted in Nawaf Salam, *The Emergence of Citizenship*, 142–43.

259. Namek Kemal, quoted in Bernard Lewis, 'Hurriyya' in *Encyclopedia of Islam*, new edn, vol. III, 592.

Glossary

ʿadālah: uprightness of character.

ʿadl: justice.

aḥkām: *Sharīʿah* rulings.

al-aḥkām al-sulṭāniyyah: rules of governance.

ahl al-ḥall wa'l-ʿaqd: those who loosen and bind, parties to the contract of *imāmah*.

amānah: trust.

amānat al-ḥukm: trust of governance.

amwāl ṣafiyyah: chosen property.

Anṣār: helpers.

al-arḥām: ties of kinship.

al-aṣl: original case.

awqāf ahliyyah: private charitable endowments.

bayʿah: pledge of allegiance.

bidʿah: harmful innovation, that which is contrary to the *Sunnah*.

bughā: rebellion.

Dār al-ʿahd: abode of treaty or of truce.

Dār al-dhimmah: abode of protection.

Dār al-fisq: country of transgression and disobedience.

Dār al-ḥarb: abode of war.

Dār al-hudnah: abode of truce.

Dār al-ijābah: abode of acceptance.

Dār al-īmān: abode of faith.

Dār al-Islām: abode of Islam.

ḍarūrah: necessity.

faḍā'il: virtues.

al-far': subsidiary case.

farḍ ʿayn: personal obligation.

farḍ kifā'ī: collective obligation, duty.

fasād: corruption, mischief.

fāsiq: transgressor, deviant.
fatwā (pl. *fatāwā*): legal verdict, legal opinion.
fitnah: sedition.
ghaṣb: usurpation.
ḥalīf: covenanted person.
al-ḥaqq: truth, right.
ḥaqq al-ādamī: right of man.
ḥaqq Allāh: right of God.
ḥaqq al-ʿazl: right of community to depose a deviant leader.
ḥaqq al-shakwah: right of complaint.
ḥaqq tarshīḥ: right to nomination.
al-ḥarb: war.
ḥarbī: the belligerent.
hijrah: migration.
ḥirābah: robbery.
ḥisbah: lit. computation or checking, but commonly used in reference to what is known as *amr bi'l-maʿrūf wa-nahy ʿan al-munkar*, that is, promotion of good and prevention of evil.
ḥudūd: prescribed penalties.
ḥuqūq al-muwāṭanah: citizenship rights.
hurriyyat al-ma'wā: freedom to reside.
ḥurriyyat al-tanaqqul: freedom of movement.
iḥtikār: hoarding.
ijmāʿ: general consensus.
ijtihād: independent reasoning.
ikhtilās: embezzlement.
ikrāh: duress.
ʿillah: effective cause.
ʿilmāniyyah: secularism.
iqtiḍā' al-naṣṣ: requirement of text.
isti'mān: lit. asking for safe conduct.
jamīʿ al-wilāyah: overall governmental authority.
jār: neighbour.
jihād: holy struggle, just war.
al-jinsiyyah: nationality.
jiwār: neighbourhood.
jizyah: poll-tax.
al-kasb: earning/acquisition.
kāshif: declaratory.
khā'in: treacherous.
khilāfah: vicegerency.

khiyānah: breach of trust.
al-khurūj: civil disobedience, revolt against the ruling government.
kufr: disbelief.
madhmūm: reprehensible.
maḥmūd: praiseworthy.
majlis al-shūrā: consultative assembly.
mandūb: recommendable.
maṣlaḥah: consideration of public interest.
mawāli: non–Arabs that resided in Arab lands under native protection.
maẓālim: grievances.
mu'ākhāt: covenant of fraternity.
muʿāmalāt: civil transactions.
mubāḥ: neutral, permissible.
mubāyaʿah: pledging of allegiance.
muḥāsabat al-ḥukkām: accountability of rulers.
muḥāsabat al-nafs: holding oneself to account.
muḥtasib: market inspector.
mursal: disconnected *ḥadīth*.
musāfir: traveller.
mushāhadah: observation.
mustaḍʿafūn: weak people.
muṭlaq: absolute and unqualified.
muwāṭanah: citizenship.
muwāṭin: citizen, compatriot.
naṣīḥah: sincere advice.
naṣrah: assistance.
niyyah: intention.
niẓām al-ḥukm al-Islāmī: Islamic system of government.
qāḍī: judge.
qāḍī al-quḍāh: chief justice.
qaṭʿ al-ṭarīq: highway robbery.
qawmiyyah: nationalism.
qiyās: analogical reasoning.
raḥim: womb.
rāʿī: custodian.
rashwah: bribery.
ribā: usury.
riḥlah: journey.
ṣabr: patience.
safar: travel.
sahm ṣafī: chosen portion.

al-salaf: predecessors.
al-sha'b: people, population.
shūrā: consultation.
ṣilat al-raḥim: ties of kinship.
al-silm: peace.
siyāsah shar'iyyah: Sharī'ah-oriented policy.
al-sulṭān al-ẓālim: oppressive leader.
al-ṭā'ah al-muḥarram: unlawful obedience.
ṭā'ifiyyah: communalism.
takhṣīṣ al-qaḍā': specification of justice.
taqwā: piety.
al-tarshīḥ: nomination.
ta'zīr (pl. *ta'zīrāt*): deterrent punishment, discretionary penalty deter-
    mined by the *qāḍī*.
'urf: social custom.
wājib: obligatory.
wakālah: representation.
wakīl: representative.
walā': patronage.
walī al-amr: ruler.
waqf: charitable endowment.
waṭaniyyah: nationalism.
wazīr al-tafwīḍ: prime minister.
wazīr al-tanfīdh: minister.
wilāyah: protection and support.
zāhidūn: the ascetics and the pious.
zakāh: legal alms.
ẓulm: oppression.

Bibliography

Abū Dāwūd, *Sunan Abū Dāwūd*. Muṣṭafā Dīb al-Bughah (ed.). Damascus: Dār al-ʿUlūm al-Insāniyyah, 1416/1995. I have also used the Eng. Trans. of this work by Ahmad Hasan, 3 vols. Lahore: Ashraf Press, 1984. I have also referred to al-Mundhirī's edition of Abū Dāwūd. Al-Ḥāfiẓ al-Mundhirī, *Mukhtaṣar Sunan Abū Dāwūd*, ed. Aḥmad Muḥammad Shākir and Ḥamīd Muḥammad al-Faqī (Beirut: Dār al-Maʿrifah).

Abū Ḥabīb, Saʿdī, *Dirāsah fī Minhāj al-Islām al-Siyāsī*. Beirut: Muʾassasat al-Risālah, 1406/1985.

Abū ʿĪd, ʿĀrif Khalīl, *Waẓīfat al-Ḥākim fiʾl-Dawlah al-Islāmiyyah*. Kuwait: *Dār al-Arqām*, 1985.

Abū Shaqqah, ʿAbd al-Ḥalīm Muḥammad, *Taḥrīr al-Marʾah fī ʿAṣr al-Risālah*, 6 vol. Kuwait: Dār al-Qalam, n.d.

Abū ʿUbayd, al-Qāsim b. Salām, *Kitāb al-Amwāl*. Ed. Muḥammad Hamid al-Fāqī. Riyad: Maṭbaʿat Muḥammad ʿAbd al-Laṭīf Ḥijāzī, 1353. Also see Eng. trans. of this work by Noor Muhammad Ghifari, *The Book of Finance*. Islamabad: Pakistan Hijra Council, 1411/1991.

Abū Yūsuf, Yaʿqūb b. Ibrāhīm, *Kitāb al-Kharāj*. 5th edn. Cairo: al-Maṭbaʿah al-Salafiyyah, 1396 AH.

Abū Zahrah, Muḥammad, *Al-ʿIlāqāt al-Dawliyyah fiʾl-Islām*. Cairo: Dār al-Fikr al-ʿArabī, n.d.

——*Al-Jarīmah waʾl-ʿUqūbah fiʾl-Fiqh al-Islāmī*. Cairo: Dār al-Fikr al-ʿArabī, n.d.

——*Al-Mujtamaʿ al-Insānī fī Ẓill al-Islām*. 2nd edn. Jeddah: al-Dār al-Saʿūdiyyah liʾl-Nashr waʾl-Tawzīʿ, 1401/1981.

——*Tanẓīm al-Islām liʾl-Mujtamaʿ*. Cairo: Dār al-Fikr al-ʿArabī, 1385/1965.

Al-ʿAbūdī, Muḥsin, *Al-Ḥurriyyāt al-Ijtimāʿiyyah Bayn al-Nuẓum al-Muʿāṣirah wa'l-Fikr al-Islāmī al-Siyāsī*. Cairo: Dār al-Nahḍah al-ʿArabīyyah, 1410/1990.

——*Raʾīs al-Dawlah Bayn al-Nuẓum al-Muʿāṣirah wa'l-Fikr al-Siyāsī al-Islāmī*. Cairo: Dār al-Nahḍah al-ʿArabiyyah, 1410/1990.

El-Affendi, ʿAbd al-Wahhāb, *Iʿādat al-Naẓar fi'l-Mafhūm al-Taqlīdī li'l-Jamāʿah al-Siyāsiyyah fi'l-Islām: Muslim am Muwāṭin?'* *Al-Mustaqbal al-ʿArabī* 22, no. 264 (February 2001), 144–159.

ʿAfīfī, Muḥammad al-Ṣādiq, *al-Mujtamaʿ al-Islāmī wa-Ḥuqūq al-Insān*, Cairo: Idārat al-Saḥāfah wa'l-Nashr bi-Rābiṭah al-ʿĀlam al-Islāmī, 1407/1987.

Aḥmad, Fuʾād ʿAbd al-Munʿim, *Uṣūl Niẓām al-Ḥukm fi'l-Islām*. Alexandria (Egypt): Muʾassasat Shabāb al-Jāmiʿah, 1991/1411.

Ahmad, Waqar & Charles Husband ' Religious Identity, Citizenship and Welfare: the Case of Muslims in Britain.' *AJISS* 10 (1993).

Al-ʿAjlānī, Munīr, *ʿAbqariyyat al-Islām fī Uṣūl al-Ḥukm*. Beirut: Dār al-Nafāʾis, 1405/1985.

Al-Albānī, Muḥammad Nāṣir al-Dīn, *Ṣaḥīḥ al-Jāmiʿ al-Ṣaghīr wa-Ziyādatih*. N.p.: Al-Maktab al-Islāmī, n.d.

ʿAlī, ʿAbd al-Jalīl, *Mabdaʾ al-Mashrūʿiyyah fi'l-Niẓām al-Islāmī wa'l-Anzimah al-Qānūniyyah al-Muʿāṣirah, Dirāsah Muqāranah*. Cairo: ʿĀlam al-Kutub, 1984.

Ali, Abdullah Yusuf, *The Holy Qur'an: Translation and Commentary*. Islamabad: Da'wah Academy.

ʿAlī, Muḥammad Kurd, *Al-Islām wa'l-Haḍārah al-ʿArabiyyah*. 2nd edn. Cairo: Majmaʿ Lajnat al-Taʾlīf wa'l-Tarjamah wa'l-Nashr, 1959.

ʿĀliyah, Samīr Qad, *Naẓariyyāt al-Dawlah wa-Adābuhā fi'l-Islām*. Beirut: al-Muʾassasah al-Jāmiʿiyyah, 1402/1988.

Al-Alwani, Taha Jabir, 'Globalization, Centralization, Not Globalism.' *AJISS* 15 (1998).

——'Naturalization and the Right of Citizens.' *AJISS* 11 (1994).

Anwarullah, *The Criminal Law of Islam*. Kuala Lumpur: A.S. Noordeen, 1997.

Al-ʿArabī, Muḥammad ʿAbd Allāh, *Niẓām al-Ḥukm fi'l-Islām*. Cairo: Dār al-Fikr, n.d.

Asad, Muhammad, *Principles of State and Government in Islam*. Berkeley: University of California Press, 1966.

——*The Message of the Qur'an*. Gibraltar: Dār al-Andalus, 1980.

Al-Ashʿarī, Abū'l-Ḥasan ʿAlī b. Ismāʿīl, *Maqālāt al-Islāmiyyīn wa-Ikhtilāf al-Muṣallīn*. Beirut: Al-Maktabah al-ʿAsriyyah, 1999.

Al-ʿAsqalānī, Ḥāfiẓ Ibn Ḥajar, *Fatḥ al-Bārī Sharḥ al-Bukhārī*. Beirut: Dār al-Maʿrifah, 1959.

El-Awa, M. Salim, *Al-Fiqh al-Islāmī fī Ṭarīq al-Tajdīd*. 2nd edn. Beirut: al-Maktab al-Islāmī, 1419/1998.

——ʿal-Muwāṭanah Hiya Asās al-ʿIlāqah Bayn al-Muslimīn wa-Ghayrihim.ʾ *Islam 21*, no. 20 (December 1999).

ʿAwdah, ʿAbd al-Qādir, *al-Mawsūʿah al-ʿAsriyyah fiʾl-Fiqh al-Jināʾī al-Islāmī*. (Being a commmmentary on ʿAwdahʾs *al-Tashrīʿ al-Jināʾī*), Commentary and Annotations by Ayatullāh al-Sayyid Ismāʿīl al-Ṣadr and Muḥammad Tawfīq al-Shāwī, 4 vols. Cairo: Dār al-Shurūq, 1421/2001.

——*Al-Tashrīʿ al-Jināʾī al-Islāmī Muqāranan biʾl-Qānūn al-Waḍʿī*. 2 vols. Cairo: Maktabah Wahbah, 1401/1981.

Azad, Muhammad Murtaza, *Judicial System of Islam*. Islamabad: Islamic Research Institute, 1987.

Bābillī, Maḥmūd Muḥammad, *Al-Hijrah fiʾl-Islām*. Beirut: al-Maktab al-Islāmī, 1416/1996.

Badawī, Ismāʿīl, *Daʿāʾim al-Ḥukm fiʾl-Sharīʿah al-Islāmiyyah waʾl-Nuẓum al-Dustūriyyah al-Muʿāṣirah*. Cairo: Dār al-Fikr al-ʿArabī, 1980/1400.

——*Ikhtiṣāṣāt al-Sulṭah al-Tanfīdhiyyah fiʾl-Dawlah al-Islāmiyyah*. Cairo: Dār al-Nahḍah al-ʿArabiyyah, 1413/1993.

Badawi, Zainab. ʿThe Dilemma of Identity in a Multicultural Europe.ʾ *Islam 21*, no.27 (2001).

Badrān, Abū al-ʿAynayn Badrān, *Uṣūl al-Fiqh al-Islāmī*. Alexandria: Muʾassasat Shabāb al-Jāmiʿah, 1404/1984.

Al-Baghdādī, Abū Manṣūr ʿAbd al-Qāhir al-Tamimī, *Uṣūl ad-Dīn*. Istanbul: Maṭbaʿat al-Dawal, 1928.

Al-Balādhurī, Abū al-Ḥasan, *Futūḥ al-Buldān*. Ed. Riḍwān Muḥammad Riḍwān. Beirut: Dār al-Kutub al-ʿIlmiyyah, 1412/1991.

Basyūnī, ʿAbd Allāh, *Naẓariyyat al-Dawlah fiʾl-Islām*. Beirut: al-Dār al-Jāmiʿiyyah, 1986.

Al-Bayātī, Munīr Ḥamīd, *Al-Niẓām al-Siyāsī al-Islāmī Muqāranan biʾl-Dawlah al-Qānūniyyah*. N.p.: Dār al-Bashīr liʾl-Nashr waʾl-Tawzīʿ, n.d.

Al-Bishrī, Ṭāriq, *Bayn al Islām waʾl-ʿUrūbah*. Cairo: Dār al-Shurūq, 1418/1998.

——*Bayn al-Jāmiʿah al-Dīniyyah waʾl-Jāmiʿah al-Waṭaniyyah fiʾl-Fikr al-Siyāsī*. Cairo: Dār al-Shurūq, 1418/1998.

Bukhārī, Muḥammad b. Ismāʿīl, *Ṣaḥīḥ al-Bukhārī*. Eng. trans. Muhammad Muhsin Khan. 9 vols. Lahore: Qazi Publications, 1979.

Constitution of Medina (known in Arabic as *Dustūr al-Madīnah*). An Eng. tr. of this document appears in Montgomery-Watt, *Islamic Political Thought: The Basic Concepts*. Edinburgh: Edinburgh University press, 1968.

Cranstone, Maurice, *What are Human Rights?* London: The Bodley Head, 1977.

Daniel, Norman, *Islam and the West: the Making of an Image*. Rvsd edn. Edinburgh: EUP, 1993.

Dāraquṭnī, ʿAlī Ibn ʿUmar, *Sunan al-Dāraquṭnī*. Ed. Al-Sayyid ʿAbd Allāh Hāshim. Beirut: Dār al-Maʿrifah, 1386.

Eickelman, Dale F. & Piscatori, James, eds. *Muslim Travellers: Pilgrimage, Migration and The Religious Imagination*. London: Routledge, 1990.

Encyclopedia of Islam, New Edition. Leiden: E.J. Brill, 1965.

Enayat, Hamid, *Modern Islamic Political Thought*. London: Macmillan Press, 1982.

Ewing, Keith, 'Citizenship and Employment.' In Edr. Robert Blackburn, *Rights of Citizenship*. London: Mansell, 1993.

El-Fadl, Khalid Abū, 'Islam and Muslim Minorities.' *Islamic Law and Society 1 & 2* (1994), 183f.

Al-Farrā, Abū Yaʿlā Muḥammad b. al-Ḥusayn, *Al-Aḥkām al-Sulṭāniyyah*. Ed. Muḥammad Ḥamīd al-Faqī. Cairo: Muṣṭafā al-Bābī al-Ḥalabī, 1357.

Gellens, Sam. I., 'Search for Knowledge.' In ed. Eickelman, *Muslim Travellers*, 50–69.

Al-Ghannūshī, Rashīd, *Ḥuqūq al-Muwāṭanah, Ḥuqūq Ghayr al-Muslim fi'l-Mujtamaʿ al-Islāmī*. 2nd edn. Herndon, VA & Tunis: Al-Maʿhad al-ʿĀlamī li'l-Fikr al-Islāmī, 1413/1993.

Al-Ghazālī, Abū Ḥāmid Muḥammad, *Iḥyā' ʿUlūm al-Dīn*. Cairo: ʿĪsā al-Bābī al-Ḥalabī, 1957, with a commentary by Ḥāfiẓ Zayn al-Dīn al-ʿIrāqī entitled *al-Mughnī ʿan Ḥaml al-Asfār fi'l-Asfār fī Takhrīj mā fi'l-Iḥyā' min al-Akhbār*.

Al-Ghazālī, Shaykh Muḥammad, *Khuluq al-Muslim*. Cairo: Dār al-Nahḍah Miṣriyyah li'l-Ṭibaʿah wa'l-Nashr, 1997.

——*Min Hunā Naʿlam*. Cairo: Dār al-Saʿādah, 1965.

——*Mushkilah fī Ṭarīq al-Ḥayāt al-Islāmiyyah*. 2nd edn. Cairo: Dār Nahdah al-Miṣriyyah li'l-Ṭibaʿah wa'l-Nashr, 1996.

——*Al-Taʿassub wa'l-Tasāmuḥ Bayn al-Masīḥiyyah wa'l-Islām*. Cairo: Dār al-Kutub al-Ḥadīthah, 1960.

Ghazāwī, Muḥammad Salīm, *Al-Ḥurriyyah al-ʿĀmmah fi'l-Islām*. Alexandria (Egypt): Mu'assasat Shabāb al-Jāmiʿah, n.d.

Ghazi, Mahmood Ahmad, *The Hijrah, Its Philosophy and Message for the Modern Muslim*. Lahore: Islamic Book Foundation, 1401/1981.

Al-Ghunaymī, Muḥammad Ṭalʿat, *Qanūn al-Salām fi'l-Islām*. Alexandria: Al-Maʿārif, 1989.

Gulap, I., 'Islamism and Turkish Nationalism,' in Tamara Sonn (ed.), *Islam and the Question of Minorities*. University of South Florida: Scholars Press, 1996.

Al-Ḥadīd, Ibn Abī, *Sharḥ Nahj al-Balāghah*. Beirut: Dār Iḥyā' Turāth al-ʿArabī, n.d.

Ḥamad, Aḥmad, *Fiqh al-Jinsiyyah*. Qatar: Jāmiʿat Qaṭar, 1406/1988.

Hamidullah, Muhammad, *Muḥammad Rasulullah: A Concise Survey of the Works of the Founder of Islam*. Karachi, Pakistan: Huzayfa Publications, 1979.

——*Muslim Conduct of State*. 3r Edn. Lahore: Shah Muhammad Ashraf, 1953.

Al-Ḥanbalī, Abū'l-Faraj ʿAbd al-Raḥmān Ibn Rajab, *Al-Qawāʿid fi'l-Fiqh al-Islāmī*. Cairo: Matbaʿat al-Ṣidq al-Khayriyyah, 1933.

Hasan, Ahmad, *Principles of Islamic Jurisprudence*. Islamabad: Islamic Research Institute, 1993.

——'The Political Role of *Ijmāʿ*.' *Islamic Studies*, 8 (1969), 175–192.

Ḥasan, Ibrāhīm Ḥasan, *Tārīkh al-Islām al-Siyāsī wa'l-Ijtimāʿī wa'l-Iqtiṣādī*. Cairo: Maktabat al-Nahḍah al-Miṣriyyah, 1964.

Ḥasan, Ibrāhīm Ḥasan & ʿAlī Ibrāhīm Ḥasan, *Al-Nuẓum al-Islāmiyyah*. Cairo: Maktabat al-Nahḍah al-ʿArabiyyah, n.d.

Hassan, Essam Mohammad (ed.), *Revitalisation of Political Thought Through Democracy and Human Rights, Islamism, Marxism and Arabism*. Cairo: Cairo Institute for Human Rights Studies, 1995.

Hassan, Kabir & Faridul Islam, 'Prospect and Problems of a Common Market: an Empirical Examination of the OIC Countries,' *AJISS* 18 (2001).

Al-Hibri, Aziza, 'Democratic Principles: An Islamic Point of View.' *Islam 21* (December 1999).

Ḥilmī, Maḥmūd, *Niẓām al-Ḥukm al-Islāmī Muqārinan bi'l-Nuẓum al-Muʿāṣirah*. Cairo: Dār al-Fikr al-ʿArabī, 1970.

Al-Hindī, al-Muttaqī, *Kanz al-ʿUmmāl fī Sunan al-Aqwāl wa'l-Afʿāl*. 4 vols. Hyderabad (Dakan, India), 1313.

Hitti, Phillip K., *History of the Arabs*. 10th edn. Basingstoke and London: Macmillan Press Ltd, 1970.

Al-Ḥuṣarī, *al-Dawlah wa-Siyāsat al-Ḥukm fi'l Fiqh al-Islāmī*. Cairo: Maktabat al-Kulliyāh al-Azhariyyah, 1408/1988.

Ḥusayn, Muḥammad Khiḍr, *Naqd Kitāb al-Islām wa-Uṣūl al-Ḥukm*. Tunis: al-Maktabah al-Zaytūniyyah, 1925.

Ibn ʿAbd al-Ḥakīm, *Sīrat ʿUmar Ibn ʿAbd al-ʿAzīz*. Cairo: al-Maṭbaʿah al-Raḥmaniyyah, 1927.

Ibn ʿĀbidīn, Muḥammad Amīn, *Ḥāshiyat al-Radd al-Mukhtār ʿalā Durr al-Mukhtār* (known as *Ḥāshiyat Ibn ʿĀbidīn*). Cairo: Dār al-Fikr, 1399/1979; and 2nd edn. Cairo: Maṭbaʿat al-Bābī al-Ḥalabī, 1386/1966.

Ibn al-ʿArabī, Abū Bakr Muḥammad b. ʿAbd Allāh, *Aḥkām al-Qurʾān*. Ed. M. ʿAlī al-Bijawī. Beirut: Dār al-Maʿrifah, 1972.

Ibn ʿĀshūr, ʿAyyāḍ, *al-Ḍamīr waʾl-Tashrīʿ, al-ʿAqliyyah al-Madaniyyah waʾl-Ḥuqūq al-Ḥadīthah*. Casablanca: al-Markāz al-Thaqāfī al-ʿArabī, 1998.

Ibn al-Athīr, ʿAlī b. Aḥmad b. ʿAbd al Karīm, *al-Kāmil fiʾl-Tārīkh*. Cairo: Maṭbaʿat al-Shaykh Aḥmad al-Bābī al-Ḥalabī, 1303 AH.

Ibn Farḥūn Burhān al-Dīn Ibrāhīm b. ʿAlī, *Tabṣīrah al-Ḥukkām fī Uṣūl al-Aqḍiyyah wa-Manāhij al-Aḥkām*. Ed. Ṭaha ʿAbd al-Raʾūf Saʿd. Cairo: Maktabah al-Kulliyah al-Azhariyyah, 1406/1986.

Ibn Ḥanbal, Imām Aḥmad, *Musnad*. 6 vols. Cairo: al-Maṭbaʿah al-Munayminah, n.d.

Ibn Ḥazm, Muḥammad b. ʿAlī b. Aḥmad b. Saʿīd al-Ẓāhirī, *Al-Muḥallā*. Aḥmad Muḥammad Shākir (ed.). Cairo: Maṭbaʿat al-Nahḍah, 1347 AH. Also Beirut edn. by Dār al-Kutub al-ʿIlmiyyah, 1408/1988.

Ibn Hishām, ʿAbd al-Malik, *Al-Sīrah al-Nabawiyyah*. Cairo: Muṣṭafā al-Bābī al-Ḥalabī, 1936.

Ibn al-Jawzī, ʿAbd al-Raḥmān Ibn ʿAlī Abūʾl-Faraj, *Sīrat ʿUmar b. al-Khaṭṭāb*. Edr. Ṭāhir al-Hamawī & Ahmad Kilan. Cairo: al-Maktabah al-Tijāriyyah al-Kubrā, 1331 AH.

Ibn Khaldūn, ʿAbd al-Raḥmān, *The Muqaddimah: An Introduction to History*. Eng. Tr. Franz Rosenthal. New York: Pantheon Books. 3 vols, 1958.

Ibn Kathīr, Ḥāfiẓ Abūʾl-Fidāʾ Ismāʿīl, *Al-Bidāyah waʾl-Nihāyah fiʾl-Tārīkh*. Cairo: Maṭbaʿat al-Saʿādah, 1351/1933.

——*Tafsīr al-Qurʾān al-ʿAẓīm* (also known as *Tafsīr Ibn Kathīr*). Cairo: Dār al-Shaʿb, 1393/1973.

Ibn Mājah, Muḥammad b. Yazīd al-Qazwinī, *Sunan Ibn Mājah*. Istanbul: Cagli Yayinlari, 1401/1981.

Ibn Qāyyim, see Al-Jawziyyah below.

Ibn Qudāmah, Muwaffaq al-Dīn Abū Muḥammad ʿAbd Allāh, *Al-Mughnī*. 12 vols. Cairo: Maṭbaʿat al-Manār, 1367 AH.

Ibn Rushd Abū l-Walīd Muḥammad b. Aḥad, *Bidāyat al-Mujtahid wa-Nihāyat al-Muqtaṣid*. Cairo: Muṣṭafā al-Bābī al-Ḥalabī, 1401/1981.

Ibn Saʿd, Muḥammad b. Manīʿ, *Al-Ṭabaqāt al-Kubrā*. Beirut: Dār al-Ṣādir, 1398/1978.

Ibn Taymiyyah, Tāqī al-Dīn Aḥmad, *Majmūʿ Fatāwā Shaykh al-Islām Aḥmad Ibn Taymiyyah*. 2nd edn., Muḥammad ʿAbd al-Raḥmān b. Qāsim (ed.). Riyadh: Dār al-Buḥūth al-ʿIlmiyyah, 1398 AH.

——*Al-Siyāsah al-Sharʿiyyah fī Iṣlāḥ al-Rāʿī wa'l-Raʿiyyah*. ʿAbd al-Raḥmān b. Qāsim (ed.). Beirut: Mu'assasat al-Risālah, 1398 AH.

al-ʿĪlī, ʿAbd al-Ḥakīm Ḥasan, *Al-Ḥurriyyah al-ʿĀmmah fi'l-Fikr wa'l-Niẓām al-Siyāsī al-Islāmī*. Kuwait: Dār al-Kitāb al-Ḥadīth, 1983/1413.

ʿImārah, Muḥammad, *al-Islām wa-Ḥuqūq al-Insān: Ḍarūrāt lā Ḥuqūq*. Cairo: Dār al-Shurūq, 1409/1989.

Iqbal, Zafar & Mervyn Lewis, 'Governance and Corruption.' *AJISS* 19 (2002), 1–34.

Al-Jaʿfar, Muḥammad Anas Qāsim, *Wilāyat al-Maẓālim fi'l-Islām wa-Taṭbīquhā fi'l-Mamlakah al-ʿArabiyyah al-Saʿūdiyyah*. Cairo: Dār al-Nahḍah al-ʿArabiyyah, 1407/1987.

Al-Jassās, Abū Bakr Aḥmad b. ʿAlī, *Aḥkām al-Qur'ān*. Beirut: Dār al-Fikr li'l-Ṭibaʿah wa'l-Nashr, n.d.

Al-Jawziyyah, Ibn Qayyim, *Iʿlām al-Muwaqqiʿīn ʿan Rabb al-ʿĀlamīn*. Muḥammad Munīr al-Dimashqī (ed.). Cairo: Idārat al-Ṭibāʿah al-Munīriyyah, n.d.

——*Al-Ṭuruq al-Ḥukmiyyah fi'l-Siyāsah al-Sharʿiyyah*. Muḥammad Jamīl Ghāzī (ed.). Jeddah: Maṭbaʿat al-Madanī, n.d. I have also used the Cairo edn. by al-Mu'assasah al-ʿArabīyyah, 1380/1961.

Kakakhel, Mohammad Nazeer, 'The Theory of Impeachment in Islamic Polity.' *Islamic Studies* 17 (1978), 93–104.

Kamali, Mohammad Hashim, *Freedom, Equality and Justice in Islam*. Cambridge: the Islamic Texts Society, 2000.

——*Freedom of Expression in Islam*. Cambridge: Islamic Texts Society, 1997 & Kuala Lumpur: Ilmiah Publishers, 1998.

——*A Textbook of Hadith Studies*. Leicestershire (U.K): the Islamic Foundation, 2005.

——'*Siyāsah Sharʿiyyah* or the Policies of Islamic Government.' *American Journal of Islamic Social Sciences*, 6 (1989), 59–81.

Karpat, Kemal. H., 'The Hijra from Russia and the Balkans,' in ed. Eickelman, *Muslim Travellers*, 131–152.

Al-Kāsānī, ʿAlā' al-Dīn, *Badā'iʿ al-Ṣanā'iʿ fī Tartīb al-Sharā'iʿ*. Cairo: Maṭbaʿat al-Istiqāmah, 1956.

Khadduri, Majid, *War and Peace in the Law of Islam*. Baltimore: The Johns Hopkins Press, 1955.

Khalid, Muhammad Khalid, *From Here We Start*. Eng. tr. Isma'il R. El-Faruqi. Washington D.C.: Council of Learned Societies, 1953.

Al-Khālidī, Maḥmūd ʿAbd al-Majīd, *Maʿālim al-Khilāfah fi'l-Fikr al-Siyāsī al-Islāmī*. Beirut: Dār al-Jīl, 1404/1984.

——*Qawāʿid Niẓām al-Ḥukm fi'l-Islām*. Kuwait: Dār al-Buḥūth, 1400/1980.

Khallāf, ʿAbd al-Wahhāb, *Al-Siyāsah al-Sharʿiyyah*. Cairo: al-Maṭbaʿah al-Salafiyyah, 1350 AH.

Al-Khuḍarī, Muḥammad, *Muḥāḍarāt fī Tārīkh al-Umam al-Islāmiyyah*. Cairo: al-Maktabah al-Tijāriyyah, 1370/1969.

Kramer, Gudrun, 'Dhimmi or Citizen.' In edr. Jorgan Nielsen, *The Christian-Muslim Frontier*. London: I.B. Tauris, 1998, 33–51.

Al-Kurdi, Abdurrahman Abdulkadir, *The Islamic State: A Study based on the Holy Constitution*. London: Mansell Publishing Ltd, 1984.

Layish, Aharon, 'Saudi Arabian Legal Reform as a Mechanism to Moderate Wahhabi Doctrine.' *The American Journal of Oriental Studies* 107: 2 (1987), 279–293.

Levin, Leah, *Human rights : questions & answers*. Paris: Unesco Press, 1981.

Lewis, Bernard, 'Hurriyyah.' *Encyclopedia of Islam*, New Edition. Leiden: E.J. Brill, 1965.

Mabkhut, Shukri & Osman, Hasan (eds.), *Maʿ Muḥammad al-Ṭālibī: ʿAyāl Allāh, Afkār Jadīdah fī ʿIlāqat al-Muslim bi-Nafsihi wa bi'l-Ākharīn*. Tunis: Dār Siras li'l-Nashr, 1992.

Madkūr, Muḥammad Salām, *Maʿālim al-Dawlah al-Islāmiyyah*. Kuwait: Maktabat al-Falāḥ, 1403/1983.

——*Al-Qaḍāʾ fi'l-Islām*. Cairo: Dār al-Nahḍah al-ʿArabīyyah, 1380 AH.

Mahmassānī, Subḥī Rajab, *Arkān Ḥuqūq al-Insān fi'l-Islām*. Beirut: Dār al-ʿIlm li'l-Malāyīn, 1979.

Mālik bin Anas, Imām Mālik, *Al-Muwaṭṭā*. Ed. M. Fu'ād ʿAbd al-Bāqī. Cairo: Dār Iḥyā' al-Kutub al-ʿArabīyyah, 1370/1952.

Mallat, Chibli & Hillary Lewis Ruttley, edrs. , *Islamic Law in the Middle East*. London: Graham & Trotman, 1995.

Manna, Haytham, *Citizenship in Arab and Islamic History*. Eng. tr. Manar Wafa & Wasim Wagdy. Cairo: Cairo Institute for Human Rights Studies, 1996.

Al-Maqrīzī, Taqī al-Dīn Aḥmad b. ʿAlī, *Imtāʿ al-Asmāʿ*. Edr. Mahmud Shakir. Cairo: Lajnah al-Ta'līf wa'l-Tarjamah wa'l-Nashr, 1360/1941.

Masud, Muhammad Khalid, 'The Obligation to Migrate: The Doctrine of Hijra in Islamic Law,' in ed. Eickelman, *Muslim Travellers*, 29–50.

Al-Māwardī, Abū'l-Ḥasan, *Kitāb al-Aḥkām al-Sulṭāniyyah*. 2nd edn. Cairo: Muṣṭafā al-Bābī al-Ḥalabī, 1386 AH.

——*Mawsūʿat al-Mafāhīm al-Islāmiyyah al-ʿĀmmah*. Maḥmūd Ḥamdī Zaqzūq (ed.). Cairo: Wizārat al-Awqāf wa'l-Shu'ūn al-Islāmiyyah, 1421/2000.

Mawdūdī, S. Abū 'l-Aʿlā, *Naẓariyyat al-Islām wa-Hadyihi*. Cairo: Dār al-Fikr, 1969.

Al-Mazarī, Abū ʿAbd Allāh Muḥammad b. ʿAlī, *Al-Muʿlim bi-Fawā'id al-Muslim*. Ed. Muḥammad al-Shādhlī. Tunis: Al-Dār al-Tūnisiyyah li'l-Nashr, 1407/1987.

McDonnell, Mary Byrne, 'Patters of Muslim Pilgrimage from Malaysia 1885–1985,' in Eickelman, ed., *Muslim Travellers*, 111–131.

Mejelle. Eng. tr. C.R. Tyser, Being an English Translation of *Majallah al-Aḥkām al-ʿAdaliyah*. Lahore: Law Publishing Company, 1967.

Momin, Abdur-Rahman, 'Pluralism and multi-Culturalism: an Islamic Perspective.' *AJISS* 18 (2001), 115–147.

El-Moudden, Abderrahmane, 'The Ambivance of Rihla: Community Integration and Self-Definition on Moroccan Traveller Accounts 1300–1800,' in ed. Eickelman, *Muslim Travellers*, 65–85.

Al-Muʿjam al-Wasīṭ, 4th ed. Cairo: Majmaʿ al-Lughah al-ʿArabiyyah, Maktabat al-Shurūq al-Duwaliyyah, 2004.

Mūsā, Muḥammad Yūsuf, *Al-Islām wa'l-Ḥayāt: Dirāsah wa-Tawjīhāt*. Cairo: Maktabah Wahbah, 1961.

Muslim, Ibn Ḥajjāj al-Nīshāpūrī, *Mukhtaṣar Ṣaḥīḥ Muslim*. Muḥammad Nāṣir al-Dīn al-Albānī (ed.). 2nd edn. Beirut: Dār al-Maktab al-Islāmī, 1404/1984.

Mutawallī, ʿAbd al-Ḥamīd, *Mabādi' Niẓām al-Ḥukm fi'l-Islām*. Alexandria (Egypt): Mansha'āt al-Maʿārif, 1974.

Al-Nabhānī, Shaykh Taqī al-Dīn, *Muqaddimāt al-Dustūr*. Kuwait, n.p., 1964.

Al-Nadwī, ʿAlī Aḥmad, *Mawsūʿat al-Qawāʿid wa'l-Ḍawābit al-Fiqhiyyah al Ḥākimah li'l-Muʿāmalāt al-Māliyyah fi'l-Fiqh al-Islāmī*. Vol. 3. Cairo: Dār ʿĀlam al-Maʿrifah, 1419/1999.

Nanda, Ved P., *Refugee Law and Policy*. Westport, Connecticut: Greenwood Press, 1989.

Al-Nawawī, Yaḥyā b. Sharaf, *Riyāḍ al-Ṣāliḥīn*. 2nd edn. by Muḥammad Nāṣir al-Dīn al-Albānī. Beirut: Dār al-Maktab al-Islāmī, 1404/1984.

Ohmae, Kenichi, *The End of the Nation State: The Rise of Regional Economics*. New York: The Free Press, 1995.

Oppenheim International Law: A Treatise. Ed. Lauterpacht, I., 8th edn. London: Longmans, 1958.

Osborn, D. L., *A Concise Law Dictionary*. 5th edn. London: Sweet & Maxwell, 1964.

Osmān, Muḥammad Fatḥī, see under ʿUthmān below.

Owsia, Parvez, *Formation of a Contract*. Leiden: Kluwer Academic Publishers, 1984.

Partington, Martin, 'Citizenship and Housing.' In edr. Robert Blackburn, *Rights of Citizenship*. London: Mansell, 1993.

Al-Qādirī, ʿAbd Allāh Ibn Aḥmad, *al-Kifāʾah al-Idāriyyah fiʾl-Siyāsah al-Sharʿiyyah*. Jeddah: Dār al-Mujtamaʿ liʾl-Nashr waʾl-Tawzīʿ, 1406/1986.

Al-Qaraḍāwī, Yūsuf, *Al-ʿAql waʾl-ʿIlm fiʾl-Qurʾān al-Karīm*. Cairo: Maktabat Wahbah, 1416/1996.

——*Fī Fiqh al-Awlawiyyāt: Darāsah Jadīdah fī Dawʾ al-Qurʾān waʾl-Sunnah*. 2nd edn. Cairo: Maktabat Wahbah, 1416/1996.

——*Fiqh al-Zakāh*. 2 vols. Beirut: Dār al-Irshād, 1969.

——*Ghayr al-Muslimīn fiʾl-Mujtamaʿ al-Islāmī*. Cairo: Maktabat Wahbah, 1977.

——*Ḥatmiyyat al-Ḥall al-Islāmī*. Cairo: Maktabat Wahbah, 2001.

——*Min Fiqh al-Dawlah fil-Islām*. Cairo: Dār al-Shurūq, 1417/1997.

Al-Qarāfī, Shihāb al-Dīn, *al-Iḥkām fī Tamyīz al-Fatāwā ʿan al-Aḥkām wa-Taṣarrufāt al-Qāḍī waʾl-Imām*, ed. ʿAbd al-Fattāḥ Abū Ghaddah. Aleppo: Maktab al-Maṭbūʿāt al-Islāmiyyah, 1387/1967.

Al-Qurshī, Ibn al-Ukhuwwah, *Maʿālim al-Qurbah fī Aḥkām al-Ḥisbah*. Cambridge edn., Matbaʿat Dār al-Funūn, 1937.

Al-Qurṭubī, ʿAbd Allāh Muḥammad Ibn Farāj al-Mālikī, *Aqḍiyah Rasūl Allāh*. Ed. Al-Shaykh Qāsim al-Rifāʿī. Beirut: Dār al-Qalam, 1408/1987.

Al-Qurṭubī, Abū ʿAbd Allāh Muḥammad, *Al-Jāmiʿ li-Aḥkām al-Qurʾān* (known as *Tafsīr al-Qurṭubī*). Cairo: Matbaʿat Dār al-Kutub, 1387/1967.

Al-Qurṭubī, Abūʾl-Walīd Muḥammad b. Rushd, *Bidāyat al-Mujtahid wa-Nihāyat al-Muqtaṣid*, 5th ed. Cairo: Muṣṭafā al-Bābī al-Ḥalabī, 1401/1981.

Quṭb, Muḥammad, *Shubhāt Ḥawl al-Islām*. Cairo: n.p., 1954.

Quṭb, Sayyid, *Al-ʿAdālah al-Ijtimāʿiyyah fiʾl-Islām*. 4th edn. Cairo: ʿIsā al-Bābī al-Ḥalabī, 1373/1954.

——*Fī Ẓilāl al-Qur'ān*. Beirut: Dār al-Shurūq, 1397/1977. Also 4th edn., Beirut: Dār al-ʿArabīyyah, n.d.

Ramadan, Said, *Islamic Law, Its Scope and Equity*. 2nd Edn. Kuala Lumpur: Muslim Youth Movement of Malaysia, 1992.

Ramadan, Tariq, *To Be A European Muslim*. Leicester: The Islamic Foundation, 1999/1420.

Al-Rāzī, Fakhr al-Dīn Abū ʿAbd Allāh Muḥammad, *al-Tafsīr al-Kabīr* (also known as *Mafātīḥ al-Ghayb*). Cairo: al-Maṭbaʿah al-Bahiyyah al-Miṣriyyah, 1357/1938, also Beirut: Dār al-Fikr, 1985.

Riḍā, Muḥammad Rashīd, *Fatāwā al-Imām Muḥammad Rashīd Riḍā*. Eds. Ṣalāḥ al-Dīn al-Munjid & Yūsuf Khurī. Beirut: Dār al-Kitāb al-Jadīd, 1919/1988.

——*Al-Khilāfah aw al-Imāmah al-ʿUẓmah*. Cairo: Maṭbaʿat al-Manār, 1341 ah.

——*Tafsīr al-Qur'ān al-Ḥakīm*, (also known as *Tafsīr al-Manār*), Beirut: Dār al-Maʿrifah, 1328.

Al-Rifāʿī, ʿAbd al-Ḥamīd, *Al-Qaḍā al-Idārī Bayn al-Sharīʿah wa'l-Qānūn*. Beirut & Damascus: Dār al-Fikr, 1989.

Al-Rīs, Diyā' al-Dīn, *Al-Naẓariyyāt al-Siyasiyyah al-Islāmiyyah*. 7th edn. Cairo: Dār al-Turāth, n.d.

Rosenthal, Franz, *The Muslim Concept of Freedom*. London: E.J. Brill, 1960.

——'I Am You: Individual Piety and Society in Islam.' In Edr. Amin Banani & Speros Vryonis Jr. *Individualism and Conformity in Classical Islam*. Wiesbaden, 1977.

Al-Saffār, Shaykh Ḥasan, 'Al-Waṭan wa'l-Muwāṭanah: al-Ḥuqūq wa'l-Wajibāt.' *Al-Kalimah*, no. 10 (3rd Year), 1996.

Salam, Nawaf. 'The Emergence of Citizenship in Islamdom.' *Arab Law Quarterly* 12 (1997), 125–148.

Saleh, Nabil. 'Company Legislation in the Gulf: Recent Developments.' In H.L. Ruttley & Chibli Mallat (eds.), *Commercial Law in the Middle East* London : Graham & Trotman, 1995.

Al-Sanhūrī, ʿAbd al-Razzāq, *Fiqh al-Khilāfah wa-Taṭawwuruha*. Eds. Nadia al-Sanhūrī & Tawfīq Muḥammad al-Shāwī. Cairo: al-Hay'ah al-Miṣriyyah li'l-Kitāb, 1989.

Al-Sarakhsī, Shams al Dīn, *Al-Mabsūṭ*. 32 vols. Beirut: Dār al-Maʿrifah, 1406/1986.

Satā, Hammād Muḥammad, *Al-Uṣūl al-Islāmiyyah li'l-Qānūn al-Idārī*. Cairo; Dār al-Ṣaḥwah li'l-Nashr wa'l-Tawzīʿ, 1411/1991.

Al-Sayed, Abdul Malik A., *Social Ethics of Islam: Classical Islamic Arabic Political Theory and Practice*. New York: Vantage Press, 1982.

Schacht, Joseph, 'Islamic Law in Contemporary States.' *The American Journal of Comparative Law*, vol.18 (1959), 133–147.

Al-Shāfiʿī, Muḥammad b. Idrīs, *Aḥkām al-Qurʾān*. Beirut: Dār al-Kutub al-ʿIlmiyyah, 1975.

——*The Risālah*. Ed. L. Bercher, 3rd ed. Algiers, 1949.

——*al-Umm*. Bulaq: al-Maṭbaʿah al-Kubrā, 1321/1940.

Al-Shahristānī, Abuʾl-Fatḥ Muḥammad, *al-Milal waʾl-Niḥal*, ed. ʿAbd al-ʿAzīz Muḥammad al-Wakīl, Cairo: Muʾassasat al-Ḥalabī, 1378/1968.

Shaḥrūr, Muḥammad, *Naḥw Uṣūl Jadīdah liʾl-Fiqh al-Islāmī: Fiqh al-Marʾah*. Damascus: al-Ahāli liʾl-Ṭibāʿah waʾl-Tawzīʿ waʾl-Nashr, 2000.

Shaltūt, Maḥmūd, *Al-Fatāwā: Dirāsah li-Mushkilat al-Muslim al-Muʿāṣir*. Cairo: Dār al-Qalam, 1960.

——*Al-Islām ʿAqīdah wa-Sharīʿah*. Kuwait: Maṭābiʿ Dār al-Qalam, c. 1965.

——*Min Tawjīhāt al-Islām*. Cairo: Dār al-Qalam, 1966.

Sharaiyra, Walid Idris Said, *Right and Freedom of Movement in Islam*. Kuala Lumpur: A. S. Noordeen, 1999.

Al-Sharbīnī, Muḥammad al-Khaṭīb, *Mughnī al-Muḥtāj ilā Maʿrifat al-Alfāẓ al-Minhāj*. Beirut: Dār al-Fikr, n.d.

Al-Shāṭibī, Abū Isḥāq Ibrāhīm, *Al-Iʿtiṣām*. Cairo: Dār al-Qalam, 1960.

——*al-Muwāfaqāt fī Uṣūl al-Sharīʿah*. Ed. Shaykh ʿAbd Allāh Dirāz. Cairo: al-Maktabah al-Tijāriyyah al-Kubrā, n.d.

Al-Shāwī, Muḥammad Tawfīq, *al-Mawsūʿah al-ʿAṣriyyah* (see under ʿAwdah).

Al-Shawkānī, Yaḥyā b. ʿAlī, *Nayl al-Awṭār: Sharḥ Muntaqā al-Akhbār*, Cairo: Muṣṭafā al-Bābī al-Ḥalabī, n.d.

Al-Shīrāzī, Abī Isḥāq Ibrāhīm b. ʿAlī, *al-Muhadhdhab fī Fiqh al-Imām al-Shāfiʿī*. 2nd Edn. Beirut: Dār al-Maʿrifah, 1379 AH.

Shīshānī, ʿAbd al-Wahhāb ʿAbd al-ʿAzīz, *Ḥuqūq al-Insān wa-Ḥurriyyatuh al-Asāsiyah fiʾl-Niẓām al-Islāmī waʾl-Nuẓum al-Muʿāsirah*. Amman: Maṭābiʿ al-Jāmʿiyyah al-Malakiyyah, 1400/1980.

Al-Sibāʿī, Muṣṭafā, *Ishtirakiyyāt al-Islām*. Damascus: al-Dār al-Qawmiyyah liʾl-Ṭibāʿah waʾl-Nashr, 1379/1960.

——*al-Takāful al-Ijtimāʿī fiʾl-Islām*. Beirut: al-Maktab al-Islāmī, 1419/1998.

Siddiqui, Mazheruddin, *Modern Reformist Thought in the Muslim World*. Islamabad: Islamic Research Institute, 1402/1982.

Sonn, Tamara, edr., *Islam and the Question of Minorities.* Atlanta, Georgia: Scholars Press, 1996.

Al-Sulamī, ʿIzz al-Dīn ʿAbd al-Salām, *Qawāʿid al-Aḥkām fī Maṣāliḥ al-Anām.* Beirut: Muʾassasat al-Rayyān li'l-Ṭibāʿah wa'l-Nashr, 1410/1990. Also Cairo: al-Maṭbaʿah al-Ḥusayniyyah, 1934.

Al-Suyūṭī, Jalāl al-Dīn, *Al-Jāmiʿ al-Ṣaghīr*, 4th edn. Cairo: Muṣṭafā al-Bābī al-Ḥalabī, 1954.

Al-Ṭabarī, Abū Jaʿfar Muḥammad Ibn Jarīr. *Tārīkh al-Umam wa'l-Mulūk.* Cairo: al-Maṭbaʿah al-Tijāriyyah, 1358/1939.

Al-Tabrīzī, ʿAbd Allāh al-Khaṭīb, *Mishkāt al-Maṣābiḥ.* Muḥammad Nāṣir al-Dīn al-Albānī (ed.). 2nd ed. Beirut: al-Maktab al-Islāmī, 1399/1977.

Al-Ṭālibī. *ʿAyāl Allāh* (See under Mabkhut edr.).

Al-Ṭamāwī, Muḥammad Sulaymān, *Al-Sulṭah al-Thālath fī'l-Dasātīr al-ʿArabiyyah wa'l-Fikr al-Siyāsī al-Islāmī*, 2nd edn. Cairo: Dār al-Fikr al-ʿArabī, 1973.

——*ʿUmar Ibn al-Khaṭṭāb wa-Uṣūl al-Siyāsiyyah wa'l-Idārah al-Ḥadīthah.* Cairo: Dār al-Fikr al-ʿArabī, 1969.

Tirmidhī, Abū ʿĪsā Muḥammad, *Sunan al-Tirmidhī.* 3 vols. Beirut: Dār al-Fikr, 1400/1980.

ʿUthmān, Muḥammad Fatḥī, *The Children of Adam: An Islamic Perspective on Pluralism.* Occasional Paper Series. Washington D.C.: Center For Muslim Christian Understanding, 1996.

——*Al-Fikr al-Qānūnī al-Islāmī: Bayn Uṣūl al-Sharīʿah wa-Turāth al-Fiqh.* Cairo: Maktabat Wahbah, n.d.

——*Ḥuqūq al-Insān bayn al-Sharīʿah wa'l-Fikr al-Qānūnī al-Gharbī.* Beirut: Dār al-Shurūq, 1401/1981.

Waṣfī, Muṣṭafā Kamāl, *Al-Mashrūʿiyyah fī'l-Niẓām al-Islāmī.* Cairo: Maṭbaʿat al-Amānah, 1970.

——*Al-Niẓām al-Dustūrī fī'l-Islām Muqārinan bi'l-Nuẓum al-ʿAṣriyyah*, 2nd edn. Cairo: Maktabah Wahbah, 1414/1994.

Yasin, al-Sayyid, ed., *Al-Qaḍāyā al-Muʿāṣirah wa'l-Khilāfah: Ḥiwār ʿUlmānī Islāmī maʿa al-Duktūr Kamāl Abū 'l-Majd wa'l-Shaykh Yūsuf al-Qaraḍāwī.* Cairo: Mīrīt li'l-Nashr wa'l-Maʿlūmāt, 1999.

Yusrī, Aḥmad, *Ḥuqūq al-Insān wa-Asbāb al-ʿUnf fī'l-Mujtamaʿ al-Islāmī. Fī Ḍawʾ Aḥkām al-Sharīʿah.* Alexandria, Egypt: Mansha'at al-Maʿārif, 1993.

Al-Ẓāhirī (See Ibn Ḥazm).

Al-Zamakhsharī, Jār Allāh Maḥmūd, *Tafsīr al-Kashshāf.* Beirut: Dār al-Kutub, 1947.

Zaman, Hasanuz. S. M., *Economic Functions of an Islamic State: The Early Experience*. Leicester: The Islamic Foundation, 1991/1411.

Zaydān, ʿAbd al-Karīm, *Aḥkām Ahl al-Dhimmah wa'l-Mustaʾminīn fī Dār al-Islām*. Baghdad: Maktabat al-Quds, 1963.

——*Al-Fard wa'l-Dawlah fi'l-Sharīʿah al-Islāmiyyah*. Gary (Indiana): al-Ittiḥād al-ʿĀlamī li'l-Munaẓẓamāt al-Ṭullābiyyah, c. 1372/1952.

——*Majmūʿat Buḥūth Fiqhiyyah*. Baghdad: Maktabat al-Quds, 1976.

——*Al-Mufaṣṣal fī Aḥkām al-Marʾah wa'l-Bayt al-Muslim fi'l-Sharīʿah al-Islāmiyyah*. Beirut: Muʾassasat al-Risālah, 1994, rep. 2000.

Zaydān, Jurjī, *Tārīkh al-Tamaddun al-Islāmī*. 4th edn. Cairo: Maṭbaʿat al-Hilāl bi-Miṣr, 1926.

Zayn al-Dīn Ibn Nujaym, *Al-Baḥr al-Rāʾiq Sharḥ Kanz al-Daqāʾiq*. Cairo: Dār al-Kitāb al-Islāmī, n.d.

Zuḥaylī, Muḥammad, *Ḥuqūq al-Insān fi'l-Islām: Dirāsah Muqārinah maʿ al-Iʿlān al-ʿĀlamī wa'l-Iʿlān al-Islāmī li-Ḥuqūq al-Insān*. 2nd edn. Damascus & Beirut: Dār Ibn Kathīr, 1418/1997.

Zuḥaylī, Wahbah, *Athār al-Ḥarb fi'l-Fiqh al-Islāmī: Dirāsah Muqāranah*. 3rd edn. Damascus: Dār al-Fikr, 1401/1981.

——*Al-Fiqh al-Islāmī wa-ʿAdillatuhuh*. 8 vols. 3rd edn. Damascus: Dār al-Fikr, 1409/1989.

——*Ḥaqq al-Ḥurriyyah fi'l-ʿĀlam*. Damascus: Dār al-Fikr al-Muʿāṣir, 1421/2000.

List of Periodicals

AJISS (The American Journal of Islamic Social Sciences)

MLJ (Malayan Law Journal)

Index

Abbasids, 108, 194; Audit and Accounts Departments, 284–285; despotism, 257; Expropriated Assets Department, 285; Hārūn al-Rashīd, 219, 266; hereditary system, 256–257; Jaʿfar al-Manṣūr, 249, 252, 257; judges, 265–266; *mawāli*, 119, 221; *mazālim*, 5, 269, 271; public officials, 221–222, 249, 255; travelling, 102

ʿAbd al-Qādir ʿAwdah, 136

ʿAbd Allāh b. Masʿūd, 43, 244

ʿAbd Allāh b. ʿUmar, 38

ʿAbduh, Muḥammad, 31

Abū Bakr, 55, 73, 159, 164, 215, 235; accountability, 199, 239; election, 152; non-selective assistance to citizens of *Bayt al-Māl*, 164

Abū Dardā', 43

Abū Dharr al-Ghaffārī, 66, 211, 217

Abū Ḥanīfah, Imām, 73, 222, 224, 247, 252

Abū Hurayrah, 67, 200, 249, 289

Abū Yūsuf, 219, 234, 266

Abū Zahrah, 49, 202

accountability, 5–8, 154; Abū Bakr, 199; ʿAlī b. Abū Ṭālib, 240; *amr bi'l-maʿrūf wa-nahy ʿan al-munkar*, 195; and consultation, 203–206; appeal to moral self, 237; *bayʿah*, 197; citizens' complaints, 233; civilian concept, 5, 6; collective duty of the society, 235; complaints, 268; criteria, 222–227; disapproval of self-nomination to public office, 153; early precedent, 198–203; al-Ghazālī, Imām, 193–194, 241; God's omniscience instilling sense of, 239; government as a Trust, 210–216; head of state, 196, 200, 234; hereditary system of succession to Caliphate, 255–257; *Ḥisbah* and *Naṣīḥah*, 207–210; history of decline in Islam, 260–262; holding oneself to account (*Muḥāsabat al-Nafs*), 237–241; Ibn Khaldūn, 197; important and neglected aspect, 7; jurists on public appointment and supervision of imam, 198; lack of emphasis in modern Arabic scholarship, 5; *maṣlaḥah*, 7; misuse of public funds, 258–262; nepotism, 254; non-transferable in government positions, 247; principles, 5, 7, 195–196, 199; Prophet's verdict in use of Jewish property, 236; self accountability of caliphs, 239; *Sharīʿah*, 198; *Sharīʿah*, no exception to the rule of law in, 195;

'Umar b. al-Khaṭṭāb, 193, 194, 249; *ummah*, 167, 195–198, 203–206; *see also Muḥāsabah* (accounting)
accountability, institutional developments, 262–288; *Ḥisbah*, 274–280; Audit and Accounts Departments, 284–285; Expropriated Assets Department, 285–286; impeachment, 280–284; overriding role of the judiciary, 263–267; *see also maẓālim*, Ottoman Constitutional Reforms
'Ā'ishah, 24, 223, 246
'Alī b. Abū Ṭālib, 240, 254, 256; benefits of affluence, 164; head of state, 230; *maẓālim*, 269; non-Muslim citizens, 37, 136; travelling in Ramadan, 58
amān (granting safe conduct), 110–112; procedure, 111; types, 36; Umm Hānī, 111; who can offer or repudiate it, 110, 112; women, 111; *see also* asylum
'Amr b. al-'Āṣ, 114, 202
amr bi'l-ma'rūf wa-nahy 'an al-munkar, 101 *Muḥtasib*, 278; *ḥisbah*, 169; government accountability, 195; head of state, 197
Arab nationalism, 105, 129–134; al-Ghazālī, Muḥammad, 129; intellectual framework, 132; Jamal 'Abd al-Nasser, 131; patriotism, 133; *see also* nation-state
Aristotle, 89
asylum, 35–37; *hijrah*, 35; *isti'mān*, *isti'jār*, 35; non-Muslims, 30, 36, 37; origins in Islam, 35; Universal Declaration of Human Rights, 10, 35; Universal Declaration of Human Rights/Qur'ān compar-

ison, 36; *see also amān, hijrah, musta'minūn*

balad, 94–96; forced eviction from, as basis for Quranic validation of *jihād*, 96; natural affinity for one's, 95; Prophet's love for Mecca, 95
bay'ah (allegiance), 5, 151–153, 197, 257; accountability, 197; citizens' duties, 168; election, 206; head of state, 6, 151, 196, 280; invalid, 252; nepotism, 254, 257; nomination and *bay'ah* distinction, 151
bribery (*rashwah*), 241 forbidden and condemned by the Prophet, 243; Ibn Taymiyyah, 244; public officials, 242–246; punishment, 247–250; 'Umar b. al-Khaṭṭāb, 244

Christianity, 47, 73, 86, 261; Egypt, 150; al-Ghazālī, Muḥammad, 155; public officials, 155, 221, 222, 255
citizen: Aristotelian idea, 89
citizen, duties, 166–170; assistance and cooperation, 168–170; *bay'ah*, 168; obedience to lawful government and *'ulū al-amr*, 166–167; right of neighbours, 169
citizen, rights, 84, 147–166; elections, 151; Iran, 148; Muslims/non-Muslims equality, 150; neglected in post-colonial period, 147; Pakistan, 149; right to basic necessities, 163; right to consultation, 157; right to criticise, 158; right to disobey unjust ruler, 160; right to employment, 164; right to nomination, 153; Saudi Arabia, 148; six rights forming basic criteria, 147; Sudan, 148

citizenship: Arabic word and concept, 92–93; Britain, 90, 91; citizens established after Arab conquest, 118; Constitution of Medina, 2; contemporary debate in Islam, 2; contemporary scholarly debate, 103; degrees, 90; disregard of open policy by modern Muslim states, 104; domicile as basic requirement, 98, 124; Egypt, 105; etymology, 88; evolution, 113–117; exclusivist agenda of nation state, 88; formal citizenship/substantive citizenship distinction, 91; France, 91; Germany, 90, 91; Al-Ghannūshī, Rashīd, 138; Hamidullah, Muhammad, 4, 85, 101–105; historical development, 87; institutionalised aspects, 89; Iraq, 106; irrelevance of religion in modern Muslim states, 107; Israel, 92; Italy, 91; Jews of Medina, 168; libertarian aspect of citizenship in Islam, 100; Malaysia, 107; Manna, Haitham, 86, 94; marginalisation and exclusion, 91; Mawdūdī, Abū'l-Aʿlā, 4, 85–87, 98–99, 138; modern Muslim states, 87; 'nation' in the Qur'ān, 94; nation state, 90, 120; no compulsion to convert, 99, 112; prohibition of marriage between Iraqis and Iranis, 91; in the Qur'ān, 97; reforms in Ottoman Turkey, 93–94, 116; requirements in Islam, 101; Saudi Arabia, 85, 91, 104, 105; Syria, 106; Tunisia, 106; ʿUmar b. al-Khaṭṭāb, 114; United Arab Emirates, 106; United States, 90, 91; universal justice and ultra nationalistic aspects, 82; universality and equality in Islam, 96, 116; *see also Dār al-Islām* vs. *Dār al-Ḥarb, dhimmī, Mawāli, musta'min, muwāṭanah*, nation-state
corruption (*fasād*), 241–242; punishment, 247–250

Dār al-ʿAhd (abode of treaty), 35, 83, 123, 145–147; al-Shāfiʿī, 33, 145
Dār al-Ḥarb, 26, 32–35, 122, 177; distinctive features, 123; *hijrah*, 26, 27, 29, 31, 32; historical roots, 34; juristic differences, 33; Mecca, 34–35; unwarranted designation, 141–145
Dār al-Islām vs. *Dār al-Ḥarb*, 17, 120–127, 137, 141, 176, 182; anachronistic division, 126; Chiragh Ali, 124; citizenship, 4, 82, 84, 120–127; difference of juristic opinion, 122; etymological interpretation, 123; Qur'ānic exegesis, 121; social justice, 142; unauthorized by the Qur'ān and *Sunnah*, 104
Dār al-Hudnah (abode of truce), 25, 33
despotism, 253–257; Abbasids, 257; history in Islam, 255–257
dhimmah, 36, 109–116; definition, 109, 113; end as legal instrument, 113, 115–116; historical circumstances behind its introduction, 114; ʿUmar b. al-Khaṭṭāb, 114; *see also dhimmī*
dhimmī, 109–117; citizenship granted to spouses, 112, definition, 109; difference between *musta'min* and, 109–110; domicile requirement, 110; etymology, 109; exempt from *zakāh*, 139; fair treatment, 136; *jizyah*, 139; revocation, 109;

ʿUmar b. al-Khaṭṭāb, 141; *see also* citizenship
disobedience and defiance, 250–254
Dīwān al-Maẓālim, 267–274

elections, 151–153; Abū Bakr, 152; *bayʿah*, 206; citizen's rights, 151; head of state, 152; non-Muslims participation, 152–153

Fatimids, 46, 276; hereditary system, 256; *mawāli*, 119; public officials, 222; travelling, 102
fiqh, 47, 179; and international relations, 103; accountability, 5; citizen's rights, 147; citizenship, 3, 82–84; *Dār al-Islām* vs. *Dār al-Ḥarb*, 104; *dhimmī*, 112, 113, 150; freedom of movement, 2; imprisonment, 67; *al-khurūj*, 251; nation-state, 104; public officials, 226; women, citizenship, 170, 171, 173–175; women, freedom of movement, 69
freedom of movement: early Islam, 12; *fiqh*, 2; free-trade history of Arabs, 40; individual freedom/utilitarian view of society, 11; Islamic jurisprudence, 9; nation-state, 13; non-Muslims, 72; outsourcing in developing countries, 11; prior to introduction of nation-states, 11; Qurʾān, 13–17; regression in modern nation-states, 10; restrictions, 12; right of passage, 51–53; right to nationality, 12; scholarly pursuit, 45–48; social visits, 53–55; Universal Declaration of Human Rights, 10; *see also hajj, hijrah*, travelling
freedom of movement, restrictions, 59–75; banishment, 64–66; conta-

gious disease, 64; imprisonment, 66–69; *maslahah*-based, 13, 64–74; non-Muslims in the Hijaz, 73–74; prohibition of espionage, 62–63; right of privacy, 60–61

Al-Ghannūshī, Rashīd: citizenship, 138; non-Muslims, 141, 153, 155, 160
al-Ghazālī, Imām, 26, 255; accountability, 193–194, 240; head of state, 282; *hisbah*, 207; travelling, 42–44
al-Ghazālī, Muḥammad, 212 Arab nationalism, 129, 130; Christianity, 155; Judaism, 155; non-Muslims, 155; public officials, 217
governance, Islamic principles, 6–7; religious leaders and ʿulamāʾ, 6; *see also* head of state

hajj, 17, 30, 37–43, 50, 236; Malaysia, 41–42; recent times, 41–42; women, 69
halīf (covenantee), 118 history in Persia, 118
Hamidullah, Muhammad, 85, 101, 103–105, 138, 154; *fiqh* and modern international relations, 103
haqq al-ʿazl, 195, 196, 262
head of state: election, 6; Abū Bakr's election, 152; accountability, 196, 234; *bayʿah* (allegiance), 6; duties, 230; election, 152; al-Ghazālī, Imām, 282; Muslims only, 154; responsible for conduct of his officials, 200; *ummah*, 197–198; *see also* governance, Islamic principles
hijrah, 16–33, 98; as mental dissociation, 26; asylum, 35; Companions, 24; contemporary world, 22; definition, 16–17; different from *safar*, 17; early history of Islam,

16–20; esoteric understanding, 25; freedom of conscience, 18; Ibn al-ʿArabī, 26–27; Ibn Daqīq al-ʿĪd, 23; Ibn Ḥajar al-ʿAsqalānī, 24; Ibn Khaldūn, 23; Ibn Rushd, 23; Islamic jurists different opinions, 22–28; Kharijites, 24; Muʿtazilah, 25; origins in Islam, 35; Ottoman empire, 29–30; principle of noble sacrifice, 18; Qurʾān, 17–19; reawakening in colonialism, 28; rejection of persecution and injustice, 18; Sayyid Quṭb, 25; al-Shāfiʿī, 24; Shaltūt, Maḥmūd, 20–22; Shīʿites, 25; types, 25; see also asylum, freedom of movement

ḥisbah: amr biʾl-maʿrūf wa-nahy ʿan al-munkar, 170; al-Ghazālī, Imām, 207

Ḥudhayfah al-Yamānī, 252

Ibn ʿAbbās, 24, 34, 252; right of neighbours, 169; travelling in Ramadan, 58; ʿumrah, 38

Ibn al-ʿArabī: hijrah, 26–27

Ibn Ḥajar al-ʿAsqalānī, 24, 74

Ibn Ḥazm al-Ẓāhirī, 69

Ibn Qayyim al-Jawziyyah, 139

Ibn Rushd, 23

Ibn Taymiyyah: impeachment, 283; punishment of bribery, 248

imprisonment, 66–69; affluent debtor, 67; civilian/criminal offences distinction, 69; fiqh, 67; Ibn Ḥazm al-Ẓāhirī, 69; only as deterrent, 68; pre-Islamic view, 67; types in Islamic jurisprudence, 68; women, 69

Iran, 155 citizen's rights, 148; Iranian revolution, 148

Jihād: Qurʾānic validation, 145

jizyah (poll tax), 139–141; dhimmī, 109, 110, 114, 139; Egypt, 116; exemptions, 139; military service, 140; Qurʾān, 139; Sayyid Quṭb, 140

Judaism, 73, 86, 92, 113, 148, 236; Constitution of Medina, 99, 135, 145, 168; al-Ghazālī, Muḥammad, 155; public officials, 155, 221, 222, 255

Kharijites, 119 hijrah, 24; rebellion, 24, 251

maṣlaḥah ʿāmmah, 64–74

maṣlaḥah, 156, 174; accountability, 7; head of state, 6, 7; public officials, 220; types, 7; see also freedom of movement

mawāli, 117–120; Arab supremacy, 117; discrimination, 119; inequality, 117; poll tax, 119; power, 119; types, 117; see also citizenship

Mawdūdī, Abūʾl-Aʿlā: nationalism/tribal fanaticism comparison, 129; non-Muslims, 149, 160; weak classification of citizenship, 138

Medina, Constitution, 2, 113, 135, 145, 168

Muʿāwiyah: accountability, 260, 261; allotment of land to family and friends, 260; first major act of disloyalty in Islamic history, 254; nepotism, 254

Muḥāsabah (accounting), 193 personal and public, 193; see also accountability

mustaʾmin, 110–112; as parallel to muhājir, 17; difference of juristic opinion, 110; legal definition, 110;

women, 111; *see also* asylum, citizenship

muwāṭanah, 113 citizenship, 92, 113, 131; created in Prophet's time, 113; legal definition, 113; *see also* citizenship

nation-state, 3, 128–134; Arabic equivalents to 'nation', 128; citizenship, 88, 90, 107, 120–127, 183; creation and creator of modern Europe, 128; divisive nature of European model, 3; emergence in Islamic world, 94; freedom of movement, 10, 11, 13, 32; Jamal 'Abd al-Nasser's Arab nationalism, 131; Mawdūdī's nationalism/tribal fanaticism comparison, 129; Medina, co-existence of Islam and, 132; national identity, 128; origins, 83, 127, 128; sovereignty, 88, 105, 128, 132, 176; threefold basis of modern Muslim identity, 134; Turkey, 132

non-Muslims: elections, 153; freedom of movement, 72; Al-Ghannūshī, Rashīd, 140, 153, 155, 160; al-Ghazālī, Muḥammad, 155; in the Hijaz, 72–74; Muslims/non-Muslims equality, 150; public office, 155; Al-Qaraḍāwī, Yūsuf, 140, 155; second class citizens, 149; status in Muslim countries, 87, 160; *ummah*, 135; *see also dhimmī, mawāli, musta'minūn*

obedience: limits, 227–233
Osmān, Muḥammad Fatḥī, 145, 156, 157
Ottoman Constitutional Reforms, 286–287; citizenship, 93–94, 116

Ottoman empire, 3, 127; formal abolition, 128; *hijrah*, 29–30

Pakistan: citizen's rights, 149
political parties, 205
public officials: Abbasids, 221–222; bribery, 242–246; disapproval of self-nomination, 153; Fatimids, 222; nomination, 153–157; selection, 216–222; Umayyads, 221; *see also* elections

Al-Qaraḍāwī, Yūsuf, 45, 126, 129, 205, 210; non-Muslims, 140, 155
Qur'ān, 131 citizenship, 97; equality, 83, 86, 136; familial unity of human kind, 143; freedom of movement, 13–17; heritage of Christian Arabs, 131; *hijrah*, 17–19; human dignity, 13, 136; *jizyah*, 139; justice, 233; 'nation', 94, 128; privacy of home, 59; validity of other revealed religions, 87, 141; women, equal rights, 171–173

Ramadan: travelling, 56–59
rebellion, 250–253; inciting violence and spreading corruption, 250; Kharijites, 251; *al-khurūj*, 251; validated by Shī'ites, 251; without a cause, as punishable offence, 250
right of complaint (*ḥaqq al-shakwah*), 233–237

Saudi Arabia: citizen's rights, 148
Sayyid Quṭb, 25, 140, 149, 157
al-Shāfi'ī: *dār al-'ahd* (abode of treaty), 33, 145; *hijrah*, 24
Shaltūt, Maḥmūd: *hijrah*, 20–22
Shī'ites, 25 *hijrah*, 25; Iranian revolution, 148; rebellion, 251
Sudan: citizen's rights, 148

theocracy, 6 Khālid Muḥammad Khālid, 130

travelling: Abbasids, 102; concessions, 55–59; conditions defining, 56; Fatimids, 102; in search of *ḥadīth*, 43–48; quest for knowledge, 48–51; Ramadan, 57–59; types according Islamic jurisprudence, 42; *see also* freedom of movement

ʿUmar b. ʿAbd Al-ʿAzīz, 52, 199, 244, 255; accountability, 203, 215–216, 237, 240, 259, 261; general affluence, 166; *mawāli*, 119; *maẓālim*, 269, 270

ʿUmar b. al-Khaṭṭāb, 52, 63, 159, 199, 237, 243; accountability, 193, 194, 249; banishment, 66; bribery, 244; citizenship, 114; *dhimmī*, 141; equality, 234; general affluence, 166; non-selective assistance to citizens of *Bayt al-Māl*, 164; pension system, 165; public officials, 220

Umayyads, 194 despotism, 255; *mawāli*, 221; public officials, 221

ummah: accountability, 167, 195–198, 203–206; head of state, 197–198; non-Muslims, 135; participation in government, 152; political unity, 135; unitarian basis, 135; *see also* nation-state

ʿumrah, 38 Ibn ʿAbbās, 38

Universal Declaration of Human Rights: freedom of movement, 10; right to asylum, 10

Universal Islamic Declaration of Human Rights, 108, 182

walā' (patronage), 117–120; Arab supremacy, 117; *walā' al-ḥilf*, 118; *see also mawāli*

women: equal rights, 72, 171, 222; equal rights in Qur'ān, 171–173; *hijāb* (veiling), 69–72; public officials, 222

women, citizenship, 170–175; discrimination in parental laws, 173; *fiqh*, 170, 171; not entitled to pass citizenship, 171, 174; second class citizens, 170

women, freedom of movement, 69–72; battle of Ḥunayn, 71; difference among jurists, 69 72; *fiqh*, 69; *hajj*, 69; imprisonment, 69

Zuhaylī, Wahbah, 112, 144, 254